Growing Up
LANSDOWNE

Growing Up LANSDOWNE

Robert L. Bingham

authorHOUSE®

AuthorHouse™
1663 Liberty Drive
Bloomington, IN 47403
www.authorhouse.com
Phone: 1 (800) 839-8640

Published by AuthorHouse 10/20/2015

ISBN: 978-1-5049-5243-9 (sc)
ISBN: 978-1-5049-5290-3 (e)

Library of Congress Control Number: 2015915921

Print information available on the last page.

To assist in the writing of this book, I reviewed the 1961-1966 editions of the Lansdowne-Aldan High School (LAHS) yearbook, The Lahian. I also consulted and freely utilized two local Lansdowne books: Views of Lansdowne by Matthew Schultz and Lansdowne: 1893-1968, 75th Anniversary edited by J. Edwin Flannery. Internet access to Delaware County and Philadelphia newspapers proved of some value as well. Additional references were drawn from Wikipedia and other online websites. Fellow Lansdowner Peter Pitts, LAHS Class of '63, also provided valuable checks and confirmation.

Contents

PART III

PART IV

In memory of Olive Lee Bingham

With love and gratitude to J. T. and Esther

Special thanks is extended to

Elizabeth Dunkle Bingham
Peter Pitts
Larry DeMooy
Nancy Gray
Mary Miller
Ed Gebhart
Kip Schlegel
Tim Taylor
Matt Schultz
Camille Doran
Matthew Stroup
Steve Kaplan
Sam Quin
Amanda Richards
Joseph Bruni
Jill McConnell-Wirth
Karl Amboz
David Baker
for their support, encouragement, and interest in the project.

INTRODUCTION

Lansdowne, a conservative, sleepy Philadelphia suburb, was my permanent home for twenty years from 1950 to 1970. I lived in three different residences but never changed schools. Lansdowne has deep Quaker roots and was known during the transition to the twentieth century as a resort community for Philadelphia, which was just six miles to the east.

The borough was founded in 1893 as a breakaway community from Upper Darby Township, which bordered much of Lansdowne's limited land mass of 1.2 square miles. The community was named after Lord Lansdowne's estate in England. Lansdowne had next to no industry when I knew it as a youth, serving primarily as a bedroom community to Philadelphia. The town was serviced by a Pennsylvania Railroad commuter line (the Media local) and four Red Arrow bus routes.

In many respects, Lansdowne was different from the suburban communities surrounding it. Because of its Quaker heritage, it was dry, containing no bars, taverns, nightclubs, or liquor stores. No alcoholic beverages in any form were available for purchase in grocery stores. It had only two permanent restaurants, and to this day it has no fast food restaurants. During my youth, the downtown section was active and serviced the community well. The Lansdowne Theater anchored the downtown and was an entertainment icon until it closed its doors in 1987. A small public library, a private swim club, and a bowling alley were also part of the community landscape. Politically, the town was heavily Republican.

Three public elementary schools and two parochial elementary schools (one Catholic and one Lansdowne Friends) provided early education. Lansdowne-Aldan High School (LAHS) was my home for both junior high and senior high years. While Lansdowne schools were integrated, the borough's small black population primarily lived south of Lansdowne's downtown. Other minority representation was largely lacking. Lansdowne also contained almost a dozen churches representing the major Christian denominations.

Distinct neighborhoods and housing styles existed, from row homes concentrated in the community's extreme northeast to older Victorian homes immediately north and west of downtown. A newer housing area known as Coral Hills evolved in the late 1950s. The borough included many heavily treed streets dominated by mature hardwoods.

When I knew it as a youth, the borough was already congested, with little land available. Lansdowne had one miniscule, isolated park, but there was little open space other than athletic fields located at the high school and at Green and Ardmore Avenue elementary schools. A major summer event was the borough's impressive Fourth of July celebration, which drew large crowds for both parade and fireworks.

The town was extremely safe, with crime almost nonexistent to me as a naïve child and adolescent. Firm in my memory is the feeling that I was always safe and secure whenever and wherever I wandered in the town.

The essays presented here are my attempt to chronicle not only my childhood and adolescent years in Lansdowne but also family life as I knew it. *Growing Up Lansdowne* is part memoir, part social landscape, part local/national history, and part love story. I have made focused and honest attempts to keep accounts as accurate as possible based upon my best recollection.

PART I

The Cast

James Truman (J. T.) Bingham
Date of birth: November 14, 1910
Place of birth: Union County, Kentucky
Place of death: Philadelphia, Pennsylvania

Esther LaRue Pitcher Bingham
Date of birth: May 7, 1916
Place of birth: Traverse City, Michigan
Date of death: May 29, 1992
Date of death, Traverse City, Michigan

William Floyd Bingham, MD
Date of birth: July 25, 1938
Place of birth: Philadelphia, Pennsylvania
Date of death: November 6, 2001
Place of death: Tigard, Oregon

Robert Laurence Bingham
Date of birth: April 8, 1948
Place of birth: Darby, Pennsylvania

1

UNION COUNTY, KENTUCKY

James Truman (J. T.) Bingham was born at home in Waverly, Union County, Kentucky, on November 14, 1910. He was the offspring of Thomas Cranston Bingham and Mary Althier Drury Bingham and the sixth of six children. J. T.'s father deserted the family before he was born, and as a result, J. T. grew up fatherless and impoverished. He was raised in a small, crowded home on Spaulding Street in Union County's county seat, Morganfield. He attended Morganfield public schools and graduated in a class of thirty-nine from Morganfield High School in 1928. He likely would have attended Catholic grade school and high school had family finances been improved.

Union County is located in western Kentucky approximately twenty-five miles southwest of Evansville, Indiana. The county is situated on almost thirty miles on the Ohio River and is bordered by Posey County, Indiana, to the north on the other side of the river. Hardin and Gallatin counties in Illinois lie to the west. County population in 1910 was almost 20,000, with the population declining slightly during J. T.'s youth and adolescence. I could not find a 1910 population total for Morganfield, but I suspect the town's population during J. T.'s childhood to be between 1,000 and 2,000. The racial composition of the county was 85 percent white, with the remaining population being primarily African-American.

Union County, then and today, is economically significant in agriculture and coal mining. The current county population is about 15,000, with Morganfield's population recorded at almost 3,300.

Please note that my parents are identified as J. T. and Esther throughout the book. I chose to use their first names for ease of identification for the reader, and I intend no disrespect. During my upbringing and into my adult life, I always referred to my parents as "Mom" and "Pop."

J. T. at age ten

2

TYLER MUMFORD

Tyler Mumford was a local businessman who wielded significant influence over J. T. during his youth and adolescence. Mumford was owner of the *Union County Advocate*, the county newspaper, which operates to this day. Mumford hired J. T. as a ten-year-old to sweep floors, run errands, answer the phone, and assist in other duties as needed. During elementary and junior high school years, J. T. would report to the *Advocate* office after school and work through the dinner hour. He also worked Saturdays during the school year and full time during summer recess.

J. T. was a quick learner who maximized the opportunity awarded him by kindly Mr. Mumford. Morganfield was a small town with fewer than 2,000 residents during J. T.'s youth, so Mumford was well aware that he was befriending a young boy who was forced to endure the ugly aftermath of an outrageous small-town scandal. Mumford also knew that J. T.'s earnings would help Mary Allie Bingham raise her six children without the benefit of their father's presence and financial support.

J. T. continued to learn and expand his knowledge base within the newspaper office, and as a junior high student, he compiled news stories over the phone, wrote minor copy, inked presses, bundled papers, and helped, as needed, as a pressman's assistant.

The work relationship between J. T. and the *Advocate* extended into high school, and while J. T. had to curb his work hours to participate in high school sports (basketball and track), he remained on the payroll as a reliable part-time employee of the newspaper.

As a graduating senior from Morganfield High School in 1928, college was not a realistic option, so J. T. secured a full-time position driving a coal wagon in a western Kentucky coal mine and worked evenings and Saturdays at the *Advocate.* About this time, Mumford approached J. T. to inform him that mechanisms could be set in motion to secure him a political appointment to the United States Military Academy at West Point or the United States Naval Academy at Annapolis. Was he interested?

After thoughtful consideration, J. T. answered yes, and in the summer of 1930, he entered the US Naval Academy as a midshipman. Why did he choose Annapolis over West Point? Strangely, I don't have the answer.

I learned the above history from J. T. approximately two years prior to his death while interviewing him for a graduate school assignment. The process included two lengthy interviews, which proved highly emotional and cathartic to my father. It was obvious that J. T. had much to say to me in order to set the record straight. At that time, J. T. knew that his prognosis was poor for colon cancer, but he took marked interest in accurately relaying the above story and answering my initial question as to how and why, at the height of the Great Depression, he had earned an appointment to the US Naval Academy.

It was during the second interview that I first saw J. T. cry as he intentionally revisited his relationship with Tyler Mumford. As he choked back tears that had been repressed for decades, J. T. cited the importance of Tyler Mumford's confidence in him as a person: "Tyler Mumford believed in me. That man believed in me."

Tyler Mumford's unselfish advocacy for a fatherless, impoverished little boy had made a resounding, lasting impact on my father, and it indirectly impacted me in turn as a father and an employer.

Understand the power and magnitude here, because in the brief twenty-nine years that my father and I shared, this second interview—born out of a graduate school assignment—was without question the base of our greatest emotional bond.

So many times during my adult life I've had opportunities to tell employees, students, and family members that I believed in them. "I'm proud of you" was a frequent response I utilized over the years. Everyone I've said that to can thank Tyler Mumford for understanding and acting upon the importance of simple encouragement.

J. T., US Naval Academy Plebe

3

THE LUCKY BAG

The Lucky Bag is the name of the United States Naval Academy's yearbook. Below is the senior profile of James Truman Bingham, class of '34. It was written in terms and references indigenous to the academy and US naval service at the time.

James Truman Bingham
"Admiral" "Bing" "Sunshine" "Bell-rope"
Morganfield, Kentucky

Little did James Truman Bingham realize what his birthplace was to do for him in 1910. Regardless, that great Commonwealth of beautiful horses and fast women produced its Candidate J. T. of old aristocratic Morganfield, Kentucky. Proceeding to the Naval Academy he was signally recognized and honored in being first in his class to board the good prison ship Mercedes. All this, during Plebe Summer before Bing had learned the innocent wiles of the non-reg as well as Navy Juniors, but then came four years of "War is Hell" and there emerges from the Academy its most finished product in that the Candidate of four years ago is lo: An Admiral! But 'tis not enough that his Commonwealth should present the only honors: athletically, Bing has gone high enough to set an unofficial Academy record in the high jump so any day now we expect the official thing and can't be particular whether it happens in a Track meet here, at the Penn Relays, or at the next Olympic games.

A true Kentucky Blue-blood couldn't fail the drags by even missing one hop so how it hurt Sunshine to initial the Watchbill which confined him to the Hall for that dance! Despite his appeal, our Bing has been true to his Cynara and deservingly earned that significant title, "Bell-rope."

Just Sunshine to the boys but Admiral to the fleet, his inherent qualities of breezy friendliness and sunshine have blossomed to give a good Navy man and infallible wife.

Track 4, 3, 2, 1, Log Board, Lucky Bag Staff
Manager N. A. Cut Exchange 1 P.O.

Esther as a child

4

ESTHER'S CHILDHOOD

Imagine one of those rare, opportune times with a parent when perfect circumstances unfold for an important and memorable conversation. I exploited that chance opportunity years ago with Esther, and I really did have that conversation.

It was late in Esther's life when she lived on the Upper Peninsula's Drummond Island, and her thought processes were not yet much dimmed by age. Her recall both to recent and distant events remained good at that time. Esther and I sat alone, late on a sunny, blue-skied afternoon on her deck as it looked out upon tranquil Pigeon Cove.

Somehow we were talking about Traverse City and her childhood. Based upon my knowledge of her upbringing and some likely cues from Esther, I remarked to her that Traverse must have been a wonderful place to grow up. Esther instantly beamed with her immediate retort: "It wasn't wonderful … it was perfect." For that fleeting moment, I saw Esther thoroughly content and at peace with her upbringing.

I know little about Esther's childhood except for the fact that her teen and young adult years were impacted by the Great Depression. Unlike the majority of Depression-era adults, Esther's parents were never out of work. They always had jobs that were steady and secure. So, when many millions of Americans and their families were struggling, all was ensured at 911 State Street.

Esther LaRue Pitcher was born in Traverse City, Michigan, on May 7, 1916. She was the oldest of three children born to Floyd and Lenora Pitcher. Esther spent her entire childhood and adolescence in Traverse City living at 911 State Street in a narrow, deep house that is still standing today.

Esther had two younger siblings: William Barnard Pitcher (1921–2000) and Jeannette "Jan" A. Pitcher McConnell (1928–2012). Both siblings graduated from Traverse City High School, as did their older sister. Bill served in the US Army in England during World War II as an airplane mechanic. After the war, he returned to Traverse City and married Nellie Wood, with that union producing five children, all girls. Bill worked for Railway Express and Milliken's Department Store in Traverse City before retiring.

Sister Jan was twelve years younger than Esther. By profession, Jan was a registered nurse, and she married Melvin McConnell in 1950. Melvin and Jan raised two girls in Grand Rapids, Michigan, and retired on Drummond Island from 1980 to 1983 until Mel passed from a heart attack. Jan spent much of her remaining years as a surgical nurse in Grand Rapids. Esther was especially fond of Jan, with whom she shared a strong physical resemblance.

During Esther's youth, Traverse City boasted a population of about ten to twelve thousand while serving as the principle city for northwestern Michigan. It was a major summer vacation center, and "Traverse," as the locals called it, was also recognized as "the Cherry Capital of the World."

Esther attended Traverse City High School, from which she graduated in 1934. I cannot speak as to her grades or classes or activities, because I have no knowledge of them. I do know that she was an accomplished swimmer, and at one point she lifeguarded on Lake Michigan at one of Traverse City's beaches. She also liked to snow ski and ice skate. She was a popular student in high school and was very active socially. Family photos reveal Esther as a beautiful teenage girl.

She was friendly with the Milliken family in town and knew William Milliken, six years her junior, who served as Michigan's governor from 1969 to 1983. She was also romantically linked to a Traverse City High School classmate, Dick Canada, with that relationship interrupted by J. T.'s momentous visit to Traverse City in the mid-1930s.

The Traverse City that Esther knew as a youth was a safe and prosperous city. While Esther's childhood may have been "perfect" in her mind, J. T.'s was not, for multiple reasons. I always found this contrast fascinating, since Esther and J. T. came from two different worlds. Esther grew up safe and secure in northwestern Michigan, while J. T. endured a tough childhood in western Kentucky.

After high school graduation, Esther briefly attended Central Michigan University in Mt. Pleasant. She had wanted to be a teacher, but she returned to Traverse City after completing only one semester. The reason for her abrupt return home is unknown.

Upon Esther's retirement to Michigan late in life, I suggested to her that despite her spending forty plus years of her life in the Philadelphia area, it was almost as if she'd never left Michigan. Her response to my observation was an impish wink.

5

J. T. AND ESTHER: THE MARRIAGE

The oral family history reveals that my parents met in Traverse City when Esther was employed working the front desk at the Park Place Hotel, the premiere hotel in Traverse City at the time. J. T. was in town on business, and apparently their meeting as he checked into the Park Place set the sparks flying. I am unclear as to where J. T. lived at the time, although I never heard either J. T. or Esther mention his working anywhere but Philadelphia prior to 1937, so I am naturally curious as to how this was all staged. J. T. initiated a major letter-writing campaign to woo Esther, an action that angered Esther's mother, Lenora Pitcher. You see, there was one little complication. Esther was engaged to marry Dick Canada at the time she met J. T.

As a youth, I had heard about Dick Canada through casual family conversation. He was billed to me as Esther's principle romantic interest in high school and not as a man she was engaged to marry. My sense is that, like Esther, he attended Traverse City High School and came from an established Traverse City family.

J. T.'s long-distance courtship obviously stirred the pot, with Pitcher relatives taking different sides in the conversation. There is even some handed-down folklore that suggests that Grandmother Pitcher actually hid J. T.'s letters to Esther, only for them to be retrieved and eventually delivered to Esther by Great-grandmother Sexton, the Quaker woman who played a major role in raising Esther and her siblings. How all of this transpired, and how the scale shifted from Dick Canada to J. T., is likely history lost. It is significant to note, however, that no reference was ever made to Bill or me about the Pitcher-Canada engagement. That news came late in my life from a cousin on the Pitcher side.

James Truman Bingham wed Esther LaRue Pitcher on August 25, 1937, in Elk Rapids, Michigan. The ceremony was performed in a small Catholic church at a time when both groom and bride were required by the Catholic Church to profess Catholicism. This mandatory conversion for Esther from the Congregational Church to Catholicism likely irritated and disappointed many within her family. I do not know who officiated or the time of the event. I do not know who was in the wedding party, including best man and maid of honor. I do know that J. T.'s mother and his three sisters drove up from Louisville to attend the ceremony.

We can speculate that the wedding was likely small and simple, since it was held in the midst of the Great Depression. Neither family, the Binghams nor the Pitchers, was well-off financially, and the depression taught and demanded prudent restraint. I doubt as well that Esther wore a traditional wedding dress because of the expense. I further speculate that the reception was likely held at my grandparents' house at 911 State Street in Traverse City. My best guess is that J. T. and Esther honeymooned for a few days in northern Michigan.

The newlyweds lived in an apartment on Spruce Street in West Philadelphia for three years, until J. T. was called up by the navy in 1941. The relocation to West Philadelphia certainly was a total shock for this small-town Midwestern girl, but Philadelphia was where J. T.'s job was headquartered. It is hard to imagine Esther liking life in a major eastern city when she hailed from such a homogenous and protected setting as Traverse City. At best she tolerated it. Less than two months into the marriage, Esther was pregnant with Bill, who was born in Philadelphia on July 25, 1938.

Prewar and wartime years in Pensacola, Florida, at the US Naval Air Station from from 1941 to 1944 were "the best years of our marriage" per Esther. Despite the start of US involvement in the conflict, Pensacola was a popular assignment because of the climate and Gulf Coast beaches. J. T. had a high-profile but demanding position as Chief Information Officer at the US Naval Air Station, and he met the likes of Eleanor Roosevelt, numerous US senators and representatives, foreign dignitaries, and popular entertainers.

The couple made tight friendships at Pensacola, with J. T. even connecting with some of his Annapolis peers. Bill enjoyed it as well, except for being hit by a car on base and breaking his leg at age five. Certainly Esther never wanted that time to end, but it did when J. T. was ordered to the Pacific as an aid to Rear Admiral William Sample's staff.

At this point, Esther and Bill headed north to Traverse City to sit out the war. Because of Bill's challenging asthmatic condition, J. T. and Esther seriously investigated a permanent move to Arizona after the war. There are actual letters penned by J. T. to Esther and Bill to two Arizona locations: Prescott and Gilbert, a Phoenix suburb.

For whatever reason, the Arizona relocation did not materialize. J. T., Esther, and Bill returned to Philadelphia upon J. T.'s decommission in early 1946 to live briefly at the Walnut Park Apartments at 63rd and Walnut Street. My parents and Bill soon moved to a red-brick row home in Darby at 122 Weymouth Road, the couple's first purchased home. I joined the family on April 8, 1948, when I was born at Fitzgerald-Mercy Hospital in Darby.

The move to Lansdowne occurred in 1950 with the purchase of the home at 22 East Marshall Road. We lived there until 1956 with the full intention of then relocating to Traverse City for J. T. to enter the small-town newspaper market. A last-minute job offer canceled the Traverse City move, most likely to Esther's chagrin. J. T. subsequently worked for nearly twenty years as general manager for Fuller Typesetting.

From 1956 to 1960 while Bill attended Franklin and Marshall College in Lancaster, Pennsylvania, J. T., Esther, and I lived in a spacious second- and third-floor apartment located at 278 North Lansdowne Avenue.

The final home purchase occurred in 1960 with the acquisition of a three-bedroom Dutch colonial home at 29 East Essex Avenue. The East Essex Avenue home is the residence that I best associate with my growing-up years in Lansdowne. J. T. and Esther bought the house for $16,500.

One of the best fortunes of my life was the ability to observe J. T. and Esther not just as parents but, more importantly, as husband and wife. Their parenting roles aside, J. T. and Esther set the highest standard as a couple. They were simply phenomenal: always deeply in love and completely devoted to each other.

Their partnership was solid well beyond parenting. At every evening meal, they always conversed for at least an hour after Bill and I had left the table. Esther did most of the listening and assuredly gave helpful counsel in regard to J. T.'s reported issues at work. Sometimes it might be as late as 9:00 p.m., and they were still at the dining-room table deep in conversation.

Their lives were never cushy, but they were comfortable in their roles and exceptional in their support of each other. Mutual respect was strong between the two of them. I never saw them verbally fight—ever. I know that is hard to believe, and while they had their spats and disagreements, conversations never got ugly or accusatory.

As a further example, they never used profane language. The toughest words out of Esther or J. T. were *damn* and *hell*—that was it. The "s" and "f" words were never, ever entertained. J. T. always claimed that you expressed your "verbal ignorance" by resorting to foul language. That high standard strongly impacted me as a man, husband, father, and employer, as I have never been a frequent user of profane language.

Both J. T. and Esther drank alcohol. It was common for J. T. to unwind with a martini upon his arriving home from work. Esther liked a bourbon mist as her choice of cocktail. Never did I see them intoxicated as a couple at home or elsewhere.

We always ate balanced meals: meat/fish and two vegetables for dinner. There was always adequate food in the refrigerator and cupboard. I was never hungry.

I was always adequately dressed.

I always felt loved. I always felt safe and secure at night in my own bed. I never went to bed worrying about any family issues.

J. T. and Esther always provided a sound moral compass, example, and direction.

There was never even a hint of unfaithfulness on either parent's part. They were simply too devoted to each other and too much in love to entertain the thought of an affair. Neither parent was wired that way. Unfaithfulness was simply not an option, not so much because of moral, societal pressure but because of the mutual love and respect that J. T. and Esther routinely demonstrated toward each other. They always slept together in a simple double bed.

As my parents entered their senior years, events were not kind. J. T. died at age sixty-seven from cancer when I was twenty-nine years old—way too premature for one's father to die.

Esther never recovered from J. T.'s death. She was thoroughly devoted to him during his painful physical decline, setting a heroic and unselfish example for Bill and me. I still recall incredibly tender and moving moments shared by the two during J. T.'s final weeks of life. Esther daily mourned J. T.'s absence from her life for fourteen and a half years until her own passing in 1992.

Esther and J. T. Bingham, 1937

6

WORLD WAR II

For my parents, World War II was the real deal. As hostilities increased in the late 1930s around the world, most experts agreed that it was simply a matter of time before the United States entered the war. However, no one really knew or could accurately predict the time, place, or circumstances that would necessitate the US entry.

When J. T. graduated from the naval academy in 1934, the United States was in the throes of the Great Depression. This massive economic downturn took its toll on the US military as well, and because both the army and navy were forced to endure significant downsizing, there simply were not enough commissioned officer slots available to all 1934 naval academy and military academy graduates.

A rigid medical criterion was used to determine which 1934 Annapolis graduates would receive commissions and which would be placed on reserve status. J. T.'s eyesight had deteriorated during his four years at Annapolis because of long hours of study. This resulted in a failed vision test, and he was not part of the limited roster that received active commissions upon graduating. While we never discussed this event, he was no doubt severely disappointed, as four focused years at the academy had primed him for an active commission. Reserve status had to suffice until March 1941 when J. T. was called up for active duty, a tangible signal that US entry into World War II was growing ever more imminent.

From what I can tell, J. T. maintained naval reserve status from 1934 to 1941 during his early days with *Country Gentleman* magazine. He served the vast majority of those years, if not all, at the US naval base located in South Philadelphia, which was, at the time, one of the country's largest and most strategic naval installations.

The 1941 call-up sent J. T., Esther, and my toddler brother Bill to the US Naval Air Station in Pensacola, Florida, where they resided for thirty-nine months before J. T. went to sea in August 1944. At Pensacola J. T. taught navigation to aspiring naval pilots while also serving as the base's chief information officer. In the CIO position, J. T. hosted and coordinated visits for political dignitaries. He also hosted a weekly radio program, was the War Bonds Promotional Officer, supervised the weekly newsletter on base, handled all press releases, and coauthored several brief texts pertinent to the Pensacola Naval Air Station's history and operations. During J. T. and Esther's three-plus years at Pensacola, they met numerous celebrities, including Kate Smith, Stubby Kay, Jerry Colona, Kay Keiser and his orchestra, and even Bob Hope in association with USO shows, which J. T. also coordinated.

Esther taught kindergarten at the base's elementary school (Bill was one of her students) and also volunteered at the naval air station hospital. German U-boats patrolled American coastal waters once Germany declared war on the United States just a few brief days after the Japanese bombing of Pearl Harbor. I recall Esther relating memories of U-boat attacks off the Florida panhandle that necessitated survivors, many badly burned, be admitted to the naval air station hospital where she volunteered. As many survivors could not physically write letters back home, Esther willingly penned letters to parents, siblings, and sweethearts in her volunteer capacity.

In August 1944 J. T. went to sea. As a result, Esther and Bill moved to Traverse City to live with her parents for the remainder of the war. J. T. served in the Pacific theater, and to my knowledge, he exclusively served on aircraft carriers, specifically the smaller carriers known as "escort" or "jeep" carriers. His principle duty during his sea years was serving on the executive staff of Rear Admiral William Sample, a battle-tested fellow Annapolis graduate whom he greatly liked and admired. Based on recollection and minor research, J. T. served on several aircraft carriers during the final two years of World War II, including the USS *Hornet*, USS *Sangamon*, USS *Suwannee*, and USS *Marcus Island.*

J. T. participated in major sea action, including the Solomon Islands campaign, the Battle of Samar, the invasion of Palau, the bombardment of Okinawa, and the epic Battle of Leyte Gulf. During the final year of the war, he was exposed to several kamikaze attacks, with one attack taking the life of his enlisted assistant.

J. T. received several decorations during World War II, including the Bronze Star, which he earned in association with his retrieval of important documents from a carrier station engulfed in flames caused by a kamikaze attack. He also received a Purple Heart because of shrapnel wounds and burns he received during this effort. J. T. played the Purple Heart down, even though he had some minor scars on his arms and back from the shrapnel. Interestingly enough, Esther repeatedly maintained that J. T. should have received two Purple Hearts for two separate incidents. J. T. was also promoted to commander under Rear Admiral Sample, who tragically died in a military plane crash a few months after the war's end.

Even after General MacArthur accepted the formal surrender from Japan on September 2, 1945, active naval service was not over for J. T., as he was part of the US military occupational force that helped Japan transition to peacetime. A few small photos exist of J. T. touring the remains of the destruction at Hiroshima or Nagasaki. J. T. was officially discharged from active duty in early 1946.

Esther always maintained that J. T.'s chronic medical problems suffered in the late 1940s were related to radiation exposure in Japan immediately following the war. She also believed that his development of prostate and colon cancer was radiation connected as well.

My personal sense is that J. T. handled well the emotional rigors of war, including the personal exposure to kamikaze attacks and the return to civilian life, despite the fact that so many of his naval academy classmates died during the conflict. Whenever he attended the Army-Navy game in Philadelphia and sat on those cold wooden bleachers with his classmates of the class of '34, those losses surely troubled him.

Many of this essay's facts are more attributed to Esther than to J. T., since J. T. was always reluctant to discuss his years at sea. To him, like millions of World War II American servicemen and servicewomen, it was simply his duty to go to war. He performed his duty without fanfare or complaint. He did what needed to be done at a time of great challenge to the nation. And he would have done it again if asked.

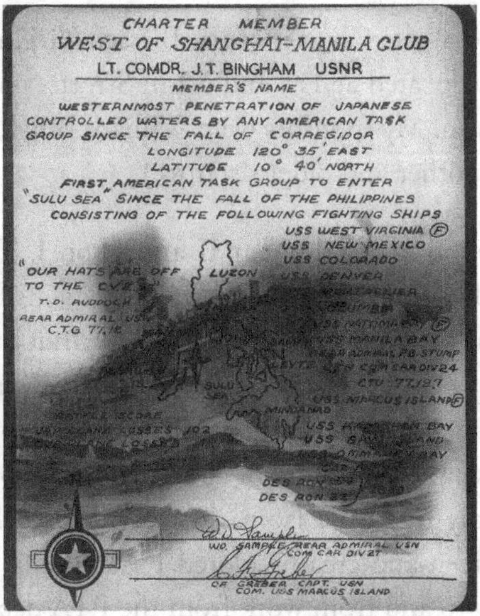

Charter Member of West of Shanghai-Manila Club

7

DARBY

I was born in Darby, Pennsylvania, at Fitzgerald Mercy Hospital on April 8, 1948, at approximately 8:30 a.m. Our family doctor, Beniah Whitman, MD, ushered me into the world as the attending physician. I don't recall my height or weight, but I know there were no complications at birth. I was physically normal and unremarkable.

I was baptized at the Church of the Blessed Virgin Mary Catholic Church in Darby, located at 11th and Main Streets, on May 23, 1948, by Rev. Leo V. Ryan. My sponsors were William Bingham and Martha Bingham, older brother and older sister to J. T.

After completion of World War II and upon J. T.'s return to his job at Curtis Publishing in Philadelphia, he and Esther briefly lived at the Walnut Park Apartments at 63rd and Walnut Street in western Philadelphia. They bought their first home, most likely in 1947: a simple, red-brick row home at 122 Weymouth Road in Darby. At that time, Darby was a working-class suburb of about thirteen thousand residents. It was located only one mile from the Philadelphia line. J. T. most likely took the green-and-cream-colored PTA (Public Transportation Authority) trolley to and from work from the PTA depot in Darby.

My parents only lived in Darby for three years, at which time they moved to another southwest suburb, Lansdowne, about two miles away.

Because of my young age at that time, I remember very little about Darby, but I do recall that the wallpaper in my room had a circus theme. I also remember a small truck that contained a mini merry-go-round on the rear of the vehicle for small children to ride. This truck would cruise the neighborhood with bells announcing its arrival in the hope that it could offer nickel rides to children. Esther hated that truck, as she said it wakened me numerous times from my afternoon naps. I also remember cruising a local candy store with my mother. I was fascinated by the roasted nut display under a heat lamp.

In researching Darby's history, I learned that it was first established in the late 1600s and has a Quaker heritage, as does Lansdowne. It is also the birthplace of famed botanist John Bartram and legendary comedian W. C. Fields.

PART II

22 East Marshall Road

8

22 EAST MARSHALL ROAD

As best I can determine, my family and I moved from Darby to Lansdowne in 1950 when I was two years old. This was a significant step up in residence for my family, as we left a row home in Darby for a Dutch colonial home in an attractive suburb and very good neighborhood. The reason for the move was twofold: Bill was having a rough time with bullying at Blessed Virgin Mary (BVM) School in Darby, and my parents desired a community with an excellent school system. Lansdowne got the call, as it was nearby and was a charming Philadelphia suburb that supported a highly reputable school system. It was a welcome adjustment for Bill as he entered seventh grade, the first year of a three-year junior high school. He was also relieved to simply get out of Darby.

Our first Lansdowne home was a gray stucco, two-story Dutch colonial with white and forest-green trim. It included a separate, stand-alone, one-car garage. The lot was small, allowing for a swing set in the narrow side yard. Mature hemlocks bordered the Hagy property to the east, and a few hardwoods stood on the south end of the lot. DelRoy and Jean Pruitt and their two children, June and Jackie, lived immediately next door across our driveway. A negative to the house was its location on Marshall Road, a busy street that separated Lansdowne from an Upper Darby neighborhood.

The house was two stories, with three bedrooms and a small second-floor room known as "the ironing room." (True to form, Esther used the room for ironing and sewing.) A living room, dining room, and kitchen comprised the first floor. The home included one second-floor, showerless bathroom; a side porch that was never used; a cold, dark, unfinished basement; a coal-fueled furnace; and an efficient living-room fireplace. An interesting feature of the small kitchen was the use of a small picnic table for dining. Looking back, I realize that the house had limited living space by today's standards, but in the early '50s, it was considered more than adequate.

Bill and I had separate bedrooms, and our family soon was surrounded by friendly and supportive neighbors, many of whom remained friends with my parents for decades. This was where I developed strong childhood ties to neighbors Susan Bartlett and the Thompson kids (Kathy, Andy, and Ray Ray). Andy and I were best friends until the summer of 1956 when he and his family moved to Newtown Square.

We lived at this property until 1956 when the Marshall Road home was sold to Glenn and Audrey Etzweiler in anticipation of my family's moving to Traverse City, Michigan, for J. T. to accept a managing position with a local newspaper. When J. T. was offered a last-minute general manager position with Fuller Typesetting in Philadelphia, he accepted. I suspect this was much to Esther's disappointment, as she undoubtedly wished to return to her hometown.

My parents quickly located a large, two-floor apartment at 278 North Lansdowne Avenue, exactly four houses away, where we lived from 1956 to 1960. During our four years on Lansdowne Avenue, I resented the Etzweilers displacing us and living in "our home." It wasn't until we moved to 29 East Essex Avenue and our second home that this feeling died.

Something else died when my family moved to North Lansdowne Avenue, and that was the tight neighborhood bond between my family and the Pruitts and the Bartletts. These three families remained close for many years, but the dynamics were now strangely different. The neighborhood link to our block on Marshall Road had been physically severed and disrupted by busy Lansdowne Avenue, and we were no longer "next-door" neighbors.

9

SUSAN BARTLETT

Susan was a close childhood friend of mine during my early elementary years. She lived at 16 East Marshall Road, just two houses down from my home. She was a key member of our five-person crowd—Andy, Kathy, and Ray Ray Thompson; Susan; and me—which ran and ruled our Albemarle Avenue domain in the mid-1950s. Susan was two years my senior, and she is pictured in many small black-and-white photos that I have from my childhood. She was smart, funny, outgoing, and very pretty. I certainly had a crush on her, then and always.

I spent a lot of time in Susan's home, which had a floor plan identical to ours—something I never realized until recently. Lot sizes were also similar, including a tiny Bartlett backyard confined by a white picket fence. There was an interesting restriction at Susan's house: no one ever entered the living room, as it was always off-limits. I only recall ever being in it one time, and that was during a holiday party where I slept over until early morning, with J. T. eventually carrying me home. The restriction reminded me of those historical homes where rooms are marked off-limits by a garnet velvet sash blocking the entry. In the Bartlett home, just imagine an invisible cordon in place.

We did spend a lot of time in Susan's small TV room upstairs, which frequently doubled as a playroom—certainly to the displeasure of Susan's maternal grandmother, Nanny. Nanny was a distant senior who never smiled. I tried to steer clear of Nanny as best I could. We also spent much time in Susan's kitchen and on her small back porch where we assisted very poorly in hand-cranking homemade ice cream, strawberry or peach, during some summer occasions. It was also on the wooden floor of the Bartlett's gray-painted back porch where Susan dropped the bombshell about Santa Claus during my second-grade year. Yes, I attribute that trauma to Susan, although I got over it in a few days.

I got to know Susan's parents pretty well too. Helen Bartlett was stately, pretty, and charming, although I did get a swat or two from her on occasion and was sent home when I misbehaved. She was an unofficial second mom to me for a few years, and I have nothing but positive memories of Susan's mom during my family's brief Marshall Road years. I also recall Helen Bartlett having a wonderful laugh. Esther and Helen were good friends as well, frequently doing each other's hair at home (on the Bartlett back porch again) or discussing the days' events as they supervised backyard play.

Susan's father, Eddie Bartlett, owned and operated an Atlantic, then Gulf, gas station on the edge of the Marshall Road commercial district. He was small of stature but compact and already balding. I have pleasant memories of him too, although they are limited. I always waved to him as I walked or biked to and from the Marshall Road stores. Eddie and J. T. were kindly toward each other as well.

Susan also had an older sister, of whom, sadly, I have next to no recall.

Susan had her dolls and tea parties with Kathy Thompson and perhaps another neighborhood girl, Pinky. But Susan was very athletic, somewhat of a tomboy, and could easily hold her own with Andy Thompson and me when it came to sports. During summers we would catch fireflies and play seemingly endless hours of hide-and-seek, a major activity at dusk and well into dark, with hiding locales extending into Albemarle Avenue yards.

Susan and I were also involved in a memorable accident during our childhood. She and I were having a spirited argument in her backyard in which neither one of us was willing to back down. Susan became so angry with me that she slammed the fence gate shut. The problem was that my right hand was in the way. It got smashed and cut, and Esther subsequently made a mad dash with me in our black Chevrolet to Dr. Ben Whitman's office in Pilgrim Gardens. My right hand, bleeding heavily, was wrapped in a white kitchen dish towel, and while I held my injured hand high per Esther's instruction, we made the fifteen-minute run to Dr. Whitman's office.

Today, this accident would surely have incurred a visit to a hospital emergency room, but in 1953 Dr. Whitman had to do. I recall little of the treatment, but when Esther referenced the incident years later, she always shook her head, marveling that Dr. Whitman was able to treat the injury without any sutures, using only a creative network of butterfly bandages and padded gauze. I believe I also got a tetanus shot.

When we returned home, Susan apologized, and for about a week, I fully exploited the benefits of the accident with adults and playmates alike. I do believe there was some permanent physical damage, as I now hold a pencil/pen awkwardly, and my hand quickly tires from writing, a condition that caused me to type at an early age.

When our family moved less than five hundred feet from our East Marshall Avenue home to our new residence on North Lansdowne Avenue, the dynamics between my family and the Bartletts and Pruitts (the in-between neighbor to our respective families) changed drastically. It is amazing what a busy street can do, how it can totally disrupt and alter relationships. The chasm was ever so evident between my parents and the Bartletts. Susan and I soon drifted apart as well, especially when she entered junior high school.

Susan and I shared the LAHS hallways for four years, and even then our relationship was reduced to a casual greeting while passing between classes. Susan blossomed athletically and was an excellent field hockey and lacrosse player. I believe she cocaptained both squads. She was very popular as well, dating Dave Thomas, a major LAHS jock. Sadly, I don't recall her plans after college.

Susan remains a major player in my early childhood, and we owe a final meeting to each other.

10

ANDY THOMPSON

My main playmate during my Marshall Road years was Andy Thompson. He and his older sister Kathy and younger brother Ray Ray lived with their parents on Wayne Avenue in a stately stone home near where Albemarle Avenue became a dead end to the east. Andy's father, Ed, was a suburban dentist and active golfer. His mother, Harriett, was a stay-at-home mom who, among other adventures, used to pile us into the Thompson car to follow fire engines to house fires. Harriett was fun to be around, because we never quite knew what was going to happen next. She was the first person I ever saw eat potato chips inside her sandwich. She was also a major fan of TV soap operas.

I most likely met Andy in the neighborhood or perhaps during the first day of kindergarten at Green Avenue. We were in class together at Green Avenue for three years and became instant best buddies. We were nearly inseparable and were usually at one of our houses or cavorting within the neighborhood. We played well together. I cannot recall any major spats between us. We played sports of all varieties, including some epic boxing matches, sledded at the golf course, played lengthy installments of hide-and-seek and Red Rover, competed in electronic football contests, did overnights, ate pancake breakfasts prepared by Mrs. Thompson, played king of the mountain, rode bikes, went to the movies, and just generally hung out together. Oftentimes, Andy's older sister, Kathy, and his very quiet younger brother, Ray Ray, would be in the mix too. When we added Susan Bartlett, we had our posse. When activities became too boyish for the girls, Kathy and Susan went off together.

What made the Thompson family connection even tighter was the fact that Andy's grandmother, Mum Mum (I do not remember the grandfather) lived on Albemarle Avenue just a few houses down the street from Andy's home, and Aunt Kate lived across the street from Mum Mum. So, in our roamings within the neighborhood, we frequently visited Mum Mum and Aunt Kate as well, not to mention our impromptu visits to the Hagy's butler, Walter.

Life could not have been any better during those early elementary years, except for the fact that I could not visit the Thompson home when Bill babysat for them. I thought that ruling most unfair, but now I understand the basis for the restriction. However, early in 1956 I learned some stunning news that I did not want to hear. The Thompsons were moving to Newtown Square during the summer between our second and third grades. I wasn't troubled by the news; I was devastated. Supposedly, Dr. Thompson wanted more land, a more rural setting, and closer access for his golfing. He had purchased land, and an expansive new home was under construction during that winter. The new home would be ready as school closed in June.

I hated Dr. Thompson up to the bitter end, and while stubbornly denying the inevitable and awful, Andy and I crammed as much as possible into our final few weeks together. But moving day occurred immediately after school was let out. Certainly Esther and J. T. knew how forlorn I would be, and they would miss Andy, Kathy, and Ray Ray as well, as they were frequent and welcome visitors to our home.

On that dreadful morning, I wandered over to Wayne Avenue and saw the movers already hard at work. I looked for signs of the Thompsons, but I soon learned that the family had already left. Possibly the parents thought it best for the children to make a quick and uneventful exit. I proceeded next to sit on the neighbor's concrete front steps for a few minutes, but then reality got the best of me. I saw no reason to further augment my agony and started walking home.

When I hit Mum Mum's front yard, I lost it. I sat on the curb immediately before Mum Mum's house and bawled my eyes out. I doubt if I ever cried harder or more passionately in my life. The world as I knew it was now drastically and cruelly different.

The good news, if there was any good news, was that our parents had agreed to weekend sleepovers at both locations to help with the transition. While the returns to Lansdowne worked well because Andy fit in immediately to the old environs, the trips to Newtown Square were disappointing for me. Andy had quickly moved on and adopted a new crowd in his new neighborhood. I was now the odd man out.

While the sleepovers were short-lived, I still saw the Thompsons for a few years during football season. Ed and Harriet had season tickets to the Eagles games, and when the Eagles played at home, the three Thompson kids spent most of Sunday at Mum Mum's. The Thompsons would return after the game and stay for dinner, which allowed even more playtime for the four of us, including memorable episodes of hide-and-seek in the chilly dark of Mum Mum's back and side yards.

I haven't seen Andy since those crisp fall Sundays at Mum Mum's. Andy graduated from Marple-Newtown High School, a much larger school that LAHS never scheduled for sports, where he played quarterback on the football team. He was also an exceptional golfer, and he went on to be a country club professional around Newtown Square upon graduation from college.

11

1948 ADMIRAL TV

Our first TV ever was a ten-inch (that's right, ten-inch), black-and-white Admiral television set. Color TV was not available until the late 1950s and initially in limited programming. It's hard to imagine life without TV, but I do remember a few occasions when I visited neighbors' houses with my mother or brother to watch a special show prior to our own TV arriving on Marshall Road. As best I can figure, J. T. bought the set used, and it joined our family in 1951 or 1952.

Early TV sets were very primitive. They used adjustable antennae, which were referred to as rabbit ears, and sets typically had poor picture quality racked by such issues as rolling picture, snow, picture without sound, sound without picture, and so on. When poor reception occurred, J. T. or Bill would spring into action, achieving limited success by adjusting the antenna and playing with dials that controlled brightness, stability, etc. Sometimes the error was not in the TV set or the reception but at the station, the source of the broadcast. It was not uncommon in those early days for lengthy delays to occur at the station due to "technical difficulties."

Early televisions looked nothing like today's models, since the technology has radically changed. Original black-and-white televisions displayed broadcasted images from a large, bulky, heavy component known as the picture tube (cathode ray tube). This principle component was supported by any number of additional components, many of which were in smaller tube form themselves. These elements included wax capacitors, electrolytic capacitors, resistors, amplifiers, coils, chokes, valves, demodulators, and so on.

If a TV set was malfunctioning, especially if it received no picture at all, the big fear was that the picture tube had blown. Replacing the picture tube equaled major expense and perhaps the purchasing of a new set altogether. Smaller tubes could be easily replaced, but someone had to determine which tube was no longer functioning. These tubes were located in the back of the set.

After removing a protective panel from the back of the TV, J. T. or Bill would do some detective work and determine potentially nonworking tubes. Most tubes had filaments that would light up and glow when working. Any unlit tubes were suspect, and on occasion, multiple tubes had blown. Tubes were typically coded by letters and numbers, e.g., GL-5, J-7, etc., and they were generally interchangeable between different makes and models.

Tubes were easily removed, and we bought replacements at nearby Owen's TV or the local hardware store, Van-De-Boe's, after testing the tubes on a device available in the store. In my latter elementary school years, I might make these runs, but I'd seek help on testing the tubes. My father would wrap suspect tubes in tissue paper and then secure them in a small bag for me to carefully transport to and from the store. Tubes were relatively inexpensive, and usually a few dollars covered the cost.

Our 1948 Admiral TV was the family's major TV set until I reached junior high school, at which time J. T. splurged on an upgraded model with a newer and larger screen. However, our family remained in the black-and-white era, even though many families were now purchasing TV sets capable of receiving limited color programming.

12

WALTER

Lansdowne was very middle class and certainly not an affluent town, but our next-door neighbors on Marshall Road, the Hagys, had a butler. His name was Walter.

Walter was a kind, handsome, and very patient black man in his late forties who was forever smiling. The neighborhood crowd I ran with and myself—Susan Bartlett and the Thompson kids (Andy, Kathy, and Ray Ray)—used to pay Walter frequent visits at the Hagy's back door. Walter patiently accommodated us with candy or cookies, with a warm and genuine smile on his face. We thought Walter was the absolute best.

I know little more about Walter. I don't know if he lived with the Hagys or if he commuted to the Hagy residence from his home. Walter was primarily employed as a caretaker, a cook, and possibly a driver.

Esther was aware of our relationship with Walter, and she halfheartedly admonished all of us to stay away and not bother him. We never much listened to her warnings, since we did not view ourselves as pests. Walter was simply our friend and a trusted contact within our neighborhood network.

Walter was the first black person I ever knew, and I have the fondest memories of waiting with Susan and the Thompson kids at the back door in anticipation of whatever treat he would provide. Black licorice seemed to be a favorite of his.

When we moved from Marshall Road to our apartment on North Lansdowne Avenue, J. T. gave the Hagys a bottle of liquor as a going-away gift. I learned in later years that the gift was actually intended as a sign of gratitude to the Hagys for their patience in tolerating my antics in their side and back yards, including my ongoing contacts with Walter. Although the gift was well intended by my parents, the liquor most deservedly should have been awarded to Walter, not the Hagys.

13

THE HANSELL ROAD ICE CREAM SHOP

Hansell Road, less than two blocks in length, is located a block south of East Essex Avenue, approximately a quarter mile from where I spent my adolescent years down the street. It was very proximate to the office of Dr. Nugent, our family's veterinarian. The street was totally residential, with row homes adorning both sides.

When I was very small (between the ages of three and five), I visited an ice cream store with Susan Bartlett, her mother, and Esther on at least two occasions. The store was operated out of a row home in this part of Lansdowne. I believe the street was Hansell Road, but it could have been any row-homed street in that part of town.

My memory is spotty in this instance, but what I do recall is an eager crowd waiting in a line outside on the front steps and sidewalk to get into the house during a sticky summer evening. The actual ice cream was scooped from refrigerated tubs in a living-room display case. I want to say that the ice cream was homemade and delicious, but I'd be guessing. I seem to recollect that everyone ate cones—no sundaes or floats.

Perhaps this snapshot remains with me simply because the model was so exotic, so unusual: a local ice cream shop operating out of someone's living room, and a tiny row home at that.

Why is Hansell Road so prominent in my memory? I was so little that I couldn't have had any sense of geography or Lansdowne's streets, so in full candor, the shop could have been in Lansdowne, Stonehurst, Drexel Hill, East Lansdowne, etc., as long as the setting was a brick row home.

I believe I held on to this obscure memory due to its pure uniqueness. I only recall visiting this store on two occasions because even in the early 1950s, zoning laws did exist; certainly the neighbors were not supportive of an ice cream store operating within a stone's throw of their homes. The last thing this tiny street needed was more traffic and parking competition as Hansell Road children played on the sidewalks and streets.

My belief is that the establishment was very short-lived, lasting less than a summer during one hot and humid Lansdowne summer in the early 1950s. And yes, this establishment could well have been in a different community altogether, but the Hansell Road imagery for some reason will not fade.

Dixie

14

DIXIE

I was two years old when Dixie, a blond cocker spaniel puppy, joined us as a family member. At the time, my aunt Martha worked for Ballard and Ballard foods in Louisville, and she was the source in securing Dixie from a company-owned kennel. I obviously had no role in naming her, but Dixie seemed like the right call because of our pup's southern heritage.

Esther stated from the very beginning that "Dixie was all Bobby's dog." Throughout my childhood, I was loyal to Dixie, and she returned the favor twelvefold. Dixie beat the terrible inbreeding curse that devastated the cocker spaniel breed in the '50s and '60s. She was a pedigree cocker spaniel with good points. She was easygoing, obedient, friendly to all, and above everything else, protective and loyal to me.

When I was able to negotiate our Marshall Road neighborhood on my own or accompanied by Susan Bartlett and the Thompson kids, Dixie was always right there by my side. Almost as if on assignment, she devotedly followed me everywhere in the neighborhood. She did not stray far from 22 East Marshall. Dixie had an uncanny understanding of cars and traffic, and if we ever crossed a busy street like Lansdowne Avenue or Marshall Road, she always followed my lead.

When I started to ride a bicycle, Dixie galloped alongside. During my elementary school years, I rode my bike to and from school. At first Dixie was frustrated and then disappointed that she could not follow me on these trips. After school was a different matter, as Dixie often joined me as I returned to Stewart Field or Green Avenue Field to play with my classmates.

A frequent destination in the fall was the Green Avenue field where we would dress up in our football gear and play with the high school football team's blocking dummies when they weren't in use. Dixie would patiently sit under one of the aged oak trees until it was time for me to return home. Again, she would gallop along on the sidewalk as I biked to and from the playground.

Dixie also accompanied me to the Marshall Road commercial district when I ran to the store for Esther. I would instruct her to wait outside during my brief absence in the store, and she always obeyed.

I fondly recall a time when Dixie went sledding with Bill and me at the nearby golf course. The feathers on Dixie's feet got so caked with snow that she almost couldn't walk. Bill and I improvised, and Dixie became a passenger on the sled ride home. To thaw her out, Dixie received a warm midwinter bath from Esther.

In the days when dogs roamed freely, Dixie knew her territory and her limitations. I cannot recall a single example where she was involved in a dogfight or altercation with any children or adults. She never roamed or disappeared.

Neighbor Ed Flannery had an older cocker spaniel named Little Guy, who was always leashed and typically irritable and snappy. Dixie, the cocker not on the leash, always gave Little Guy a wide berth so as to avoid any confrontation.

Dixie lived in two Lansdowne locations: 22 East Marshall Road and 278 North Lansdowne Avenue. In order to alert us that she wanted to be let in, Dixie would politely bark at our first-floor entrance on Lansdowne Avenue so we could take the steps down from our second-floor apartment to let her in. Smart dog, that Dixie.

I was a sixth-grader at Highland Avenue School when Dixie ran into a serious medical issue. She was now ten years old, graying on the face, lacking energy, and slowing down in general, and she now infrequently accompanied me on my neighborhood exploits. One morning Dixie could not walk. I did not sense that anything was terribly wrong, although my mother knew otherwise. I kissed my faithful companion on the head as I trotted off to school with the confident belief that our vet would make Dixie better. The vet diagnosed Dixie with stomach cancer, and my mother correctly made the call to put her down while I was at school.

Upon hearing the news from my mother, I was overwhelmed, disbelieving, bursting into tears. I cried for hours in my room. I had not seen this coming. Words of consolation from my parents helped, but the promise of a new puppy was not a comfort. Perhaps the hardest adjustment was not feeling Dixie's snuggled body at the foot of my bed, her standard sleep station, as I slept.

Eloise, our beagle puppy, joined us in about a year's time, and while I was glad to have a dog back in the house, I understood, even at age thirteen, not to expect another Dixie.

15

HARVEY CEDARS

Harvey Cedars, in the early 1950s, was a quaint, undeveloped beach town on Long Beach Island, New Jersey, located about halfway between Atlantic City and Toms River. Back then it contained a few scattered beach houses, but much of the landscape was undeveloped sand dunes dotted by sea oats. One of my earliest childhood memories, and easily the most frightening, occurred there in the summer of 1952. I was four years old, and my older brother, Bill, was fourteen.

On an unremarkable summer's day, my family was visiting a business associate of J. T.'s, who owned a beachfront summer home in Harvey Cedars. This was the only time I can ever recall our family spending time together at the Jersey Shore. According to Esther's account and my limited recall, she and I were resting on the beach, while Bill, a competent swimmer, was enjoying the surf. J. T. had remained indoors back at the beach house with our hosts.

Suddenly Bill emerged from the water in dazed distress. He was gasping for breath as he frantically pointed to his face as if to display the cause of his distress. As Bill collapsed on the sand, struggling to breath, Esther desperately called toward the beach house for help, but her calls were drowned out by ocean and wind. Other than me, no one else was present on the beach when my mother made a spontaneous decision.

As I was already scared and crying, I could not be entrusted as a reliable or timely messenger. Seeing no other alternative and understanding that she had little recourse, Esther left me and darted to the beach house about fifty yards away to seek help. Soon J. T. and other adults arrived at the scene as Bill's status worsened. His face was red and swollen, especially around his nose and eyes. An ambulance was summoned.

Upon arrival and quick diagnosis, the paramedics deemed Bill's condition so serious that they decided to immediately transport him by ambulance to a Philadelphia hospital, a distance of approximately seventy miles. I have no recollection of the paramedics' initial response to Bill's condition, but the general sentiment of J. T. and Esther over the years was that the paramedics saved Bill's life.

With ambulance sirens blaring and lights flashing, Esther accompanied Bill in the ambulance to Philadelphia's Hahnemann Hospital where Bill was admitted. J. T. and I followed in our black 1950 Chevrolet. Bill's condition stabilized during the ninety-mile ride to Philadelphia. The medical explanation at Hahnemann was that Bill had suffered an allergic reaction to being struck in the face by the tail of a stingray. He was released from Hahnemann the following day after medical treatment had countered the allergic reaction and his breathing had returned to normal.

A final observation from this disturbing incident is that it was the first and only time I ever saw my parents run.

16

ASTHMA

I had asthma as a small child. This was not a big surprise, since Bill had had it early in life as well. Bill's version lasted into his teen years, nearly prompting a family relocation to Arizona after J. T.'s return home from World War II. Several of my paternal relatives were afflicted with the disease as well, with my Grandmother Bingham having a particularly nasty and nagging form of it well into her senior years. Oddly, it was never an issue for J. T. My good fortune was that I outgrew it during my early elementary school years.

Easily, my earliest ugly memory was that of having an asthma attack while visiting relatives in Louisville. I was three or four years old, and I recall that the episode occurred in the evening. My parents and an aunt or two rushed me to a nearby hospital emergency room for treatment. I have no recall of the treatment, but I do remember how frightening was the sensation of not being able to breathe. I could not catch my breath. As I continued to gasp for air, my anxiety elevated to near panic. I recall helplessly looking at my mother from the gurney for some semblance of relief, for a sign or some reassurance that this challenge would end.

This was the only attack I recall. One was certainly enough. In the early 1950s asthma killed people, especially small children and the elderly. I didn't know that at the time, and in retrospect, I don't know how truly serious the incident was. I'll never know, but I do vividly recall the incident some sixty years later: the fear, Esther's attempt to calm and comfort me, and as much as anything, the horrifying sensation of not being able to breathe.

17

RANDOM REMEMBRANCES I

Looking east from my bedroom window on Marshall Road, I could see a line of tall hemlock trees that separated our property from the Hagys. If snow was forecasted overnight, these trees were the first sign I checked upon rising the following morning. If it was a school day and the hemlocks received a light dusting, school would be held as usual. If the hemlock branches sagged from a heavy accumulation of snow, there was a better chance that school would be canceled.

Many of Lansdowne's residents lived within a half mile of the town's principle intersection: Lansdowne Avenue and Baltimore Pike (US 1). At noon on Saturdays, a civil defense siren routinely blasted from the police/fire station in downtown Lansdowne. You could easily hear the siren from our home on Essex Avenue and most other parts of the town. The siren was irritatingly loud, and it left no question in your mind as to the actual time. Any activities that I had in downtown Lansdowne on Saturdays were generally scheduled to avoid the civil defense siren testing at noon.

The Hot Shoppe was a restaurant that we occasionally frequented as a family when Bill was still in high school. It was located on Market Street just east of the 69th Street terminal in Upper Darby. It was akin to a Big Boy restaurant in appearance and menu. At one time they may have offered curb service as well. What stands out in my memory is that

Bill constantly and deliberately reminded me that, because of my age, I was required to order from the "kiddie menu." Bill took great delight in teasing me on this technicality to the point where I resorted to fierce kicks under the table to retaliate.

Standard elementary school field trips took me to the Philadelphia Zoo, Franklin Institute, Lenape Park, Turner and Wescott Dairy (now Wawa), Valley Forge, Independence Hall/Betsy Ross House/Carpenter's Hall, and the University of Pennsylvania Museum.

When I was a very small child (age three or four), Esther would occasionally take me to a site she called "the duck pond." It was situated near Darby Creek on the north side of Providence Road just outside the boundaries of Lansdowne. It was located on private property with the ducks separated from visitors by cyclone fencing. If she had the forethought, Esther would bring bread that we would feed to the ducks through the fence. The site was extremely popular with me and a great treat to visit.

When I attended Green Avenue School, our crossing guard was Mr. Jimmy, who was stationed at Plumstead and Green Avenues. He was there to assist students crossing Plumstead in the morning, to and from home during the lunch hour (Green Avenue had no cafeteria, and students were not allowed to bring a sack lunch to school), and after school was dismissed. He was an amiable and kind senior citizen who wore a standard police-officer-type hat and role-identifying clothing. He also handed out small Tootsie Rolls to us on a regular basis. As I recall, my fellow classmates on these walks were Andy and Kathy Thompson, Sally Cheeseman, Sarah Wool, Jack Campbell, and sometimes the Glotfelty children.

As a little boy, I recall my parents having a small RCA record player. They only had a few 45 records. These are the titles and artists I remember:

- "Hold That Tiger" by Les Paul and Mary Ford
- "The World Is Waiting for a Sunrise" by Les Paul and Mary Ford

- "Muskrat Ramble" by Phil Harris
- "Whispering" by Paul Whiteman
- "You're Driving Me Crazy" by Paul Whiteman
- "Goodnight Irene" by The Weavers
- "Tennessee Waltz" by Patti Page

My particular favorite of this group will always be "Goodnight Irene," a classic American folk song written by Huddie "Lead Belly" Ledbetter, which was number one on the pop music charts in 1950 for thirteen straight weeks.

When I recall the early days of television, I remember Esther regularly watching a show that ran from 1951 to 1957 known as *Life Is Worth Living.* This weekly religious show, a precursor to today's televangelism, was hugely popular. It was hosted by an unpaid Catholic priest Bishop Fulton J. Sheen before a live studio audience in New York City.

At that time Bishop Sheen was a rising figure within the Catholic Church. At the height of the show's popularity, it reached thirty million American viewers. Sheen even received an Emmy award one year for "outstanding personality." While Sheen's messages were always over my head, I was fascinated by his delivery. He used no script or cue cards, only an occasional blackboard to emphasize his message. He was as polished and smooth an orator as one could ever imagine. I never fashioned Esther as a rapt Catholic, but she was glued to Bishop Sheen's presentations during his weekly shows, as was much of America in the early to mid '50s.

Lansdowne's three elementary schools utilized a network of student "safeties," who wore reflective badges on sashes at their posts as they assisted children in crossing intersections located close to the school. Safeties were on post before school, at lunch time, and at dismissal. Safeties were usually the more responsible, teacher-nominated students, who received limited training and took their tasks seriously. I was a safety at both schools. If students were disrespectful or disobedient, the safety could report them, which was the case in fifth grade when

I reported Susan McCain for kicking me in the shin. She got me good. I also remember my disappointment when I was not promoted to lieutenant at Highland Avenue in sixth grade.

Both J. T. and Esther wore false teeth. Esther had a complete upper plate; J. T. had a major bridge connected to his bottom teeth. My parents' dental apparatus was not unusual for the times. Root canals had yet to be introduced and standardized, so before the 1970s, infected, heavily decayed, or dead teeth were extracted and replaced with bridges, partial or complete plates of teeth, or nothing at all. Yes, their dentures resting in separate glasses of water on the nightstands next to their double bed was a common sight in the late evening and early morning during my growing up years.

Carlton Abbott was the long-standing superintendent of schools for the Lansdowne-Aldan School District. He was also a native of Vermont and a veteran of tough winters. He was not prone to cancel school because of snowstorms. Dr. Abbott typically held out to the last minute before canceling school. The end result was that it was not unusual for most school districts proximate to Lansdowne-Aldan to be closed while LAHS and the district's elementary schools remained open. Anything less than six inches usually meant school as usual for students and teachers. There were also no late starts, two-hour delays, or early dismissals that I can recall.

Nearly every year, my parents and I would attend the traveling show of the Ice Capades or the Ice Follies, usually at the Philadelphia Arena. This outing was assuredly scheduled to please Esther, who had enjoyed ice skating as a child and teenager. Ironically, I only saw Esther skate as an adult once while we were visiting some family friends in Newtown Square. Having not skated for years, she did right well on a roughly iced farm pond.

I came very close to being named Frederick Barnard Bingham. Within a few weeks prior to my birth, there was a change to Robert

Laurence. Initially I was to be named after an uncle Fred on the paternal side of Esther's family, my mother's favorite uncle, who had died prematurely at age forty-two. Barnard was a middle name common to many Pitcher men, my grandfather included. J. T. and Esther decided at the last minute that my first name should now be Robert after an Annapolis classmate of my father's, Robert Brinker, a World War II submarine commander of the USS *Grayling* who died at sea off the Philippines in early September of 1943. My middle name, Laurence, is the masculine form of Laura, the middle name of Martha Bingham, J. T.'s sister.

In the mid '50s my parents made a concerted attempt to play contract bridge as partners. Esther was a decent bridge player, having learned the game during World War II. The experiment lasted about a year, but the tandem was curtailed by Esther because of J. T.'s ineptness with the game. My mother rarely criticized my father openly, but one morning following a disastrous bridge outing the previous evening, she claimed (paraphrasing), "Your father is good at many things, but playing bridge is not one of them." Esther then went on to play bridge for a few more years with a female partner.

I was a fan of Golden Books as a small child. My particular favorites were *Day at the Circus*, *Scuffy the Tugboat*, *Little Black Sambo* (sorry), *The Little Red Caboose*, *Tootle*, and *The Little Engine That Could*. One can now see that an interest in trains was already evolving.

My first bicycle was a birthday gift, most likely for my seventh birthday. It was a used bike with chrome fenders, a Pee Wee Herman–type bike with big, fat tires. Bill taught me to ride it on Albemarle Avenue. Kids in those days generally rode their bikes on sidewalks, and that bike covered dozens of miles on the rectangular block defined by Marshall Road, Lansdowne, Albemarle, and Wayne Avenues.

To the best of my memory, my first exposure to a black person was at Wanamaker's Department Store in Philadelphia during the

Christmas holiday season. I was three years old and was most certainly at Wanamaker's with Esther to visit Santa Claus. As I was prone to do, I got lost. The Wanamaker's employee who consoled me until Esther was located was a very kind and reassuring, middle-aged black salesperson who made a very positive, lasting first impression. I also recall getting lost at the Philadelphia Zoo and at Wawa Dairy on school class trips.

Throughout grade school, we were regularly exposed to art and music. Each grade in Lansdowne's three elementary schools received weekly visits from Mrs. Russell for art, while we visited Miss Herr in a multipurpose room or separate classroom fitted with a piano.

I enjoyed art. Mrs. Russell was creative and comfortable in her specialized teaching role. She was heavily engaged during class going from one student to the next as she offered technical guidance and support.

When I recall Miss Herr, I think of Ralphie's teacher, Miss Shields, in *The Christmas* Story. They are dead ringers for each other in appearance and dress, although Miss Herr wore glasses. Music class was a drag; there are just so many times one can rattle a tambourine and sing *Erie Canal*. Unlike Mrs. Russell, Miss Herr seemed distant and unenthused. Perhaps it was because so many of us felt forever trapped on the Erie Canal: "Low bridge, everybody down … low bridge 'cause we're going through a town."

I recall only two spankings in my life—both from J. T. One had to do with my running through traffic as a five- or six-year-old to greet my father at the bus stop on Marshall Road as he came home from work. He was furious with me for my recklessness, and he paddled me on the spot in full view of the world. The other time I was spanked early on a Sunday morning by a sleepy and irritated J. T. as I had attempted to balance a table lamp on the arm of a living-room chair. The lamp broke, I was spanked, and J. T. promptly returned to bed. While not officially billed as spankings, I did receive my share of swats from Esther's dreaded wooden spoon as a young grade schooler.

Victory at Sea was a popular NBC television documentary series that was originally aired in 1952–1953 in twenty-six half-hour segments on Sunday afternoons. The series chronicled the US Navy's exploits during World War II. It was narrated by Leonard Graves with a popular musical score composed by Richard Rodgers and Robert Russell Bennett.

Bill was enthralled with the series, since J. T. had been a deployed naval officer in the South Pacific from 1944–1946 and had fought in many of the battles portrayed within the documentary. Because of Bill's interest, I watched as well as an impressionable four- or five-year-old could, unable to grasp any real understanding of this cataclysmic event and J. T.'s involvement in it.

I cannot recall J. T. watching a single episode. It was most likely too painful for him to revisit and relive, since he had witnessed such brutal fighting during the final years of the war and had lost many Annapolis classmates and naval comrades to the process.

I have listened to the musical score for *Victory at Sea* for over sixty years, and it remains one of my favorite pieces of music, regardless of genre.

Kathy Hughes, my nemesis during my Albemarle Avenue days, was a year older than me and routinely bullied me for several years. The only positive aspect was that I could run faster than Kathy. Kathy attended St. Philomena School, so we just ran into each other in the neighborhood. An irony here is that Bill was friends with Kathy's older brother, Tony.

Lansdowne had little wildlife. The town was simply too crowded and had little open land. Our wildlife pretty much consisted of squirrels, raccoons, and opossums. I recall a confused and very lost deer on one occasion crashing through a service station window near Pepper's, and the event caused quite a stir. Everyone naturally asked, "Where'd that deer come from?"

A sick and immobile opossum resting in the McCollum's driveway caused a similar commotion in our Marshall Road neighborhood one Saturday morning. Rumors that the opossum could be rabid spread like wildfire. The Lansdowne Police Department was summoned. Animal control, or whatever it was called in those days, received calls. The Vatican was contacted. The National Guard went on alert status. You would have thought that King Kong was on the loose in our backyard.

With perhaps more than a dozen concerned, if not scared, adults and children looking on, the opossum made a dash (correction: opossums don't ever dash anywhere. The movement more resembled a slow, desperate gallop) for sanctuary behind Ed Flannery's woodpile. We never saw the opossum again, and Esther claimed that it most understandably died from fright.

When I was a small child, I suffered terrible foot cramps. They usually occurred at the end of the day, and they were awful. I would soak them in hot water and Epsom salts, and poor Esther would rub them for hours as I tried to go to sleep.

Dr. Whitman, our family doctor, recommended that I wear special shoes. The shoes, which looked like regular school shoes, must have had some type of orthopedically designed arch installed in the shoe. These shoes were only available at a specialty shoe store, Karl Dillman's, located in center city Philadelphia. Esther did not like to drive in the city, so she and I would take the Market Street el/subway into Philly from the 69th Street terminal twice a year to visit Karl Dillman's for my shoe fitting and next pair of shoes.

On one memorable excursion with Bill in attendance, we were sitting in the subway car in seats where our backs were against the side of the car so we could fully view fellow passengers sitting on the opposite side of the car. Sitting across from us was an elderly, well-dressed Asian man. I remember him well despite the lag in years. He wore glasses, carried a cane, wore a brimmed hat, and could not have been more pleasant. He smiled softly during our rail commute into the city and seemed to have taken a special liking to me. This person may well have been the first Asian person with whom I had ever had contact.

About the time that our Philadelphia Transportation Company (PTC) train entered the subway portion of the route, I inexplicably started to cry. I was focused on the elderly Asian gentleman, and something about him made me feel uncomfortable, even threatened. Esther and Bill were both embarrassed, as it appeared that my discomfort was directly linked to this kind gentleman who meant me no harm.

Decades have passed, and I have often questioned my actions in that situation. Prejudice is learned; we are not born with it. So where did my aversion—even fear—of the elderly Asian man develop? Playing armchair psychologist, I have a theory. Bill and I used to watch movie serials on television and at the movies that were produced in the 1940s and 1950s. One of our favorites was *Don Winslow of the Navy*, a World War II–based serial where Commander Don Winslow fought the evil saboteur, the Scorpion, and his band of thugs. The mysterious and sinister Scorpion was Asian and was very scary to the likes of a small child. Could I have projected that connection to the elderly Asian man on the Market Street subway?

Green Avenue School

18

GREEN AVENUE SCHOOL

When I was elementary school age, Lansdowne had three grade schools: Green Avenue, Highland Avenue, and Ardmore Avenue. The three schools were well dispersed geographically within Lansdowne's 1.2 square miles.

Green Avenue was clearly the newest school, having been built in the early 1950s of blond brick with green trim, naturally. It was a one-story building with dark hallways, approximately six classrooms with full windows on exterior walls, plus administrative space, a teachers' lounge, a nurse's office, and a multipurpose room (for music class and special assemblies) complete with stage and curtain, but no cafeteria (no need to have one, since we all went home for lunch). I believe we had an hour for lunch—noon to 1:00 p.m.—but that included walking or biking to and from home.

I attended school at Green Avenue from kindergarten through fifth grade. They were good and fun years. We students hated the fact that we would spend sixth grade at Highland Avenue—an ancient, dungy, two-story, brown-brick firetrap located in downtown Lansdowne—as opposed to the familiar and modern confines of Green Avenue. We also knew we would have to blend with new students at Highland Avenue, a thought that was not attractive to the majority.

Each classroom at Green Avenue School had the luxury of its own cloak room and gender-specific bathrooms. Characteristic of most secondary schools at the time, the school was not air-conditioned.

On a few special occasions, students from Ardmore Avenue School would walk over to Green Avenue for special assemblies. One of these assemblies featured a character education puppet show created by Mrs. Dorothy Waldo Phillips of Lansdowne. The presentation starred a poorly mannered character known as Sammy Spivens, and the theme for students was to replace their "bad weeds" with flowers. This series gained national attention and was even featured in many editions of *Highlights for Children* magazine in the 1950s.

A playground complete with playground equipment (swings, sliding board, sandbox, jungle gym, etc.), one basketball standard, and a large athletic field occupied the east side of the school property. Green Avenue was one of the first schools in the nation to install rubberized safety padding underneath the major playground equipment. On several occasions, I recall taking the initiative of using waxed paper to treat the sliding board to cause slicker, faster rides.

Kickball was an extremely popular sport for both boys and girls. A basketball standard stood in shallow center field, and a local ground rule was that if your kick somehow went through the basketball hoop, you automatically scored a grand-slam home run. It only happened once to my witness. Classmate Bobby Schafer claimed the honor, and we celebrated that feat for days. The school's popular principal,

Mr. Buffington, periodically would partake of kickball, a move that delighted us all.

As many classrooms bordered the playground, broken windows were fairly common, so our janitor replacing a broken window was a common sight. On too many occasions, balls found their way to Green Avenue's rooftop, which frustrated us all. A major annoyance was the fact that the playground's only drinking fountain was usually clogged and inoperable from being overloaded with sand from the nearby sandbox. Probably nine and half times out of ten, the fountain did not work.

In my latter years, I rode my bike to and from school, but in the lower grades, I generally walked home with Sally Cheeseman, Sally Wool, Jack Campbell, Andy and Kathy Thompson, the Glotfelty children, and JoEllen Franz.

A popular game we played in the front of the school was Green Tag. Some of Green Avenue's exterior was not tan brick; window frames, posts, doors, etc., were painted a dark forest green. We usually played this modified version of tag after school as students were awaiting rides from their parents. Anything green was home base; you could not be tagged "it" if you were touching green, but you needed to abandon your current base on a break, at which time you were vulnerable to being tagged.

First-Grade Class, Dibby Koller)
Dibby Koller's first-grade class, Green Avenue School, Lansdowne, Pennsylvania, 1954–1955

First row: Unknown, Bobby Jeffers, Jack Campbell, Gary Goodyear, Bob Bingham
Second row: Lorraine Nasuti, Andy Thompson, Sally Cheeseman, Wayne Foster, Sally Wool
Third row: Mary Crouthamel, Miss Koller, Unknown, Denise Kane, Margaret McCullough, Bobbie Deible (?), Judy Jackson

Green Avenue School Teachers

Kindergarten: Miss Edwards
First grade: Miss Koller
Second grade: Miss Wilson
Third grade: Miss Huruda
Fourth grade: Miss Michaels
Fifth grade: Mrs. Freas

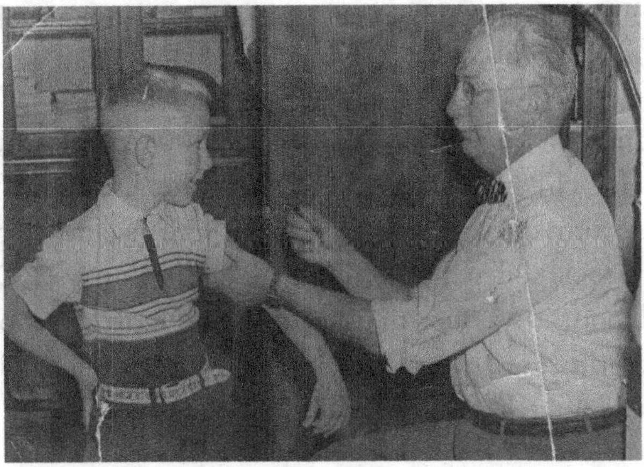

Polio injection, 1954

19

POLIO

One of my earliest childhood memories is one of staring out a St. Paul high-rise hotel window at the Minnesota State Fair in the summer of 1952. J. T. was on assignment for *Country Gentlemen*, the farming magazine for which he worked, and Esther, Bill, and I had accompanied him on this summer business trip. I assume we were in Minnesota for my father to cover the fair or to research articles with local farmers and agricultural professors at the University of Minnesota.

While the Minnesota State Fair midway and all of its allure bustled a few short blocks away, I was confined to our hotel room, reduced to tears, because of a local polio scare. I naturally did not understand my quarantine, since Bill, age fourteen, was able to accompany J. T. to the event, while I was restricted from attending because of my age. Esther drew the fun assignment of somehow attempting to console me and occupy my attention for a few days until we left St. Paul.

According to *www.PolioToday.org*, 58,000 Americans, the vast majority being children, were infected with the disease in 1952. That year, 3,145 victims died of the disease, the majority again being children, plus 2,269 people suffered from mildly disabling paralysis. During my early childhood, it was not unusual to know individuals or families impacted by the disease. A close friend during my junior high school days had mild aftereffects from polio.

In spring of 1954 a polio vaccine was finally approved for national immunization. As a first-grader at Green Avenue Elementary School, I was the first child to receive the vaccine within the school district. Green Avenue actually had two first-grade sections; a true alphabetical purist would insist that Jessica Adams, a student in the other section, should have received the first shot, not Bobby Bingham.

Dr. Harry B. Fuller, the school district's legendary physician ("turn your head … cough … again"), gave me the shot with the local newspaper taking a photo of the occasion.

20

CHRISTMAS EVE, 1952

A lasting memory of my childhood is the first direct exposure to Santa Claus that I can actually remember. I was four, and my parents, older brother, Bill, and I had lived in our current Lansdowne home on Marshall Road for two years. My parents, wishing to be well received as new neighbors, were socially active in our new neighborhood. I was told a few days prior to Christmas that Santa Claus was going to pay me a personal visit on Christmas Eve.

As I anxiously waited after dinner that December 24th, Santa Claus did appear, and upon his arrival, I sat on his lap in our living room for several minutes while I recounted my Christmas list. The passed-down family recollection is that I was totally captivated, completely mesmerized by Santa, that I could not take my eyes off of him as I sat on his lap.

I recall that during this meeting our blond cocker spaniel, Dixie, was extremely agitated, barking nonstop at events that were happening outside our house. This was unusual behavior for Dixie, who was generally easygoing and mild mannered, and subsequently I inquired of J. T. about Dixie's alarm. I then heard jingle bells outside, which proved to be the obvious source of Dixie's irritation. J. T. revealed that Dixie might be barking at Santa's reindeer on our roof.

In response, I bolted from the house in my pj's and looked upward toward the roof. Though jingle bells still sounded, I saw nothing. My father, joining me with my winter coat, suggested that we check the rooftop on the other side of our house, as the reindeer might have shifted position. We maneuvered to the new vantage point, and there were still no reindeer on the roof, but annoyingly, the jingle bells continued.

At this point, Santa appeared on our small front porch. J. T. carefully helped Santa down the three concrete steps from our front door. I was hurriedly ushered inside after hugging and thanking Santa Claus for his visit, but I was still extremely frustrated that I had not observed the reindeer. Years later I learned that Santa had been played by Ed Flannery—imbibed neighbor, Lansdowne historian, and local banker—whom my father saw cause to physically escort home a few doors down. The jingle bell ringer was Bill.

A point of ongoing amusement to my parents and Bill was my ignorance as to Santa's intoxication. However, I did make the revealing statement, while squinching my nose, that Santa smelled funny. What I most recall was the thrill of Santa personally visiting our home to inquire about my Christmas list. My parents and Bill recalled a drunken neighbor, who continued to admonish me in future years against using his backyard as a neighborhood shortcut, an instruction I rarely heeded.

21

FRIDAY NIGHT TREATS

Until I was about eighteen years of age, J. T. worked in center city Philadelphia, first at Curtis Publishing Company until 1956, and then later at Fuller Typesetting near 8th and Market. During the workweek, Esther drove J. T. to the 69th Street terminal in Upper Darby, where he caught the Market Street–Frankford elevated/subway train to center city. On the return home, he again took the Market–Frankford line to 69th Street where he rode the Red Arrow Lansdowne–Darby bus home. Occasionally on a Friday evening, J. T. would stop at a terminal vendor to purchase breaded flounder for dinner or hot raisin-cinnamon rolls as special treats.

Both of these selections were outstanding in both aroma and taste. I was never a big fish-eater as a child, but the breaded flounder from the terminal was wonderful. I easily could have eaten the entire package. The raisin-cinnamon rolls came in a square white box, which was neatly secured by tightly drawn string. The rolls were heavenly, all gooey and cinnamony with plump raisins, and typically still warm. They never lasted till the next morning and were usually consumed after dinner as dessert.

These culinary novelties always arrived unannounced, and on those distinct occasions, J. T. assumed superhero status. These foods were always unexpected, especially during my early grade school years. And even though our family undoubtedly thanked him for his kindness, J. T. likely never realized the delicious memory that he had created for his youngest child.

22

MARSHALL ROAD A&P STORE

A&P grocery stores were a fixture in thousands of communities across the United States in the 1950s and 1960s. Lansdowne was home to two A&P stores for many years: a large one located in downtown Lansdowne just north of the Lansdowne Theater, and a smaller one housed within the Marshall Road commercial district. The downtown A&P was typical for many A&P stores around the country as to size, stock, and services. The Marshall Road A&P was the extreme opposite. It was extremely small in size, and it relied on limited street parking and walk-in business. It was within this store that I received my first glimpse of a retail chain grocery store. It may well have been the smallest A&P store in America.

The Marshall Road A&P more resembled a grocery found in a remote, rural, small town as opposed to a well-established suburb. I believe it had three short aisles (thirty feet in length, I would estimate), wooden floors, ceiling fans, and one ancient cash register, which key recorded purchases by cents, tens of cents, and dollars. For example, a nineteen-cent loaf of bread would require the cashier to depress a ten-cent key and a nine-cent key. A package of ground beef costing $1.23 would require three keys to be depressed by the cashier: a one-dollar key, a twenty-cent key, and a three-cent key. The checkout process was laborious and time-consuming, especially if the shopper had a large order. There were no express aisles in those days.

On all levels, this store would be considered primitive by today's standards. The Marshall Rood A&P carried boxed and canned groceries; selection as to brand and size was severely limited. As for cereal, the Marshall Road A&P may have sold only corn flakes and Rice Krispies. Flour selection was most likely limited to one brand. To maximize retail space, the A&P had high shelving, which employees or customers could only reach with a wooden, extended-reach pick-up tool. In this store I heard and smelled coffee being ground by a machine for the first time.

The meat counter was minuscule by any standard. If you needed ground beef, you requested it, and it was ground and packaged on the spot. Esther had a peculiar need for her ground beef to be ground twice (which supposedly helped with digestion), a request not necessarily well received by A&P workers. Dairy product stock was limited, but keep in mind that the majority of residents received home milk delivery in that day. Produce variety was sparse as well.

I must pay special homage to Joe, the store's manager and the only employee of whom I hold any memory. Joe was in his mid to late forties, and he wore glasses and combed his greased salt-and-pepper hair straight back. Joe did everything: checkout, bagging, inventory, deliveries, shelf stocking, phone answering, broom sweeping, merchandise cleanup, meat cutting, etc. He had coworkers, but Joe typically was front and center—always helpful and efficient, sometimes wearing a bloodstained, white apron earned at the meat counter—while he continually shifted gears from one task to the other.

An odd spin to the A&P's presence was a competing family grocery story, the Mar-Win Market, which was located immediately adjacent in the same strip of stores. Esther preferred the Mar-Win for meat, and we got to know the senior owner and his two younger sons during the mid to late '50s. More likely than not, it was simple schmoozing with the customers, but one of the sons told my mother that he would like me to work at the store part-time when I turned sixteen. That never happened, but what did happen was that Mar-Win assumed the existing A&P space in the late 1950s when the A&P closed its doors. This acquisition nearly doubled the Mar-Win's square footage, and it remained a viable community grocery until 2015 when it ceased operation.

23

BILLY ERNST

During my early childhood, it was not unusual for my father, who was still active in the US Navy Reserves, to connect with some of his former service buddies from World War II. In the early to mid-1950s, the Philadelphia naval base was a busy and vital military installation along the east coast. Thousands of naval and civilian personnel worked at the base. There was also frequent passage to and from the base from servicemen around the country.

On one occasion, a naval officer, Captain Ernst, and his wife visited us briefly on Marshall Road with their seven-year-old son, Billy.[1] The Ernsts most likely spent one or two nights with us—again, not an unusual practice. But on one occasion, they left Billy in the care of Esther while J. T. accompanied Captain and Mrs. Ernst to the naval yard on a weekend afternoon. My older brother, Bill, was absent from home at the time for some reason, so it was just Esther babysitting Billy Ernst for a few hours while caring for me. This should have been a piece of cake, right? Wrong … most definitely wrong.

Billy Ernst was two to three years my senior and was physically much bigger than I was. He was also a bully—a mean-spirited, physically aggressive bully. Details are very sketchy at this point as to Billy's intent,

[1] Names have been fictionalized here to protect individuals' privacy.

but he formed an evil plan to splash our green-wallpapered second-floor landing with Bosco chocolate syrup. Initially, Esther thought I was the culprit, but I soon convinced her that I had no knowledge of or role in Billy's handiwork. After Esther severely reprimanded Billy and cleaned up the mess, we learned that Billy was teasing and attempting to hurt our cat, Sylvia. Had solitary confinement been an option to Esther at this time, Billy would have been an instant candidate.

The final blow came when Billy ripped off the head of my pet stuffed dog, Pepsi, most likely for my snitching on his Bosco and Sylvia misdeeds. Around this same time, the Ernsts and J. T. returned from the naval base to the chaos on Marshall Road. I was sobbing major tears upon witnessing the decapitation and death of my favorite stuffed animal. There were absolutely no words, no comforting gestures available to lessen my grief. However, as the Ernsts most certainly apologized and ushered Billy out of our home, never to return, Esther had other plans.

Esther got my attention and requested my help as she hurriedly cleared the dining-room table. As my tears subsided, Esther spread a white sheet over the table and announced that she was performing surgery on Pepsi; I was to assist. I was completely enthralled by what was happening. With discarded stuffing gathered from the living-room floor and couch, I joined my mother in returning the stuffing to Pepsi's limp torso. Once that was accomplished, Esther artfully sutured Pepsi back to full life. My favorite stuffed animal was now as good as new. Pepsi's demise had been averted by Esther's quick and creative response.

So much of what we experience as children fades and is quickly forgotten. Esther's focused actions that weekend afternoon over sixty years ago underscored her sharp thinking in the midst of a mild crisis. More importantly, it demonstrated in graphic style an instant reaction driven by a mother's love. Esther totally understood my horror and anguish in witnessing Billy's vindictive mutilation of my beloved pet, and as a result, she innovatively sought to right the wrong.

This was Esther at her glorious best. She never stood taller in my memory.

24

JANE FAIR

Jane Fair was a speech therapist employed by the Lansdowne-Aldan School District. I had a significant speech impediment (lisp) during my elementary school years. While school was in session, I attended treatment sessions with Mrs. Fair from kindergarten through seventh grade. Sessions were about a half hour in length once a week, with their frequency decreasing as I grew older and the impediment lessened.

I mainly remember meeting with Mrs. Fair at Green Avenue School, which I attended from kindergarten through fifth grade. Mrs. Fair would guide me in exercises, many of them in front of a mirror. I remember her as an extremely patient and kind woman whose encouragement and support I welcomed. Going to see her was not bothersome to me, as I knew she was genuinely trying to help.

I recall some mild teasing from my classmates, mainly boys, in the lower elementary grades. I only remember one incident where I was reduced to tears. That criticism came from an older elementary-age boy as school was being released and I started my walk home. I also recollect that the lisp seemed to worsen when I was tired or excited.

My memory recalls some supportive and patient intervention by Esther at home. I recollect no response from J. T. Certainly Mrs. Fair gave them advice on how to handle the issue, but I do not remember any pointed dialogue with them on the subject. Perhaps the advice was to downplay the issue. Bill, on the other hand, the ever-so-sensitive older brother, did rag on me occasionally. This was offered in insensitive comments, such as: "Why can't you talk right?" or "Stop talking like a baby."

Jane Fair worked with me for over seven years; her skilled instruction permanently corrected my speech deficit. I remain grateful to her and the school district for offering this service, as I doubt that I would have outgrown it on my own. Because of the experience, I have always looked at the "special ed" label differently from most people.

A side note here is that Jane Fair's only child, Don, whom I knew fairly well, became a news reporter and evening talk show host on Philadelphia radio in the early 1970s.

25

PENNSYLVANIA TURNPIKE

America's first superhighway was a significant roadway for my family as we made our annual summer treks to Michigan and/or Kentucky. During most trips, we only went to Michigan or Kentucky, but on a few occasions, the trips included both destinations, with an all-day drive between the two states through Indiana. Until Bill graduated from college in 1960, the family Chevrolet would carry the four of us through southern Pennsylvania via the turnpike to and from our trips to Louisville and Traverse City/Drummond Island. On several excursions, our family dogs, Dixie and Eloise, made the journey as well, helping to break up the tedium of travel.

The Pennsylvania Turnpike from New Jersey to Ohio was completed in 1956, so we used the road westward, from the Valley Forge toll booth until we exited for Kentucky in Washington, Pennsylvania, or where it eventually intersected with the Ohio Turnpike in western Pennsylvania for the ride to Traverse City. Whenever a vehicle entered the turnpike, the driver was issued a ticket that marked the entry point and calculated mileage and toll from entry to designated exit. (Vehicles exclusively entered and exited the turnpike at state-controlled tollbooths.)

On more than one occasion, there was near panic in our car when the toll ticket was temporarily misplaced. Drivers who were unable to produce the ticket at the exit had to pay the full cost of utilizing the system. These rare instances led to the glove compartment earning distinction as the official depository for all toll tickets. Despite the turnpike's cost, my parents never complained, since the road significantly cut travel time across the state.

The four-lane, divided road traveled the path of abandoned Pennsylvania Railroad track, but it was not as well engineered as today's modern interstates. The road was extremely curvy at points going through the Allegheny Mountains, which demanded lowered speed in many sections. Although tunnels are now reduced in number, the turnpike originally utilized seven of them (Blue Mountain, Kittatiny Mountain, Allegheny Mountain, Sideling Hill, Ray's Hill, Tuscarora Mountain, and Laurel Hill) to traverse the Allegheny Mountains in south central Pennsylvania. Passing through these tunnels was a high point, since they interrupted the tedium of the journey. I soon learned their order and length, and my parents would often quiz me on which tunnel was next. A dreaded event, however, was when a section of tunnel was being cleaned, thus causing excessive backup and lengthier travel times.

A unique feature to the turnpike was the fact that food, fuel, and bathrooms were found at designated rest plazas along the way. Howard Johnson's operated all turnpike restaurants. I was very partial to their hotdogs and ice cream.

Mileage for our family trips across the state was over three hundred miles, but the distance seemed much longer in those days. Air conditioning did not exist, and AM car radios received spotty reception, especially in the mountains. To entertain myself, I generally read, colored, or bothered my parents.

I recall two memorable travel events. On one trip, Esther had forgotten the bag that contained her makeup and required medications. She made this determination about forty-five minutes into the trip as we neared the turnpike entrance at the Valley Forge toll booth. This oversight demanded an immediate, hurried return to Lansdowne and then backtracking to Valley Forge, adding ninety-plus unnecessary minutes to the trip. To say that J. T. was displeased is a gross understatement. There was no need for air-conditioning on that day, for it was very chilly inside our 1954 Chevrolet until dinnertime.

On another occasion, J. T. missed the Valley Forge exit after a long day's drive from southern Michigan. He dared to double back to the missed exit using the crossover marked "For Official Use Only." After I was admonished by Esther to say nothing, and after J. T. had carefully surveyed the traffic flow and calculated his chances, he made his illegal move—only to be promptly pulled over and ticketed by a Pennsylvania State Trooper. The man deserved better, and much to Esther's surprise, I kept my mouth shut as J. T. was ticketed.

Grandmother Mary Althier Drury Bingham
and her only two grandchildren

26

MARY ALTHIER DRURY BINGHAM

My grandmother on J. T.'s side, Mary Althier Drury Bingham (frequently referenced as Mary Allie) was born in western Kentucky in 1878. She was the third of four children born to George Hamilton Drury (1846–1919), a farmer, and Margaret Ellen Harris (1847–1918). I know little of Grandmother Bingham's childhood and young adulthood or her parentage and siblings. At age twenty-four in 1902, she married my paternal grandfather, Thomas Cranston Bingham (1868–1954), and in eight years gave birth to six children:

- George Hamilton Bingham (1902)
- Margaret (Peg) Ellen Bingham (1904)
- William Truman Bingham (1905)
- Martha Laura Bingham (1907)

- Mary Cornelia (Connie) Bingham (1909)
- James Truman (J. T.) Bingham (1910)

In 1910 and prior to J. T.'s birth in November of that same year, a small-town scandal rocked Morganfield, Kentucky, when Thomas Cranston Bingham, a local banker, abandoned his family, fled the state, and relocated to Montana with a married mother of three children who resided in Morganfield. The matter was made even more sensational by the fact that several thousand dollars was missing from the bank that employed Thomas Cranston Bingham. In 1910 states rarely pursued noncapital felons except for neighboring states. My speculation is that my grandfather knew of this practice, which was why he chose distant Montana as his new home.

This event no doubt had a dramatic and lasting impact on Mary Allie and her six children. With five children in the household under the age of ten and one soon to be born, Mary Allie had no choice but to lean heavily on family for help. During my father's childhood, Mary Allie supported the family by being a laundress and seamstress. J. T. grew up fatherless and poor, and by age ten, he was already working part-time after school at the county newspaper. A divorce was finally obtained in 1920, a tricky accomplishment at the time for a couple of Catholic faith.

As the Bingham children matured and reached adulthood, all three Bingham brothers, interestingly, sought to leave Morganfield and their immediate family. The three Bingham sisters eventually moved to Louisville for better employment opportunities, with Mary Allie accompanying them. Mary Allie never worked upon moving to Louisville with her daughters. For more than thirty years of residence in Louisville, Mary Allie and her three daughters lived in rented homes with household head Mary Allie clearly calling the shots.

All three daughters had romantic interests with which Mary Allie interfered. Martha Bingham was married from 1943 to 1946, but that marriage ended in divorce. Connie Bingham was happily engaged, but Mary Allie became a divisive factor in that relationship, causing the couple to part ways. Esther even commented that Mary Allie attempted to be a disruptive force in her marriage, despite the sizable mileage between Louisville and Philadelphia. I recall Esther telling me once that she "dreaded" summer trips to Louisville when Mary Allie was alive, as unnecessary and petty controversy frequently arose.

Even as a small child, I was grateful that my interactions with Mary Allie were minimal. Bill felt likewise. I only recall three or four meetings with her, the last contact being in a Louisville nursing home. Even small children can sense when attending adults, especially relatives, are disinterested and put out by youthful presence. I read Mary Allie loud and clear: five minutes on her lap for a few photographs every two summers was her limit. She had absolutely no interest in Bill or me.

My overall perception is that Mary Allie was understandably humiliated and deeply embittered by her husband's desertion of the family and the far-reaching ramifications. Keep in mind that this was small-town, western Kentucky in 1910. The emotional scars from this ugly experience would have severely impacted anyone, but my speculation is that the scars within Mary Allie were especially deep, stinging, and long lasting. Mary Allie chose never to recover and move forward from her embarrassment, and as her children reached adulthood, she perfected a selfish, troublesome, and dictating persona, which she masterfully orchestrated to bully and control her children. In her final years, it was as if her life's focus was to make her children as miserable as she was. Mary Allie especially tried to lure J. T. back to Kentucky in the 1950s, but my father wisely understood that any relocation of our family would surely doom the marriage.

Mary Allie died in Louisville in 1961 of a heart attack. J. T. and his five older siblings were all in attendance, as was Esther, for the funeral services. Fortunately, I was spared the ordeal.

27

THOMAS CRANSTON BINGHAM

J. T.'s father—my paternal grandfather, Thomas Cranston Bingham—was born in western Kentucky in 1868 to Silas Henry Bingham (1843–1923), a local farmer, and Margaret Ellen Gardner (?–1901). Thomas Cranston Bingham was the second oldest of nine children, the oldest boy. I know nothing of his early years. He married my paternal grandmother, Mary Althier Drury, in 1902 and fathered six children during the first eight years of marriage.

His desertion of his family and the related scandal is well documented in the previous essay. J. T. never knew his father, and the impact on him as a child and adolescent was formidable. Considering the era and the rich fodder created by Thomas Bingham's scandalous affair, embezzled funds, and cruel desertion of his wife and children, J. T. and his siblings grew up in a town where they were ostracized and blacklisted to varying degrees. This cloud assuredly lifted somewhat over time but not completely, as the hurt and humiliation caused were assuredly lifelong.

J. T. and his siblings grew up poor in a wood-framed house on Spaulding Street in Morganfield, and I know from conversations with J. T. late in his life that clothes were hand-me-downs and birthdays were nothing special. He shared a bedroom with two older brothers. He told me once that his Christmas gift one year was an orange.

In a family photo that was not discovered until after J. T.'s death, J. T. is clothed in a long-sleeved shirt, bib overalls, and hat. He is also shoeless, which was not unusual for the time. What is most striking to me about this image is J. T.'s aloof and bland expression. My emotional response to the photo has always been, "That is one sad little boy."

Ironically, I never heard J. T. complain about his childhood or even the physical absence of a father. The real ramification was the lack of an appropriate role model. Sure, some male relatives kicked in periodically, but extended family can be very cruel at times. J. T. once related a story about winning a fist fight in response to a peer calling him a "bastard." That peer was cousin Snats, a same-age relative who was more brother than cousin.

While J. T. was directly impacted, Bill and I were affected as well. Quite simply, J. T. was uncomfortable in the role of father. His understanding of his role—as was the case with many American men at the time—was to be the very best provider possible, to work hard, to provide the material necessities, and to live in a comfortable home in a solid community. He undervalued—and perhaps even failed to recognize the need for—a baseball catch in the backyard, a spontaneous father-and-son trip to the zoo, a lesson in riding my first bicycle, or an outing to a Phillies game.

There were notable examples where we did spend time together, and many of them were memorable: trips to Annapolis, the dozen-plus Army-Navy games we attended, train excursions to Washington, DC, accelerated help with a school leaf project in junior high, and so on, but they were few and far between. J. T. was never comfortable in the nurturing role; that was pretty much left to Esther, as she was always the bedtime reader, the medic, the listener and go-to problem solver, and more typically the "fun" parent.

I was very aware of J. T.'s uneasiness as a father. As I matured, I understood the basis for the gaps, the unintentional shortcomings in his fathering style. Well before I assumed my role as father, I pledged not to replicate J. T.'s underdeveloped parenting style. I wanted to be the complete father that he never was.

I hold no malice or grudge toward J. T.'s rearing of me. He did the best he could. He cared for me, loved me, and wanted the best for me, but his performance, as I referenced previously, was shortsighted because of the lack of a physical role model.

The person I do criticize and hold accountable is my grandfather, Thomas Cranston Bingham. He was the selfish individual who thoroughly reneged on his parental responsibilities, permanently scarring his wife and six children.

Late in his life, Thomas Cranston Bingham wished to reunite with his children, including J. T., whom he had never met, written, or spoken to. As he was in his final years in Montana, he reached out for conciliation with the children he had so severely wronged. I know few details here, but all siblings were unified in rejecting his offer. Good for them.

Having lived in Montana as a sheep rancher for over forty years, Thomas Cranston Bingham died in 1954 from a heart attack. He is buried in the Mt. Olivet Cemetery in Great Falls, Montana. Before I die, and despite the physical distance, I am committed to paying his gravesite a visit. I have unfinished business to address.

28

KINDERGARTEN CHRISTMAS PLAY

It was December of 1953, and our kindergarten class was responsible for producing a Christmas play that portrayed the nativity scene and Christ's birth. I was chosen to play Balthasar, one of the three wise men. The play was performed in front of an all-school Christmas assembly in the auditorium at Green Avenue School.

My lines were certainly minimal, but when I was cued to deliver my scripted words, I froze. Miss Edwards, my kindhearted kindergarten teacher, and my mother quickly rose from the front row and leaned on the stage, whispering the simple lines to me. I still froze. Panic struck. I was soon between sobs and major tears. I can't recall if I gutlessly bolted from the manger or somehow managed to console myself enough to conclude the scene with my fellow thespians, but the play did conclude without meaningful contributions from me. However, the three wise men, one being severely muted, did bear and deliver their gifts to honor the birth of baby Jesus.

Esther and Miss Edwards consoled and comforted me afterward, but any misplay on my part was soon forgotten, since the star of the play was actually our family's blond cocker spaniel, Dixie, the only live animal appearing in the production. Understandably, Dixie stole everyone's heart, and my popularity soared from Dixie's performance.

Although it was a nearly forgotten childhood event, I believe the experience had a lasting impact on me. I have generally been comfortable in the role of public speaker. My skills and confidence matured during my professional career, and I was typically not anxious or nervous in speaking before large audiences. However, I have never been comfortable or capable in reciting memorized lines in public. In such instances, I have always been forced to read from prepared, written notes. This is the result of a complete lack of confidence.

As an undergrad, I was considered for a minor role in a university Shakespearean production, but I turned it down despite my interest because of a marked lack of confidence in memorizing the written word. To this day, I am in awe of stage actors and their ability to memorize lengthy scripts, a talent for which I am totally lacking. Maybe there is no connection between my botched Christmas pageant performance and poor select memory, but that has always been my association.

29

THE MARSHALL ROAD COMMERCIAL DISTRICT

When we lived on east Marshall Road and north Lansdowne Avenue, this small neighborhood shopping cluster served as a convenient commercial lifeline for our family. The grouping of stores was small in number, but many useful businesses were contained there within easy walking distance from home: grocery store(s), bank, hardware, pharmacy, gas station, barber shop, deli, tavern, etc.

Marshall Road split the district in two between the Lansdowne and Upper Darby sides, less than one block in length between Windermere and Owen Avenues. My family and I frequented this area primarily from 1950 to 1960. When we moved to east Essex Avenue in 1960, the reliance dipped considerably simply because of geography, but the area continued to remain familiar, less frequented turf.

An incomplete list of the Upper Darby stores included:

- Coffman's Drug Store
- A butcher shop (which we never frequented)
- Stewart's tavern
- Van-De-Boe's hardware
- Windermere Delicatessen (Sam and Momma's)

- A gift shop
- An ice cream parlor in my younger days
- Possibly a beauty parlor at one time
- Gulf/Atlantic gas station

An incomplete list of Lansdowne stores included:

- The world's smallest A&P store
- Mar-Win Market
- Chamberlain's Realty
- A dry cleaners perhaps?
- Pete's Sanitary Barbershop
- A veterinary office
- Owens TV repair
- Fidelity Bank with Lansdowne's first drive-through service

Coffman's was our drugstore until an unfortunate incident (separate essay) ended our family's patronage. Esther shopped at both the A&P and the Mar-Win. Van-de-Boe's was a tiny hardware store that J. T. relied upon as needed for home repair items. I frequented it often for baseball cards, model airplanes, rubber balls, assorted toys, school supplies, and so on. Stewart's was an extremely popular tavern with former LAHS athletes. (Remember, Lansdowne was a dry town with no bars or taverns.) We also occasionally used Owens TV for tubes and repairs.

Neighbor Eddie Bartlett owned the gas station and operated it as owner/mechanic for years. Esther valued the drive-through service at Fidelity Bank, getting to know the tellers by first name. As for me, the Windermere Deli was close to a second home.

I certainly visited this business area several hundred times as a youth, either on my own or running errands for my mother or even neighbors. While some of the stores had short lives, many of the stores remained staple businesses that continue to operate to this day. Whenever I return to Lansdowne, I always pay this block a visit to determine what has changed and what has remained constant. In doing so, it's like I never left.

30

J. T.'S ATTIRE

J. T. would never be confused with someone making a fashion statement. His work attire was business conservative and highly predictable: white, starched dress shirt (I never saw him wear a colored or striped dress shirt, as he never owned one, to my memory), conservative business suit (gray, brown, or perhaps blue) with a herringbone or light, subdued stripe pattern, business tie and tie bar, socks, and plain, laced oxford shoes, preferably brown. He also owned a few tweed sport jackets that he wore casually, never to work.

I never saw J. T. in a pair of loafers or casual shoes. He owned about twenty unremarkable ties, and he routinely rotated them for business use. Late in life, he started wearing western string ties around the house. He never wore a T-shirt around the house, to my recollection. When he got up in the morning, he religiously got dressed. There was no lounging around for this man in pajamas, bathrobe, and slippers.

Men's socks in my father's day had poor elastic, and after two to three wearings, they would not hug the legs but drooped down to the ankles. A classic line from the nostalgic Statler Brothers' classic, "Do You Remember These?" comes to mind as befitting J. T.: "My daddy's socks rolled down." So, when my father sat down at home after a long day's work, one saw a lot of his shiny, hairless lower calves. He also never wore white athletic socks.

I often thought that J. T. was the model for the opening scene of TV's "Mister Rogers' Neighborhood." Upon arriving home from work, J. T. promptly removed and hung his suit jacket in the master bedroom closet. In colder months, he would don a substitute: a Pendleton jacket with frequently worn, patched elbows.

The really strange aspect to all of this is that J. T. never removed his tie upon arriving home from work. In fact, he never even loosened it. I always thought that this response was connected to his naval academy and military days during WWII.

Weekend attire was somewhat relaxed: a sport shirt, no tie, a Pendleton jacket—or possibly a button-down, Mr. Rogers–style sweater in fall and winter—and dress pants. Yes, dress pants. I think he'd had enough of khaki pants in the navy so we never saw J. T. in khakis. J. T. had one pair of jeans, and he only wore them infrequently when he was determined to do some gardening or serious outdoor work. I never saw J. T. in sneakers or boots; he wore old dress shoes when he worked outdoors. He also never wore shorts. During colder months, J. T. wore an overcoat and fedora-style hat to work.

31

LANSDOWNE ICE & COAL

During my youth, this long-established business was located at 500 East Baltimore Pike. I recall going there numerous times with J. T. to pick up ice for neighborhood picnics and gatherings. Convenience stores did not yet exist, so they were not an option for ice. Nor did supermarkets sell ice. Crushed ice, packaged in large brown-paper bags, and block ice were available from a machine at any time at Lansdowne Ice & Coal. During business hours, you could go through the office and collect purchased ice from the loading dock. I seem to remember paying twenty-five cents for a large bag or single block.

I recall that we got a combination of both, but I believe J. T. was more partial to the block ice. You'd hurry home to place the block ice in a galvanized aluminum tub (coolers, as we know them today, were not yet popular), which was used to hold and chill the beer and soda (it was called soda back East). With less than a dozen carefully targeted strokes of the ice pick, J. T. would reduce the block to chopped, icy rubble. The man knew what he was doing with an ice pick.

Lansdowne Ice & Coal also had a small skating rink. The Lansdowne Boys Club sported a boys' ice hockey team at the rink for at least one year in 1959. Ken Dunkle was a team member, as were some childhood friends of mine: Don Petrosa, Eddie Cope, and Chris and Dan Greening.

Even though our house on Essex Avenue was heated with fuel oil, my father and I still made autumn trips to LI&C to purchase baskets of cannel coal. Cannel coal is a type of bituminous coal, which was actually used in fireplaces to help heat homes both in England and America. We would buy two to three baskets every fall and use it sparingly during the colder months as an addition to firewood. Cannel coal generated a great amount of heat and burned very, very slowly. The coal hissed, crackled, and popped as it burned, and it also gave off beautiful, multicolored flames from the natural gas that escaped as it burned. It was not unusual for some of the coal to burn through the night and still be burning in the hearth the following morning.

J. T. seemed very knowledgeable about this type of coal, and I wonder if it was because he learned of it when he worked in a coal mine in western Kentucky County in 1928–1930 after graduating from high school. Today, cannel coal is not available for home purchase, as I suspect it simply gives off too much heat for today's contemporary home fireplaces.

Lansdowne Ice & Coal still operates today at the same East Baltimore Pike location, although the ice skating rink is just a distant memory.

32

HURRICANE HAZEL

Anyone who grew up in the Philadelphia area in my age range will remember this storm that monumentally arrived on Saturday, October 16, 1954. I was six years old at the time, and our family was still living on Marshall Road. Hurricane Hazel was a class-four hurricane that entered land just south of Wilmington, North Carolina, and then traveled due north through North Carolina, Virginia, Maryland, and Pennsylvania, eventually veering northwest into New York State and Ontario. It was considered one of the worst hurricanes in North Carolina history, and in researching the storm, it is amazing to learn how little it slowed once it hit land mass in North Carolina.

The storm's impact was so severe that Hazel's name has been permanently removed from the national registry of hurricane names. Hazel killed over a thousand people in Haiti before it traveled to the United States. In North America alone, six hundred people died from the storm, with winds at the Philadelphia airport being clocked as high as ninety-five miles per hour.

Hazel did not hit Philadelphia directly, as it traveled more westerly through central Pennsylvania, but it caused severe power outages, extensive property damage, and flooding. From our front door, I saw darkened skies, fallen tree limbs, and downed power lines that twisted and sparked on the ground. I was eager to go outside, but Esther wisely kept me inside for the entire weekend. I cannot recall if school was called off on the following Monday and possibly Tuesday, but certainly some districts canceled classes. I also remember brief power outages and candles lighting the house.

Such excitement was seen through the eyes of a naïve six-year-old who did not know about lost lives or the severe economic impact experienced across the eastern United States and into Ontario. To me the storm was novel and pure excitement, void of negative consequences.

33

ABRAHAM LINCOLN BIRTHPLACE NATIONAL HISTORICAL SITE

During one of our annual summer treks to Louisville to visit Grandmother Bingham and J. T.'s sisters, we scheduled a day trip to Hodgenville, Kentucky, approximately fifty miles away. We toured the Abraham Lincoln Birthplace National Historical Site and then had a picnic at the park with some local distant relatives. I was probably seven or eight years old at the time.

An older, never-to-be-seen-again boy relative of mine had brought a BB rifle to the picnic. He and I were in a nearby field of high grass, shooting the rifle at cans mounted on a fence. As I ran to the fence to reset some cans, a long-abandoned, rusted horseshoe spike gouged my left lower leg near my shin. Despite the fact that one of my aunts suggested that a Band-Aid would suffice, the picnic was cut short by J. T. and Esther's insistence that we immediately visit a hospital emergency room for medical care. While the wound was deep, jagged, and painful, bleeding was minimal, and I did my best to put up a good front.

For some reason, we wound up a local doctor's office where the wound was cleaned, medicated, repaired using six clamps, and wrapped. I also received a tetanus shot because of the rusty stake.

I walked with a limp for several days while wearing a medicated dressing that extended from knee to ankle on my injured leg. Prior to the accident, and at my insistence, my parents had purchased a Confederate soldier's cap for me (my mother was an admirer of Robert E. Lee) at the site's gift shop. As we journeyed back home to Pennsylvania, I wore the cap proudly. I recall J. T. chuckling at a fellow traveler's comment to me as we left a Howard Johnson's on the Pennsylvania Turnpike. It was something like "Had a rough time at Gettysburg, did you?"

34

SUPERMAN

"Faster than a speeding bullet … more powerful than a locomotive … able to leap tall buildings in a single bound … Look … up in the sky. It's a bird. It's a plane. It's Superman. Yes, Superman … strange visitor from a faraway planet who came to earth with powers and abilities far beyond those of mortal men … Superman, who could change the course of mighty rivers, bend steel in his bare hands, and who—disguised as Clark Kent, mild-mannered reporter for a great metropolitan newspaper—fights a never-ending battle for truth, justice, and the American way."

Above is the narrated introduction to the weekly television program *Superman*, which ran from 1952 to 1958. Superman was sponsored by Kellogg's, "the greatest name in cereals," and it aired in prime time. I knew this intro by heart as a small child, and I still know it word for word.

TV's Superman was played by journeyman film actor George Reeves, whose most noteworthy previous role was as one of Scarlet O'Hara's suitors, Stuart Tarleton, in the 1939 film classic, *Gone with the Wind.*

Like many of my playmates, I was hooked on Superman from the start. I rarely missed an episode. I was familiar with all key characters: Perry White, Lois Lane, Jimmy Olson, Inspector Henderson, and of course, Superman. Esther got into my fascination as well, as she crafted a Superman cape for me from an old white dish towel by crayoning in a red-and-blue Superman emblem. I didn't care that I was wearing an inaccurate replica of Superman's red-and-blue cape. My mother would safety-pin the cape around my neck, and I was off, flying around the neighborhood.

My Superman enthusiasm approached disastrous heights one summer evening. After watching an especially inspiring weekly episode, I secured and somehow positioned a stepladder next to our one-car garage on Marshall Road. As I was transitioning from the top of the ladder to the roof, Esther caught me and intervened, likely preventing a serious accident.

I don't recall Esther's precise discipline that night, but I would suspect a brisk escort to my bedroom, possibly with Esther leading me by my ear, a very strong reprimand, and an early bedtime. Also, if my memory serves me correctly, my Superman cape was officially and permanently retired later that evening. I was grounded, never to fly again.

35

"A CORNFIELD AT SUFFOLK"

My family's association with the watercolor of this title dates back to 1950 when J. T. bought the painting at an auction at Freeman's in Philadelphia. The purchase price was fifty dollars.

The artist is Henry J. Kinnaird (1880–1920), a British artist who painted both in watercolor and oil. He is known primarily for his rural scenes of rivers and farms in early twentieth-century England.

While the details of the purchase are clear, J. T.'s motivation was not. J. T. and Esther were certainly not art lovers. During my childhood and adolescence, all that adorned the walls within our homes were some framed magazine poster covers (beagle, mare and foal) from J. T.'s employment years with *Country Gentlemen*, some oil paintings completed by family friend Ben Marcune, assorted family photos, and surprisingly, "A Cornfield at Suffolk."

This painting is impressive as a carefully crafted, original watercolor, but we have no understanding as to why J. T. bought it back in 1950. We were not a wealthy family, and neither parent was known for frivolous buying. A fifty-dollar purchase of a nonessential item in 1950, especially art, was inconsistent and totally out of character with J. T.'s pragmatic ways.

Regardless, I am pleased that he did acquire the painting. It has been a constant comfort to me all of my life. The serenity of the scene helped soothe many a difficult day at school or work or a trying circumstance within the family. During my childhood and adolescence, the painting always maintained a prime location on the family living-room wall over the sofa.

The painting was treated and rematted in the late 1990s. The gold frame is believed to be the original and adds much to the presentation and charm. Overall, the painting is in excellent condition.

Based on its condition, size, frame, and additional research I've completed on recently auctioned/sold watercolors by Henry J. Kinnaird, current value is estimated at $1,200 to $2,000. Despite his short lifespan, Mr. Kinnaird produced hundreds of original paintings, thus significantly lowering the value of the painting. The painting's size, roughly seventeen inches by twenty-nine inches, is a major plus.

The directive within the family is that "A Cornfield at Suffolk" is to forever stay within the family; it is never to be sold. In hindsight, I believe J. T. would be pleased with that decision.

36

THE PRUITTS

The Pruitts were next-door neighbors to us on Marshall Road. Their friendship with my parents lasted for decades.

DelRoy was once and always a character. He was a native of tiny Monterey, Virginia, which is nestled in northwest Virginia in Highland County near the West Virginia state line. I hold no history as to DelRoy's migration to Philadelphia from Virginia, although he did try his hand at the ministry early in life. He left divinity school within the first few weeks, claiming that he was astonished to learn that ministers were supposed to be against sinning.

Physically, DelRoy was tall, gangly, and bald. He was about the same age as J. T., and he and J. T. enjoyed the common bond of being rural southerners living up north. The two of them liked to swap stories and jokes. DelRoy owned a small network of five-and-dime stores in West Philadelphia and the nearby Philadelphia suburbs of Yeadon and Stonehurst. He also owned one extremely profitable store on the boardwalk in Ocean City, New Jersey, near 9th Street, and he claimed that his Ocean City store made more money from June to August than his other stores made combined in a year.

DelRoy worked hard. He was never unwilling to do dirty or menial work to get the job done. He was also extremely strong physically, using his large hands and long arms and legs to his advantage. He drove a large brown truck to and from work (similar to a modern-day UPS truck), which was a familiar parked fixture in his neighboring driveway for years.

Also a musician, DelRoy was active in Yeadon Kiwanis, and for years he organized a "Hillbilly Band," as he called it, which would put on musical comedy shows at nursing homes and community centers in the area. On an ongoing basis, he attempted to recruit Esther to play the piano for his band. However, Esther always refused his offer, as it demanded too much time away from the family.

DelRoy was married for many years to his wife, Jean, who, like Helen Bartlett, grew very close to Esther. Jean Pruitt did not work. She was an avid, voracious reader during the daytime, and she is the first person I ever knew who wore her glasses on a string around her neck. Jean Pruitt was also a devotee of Christian Science, and our family even got to know Jean's Christian Science practitioner, white-haired, kindly Mrs. Warren, who all too often visited when Jean suffered migraines.

While Jean was quiet and reserved, DelRoy was far from it—the exact opposite, in fact. He was loud, outgoing, even boisterous, yet always friendly and very loyal to his friends. The Pruitts had two children, June and Jackie, who were both much older than I. Jackie was closer in age to Bill than I was.

The Pruitts liked to throw elaborate summer picnics in their backyard. They were some of the best family picnics I ever attended, gala events frequented by neighbors, friends, and extended family members.

It was clear that I was a favorite child neighbor to DelRoy. He got the biggest kick when I played Catholic priest and held Mass in our living room with the sole intent to collect money from the offering. One time he set me up by paying me twenty-five cents to supervise some drying concrete in his backyard patio—only to return fifteen minutes later to find me making handprints in the wet cement. He told that story for years, claiming that it was the best twenty-five cents he ever spent.

DelRoy also had a serious side to him. His commitment to Kiwanis was genuine and ongoing, and he volunteered hundreds and hundreds of hours to his band and other Kiwanis projects. He was also a serious and learned collector of small Asian figurines sculpted in ivory. Hundreds of intricately carved pieces adorned multiple glass display cases in the Pruitt living room.

When I think of my parents' best friends during my lifetime, I think first of the Pruitts. My own personal relationship with DelRoy extended well past my high school years.

37

PETE'S SANITARY BARBERSHOP

Even as a child, the "sanitary" reference in the title, which was stenciled on the shop's front window, was strange to me. Perhaps it was intended to avoid anyone's confusing the establishment with "Pete's *Un*sanitary Barbershop." Who will ever know?

Pete's was located at 54 West Marshall Road. It was a separate building clumped in the Marshall Road commercial district, and it looked like it was specifically designed and constructed as a barbershop. Pete ran the place with his two sons: one who was prematurely balding and the other who had buckteeth. Pete was probably in his late fifties to early sixties when I went there from about 1950 to 1959. My father accompanied me in my younger years. There were three barber chairs. Pete and his sons always wore customized white shirts with buttons up the neck, which made them appear like they worked in a hospital.

There was one cardinal rule in patronizing Pete's: you never wanted Pete to cut your hair, because Pete did not use electric trimmers. Pete used manually operated hand trimmers, which pinched your hair when he pulled the lever. The process was actually painful. Pete never caught on that he had alienated the majority of the shop's patrons by his use of such a crude and outdated instrument. Pete's sons used electric trimmers, so I soon learned how to position myself in the Saturday morning queue so as to avoid Pete.

One of Pete's sons commuted from New Jersey every day. What a drag that must have been! He battled traffic and congested, noninterstate, urban highways for at least an hour, only to stand on his feet for eight to nine hours cutting hair. Then he battled similar traffic returning home at the end of a long day in order to repeat the lovely process the following day.

A big day in the life of a small boy at Pete's was when you no longer had to sit on the board to get your hair cut. This rite of passage usually occurred around age five or six. Men could also get a shave at Pete's, but it was not a full shave, just around the ears and back of the neck.

Pete's introduced me to such manly publications as *Sports Afield*, *Field and Stream*, and *Outdoor Life*. I cannot recall the price of a haircut, but the entire process of waiting, avoiding Pete, and getting my hair cut, usually took an hour. I believe kids got a lollipop out of the deal as well.

When my family moved to 29 East Essex Avenue in 1960, my allegiance in barber shops shifted to Bob's Barber Shop, which was located on South Lansdowne Avenue adjacent to the train station. I had no real reason for the move other than the fact that Pete was most likely still using the manual clippers, and I had grown weary of the queue game.

A final note: at Christmastime, a Lansdowne Boy Scout troop sold Christmas trees on the property just outside the barbershop. J. T. bought many a scrawny Christmas tree there a day or two prior to Christmas.

Floyd Barnard Pitcher

38

FLOYD BARNARD PITCHER

Floyd Barnard Pitcher, my maternal grandfather, was born in 1892 in Sheridan, Michigan (Montcalm County northeast of Grand Rapids). He was the third of seven children born to Barnard Pitcher (1853–1917) and Lydia Lodema Greenhoe Pitcher (1864–1959). Grandfather Pitcher grew up in Traverse City, a town he never left. After high school, he worked in a grocery store, but later in life he was employed for over twenty years with Railway Express. He did not serve in the military, to my knowledge. He married Lenora Leone Sexton when he was twenty-three.

Grandfather Pitcher was a thin and slight man, less than six feet tall. He had black hair with very little gray on the edges, even in his senior years, and he wore glasses. I only saw him six to eight times in my life. He was a quiet but fun guy. A bit of an imp, he was mischievous and liked to playfully tease and joke. Bill and I were his only grandsons out of nine grandchildren. Bill received direct benefit of that father-substitute relationship when he and Esther lived in Traverse City during J. T.'s naval deployment during World War II.

I recall accompanying Grandfather Pitcher as he dutifully worked his vegetable garden in the back of the house. He liked baseball, especially the Detroit Tigers and all-star outfielder Al Kaline. We played baseball catch in the side yard on a few occasions. In many ways, Grandfather Pitcher acted younger than J. T., even though he was eighteen years his senior. He religiously drank one can of Detroit-brewed Blatz Beer daily, usually after work while reading the paper or listening to a Tigers game on the radio.

One summer morning, quite early, he took me fishing. We drove to a nearby beach on Lake Michigan, and he oared our rowboat to a specific spot not far from shore. He definitely knew what he was doing, because we effortlessly caught one yellow perch after another. In ninety minutes, we had a full bucket, which comprised the evening meal.

While his employment career was unremarkable, Grandfather Pitcher was an avid naturalist and pioneer conservationist in northern Michigan at a time when conservation as a concept and cause was barely known. He even bought me a subscription to *Michigan Conservation*, a monthly magazine, which I enjoyed receiving in the mail.

Grandfather Pitcher was an avid hunter of deer and rabbit. Esther's family routinely had beagles in the house, and King and Queenie were used for rabbit hunting. Esther gleefully recounted on one occasion when she dressed Queenie in doll clothes and paraded her in a baby carriage around the neighborhood. Venison and rabbit were common dinner dishes for the family during Esther's childhood and adolescence.

Grandfather Pitcher had the luxury of walking to work when he was employed at Railway Express. Occasionally he would forward to us unclaimed, abandoned items. The literary series *Harvard Classics* was an example, and it has been in our family for nearly seventy years.

Grandfather Pitcher suffered a second major heart attack in 1964 while shoveling snow. He died a week later in a Traverse City hospital at age seventy-two. My mother and father flew to Traverse City and attended the funeral while I remained in Lansdowne.

I have good memories of this kind and decent man. I only wish that I had known him better.

Lenora Leone Sexton Pitcher

39

LENORA LEONE SEXTON PITCHER

My maternal grandmother, Lenora Leone Sexton Pitcher, was born in Traverse City in 1893. She was the youngest daughter of four siblings born to William Sexton (1851–? in Lexington, Virginia) and Margaret Ann Cook (1855–? in Lancaster, Ohio). Margaret Ann Cook Sexton was raised as a Quaker in southern Ohio, and this Quaker heritage had a direct impact on her during her youth.

How the Sextons met and arrived in Traverse City is not known. The Sexton-Cook marriage ended in divorce in 1906 when Lenora was thirteen years old. William Sexton was an attorney by profession, and he eventually migrated to Oregon where he became involved in the timber history. Family oral history claims that William Sexton lost all family income and property on a horse race in Saratoga, New York. This fiscal calamity may have related directly to the Sextons' divorce and William Sexton's move westward.

I remember Grandmother Pitcher (Lenora) as short in height but strong in conviction and opinion. She had snow-white hair, wore glasses, and was dependent on false teeth. Unlike her husband (Floyd), Grandmother Pitcher seemed much older than her years. She typically wore drab dresses and laced black shoes with stacked heels. I never recall seeing her in leisure or recreational clothing, and I doubt she owned any. She was more serious and focused than her husband, and my brief exposure to her gave the impression that she ran the household.

For practically all her adult life, Lenora Pitcher was a dedicated school teacher who taught kindergarten through twelfth grade in a rural, one-room schoolhouse. Because she was married, local practice disallowed her from teaching in city schools; she was required to teach in rural areas where many of her students came from poor cherry-growing families. Her actual one-room schoolhouse has been refurbished and is now utilized by a winery/tasting company. Family lore includes references to Grandmother Pitcher taking homemade pots of soup to school to feed hungry students, and providing treat baskets for them at holiday time.

Grandmother Pitcher received her education from Central University, now Central Michigan University in Mt. Pleasant. After spending several summers in study, she was qualified to be a principal of a Traverse City School. The educational process was complicated by Grandmother Pitcher's lack of a driver's license. Because of Lenora Pitcher's frequent absences from the home while teaching and schooling in Mt. Pleasant, Esther's grandmother, Margaret Ann Cook Sexton, is credited with a significant caretaking role to Esther, brother Bill, and younger sister Jan.

Grandmother Pitcher rarely rested. After completing a full day's teaching, she would return home and cook the evening meal. After washing, rinsing, and drying the dinner dishes with my grandfather's reliable assistance, she would frequently prepare and bake some bread, cake, muffin, or cookie for the next day's consumption. By the way, Grandmother Pitcher baked solely with butter. Then came papers to grade and lessons to prepare for the next day's class.

Occasionally, I would receive a short, handwritten letter from Grandmother Pitcher in the mail. It was intended as a catch-up letter, as she inquired about school and my current interests. The theme of these letters was simple: she wanted me to know that she thought of me and cared for me despite the hundreds of miles that separated us. The most unique aspect of her letters was her signature act of enclosing two sticks of Beeman's gum in the envelope. I enjoyed that gesture then, and I still recall it with fondness. To this day, whenever I see Beeman's gum in a store display, I instantly think of Grandmother Pitcher and smile.

I remember Grandmother Pitcher less than her husband. While pleasant and attentive, she did not hesitate to act or voice her opinion. Esther's parents only visited us in Lansdowne on one occasion during my childhood when they traveled by train, as one of them was fearful of flying. During this visit to our Marshall Road home, I returned home from school one day after having had an altercation with classmate Jack Campbell. I was upset and angry and loudly announced that I hated Jack Campbell. Without consulting with her daughter, Grandmother Pitcher instantly grabbed me by the ear and marched me to the living room where she sat down next to me on the couch and boldly lectured me that I was never to use that word again in her presence. She said that I could dislike people very much, as much as I wanted, but hating people was not an option or choice. Wow. Impression most definitely made.

On that same visit, I used some language inappropriate for a seven- or eight-year-old. This time I was led by the ear to the basement washtub where I received a washrag in my mouth, flavored in Fels-Naphtha hand soap. Lesson learned. Ralphie Parker had nothing on me.

Floyd and Lenora had some interesting habits. In military precision, they washed dinner dishes as a team. Lenora washed while Floyd readied for his role. The rinsing process was unique. After having boiled water in a teapot, Floyd would carefully pour the scalding water over the soaped dishes resting in the dish rack. Then, approximately five minutes later, the dishes were dried and stored in the cupboard.

One of the strangest aspects to their relationship was that they referred to each other not by first name or endearment but as "Mother" and "Dad." Lenora's memorable nagging of Floyd was frequent and ongoing. While paraphrasing, a typical exchange would sound like this:

Lenora: "Dad, is brown sugar on the shopping list?"

Floyd: "Yes, it is, Mother."

Lenora: "And Dad, don't forget to get the light-brown sugar, not the dark."

Floyd: "Yes, Mother, I won't forget."

Lenora: "Be sure not to forget, because I need it for the cookies."

Floyd: (showing increased agitation) "Now, Mother, I said I'd get you your brown sugar—your light-brown sugar, and I will."

Lenora: "Well, Dad, I just didn't want you to forget so as to avoid a return trip to the grocery."

Floyd: "I understand, Mother."

To their complete credit, Floyd and Lenora were both gainfully employed during the entire extent of the Great Depression. They successfully raised three children through the Depression and World War II in a narrow three-bedroom home, which still stands at 911 State Street in Traverse City. They were married for forty-nine years until Floyd died of a heart attack in 1964. The following year, Lenora died of the same cause.

My seven female cousins on Esther's side, all raised in Michigan, were much closer to my maternal grandparents, and they certainly have deeper and more pronounced memories than I hold. Bill too was closer to them because of his living in Traverse City from 1944 to 1946.

Christmas Day, 1953

40

CHRISTMAS

During my childhood and adolescence, the entire holiday season was simpler and far less developed than today. The traditional Christmas buildup did not begin until the day after Thanksgiving. Stores were not decorated until late November, and then the blitz was on. That model is far more comfortable to me than what has evolved since the 1960s.

My family was not unique from the standpoint of holiday decorating. During most years, J. T. would wait till nearly the last minute and then buy a scraggly, neglected balsam tree from the Boys Scouts' lot next to

Pete's Sanitary Barbershop on Marshall Road. J. T. detested buying a Christmas tree (I believe he felt it was a poor investment for his dollar), and he paid the minimum for the times, usually in the three- to four-dollar range. There were a few years when my father's boss, Vincent B. Fuller, a native of upstate New York, transported Christmas trees from the Fuller Christmas Tree Farm near Oneonta, New York, to administrative employees in and around Philadelphia. Those trees were freshly cut, full, and near perfect in size and shape. They were easily the most handsome Christmas trees we ever had.

Trees went up and were decorated very close to Christmas Day. Ours was generally decorated the week before Christmas but never on Christmas Eve as was the tradition with many families in the eastern part of the country. Erecting and decorating a tree immediately following Thanksgiving was not customary at all. In general, trees were taken down shortly after New Year's.

On Essex Avenue, our tree stood in the living room near the passage to the dining room. It was usually five to six feet tall and was illuminated by strands of replaceable screw-in colored bulbs. I recall one year when J. T. experimented with blinking, nonreplaceable colored lights, which Esther referred to as "nervous" lights. That experiment was instantly called off by Esther after only one or two days.

Tree decorations consisted of solid-colored Christmas balls, pine cones, clear plastic icicles, and decorations made during my Green and Highland Avenue elementary days. There was no tinsel, as Esther detested tinsel on trees, thinking it to be "trashy and cheap."

Aside from the Christmas tree, there were few indoor decorations, although Esther did like to light winter-themed candles indoors, such as evergreen and berry. A fresh evergreen wreath adorned the front door, usually with a big red ribbon. J. T. would also install a strand of colored lights around the front door, complete with fresh garland, another requirement of Esther's.

Separation of powers of church and state was largely unaddressed during my Lansdowne school years. Therefore, Christmas was a celebrated holiday within school environs from kindergarten through twelfth grade. The few Jewish students simply went along for the ride, although I do recall some designated attempts at explaining Hanukah. Bulletin boards were decorated with Christmas/holiday themes. Both junior high and senior high students attended an annual Christmas concert held by the school orchestra and choir, and both religious and popular Christmas music was performed. Similar Christmas assemblies were scheduled at Lansdowne's three grade schools.

Lansdowne did not sponsor a Christmas parade, but they did erect a borough Christmas tree next to the post office across from the Lansdowne movie theater. The downtown commercial district was appropriately decorated with Christmas lights and other holiday decorations.

A major project prior to Christmas was the addressing, stamping, and mailing of Christmas cards by my parents. While this tradition has declined in recent years, it remains a major component of my childhood recollections of Christmas. The process took several evenings of J. T. and Esther being stationed at the dining-room table. From carefully kept mailing lists, dozens and dozens of Christmas cards were addressed to relatives and family friends in Michigan and Kentucky, naval academy alums, World War II comrades, J. T.'s business associates, current and former neighbors, Lansdowne-Aldan School Board members, and other assorted friends. All in all, I conservatively estimate more than 150 Christmas cards being mailed annually in the '50s and '60s. We likely received the same number in return, with incoming cards deposited in a large wooden bowl on the living-room coffee table.

Because of J. T.'s contacts within the printing business, the family Christmas cards were of the highest quality. J. T. also penned a family Christmas letter, which was included in the mailing as well. J. T. was very creative in his style, sometimes writing in prose and also in verse. Authors included not only J. T. but beagle Eloise, tortoise-shell cat Cassandra, and me. I only wish more examples of these letters still existed, as J. T. was extremely clever and imaginative with their presentation.

A quick, interesting note: during the late '50s, home mail delivery prior to Christmas was conducted twice daily due to heavy volume. I remember this activity well, because Bill worked part-time during several Christmas seasons as a letter carrier for the post office during his break from F&M. Can you believe it? Mail delivery twice a day!

In a separate chapter, I mentioned the fruitcake project, but Esther also baked holiday sugar cookies using a metal cookie press. A large batch of sugar cookie dough, sometimes colored red or green with food coloring, was prepared and then chilled in the refrigerator. Esther and J. T. were both proficient in configuring the chilled dough through the cookie press's assorted design dials: Christmas tree, snowflake, star, etc. Out of the oven, cookies were then accented with sprinkled colored sugar, nonpareil candies, raisins, or quartered maraschino cherries. Esther also concocted for J. T. at least one batch of divinity, a white fudge-like candy.

Prior to Christmas, Bell of Pennsylvania sponsored two special television programs. They were only aired once or twice a season and were broadcast in early evening, as they were intended for children. The programs were *The Nativity* and *'Twas the Night before Christmas*. What made the shows so memorable was that they were acted out not by actors or cartoon figures but by marionettes. The narrator was Alexander Scourby, a well-known American actor whose voice was readily recognized for its clear and soothing delivery. Why I was so enthralled by these programs remains a mystery, but I so looked forward to their broadcast each Christmas season. I also enjoyed the cartoon version of *Frosty the Snowman*.

I do not recall Christmas Eve ever being very eventful, save for that one memorable visit by Ed Flannery in the early 1950s. Like many families, we did not attend any religious service (not yet that popular an event), and we usually stayed at home as a family watching TV by the fire or wrapping last-minute gifts. I generally was allowed to open one "lesser gift," as Esther called it, on Christmas Eve. Esther, on occasion, would play holiday songs and Christmas carols on the piano, and she would beam when carolers appeared on our front porch sometime during the evening. She always invited them inside from the cold for candy and cookies.

Christmas morning eventually arrived, and we usually opened gifts that morning after 8:00 a.m. A box of Russell Stover chocolates was readied, and as J. T. sipped his tea and Esther drank her black coffee, gifts were distributed for opening. I typically received two or three gifts from Santa and two or three gifts from my parents. There was usually a major gift on the line that I wanted, i.e., a train set, bicycle, microscope (figure that one out), and so on, but then there was a major drop-off with less-requested gifts and the inevitable and dreaded boxes of sweaters, shirts, and socks. Bill and I must have exchanged gifts as well, but my memory on that point is blank. I also typically received very welcome checks from Michigan and Kentucky relatives. My most memorable Christmas gift ever was a Lionel train set, which I received at age six or seven while still living on Marshall Road.

My parents' gifts to one another were generally of minimal value. This is where their Depression-era roots intervened, cautioning them both not to be extravagant, even though family finances disallowed that possibility. J. T. was a poor judge of Esther's needs and wants; he usually had no clue as to what to buy her. I even recall one instance in high school where he actually came to me, near desperate for ideas.

The rest of Christmas Day was devoted to cleanup, early afternoon phone calls to Michigan and Kentucky, and preparation for Christmas dinner. Esther always had the dinner duty under steady command.

The meal was very similar to Thanksgiving, if not identical: iceberg lettuce wedge, roast turkey, traditional and oyster dressing (for J. T.), cranberry sauce, mashed potatoes, peas/carrots or green beans, and rolls. Dessert was usually homemade apple pie and Christmas cookies. Familiar attendees at Christmas dinner were Harry and Maude Quinn (Harry actually gave me a lump of coal as a gag gift one year) and Ed and Gladys Berman.

Here are some miscellaneous memories:

J. T. and Esther especially liked Perry Como and his Christmas special. Como always performed *O Holy Night* on the show, which happened to be my parents' preferred version of their favorite Christmas carol. On the contrary, J. T. was a big Bing Crosby fan, but he strongly disliked *The Little Drummer Boy*, which Crosby released in 1962. However, Crosby returned to good standing with J. T. upon the release of *Do You Know What I Know?*, a song that he much enjoyed.

When I was two and a half, I woke early on Christmas morning and opened all the gifts under the Christmas tree while my parents and Bill slept. When they awoke, the living room was a mess, and no one knew, courtesy of my help, who had given what to whom. Fortunately, the details of that event have been totally canceled from my memory vault.

And my worst Christmas? Easy. 1959. By accident, I had discovered where my parents had hidden my Christmas gifts. I opened them all, including my prize gift, a battery-powered tank, which I played with on several occasions prior to Christmas Day. My parents never discovered my antics, and when Christmas morning arrived, I knew exactly what was under the tree. It was horrible—just plain horrible—and I had only myself to blame. It was as if Christmas Day did not exist. This is why, to this day, I purposely ignore eyeballing any gifts under the Christmas tree prior to Christmas Day.

I do recall one white Christmas. It was in the early '60s. It snowed in the early morning through midafternoon on Christmas Day, necessitating a major shoveling of the sidewalk and driveway on Essex Avenue.

An ironic remnant from pulling together these memories of Christmas is the major void that I hold toward Bill's presence and involvement. He was a part of these activities and events up until I was thirteen, but sadly I remember little of his participation.

29 East Essex Avenue
Lansdowne, Pennsylvania
Christmas, 1961

A Holiday "Howdy" to You and Yours!

Here's hoping that 1961 proved to be a banner year for you. For us Binghams, it was a mixture of good and bad with the accent on the good.

While the tragedy column really had only one entry, it couldn't have been a more serious one and more than made up for a host of lesser ones. We refer, of course, to the death of Bing's Mother on February 16 last. The two of us flew down for the funeral and the for the first time in 39 years, all six of the kids were reunited in death. Until this unhappy event came to pass, Bing and George, who resides in Seattle, never could make it home at the same time.

The highlight of the year followed some two months later when Bill, now in his second year at Jefferson Medical College, was married to Miss Letitia Henderson, a high school classmate, who lived around the corner from us ever since we moved to Lansdowne in 1950. Tish, a University of Pennsylvania graduate, is currently Program Editor for the New York Metropolitan Edition of TV Guide. The two have an apartment here in Lansdowne at Stratford Court Apartments which is but five blocks from here.

Another highlight of the year was Esther's election to the Lansdowne School Board on Tuesday, November 8. She was sworn in for a full six-year term on Monday, December 11.

Bobby, now 13 and an eighth-grader, reports that his teachers treat him with no more deference than before. Already he is beginning to wonder what the point of Esther's election was.

Business-wise, the "bread winner" half of our team couldn't have been busier. All five graphic arts companies of which Bing is Secretary expanded in one or more ways. One recently moved into a new 10,000 square foot plant while a 3,600 square foot addition was yet a-building. And another is in mid-flight in its move to 6,300 additional square feet of space. Strong in the fields of magazine and book composition, we are getting stronger in the fields of technical publications, business forms and check imprinting with magnetic inks. At the moment, greeting cards appear to be next on the list.

Pet-wise, Cassandra, our Calico cat, and Eloise, the family Beagle, are well and apparently happy. With "softies" like Esther and Bobby to cope with, no two animals ever had it more plush.

We can but hope that you are up to your ears in similar trivialities and enjoying them to the full, as we are. Toward that end, we send our best wishes for a Merry Christmas and a Happy and Prosperous New Year.

Esther & Bing

41

BLUE LAWS

I had to do some research on this topic, and in the process I learned that "blue laws" were not common only to Pennsylvania. They existed and still exist to some extent in most of the fifty states. Even though there is reference to them dating back to 1682 in Pennsylvania, they were primarily established in the 1920s and 1930s during Prohibition and were designed to encourage and even enforce religious standards. They also were intended to "regulate industry and shopping on Sundays." One source suggested that Pennsylvania blue laws were even more limiting than those in Utah.

Blue laws primarily restricted the sale of certain items on Sunday, including alcohol, some groceries, office supplies, housewares, and beauty supplies. I recall specifically that Esther was upset one Sunday when she needed a new pair of nylons for going out to dinner, but the blue laws' restriction disallowed the purchase. Blue laws also limited the Sunday operating hours of some businesses (such as restaurants) or blocked their being open for business altogether. It appears that the underlying theme of the blue laws was to reinforce religious focus and church attendance on the Lord's Day.

While many blue laws have been eliminated or severely curtailed, several remaining ones are ignored or loosely enforced. However, during my childhood, blue laws were active, and they occasionally produced a frustrating impact.

Certain businesses that were closed on Sundays included car dealerships, bars and taverns, and certain movie houses. In some instances, operating hours restricted sporting events. In 1931 changes in the blue laws had to be implemented to allow the Philadelphia Athletics professional baseball team to play baseball on Sundays. In 1933 an additional change was required to allow the Philadelphia Eagles professional football team to play on Sundays.

As a teenager, I occasionally attended Sunday doubleheaders at Connie Mack Stadium, and for years there was a restriction on length of play, where the second game on Sundays could not extend past 7:00 p.m. In the event that a game was long and extended, this restriction obviously made an impact. I don't know if the 7:00 p.m. cutoff was a blue law restriction or not, but the intended spirit was the same. I also don't recall how games in progress at 7:00 p.m. were continued at a future date.

Fishing was not prohibited on Sundays, but hunting was—except for the hunting of fox, crow, and coyote (figure that one out). You could buy new carpets on Sunday but not antique rugs.

Noting the unevenness and capriciousness of the laws, the Pennsylvania State Supreme Court ruled the blue laws unconstitutional in 1978. The majority of the restrictions then went by the wayside.

42

COFFMAN'S

Coffman's was the established pharmacy that occupied the northeast corner of the Marshall Road Commercial District. The owner/proprietor was Nate Coffman, a short, very tanned man in his midforties, who combed his thinning, greased black hair straight back. I recall that I wondered back then how a man could be so tanned as he always looked like he had just stepped off a Florida beach. Coffman also wore distinctive black-framed glasses and a white medical jacket.

Coffman's was typical for a Philadelphia area neighborhood pharmacy of the 50s and early 60s. It was a compact store that included a small soda fountain. Aside from the fountain, one could also buy newspapers, assorted magazines, greeting cards, cigarettes, candy, over-the-counter medications, and of course, prescribed drugs.

After the move from Darby to Lansdowne in 1950, Coffman's became our family pharmacy. However, on a summer evening in 1954, my parents were no longer loyal patrons because of a store incident involving Nate Coffman and me.

I had finished dinner and just received my twenty-five cents weekly allowance. Personal protocol dictated that I would then promptly walk down to the Marshall Road stores and blow my quarter on five candy bars. That was exactly what I proceeded to do. I chose Coffman's that evening for no particular reason.

After receiving payment, the Coffman's clerk bagged my candy in a small brown-paper bag. However, as I turned from the counter, I accidentally knocked over a cardboard display of Life Savers candy. With much embarrassment, and while teenagers at the counter giggled at my clumsiness, I retrieved the numerous rolls of candy from the floor, correctly stocked the display, and returned the stand to its previous position. With all back to order, I started to exit the store while clutching my bag of goodies.

To my surprise, Nate Coffman physically blocked my exit as he sternly announced, "I saw what you did." In full view of the store's customers, he accused me of shoplifting. He inspected my bag and found twenty-five cents' worth of candy, the purchase nervously verified by the teenage cashier. He then demanded that I empty the pockets of my shorts. I turned my pockets inside out, revealing no additional candy, no additional anything. By this time, I was welling with tears. Having proved my innocence, Coffman had no other choice but to back off and allow me to leave the store. I immediately ran the three blocks home, and in full tears, with labored breathing, I divulged to my parents what had just taken place.

I certainly was no perfect little boy by any standard, but both Esther and J. T. knew I wasn't a thief. They also knew that it made no sense for me to voluntarily reveal the incident if I were guilty. In calculated fashion, J. T. rose from the dining-room table and promptly walked to Coffman's pharmacy with me in hand prior to the store's closing. What followed was J. T.'s finest example and my childhood's most valued memory of my father.

Upon arrival and without aggression, J. T. simply called Nate Coffman out in the full company of the store's half-dozen patrons, including the same teenagers still parked at the soda fountain. J. T. did not speak to Nate Coffman privately because, I assume, he wanted to treat Coffman precisely the way I had been treated. J. T. politely but firmly demanded that Coffman apologize to me. The store suddenly got very quiet as all attention shifted to Nate Coffman.

Remaining behind the counter during the exchange, Coffman knew that he had erred badly. He also knew that he had only one route to take. He very sheepishly apologized, at which point my father informed him that, as a result of this incident, he had permanently lost our family business, and that we would no longer patronize his store on any level. Quietly and uneventfully, we exited the store, my father's hand in mine as we walked home.

I have to be careful here not enhance or enlarge what transpired that summer evening sixty years ago. Many details are now vague or lost altogether, but what I do recall was my father's firm and confident advocacy, his courage, and the love demonstrated by his direct challenge of Coffman. J. T. was not a confrontational man, but his family had been wronged. It was necessary for him to challenge and correct the error. Even though time has dulled my memory on many events, J. T.'s performance that day was masterful, a minute sliver in time that I have always treasured.

The aftermath of the event was that we changed pharmacies. J. T. wrote a check, closing out our Coffman's account, and the family was never to patronize the store again on any level.

Undeterred, I simply took my candy business elsewhere.

43

FAVORITE ELEMENTARY SCHOOL TEACHERS

Isabelle Koller

Isabelle "Dibby" Koller was my first grade teacher. She was not only my first-grade teacher, but she became a family friend for over twenty years. Miss Koller was from the Harrisburg area and was a veteran teacher, probably in her midforties when she taught me. Dibby possessed all the major qualities you would ever want in an elementary school teacher. She was attentive, creative, in control, patient, personable, knowledgeable, caring, and reassuring. Miss Koller was also single, and she truly looked upon her classroom kids as *her* kids. Above all, the woman knew how to teach, and she made the process fun from 8:30 a.m. to 3:00 p.m. I actually felt sorry for the other section of first-grade students at Green Avenue.

I quickly became a favorite, as did Andy Thompson and Sally Cheeseman. I recall that as Thanksgiving approached we made candles by walking around a newspaper-covered rectangle on the classroom floor, dipping wicks into four separate buckets of hot wax. I also recall Miss Koller during winter playground duty. She wore a long raccoon coat, in which she would periodically nestle chilled students for temporary warming.

Even though I was nearly forced to repeat first grade because of health issues, I blossomed under Miss Koller's tutelage and received high marks in all subjects, especially reading. About ten years later, she joined my parents and me for dinner at a local restaurant. The restaurant door was clearly marked "pull" on the door handle. I naturally pushed instead, causing Dibby to joke: "Whoever taught you to read?"

Miss Koller lived in a spacious, second-floor apartment in a large house on Owen Avenue near Bryn Mawr Avenue. Esther would periodically visit her there after I had advanced in elementary school. Dibby was also a familiar face at the Marlyn Restaurant when we ate there as a family. She attended many family dinners at my house, including the Fourth of July picnic. Both J. T. and Esther were very fond of Dibby.

Dibby Koller taught at Green Avenue for several decades, and when former students of that era and school mention Green Avenue, they typically smile when her name comes up. They know they were taught by the very best the school system had to offer.

Mrs. Freas

Unlike Dibby Koller, Mrs. Freas was young and relatively inexperienced. She was extremely attractive, and her blonde hair was frequently set in a ponytail. She also wore glasses.

She was enthusiastic, and we started each school day doing stretching exercises at our desks, an activity totally new to us. Again, I was an early favorite of hers. She considered me a leader within the classroom, and occasionally she would subtly query me for information about another student who might be emotionally distant, disruptive in class, etc.

I naturally compared her style with former elementary teachers at Green Avenue in kindergarten through fourth grade, but the woman was unique. I don't know if it was her academic training, her energetic personality, or a combination of the two, but Mrs. Freas was different and "outside the box," using refreshingly new techniques and strategies. Her class did not flow or process as previous classes had. Each day could mean a new approach or exercise, and it was an alternate, fun way of learning. This style made instruction more enjoyable and memorable.

I also remember that Mrs. Freas was recently married, and that she and her husband liked to ski in the Poconos on winter weekends. Monday mornings for her were rougher than usual during the winter months, with Mrs. Freas frequently needing those morning calisthenics more than her students.

44

MADISON 3-2754

As a youth growing up, local telephone numbers frequently began with the first two letters of a common word. Famous last names were regularly used, as were trees, events, and so on, e.g., MAdison, WAlnut, LOcust, FLanders, HOliday. It wasn't until later that the phone company (there was only one, Bell of Pennsylvania) dropped the first-two-letters emphasis in favor of all numbers. For thirty years from 1950 to 1980, our family phone number was MAdison 3-2754.

All phones available during my childhood were landlines connected to rotary black telephones. We always had two in our home: one in my parents' bedroom and one at a more common location, such as the living room or kitchen. There were no features like call waiting or phone messaging. If you called a number and it was busy, you simply kept calling back. In the event of an emergency, your option was to call a neighbor to your party and request that neighbor to physically contact the needed person.

Long distance was expensive, and before direct dialing, we had to go through an operator. Station-to-station calls were cheapest and were usually best made during evenings, weekends, and holidays. Another option was the more expensive person-to-person calling. This option was frequently manipulated to the customer's advantage. For example, a customer might request a person-to-person call to his brother. This call would be rejected, because the called brother would recognize the source of the call, and then a cheaper station-to-station call would be placed, knowing that both parties were available. The person-to-person games were common practice until direct long-distance calling was fully implemented later in the '60s and '70s.

In a pinch, you could also call collect, but those calls were also more expensive to the receiving party because of the need for operator assistance. Toll-free numbers and phone cards did not yet exist. If you needed to make a phone call while away from home, you had to be sure to have an initial dime or some loose change available in order to make a call from a pay phone and/or that forgotten artifact known as a phone booth. Bell of Pennsylvania also issued phone books (white-page versions for residences, yellow-page editions for businesses) as essential resources that were kept close to the phone. You could also call a Bell operator at no cost, which was a highly valuable service when the local phone books failed or the call was out of the calling area.

I wish both J. T. and Esther could hear this, but I was notorious for tying up our family phone line in high school. I apologize for that injustice, not to mention the expense generated. J. T.'s "fifteen minutes" rule was recklessly broken on a daily basis, with most of my calls directed to and from girlfriends.

45

BENIAH WHITMAN, MD

Beniah Whitman was our family physician for most of my upbringing. His first office was conveniently located in the Pilgrim Gardens section of Upper Darby. I went to him often as a sick youngster before Dr. Wallace got involved with all of my ENT and allergy issues. He brought me into the world on April 8, 1848, when he delivered me as the attending physician at Fitzgerald-Mercy Hospital in Darby. It was not unusual at all during this time for general practice physicians to also deliver babies, since obstetrics was in its infancy as a specialty.

I have no rationale as to why Dr. Whitman was chosen as our family doctor. He was a quiet, friendly, and competent family doctor, whose office consisted of a small waiting room with receptionist and his private office, which also doubled as an examining room. Facially, he resembled Dr. Billy Graham. Usually when I saw Dr. Whitman, I was treated to a penicillin shot in my butt. He also treated and bandaged my right hand after the bloody gate incident with Susan Bartlett.

Dr. Whitman made house calls when his office was in Drexel Hill, and he most frequently visited us when my mother had a migraine headache. Esther's treatment at that time included a major injection of morphine and several days of bed rest in the darkened master bedroom. He also visited me at home on one occasion when I suffered a very painful twisted testicle injury, which occurred in my sophomore P.E. class (wrestling). Oh, the embarrassment.

Dr. Whitman relocated during my late elementary school and early junior high school days. For this brief respite, we saw a Dr. Robert Hekking, whose office was conveniently located on the northeast corner of Plumstead and Lansdowne Avenue.

During my high schools days, Dr. Whitman surfaced again, and we were reconnected. However, his new office was located in Chadds Ford, Pennsylvania, a good fifty-minute car ride one way from Lansdowne. About that time, I was soon off to college, and my parents found other physicians for medical care.

Beniah Whitman, MD, was a good man and a good doctor.

46

SUMMER TRAVEL

Summer travel did not necessarily mean vacationing for our family. It meant annual visiting of relatives in Kentucky and Michigan.

J. T. captained our epic two-week treks to and from Louisville and Traverse City/ Drummond Island with well-organized assistance from Esther. More times than not, the two-week trips consisted of overnight stops in both Michigan and Ohio. That meant four to five days on the road, since the vast majority of interstate highways had not yet been built (the Pennsylvania and Ohio Turnpikes were exceptions).

Long-distance driving was simply more challenging back then. There were few interstates, and bypasses around major cities and large towns had yet to be designed and built. Cars had no air-conditioning, and vehicles were less reliable. There was poor road signage, more frequent flat tires, and so on.

The one-way trip to Traverse City/Drummond Island from Lansdowne meant an overnight stay in southern Michigan. If we were returning home from Michigan, we typically stayed in eastern Ohio (J. T. liked Canton) or western Pennsylvania southwest of Pittsburgh. The one-way trip to Louisville from Philadelphia typically included an overnight at a tourist home in Washington, Pennsylvania, or Ohio's hottest hotel in Washington Courthouse. If we were traveling between Michigan and Kentucky, Battle Creek, Michigan, was a likely stop.

The hotel in Washington Courthouse remains highly memorable to me. It was an old multistory hotel, a downtown fixture of the city, which was in its final days. Recall the hotel featured in the movie *Paper Moon*, and you'll get the right image. Our huge room was not air-conditioned, but it was cooled(?) by a noisy and ineffective window fan. We attempted to sleep in this room, stuck to our sheets. We ate breakfast in the hotel's coffee shop, and I recall being fascinated by a large wall map of the United States, with each state being represented by a tree wood common to that state. Ohio was naturally represented by a buckeye.

In the 1950s and early 1960s, national hotel/motel chains were first being developed, so most travelers relied on local, mom-and-pop-operated motels, which included exterior entrances to rooms from the parking area outside. Most of these motels were small, containing fewer than twenty units. They had few of the amenities associated with today's modern motel/hotels chains. Since we were never certain of the distance we could complete in a day's travel, J. T. would wait until early evening to select an overnight site. Travelers relied on neon motel "vacancy" signs to determine if beds were available, since cell phones were half a century away.

When we saw a motel that seemed acceptable and was flashing a "vacancy" message—and after receiving Esther's blessing—J. T. would enter the motel's office to secure a room. There was no guarantee here. If the price was too high, J. T. quickly left and looked for another option. If J. T. accepted the cost, Esther would then inspect the room beforehand, which was not an uncommon practice for the times, since quality varied greatly from motel to motel.

Another variable that came into play was that motels lowered their prices as the evening advanced. J. T. poorly played this card on a few occasions—a major irritation to Esther—when we were desperate late at night and needed to accept less than ideal accommodations.

I especially recall one occasion in Tennessee after I had interviewed for college admission at Vanderbilt. The building was a former stable converted to a motel. With all other local possibilities exhausted, J. T. had no choice but to rent two rooms, since the rooms were very small. I was by myself next door to my parents, but we all soon learned that this motel was frequented by locals more than nonresidents. I learned much that evening from love messages left on my room's wallpaper and from romantic antics that were easily heard from next-door strangers.

Another memorable stay was in eastern Ohio at a small tavern/motel combination. It was pretty clear whom this motel catered to, but J. T. again had no choice because of the late hour. This motel did not take pets, so we were forced to smuggle our mouthy beagle, Eloise, into our room. As the local lovers were leaving their rooms early and midmorning, Eloise would erupt in howling to the point that I had to quickly muzzle her barking and growling for fear that we would be evicted.

Meals on the road were less eventful. Fast-food did not exist, and J. T. liked diners for breakfast and lunch. Over the years, he developed restaurant favorites. He loved a small cafeteria in Carrolton, Kentucky, along the Ohio River, and a diner in Xenia, Ohio. He also liked "Ma's Dinner Bell" in Canton, Ohio, and a hotel dining room in Indian River, Michigan. On occasion, Esther would determine that J. T. was geographically off course, and the rerouting was most frequently associated with a favorite meat loaf, chicken croquettes, or apple pie available somewhat off course from our main route. I recall one summer Sunday when we ate at Win Schuler's in Marshall, Michigan, a well-known restaurant that operates to this day.

If we were on state or county roads, J. T. was a sucker for fruit stands, especially those that sold peaches. These stops were legendary.

Despite a guaranteed allergic reason to peaches, J. T. would down two or three peaches of his personal choosing while pivoted to the left in his driver's seat, hunched over so that the errant juice would drop to the ground. Within thirty minutes or less after having left the fruit stand, J. T. would calmly pull our Chevrolet over to the side of the road, exit the vehicle, and promptly vomit the recently devoured peaches. With Esther lightly shaking her head, and as if nothing had happened, J. T. quietly returned to the car, and we were once again on our way.

For three to four years while stationed at the US Naval Air Station in the early 1940s, J. T. taught navigation to pilots in training. This skill was not forgotten or relaxed after the war, as he used his knowledge at night when redirected by road construction, a downed bridge, or simply being lost after missing a turn. He would exit the car, check the constellations, and then return, knowing full well in which direction we were headed. As a child, I was always amazed at this seemingly mystical talent.

One final recollection: we most certainly traveled with a large Hawaiian Punch can in the backseat, intended for my bathroom emergencies.

47

HALLOWEEN 1954

To the horror of many people today, we trick-or-treated in the 1950s without parental escort. When I lived on Marshall Road, my Halloween partners were typically Susan Bartlett and the Thompson kids. Like a small, constantly moving swarm of bees, we would flit from house to house in homemade costumes or cheap store-bought versions in search of our Halloween loot. We pretty much stayed close to home and rarely strayed more than one block from our immediate neighborhood. Total time on trick-or-treat offensive was about an hour.

While trick-or-treating on Halloween evening in 1954, my crew and I were assaulting Albemarle Avenue residences on a raw, drizzly evening. Our complete focus was on filling up our brown sacks with Halloween goodies. Nothing else mattered, including our physical safety. We had just visited the McCollum home, which was situated directly behind our home on Marshall Road. As we scurried to our next house, I unknowingly ran into a thin supporting wire installed for a newly planted tree. The wire won, and I was flung to the ground and briefly knocked unconscious.

Subsequent details are limited. An adult or child summoned my nearby parents, and I was taken to the Delaware County Memorial Hospital Emergency Room. I know I suffered a mild concussion from my head being whipped to the ground by the support wire. The next day, I had an ugly, red diagonal mark on my throat, which looked like someone had tried to slit it with a knife. My neck was extremely stiff and sore for several days. I also had a headache the morning after the accident.

That evening as I went to bed, I started crying, as I suddenly realized the essential loss of the evening. Esther misread my tears, thinking that I needed to be comforted and reassured because of the neck pain and general trauma. Wrong. That wasn't it at all. "What about my candy?" I cried. "Where's my candy? I left my candy. Somebody get my candy!"

The following morning, I awoke to a bowl of Halloween treats resting on the nightstand next to my bed. I was both relieved and very happy. The Halloween loot had been recovered by J. T. later that evening from a soggy brown-paper bag abandoned in the McCollum front yard. With flashlight in hand, J. T. had surveyed the ground at the scene of the accident to recover as much of my trick-or-treat goodies as possible.

There are times in a child's life when a father stands particularly tall and heroic. This was one of those times for J. T.

Some other notes on Halloween in the '50s: We frequently received homemade treats (cookies, candy corn, licorice pieces) wrapped in a napkin. Homemade popcorn balls were also popular, and so were apples. A few neighbors even gave away pennies or a nickel. Some schools supported UNICEF donations as a Halloween project so we would trick-or-treat with candy in mind while also seeking coin donations in a UNICEF cardboard box.

48

WINDERMERE DELICATESSEN

For more than a dozen years, my family and I lived within walking distance of the Marshall Road commercial district, which included the Windermere Delicatessen or "Sam and Momma's," as we were prone to call it. This wonderful little store was situated in a Drexel Hill neighborhood, on the north side of Marshall Road. I was a regular customer by the time I was an early grade schooler, and I frequently undertook assigned runs for Esther, typically after hours and on Sundays, for cold cuts, rolls, milk, pickles, etc., when the proximate A&P Store and Mar-Win Market were both closed. My personal visits focused on candy, soda, ice cream, and baseball cards. I bought a lot of baseball cards at the Windermere Delicatessen.

The proprietors, Sam and Momma Hoffman, were European born, in their midfifties, and most likely German or Austrian, as they spoke with slight accents. Momma pretty much ran the store, with the high-belted Sam as her overseer. As I grew older, occasionally a neighborhood teenager also worked the store. I believe Sam and Momma lived over the store in a small second-floor apartment. While Sam was somewhat distant, Momma knew me by name. She was kind, personable, and helpful, putting in long hours working the store throughout the week. I also recall that Momma wore strange shoes, the kind that Esther's hair stylist wore, shoes designed for people spending long hours on their feet at work.

This tiny neighborhood store sold cold cuts, bread, rolls, soda, custom-made sandwiches, and even some items common to a grocery store. There was no excessive inventory, but if you needed some emergency toilet paper or applesauce or aspirin, Sam and Momma's usually could supply it. How many times did I offer Momma a handwritten note from my own mother calling for half a pound of boiled ham, some sandwich rolls, or a can of mushroom soup? Too many to count.

I hit it off with Momma early on and could soon tell that I was a favorite. She used to get anxious when too many kids were in the store at once, as she feared shoplifting. However, I had earned special status, since she trusted me. I was never hurried out when the store was too populated with kids.

The Windermere Deli also sold beer, which opened up a whole new world to me. As well as cartons of beer, one could buy chilled individual cans or bottles of beer out of the cooler and drink them in a mysterious backroom with a custom-made sandwich (a small, mediocre hoagie cost thirty-five cents). Popular indigenous and regional beers common to Philadelphia (Ortleib's, Ballantine, Eslinger, Piel's, and Schmidt's) were the standard selections. My parents never drank beer, and I was rarely around it, so I took special notice of the male customers who came in at lunch or dinnertime to imbibe in the backroom. I remember that postal workers were frequent customers to the backroom.

I saw my first drunks in Sam and Momma's, but they were happy drunks. On one occasion, a fairly well-lit elderly man bought me a bag of candy at his request. Upon my mother hearing the story, she promptly called the store and inquired as to the details. Momma assured her that neither her son nor the patron had crossed any lines.

The Windermere Deli contained a unique smell, most assuredly a glorious combination of deli meats and cheeses, freshly baked rolls, cigarette and cigar smoke, beer, and kosher pickle barrel. I have never been a pickle fan, but the exotic aroma from that barrel remains a delicious memory for me. On occasion, my mother would eagerly summon me to fetch her a pickle from Sam and Momma's. Momma would carefully make the selection with the understanding that I did not know what I was doing. Upon my return home, Esther was a blissful housewife, as she usually gobbled down her prize in one sitting.

The Windermere Deli has changed ownership several times since the days of the Hoffmans. Whenever I return to Lansdowne, I usually pay it a pilgrimage, even though the store little resembles my memories from childhood. While I am always disappointed that both the pickle barrel and that wondrous store aroma are long gone, the fondest memories remain of Sam and especially Momma. They were as close to substitute grandparents as I encountered outside of my family's circle of adults. I lost touch with Sam and Momma in my later teens, and I now recognize that it would have been a fun part-time job for me as a high school student. They certainly would have hired me.

49

TRAVERSE CITY, 1955

When I was in second grade (1956), Grandpa Pitcher had a serious heart attack in Traverse City while shoveling snow. Grandma Pitcher was teaching full-time, so an arrangement was made for Esther to travel to Traverse City to assist in Grandpa's recovery at home.

Keep in mind that this was 1956. Quiet bed rest for several weeks was the prescribed treatment at that time for surviving heart attack patients. The plan included my accompanying Esther to Traverse City for the duration of her stay during the months of mid to late winter.

Study plans were developed by my second-grade teacher, and Esther assured Miss Wilson that her instructions would be diligently followed as supervised by Esther, a former kindergarten teacher, and Grandmother Pitcher, a current first-grade teacher.

A great thrill for me was flying to Traverse City. Esther and I flew a Vickers Viscount prop jet from Philadelphia to Detroit, and most likely a small prop plane, DC-3, on to Traverse City. I recall seeing my first industrial snowplow at the Traverse City Airport as it cleared a runway, and I asked Esther what it was, since I had never seen such equipment.

My role during our six- to eight-week stay was to complete my assignments in the morning and be as quiet and invisible as possible, quite the task for a displanted seven-year-old. I saw little of Grandpa Pitcher, as he remained bedridden in his darkened bedroom for most of my stay. However, he did get up for dinner. After dinner dishes were washed and dried, Grandma Pitcher sat down with me, reviewed my completed work for the day, and provided even more assignments. I recall her being a stern, no-nonsense taskmaster.

That winter in Michigan was brutal by Lansdowne standards, and I remember walking my grandparents' Jack Russell terrier, ironically also named Dixie, down cavernous sidewalks with snow piled up well above my head. Cars sported flags on their radio antennas so as to be better seen at street intersections. It was also very cold, much colder than anything I had known in Pennsylvania.

I was actually glad for the time in Traverse City to end. It was a lonely time, and I missed my father, brother, and school classmates. The return flights to Detroit and Philadelphia were a thrilling finale. Grandpa Pitcher recovered and survived another nine years, after which a second heart attack took his life in 1964.

Don Winslow of the navy

50

SERIALS

This movie-related interest I learned from my brother. He was more directly exposed to this special movie feature than I, as the heyday of the movie serials was in the 1940s and early 1950s.

Movie serials were adventure series. Their themes and subjects, frequently drawn from pulp fiction of the times, were shown in twelve- to fifteen-minute sequential installments at local movie houses. They were shown prior to the main feature, along with newsreels, cartoons, and other short subjects. If you wanted to follow the course of the serial, you naturally had to regularly return to the same movie theater to see the next episode. That was the hook. It was not out of the ordinary for someone to attend an average main feature simply to stay abreast of the serial's progress.

Serials were cheaply and quickly produced. The emphasis was on action. Many relatively unknown actors, such as John Wayne and Buster Crabbe, got their start in serials. The scripts and acting were poor, as was overall production quality. Science fiction (Flash Gordon and Buck Rogers) was a familiar focus, as were superheroes (Green Lantern and Batman), detectives (Dick Tracy), espionage (Don Winslow of the Navy, fighting the evil Scorpion in a 1941 series, which already demonstrated concern for potential conflict in the far Pacific), jungle series (Tarzan and Jungle Jim), and westerns (Red Ryder, Zorro, and the totally ridiculous Gene Autry and the Phantom Empire, a 1935 serial that attempted to combine science fiction with a singing cowboy.

Serials typically involved a cliff-hanger at the end of each chapter. The cliff-hanger always portrayed a life-ending, perilous event involving the serial's hero—and sometimes heroine—such as a building explosion, car crash, bridge collapsing, runaway boat, dam bursting, or exposure to some horrible monster. In watching the cliff-hangers, you always wondered how on earth the hero would survive. You mumbled to yourself, "No way he's getting out of this mess."

But eventually, even the dumbest of the dumb figured out that the ending of the current episode was not the same as the flashback beginning of the upcoming chapter. Just call it creative editing, since the upcoming chapter included previously unseen footage, which explained how our hero had avoided disaster. The end result was that the cliff-hanger scenes always included two versions, thus allowing the hero of the series to survive.

Bill was exposed to serials from movie attendance as a child, but in the early 1950s, television started airing them as well. My most immediate exposure was through TV where I primarily viewed them in conjunction with children's programming. I have a very faint recollection of viewing serials in some select movie theatres (Stonehurst and Yeadon) at Saturday afternoon matinees, which were exclusively designated at that time for children. I have no memory of them being shown at the Lansdowne Theater, but certainly at some time they were featured for evening audiences in the '40s and early '50s.

I much enjoyed the Flash Gordon serials, as did Bill. We especially liked Flash's dastardly enemy, Ming the Merciless, as played by actor Charles Middleton. No doubt, movie producer George Lucas envisioned Darth Vader after Ming. Don Winslow of the Navy was also very popular with Bill and me (oh, those epic speedboat chases). Another favorite serial was the Rocketman or Commander Cody series, where a helmeted scientist-hero flew by use of a jet pack attached to the back of his leather jacket. Rocketman/Commander Cody frequently fought aliens from other planets, who were intent upon conquering Earth.

Bill was so enthralled with Rocketman that he contrived a fake set of wooden rockets and a control box in J.T.'s basement workshop. He attached them to my chest and back with leather straps and buckles. Complete with football helmet and pseudo-Rocketman propulsion gear, I was a well-known yet underappreciated force in the early 1950s as I fought interplanetary villains threatening our Marshall Road neighborhood.

51

MARGARET ANN COOK SEXTON

Margaret Ann Cook Sexton (1855–1942) was my great-grandmother on Esther's side. She was born in Lancaster, Ohio, in 1855 and was raised by Quaker parents on a farm in southern Ohio. The following account is directly attributed to Esther, and to my knowledge, it is the oldest folklore known on the Sexton-Pitcher side of the family.

Esther and her maternal grandmother, Margaret Ann Cook Sexton, were very close during Esther's childhood, since Margaret often assumed a caretaker role. Esther related this story to me at least twice, once very late in her life with no loss of detail or consistency. The Quaker influence on Esther—and indirectly on me—is specifically tied to Margaret Ann Cook Sexton. The story goes as follows:

Margaret and her family lived in a section of southern Ohio that was subject to periodic raids by bands of Confederate soldiers. Margaret and her two sisters were curiously observing a small detachment of rebel soldiers marching down the dirt road that bordered their farm. In playful defiance, Margaret began singing the Yankee tune "Hang Jeff Davis from a Sour Apple Tree" from behind their farm's wooden fence.

In response, a handsome Confederate lieutenant halted his troops and dismounted his horse. Wearing a kind smile and with no sense of malice, he approached a now silent and concerned Margaret, who had ceased her singing. The officer dropped to one knee, gently tilted back Margaret's sunbonnet, and said, "Little girl, you can sing any song you wish, but I'd be obliged if you didn't sing that one." The gallant lieutenant then returned to his mount, and the detachment slid into the Ohio countryside.

The 1956 movie, *Friendly Persuasion*, starring Gary Cooper and Dorothy McGuire, was one of Esther's favorites. The movie depicts a southern Indiana Quaker family's response to the Civil War. Esther often commented that the circumstances experienced by the film's family, the Birdwells, appeared similar to those impacting her grandmother's family in southern Ohio.

As a side note, Esther knew the theme song from *Friendly Persuasion*, both music and lyrics. It was one of her standards, which she played on the piano and sang over the years. Esther also borrowed Dorothy McGuire's "pure pet" reference toward a pet goose named Samantha, lovingly using it for decades in her dealings with the Bingham family dogs and cats.

52

WHAT IN THE WORLD?

What in the World? was a Philadelphia-based television show that was broadcast in the 1950s and early 1960s. It was produced by WCAU, channel 10 on the CBS network. PBS later picked up the show in the early 1960s. I remember that it usually aired on weekends. The show's narrator was either Barry Cassell or Gene Crane, both familiar Philadelphia TV announcers at the time.

The format was odd and intriguing. The program resembled a quiz show and featured the learned and likeable emcee Froelich Rainey, director of the Pennsylvania Museum of Archaeology and Anthropology at the University of Pennsylvania. Panelists were fellow PhDs from the disciplines of archaeology and anthropology. Carlton Coon, a noted and controversial expert on racial theory and origins, was a regular, as was Alfred Kidder, a New World specialist. The three-person panel always included a guest panelist as well.

The challenge to the panel was to identify archaeological objects and anthropological artifacts from around the world as to substance, location, age, and purpose. A whispering, off-screen announcer revealed the object's identity to the television audience immediately prior to the object's exposure to the panel. I viewed a YouTube excerpt of the show in which a panelist correctly identified a piece of volcanic glass from northern Iraq, detailing its value striking hunting blades. On another show, the panel identified an iron object worn by a Siberian Shaman. Panelists not only engaged their diverse, extensive subject knowledge, but they might also smell the object or possibly even taste the texture to determine the item's substance and use, e.g., a tobacco vessel.

I was seven or eight years old when I first watched the show, and it was one of the few TV shows that my brother and I might watch together. I acknowledge that it was not typical fare for a seven- or eight-year-old to watch, but I loved it. It most certainly fueled my interest in anthropology, which was my major in college. I was fascinated by how knowledgeable the panel was and how accurate they were in pinning down specifics. Rarely were they wrong or stumped, but when they were, it was usually because they could not determine the object's purpose.

Dr. Rainey got much pleasure in needling the panel, but he also gave them due credit, which was often, when they nailed the item. At times panelists were challenging toward one another, but it was all in good fun. Carlton Coon was a favorite of Bill's and mine because of his eccentric—and at times argumentative—nature with Dr. Rainey and fellow panelists. Imagine my response in college when I was assigned a reading authored by none other than Carlton Coon.

Interestingly enough, Great Britain broadcast a somewhat similar show at that time. It was known as *Animal, Vegetable, or Mineral?*

53

JOSEPH WALLACE, MD

Joseph Wallace was an ear, nose, and throat specialist who treated me for the majority of my childhood and adolescence. His office was in his home located on the northeast corner of Owen Avenue and Baltimore Pike. He was a native of Northeast Pennsylvania, and he attended the University of Maryland for his medical degree. He operated on me on three occasions: for a tonsillectomy/adenoidectomy when I was in first grade, and for additional adenoidectomies in the fifth and ninth grades.

My most memorable surgical experience occurred in 1958 when I was in fifth grade. On the evening prior to my morning adenoid surgery, I became very angry at the unresponsiveness of hospital nursing care despite my multiple rings for attention. It was as if the nursing staff had taken the night off. I became enraged to the point that I made a bold decision for a ten-year-old. I subsequently donned my winter coat and walked the half mile home from Delaware County Memorial Hospital to our apartment at 278 North Lansdowne Avenue. My astonished parents immediately returned me to my surgical floor—and a very rattled and apologetic nursing staff. Dr. Wallace was less than pleased with me and with the nursing staff when he learned of my exploit the following morning.

Dr. Wallace's waiting room was dark, dated, and uninteresting, but it had adequate seating. I especially recall that the magazines were not popular publications of the day but more esoteric reads that held no interest for me, as the selections were geared toward adults. His immediate office was again very dated, with equipment and furniture that begged for replacement.

What his waiting room and office lacked in ambience and décor, Dr. Wallace compensated with medical skill and patience. I almost repeated the first grade because I was so frequently ill with strep throat. I got to know strep throat so well that I could sense the onset by taste and smell. In those days, a large dosage of penicillin by injection was the initial treatment, and whenever I see that Norman Rockwell illustration of the boy dropping his pants while waiting for an injection, I think of Dr. Wallace, because the needle used for penicillin was long and thick and best applied to one's bottom.

For years Dr. Wallace also gave me weekly allergy shots. When I had mononucleosis as a junior high student, Dr. Wallace gave me weekly injections of crude liver extract (that needle made the penicillin needle look puny), which was a form of treatment at the time. When our gas stove exploded on New Year's Day as I attempted to light it, who was summoned to check my eyes for damage? Dr. Wallace.

When I was an elementary school student, Dr. Wallace requested permission from my parents to drive me to Johns Hopkins Medical School in Baltimore for my throat to be photographed for a medical textbook. Dr. Wallace stated that my throat best fit a condition known as "allergic throat." The day was quite the adventure for me, and for my time, trouble, and "allergic throat," I was compensated fifty dollars, so naturally my parents said yes. I recall actually viewing the photograph with enormous pride in Dr. Wallace's office when the text was eventually published.

Dr. Wallace had no receptionist. You simply walked in, and he would take you in turn for your appointment. I also knew his wife, who was an attractive, dignified woman, who assisted the practice behind the scenes. Mrs. Wallace was very proper, as was Dr. Wallace, so they seemed a solid match as a couple. I even got to know the Wallace children: LeRoy, a year older than me, and twins, Brandon and Lewis, two years younger.

Dr. Wallace gave me two expressions I have used my entire adult life: "Thank you kindly" and "You're welcome, I'm sure." But more than anything, he gave me reliable and competent medical care.

He was also one of the kindest men I have ever known.

54

RANDOM REMEMBRANCES II

The only musical talent in the family lay with Esther. She was accomplished at piano and had a good singing voice. Bill dabbled at both piano and guitar but never got serious. All three Bingham males were poor singers.

Esther did not knit or stitch, which was surprising for her generation and background.

J. T. shaved every morning, including weekends and holidays. His standard cologne, which he wore daily, was traditional Old Spice. His hair lotion was Vitalis. He also bathed in the evening, perhaps because we only had one bathtub.

One of the Curtis publications was a children's magazine called *Jack and Jill*. I always looked forward to J. T. bringing home my monthly copy from his office.

J. T. never golfed or played tennis. He rarely went swimming either. Physical exercise was not on J. T.'s agenda, and the same went for Esther.

For most of my life, the Lansdowne Post Office was located in downtown Lansdowne on Lansdowne Avenue across from the Lansdowne movie theater. It was built in the late 1950s. I still hold a memory of the original one, but barely, as being located just west of Lansdowne Avenue on Scottdale Road. I remember it from Christmas fruitcake runs to the post office as a small child. Jimmy Bower's father worked the counter at the Lansdowne Avenue location, and I always enjoyed seeing him whenever I was in the post office to do business.

Karen Anderson, was a 1956 classmate and a friend of Bill's at LAHS. Karen won a gold medal in the javelin throw in the 1955 Pan American games. She was an Olympic athlete, finishing eighth in the javelin at the 1956 Olympic games in Melbourne, and thirteenth at the 1960 Olympic games. She achieved this success despite the fact that LAHS did not have a girls' track team. She was a three-time AAU champion in the javelin (1954–1956), setting four national records in the event in 1955, 1956, and 1960. What is perhaps most amazing is that Karen was only five foot four and weighed 117 pounds. She attended the University of Pennsylvania and eventually married Ned Oldham, who played halfback at the US Naval Academy and captained the 1958 team that won the Cotton Bowl. Later in life, Karen became an accomplished golfer.

It was likely due to J. T.'s initial employment in the magazine business, but our house always had assorted magazines available on the coffee table and end tables. When J. T. worked for Curtis Publishing, there were always current copies of Curtis publications lying about the house, including *Saturday Evening Post* and *Country Gentlemen,* the farming magazine for which J. T. served as associate editor for several years. Current copies of *Life* and *Time* were also displayed.

Most likely because of my fixation with airplanes as a young child, my parents, as a special treat (birthday?), arranged for me to fly one way with my mother from Philadelphia to Atlantic City on a commercial airline in a piston-powered DC-3. My best guess is that I was five or six years old, and I was thrilled beyond belief with this opportunity. J. T. dropped us off at the Philadelphia Airport and then proceeded to drive the approximate sixty miles to the Atlantic City Airport to meet our flight.

Before our flight had even crossed the Delaware, I had motion sickness. Throughout the twenty-minute flight, I was nauseated, vomiting several times in those small paper bags that the airlines hope you will never have cause to use. I remember pathetically looking out the plane's window, my only concern being how quickly we would land. Kudos to J. T. and Esther here for their effort. I only wish that the gesture had not backfired.

Lansdowne had a symphony orchestra, which periodically performed in the LAHS auditorium. I went with parents or classmates to several performances, which I recall were usually held on Sunday afternoons. While this orchestra wasn't the renowned Philadelphia Orchestra, they held their own. Not bad for a community of twelve thousand.

In the '50s and '60s, Lansdowne was serviced by four Red Arrow Bus (now SEPTA) routes. The routes we typically took to and from the 69th Street Terminal were Lansdowne–Darby ("M") and WestBrook Park ("B"). The Lansdowne–Darby route was typically accessed at the corner of Wayne and Plumstead. On the return route, we generally exited at Essex and Lansdowne Avenues or on Marshall Road at Wayne Avenue. The heavily ridden Chester route ("O") also went through Lansdowne, as did the Oakview route. J. T. typically took the "M" route home at the end of the work day.

For many years, my parents had an interesting morning tradition during the workweek: Esther would drive J. T. to the 69th Street Terminal to avoid his taking the morning bus. As a small child, I accompanied them on hundreds of these short trips. I especially recall the gentle kiss they always shared in the front seat upon arrival at the terminal.

In the mid-1950s Grandmother Bingham was living in a nursing home in Louisville. It was a scary place for a first- or second-grader, but when we visited Louisville, we obviously had to pay our respects by visiting her. On one occasion, I was standing in the hallway apart from my parents and other relatives when I felt a tap on my shoulder. I turned around and was face-to-face with a dwarf wearing a birthday hat. He asked in cartoon-voice fashion, "Hey, little boy, you want to come to my hundredth birthday party?"

I totally freaked out. I ran down the hallway, out the door, and down the street, crying hysterically. Esther or J. T. eventually caught up with me and settled me down. I eventually returned to the nursing home after much coaxing. I even met the comical dwarf, who, we learned, had been a circus performer for much of his life. He apologized for startling me. But whenever people claim that they are uncomfortable around clowns, I certainly understand why after this nursing home experience.

Albemarle Avenue between Lansdowne and Wayne Avenues was a major playground for the Thompson kids, Susan Bartlett, and me in the mid '50s. Fortunately, the street saw little traffic and few parked cars. We rode our bikes on this three-hundred-plus-feet stretch of concrete, played baseball and football in the street, traded baseball cards while sitting on the curb, consumed sticky orange and cherry popsicles, and shot our cap guns while playing cowboys and Indians.

Albemarle was our neighborhood course for evening games of hide-and-seek. During summer months we used to hide in the hydrangea bushes and spy on the adults enjoying the Eshams' small inground pool. We had no clue that one of Lansdowne's oldest buildings, a former farmhouse now converted to apartments, was situated within our Albemarle Avenue playground. We knew most of the street's neighbors, so this was naturally major trick-or-treat territory on Halloween night.

It wasn't all happy memories. Sometimes we competed with older kids for street time, especially when it came to baseball. There were periodic skinned knees and elbows, a bloody nose or two, bike accidents, an occasional disagreement that evolved into a temporary declaration of hostilities between playmates, my frequent running away from Kathy Hughes, and cranky Ed Flannery's admonishments to stay off his property.

Esther generally shopped for groceries at various Acme markets during my school years. Acme remains a major food store chain in southeast Pennsylvania and south Jersey today. In the early '50s there were three other major food chains: A&P, Penn Fruit, and Food Fair. Esther occasionally shopped at these stores when I was very young and prior to Acme's major growth in the '50s and '60s. I vaguely recall her shopping in Darby at a Penn Fruit store, which must have been her grocery store of choice when living in Darby from 1947 to 1950. For the times, the Darby Penn Fruit store was a major supermarket.

The only individuals who ever referred to J. T. as Jim were Esther's parents. For some silly reason, they just couldn't make the transition to Bing or J. T. My father was known as Bing or J. T. in the workplace. He signed checks and documents as James T. Bingham or J. T. Bingham. When he returned to Kentucky, either Louisville or Morganfield, relatives and friends always referred to him as J. T. The "Bing" nickname was earned at the naval academy.

J. T. was not a cook, and he rarely helped out in the kitchen, with the exception of washing and drying dishes and pots and pans. However, he did have some unusual tastes. With the possible exception of scrambling an occasional egg, his only culinary contribution was making okra soup in the summer. That's right: okra soup. I remember that it had a tomato base, and it included both okra and lima beans as main ingredients. Certainly his fondness for this dish was learned during his childhood years in western Kentucky.

This kitchen event was an annual summer ritual in which a large pot of okra soup commanded our small refrigerator for over a week. J. T.'s recipe was unknown, and he likely secured the fresh okra from a Mennonite vendor at the Farmer's Market on 69th Street. J. T. experienced no competition from Esther or me for his okra soup, as we were not fans (understatement). J. T.'s other craving was peanut butter milkshakes, which he would concoct several times a summer. They weren't bad.

My family subscribed to *The Philadelphia Inquirer*, which was delivered to our home in the morning seven days a week. J. T. frequently purchased a copy of the evening paper, *The Philadelphia Bulletin*, on his way home from work. Philly also had a third paper at that time, *The Philadelphia Daily News*, which was more a working man's daily that emphasized city news, sports, and entertainment. The *Inquirer* and *The Daily News* continue in publication today.

Esther's main baked goods were apple pie with made-from-scratch crust, brownies (not from a box), oatmeal raisin cookies (J. T.'s favorite), homemade spice cake, and homemade angel food cake. When icing a non–angel food cake, she frequently made seven-minute frosting, which was positively wonderful.

Esther and J. T. occasionally traveled during the school year. Sometimes the trip was business related, a conference or a convention, and Esther would join J. T. at the event. Sometimes it was pleasurable, including two cruises to Bermuda. As we had no relatives in the area, Alice, a middle-aged black woman from Darby, would stay with me. Alice was kind, quiet, and a wonderful cook, who introduced me to the use of paprika on mashed potatoes and wonderful homemade fried chicken.

During a convention trip to New Orleans, J. T. had his wallet stolen by a pickpocket. As a result, he anxiously called home one evening from New Orleans and gave me specific instructions in order to locate needed paperwork, phone numbers, etc., so that he could secure money and a needed ID. I came through for him, and I recall the incident primarily because it was the first time my parents were dependent upon me. I was nine or ten years old at the time.

J. T. paid bills biweekly, in timely fashion, from the dining-room table, not the card table, which he erected nearly every evening in our living room for his take-home work from the office. He kept all bills in a shoebox and never opened the bill's envelope until he was in his check-writing mode. Occasionally, he would inquire of Esther as to the need for a department-store purchase, but the process never got confrontational or ugly. To my parents' complete credit—and this is a major observation—I never, ever heard them even once argue openly about finances.

When we lived on North Lansdowne Avenue, my parents invested heavily in living-room and dining-room furniture. The living room received a new coffee table and end tables, and the dining room got a new table with six chairs. Esther was thrilled with the acquisition, since most of the family furniture was old, worn, and out of style.

As a fourth-grader, I suffered a knucklehead moment after I made some popcorn in our iron popping pot. After I'd emptied the popcorn into a bowl, I proceeded to rest the hot pot on the edge of the new dining-room table as I scurried into the kitchen to fetch some salt. When I returned, I knew something was instantly wrong from the smell of burning wood. I quickly removed the pan to observe the terrible, lasting damage I had caused. At that same moment, Esther arrived in the dining room, obviously drawn by the smell of something burning.

When she observed what had happened, I thought my life was over. In my recollection, I never saw her more angry—angry and hurt. She burst into tears and directed me to my room. Once she was finally composed, she entered my room to give me the tongue thrashing of my young life. I don't recall a spanking, but that well may have occurred as well. Grounding for a month, most likely reduced to two weeks for good behavior, may well have been the punishment. I felt so horrible about my deed that I thought coloring the exposed raw wood with brown crayon might help. It didn't. Esther and J. T. did have the table spot repaired, but the corner edge still held a small two-by-three-inch blemish that was barely noticeable.

A few years later as a young teenager, I was setting that same table with Esther for a holiday meal. Esther pointed to the damage and then smiled affectionately, pinching me on the cheek and claiming that I had done nothing more than "give the table some character." What a difference a few years made.

When I lived on North Lansdowne Avenue, I discovered a senior neighbor who worked part-time in the gumball machine business. His East Marshall Road garage was used as an assembly station and was thoroughly stocked with machines, charms, and gumballs. I occasionally helped out for fifteen- to twenty-minute spurts loading the machines into his truck—with my salary earned in gumballs.

When I was elementary school age, J. T., Esther, and I spent some time on two occasions staying in Otego, New York, in the boyhood home of my father's boss, Vincent Fuller. It was a kind gesture on Mr. Fuller's part. The home was a simple white-clapboard, black-shuttered home similar to the other homes in that small, sleepy, upstate New York town. I had much free time on my hands, and I frequently traversed the town by bicycle.

Otego is on the banks of the Susquehanna River, so several times I rode by the river, the elementary school, quaint homes on shaded streets, the community swimming pool, and the tiny business district that included a charming family-operated market. For the first time in my life, I imagined what life would be like had I grown up in small-town Otego as opposed to suburban Lansdowne.

It was on one of these occasions in 1959 when we visited the Baseball Hall of Fame in picturesque Cooperstown, New York, less than an hour's drive from Otego. I loved the museum experience and the town of Cooperstown as well, which has far more to offer than just the museum. We also attended the annual Hall of Fame Classic exhibition baseball game scheduled between the Pittsburgh Pirates and the Kansas City A's, which was held in an old ballpark associated with the museum. The small ballpark had reduced field dimensions compared to major-league parks of that era, and the home runs were flying. The game was called in the sixth inning because of rain with the score tied at five runs each.

I also recall that J. T. and I went fishing in a rowboat on one hot day on the Susquehanna River. I obviously inherited my lack of fishing skills from J. T., as all we did that day was eat sandwiches, get baked by the summer sun, and feed the fish. We caught nothing. As an exasperated

J. T. rowed the boat in after a futile outing, we saw two local boys catch a large catfish from a nearby riverbank. I had eyed the boys previously, and they had only been fishing for about ten minutes before they made their catch. This success did not sit well with J. T. and only further fueled his frustration.

PART III

278 North Lansdowne Home

55

278 NORTH LANSDOWNE AVENUE

The abrupt move to 278 North Lansdowne Avenue in 1956 came about because of a major job change for J. T., who had worked for Curtis Publishing's farming magazine, *Country Gentleman*, since being discharged from the navy in early 1946. He had worked his way up to associate editor and enjoyed his position with the magazine. Unfortunately, *Country Gentleman* was the first Curtis publication to fold in the 1950s, with several more to follow. Curtis generously gave my father a year's notice to find new work. The plan that evolved was for our family to move to Traverse City, Michigan, where my father would work as an editor/executive for a local newspaper.

Our house had been sold to Glenn and Audrey Etzweiler, and we were within a few short four weeks of moving to Michigan (I recall cardboard boxes already packed and stacked in our dining room). In a gesture of good will to our neighbors, the Hagys, J. T. visited them one evening to give them a bottle of liquor, supposedly offered in part as a peace offering for all that I had put them through as a rambunctious neighborhood youngster. (By the way, I never deserved this reputation.)

By chance meeting, Gladys Fuller was also visiting the Hagys that evening, and upon hearing of my father's background, she was convinced that J. T. should interview for a general manager position with a growing printing company that she and her husband owned. Within a few days, J. T. had a new job, our move to Michigan was canceled, and our family was quickly in need of a new Lansdowne residence.

I hold no history as to why the large apartment at 278 North Lansdowne Avenue was selected, but my parents and I lived there from 1956 to 1960 during Bill's college days at Franklin & Marshall. We leased the apartment from Harry and Maude Quinn, who lived on the first floor. The Quinns remained good friends with our family through my high school and college years.

The living space was huge by apartment standards, offering more square footage than our home on Marshall Road. Our primary living area was on the second floor, which was accessed by a stairway leading to and from the apartment's only entrance. The stairway lead to a central foyer from which other rooms were accessed. The living room was large and rectangular and was accented by many windows. J. T. and Esther's bedroom was a good size and contained a small cedar closet. A large bathroom included both a tub and a walk-in shower. A narrow kitchen and dining room proved sufficient.

My bedroom was actually larger than the master bedroom, which allowed me to keep my model train platform up year-round. Bill's third-floor bedroom was the largest of all: a long, rectangular room with a slanted ceiling. My nerdy brother actually had a periodic table thumbtacked to the ceiling over his bed for study and memorization when he was home from F&M.

Our laundry was washed in the owner's basement, and Esther dried clothes in the basement or on a clothesline located in a remote section of the backyard. It was at this backyard clothesline where my mother and I met a neighbor across a hedge: a kind, elderly Italian man who had recently immigrated to the United States. I do not recall his name, but he was extremely active in the summer, tending his large vegetable garden. This respectful and humble gentleman, who spoke very limited English, frequently offered us vegetables across the hedge, including tomatoes, green peppers, and eggplant. The garden setting in *Godfather I* is strikingly reminiscent of this neighbor's garden.

The property's yard was far more adequate for play than Marshall Road, and Wiffle ball, football, stepball, and baseball were major activities for me during our four years at the apartment. Few kids my age lived in this neighborhood, and this was a lonely time for me.

56

THE QUINNS

Harry and Maude Quinn became friends with J. T. and Esther when we rented our North Lansdowne Avenue apartment from them from 1956 to 1960. The Quinns occupied the first floor of the home, while we rented the second and third floors.

Harry was short and stout and had a ruddy complexion. He had thinning silver hair and wore heavy, black-rimmed glasses. He was of Irish descent, having been born and raised in Brooklyn. He was a US veteran of World War I who saw infantry action in France. I know nothing of his early background, but he was in the wholesale furniture business and often worked out of an office located over the property's two-car garage. He was good-natured and jolly and had a boisterous laugh, but he was very serious about his business and his passion for golf. He always drove a current-year Cadillac.

His wife, Maude, was a sharp contrast. I never felt they went together as a couple. Maude was extremely thin, frail, and unsteady on her feet. Her skin was very wrinkled, her lips were always peeling, and she frequently did not wear her dentures. Despite her physical shortcomings, Maude was always well dressed. Even though she infrequently left the house, her clothes and jewelry were top-of-the-line. Maude watched TV most of the day, smoked and conversed back and forth with a pet parakeet. Again, I know absolutely nothing of her background and marital history with Harry. The Quinns were childless, but they generally treated me well, and I was a welcome visitor anytime.

Even after we moved to Essex Avenue, the Quinns were frequent visitors to our home for holiday dinners. J. T. and Esther got along well with both Harry and Maude.

Harry served somewhat as a surrogate uncle for me when we lived in the apartment, and I referred to them both as Uncle Harry and Aunt Maude. We watched a lot of TV golf together when coverage of the sport was in its infancy, and he taught me a fair amount about the game. His favorite player was a young Jack Nicklaus. He tried to interest me in caddying at his county club, but transportation to and from the club was an issue, as was my age. Oftentimes he would hit Wiffle golf balls off of a welcome mat in the side yard, and I would catch them like a baseball outfielder and throw them back.

I did errands for the Quinns as well, such as burning their trash and picking up a daily copy of *The Philadelphia Bulletin* for a slight tip. Uncle Harry nicknamed me Nijinsky after the Russian ballet dancer because of my boundless energy and leaping ability one floor up. He also gave me a lump of coal for Christmas as a gag. He even allowed me to grow pumpkins one autumn that almost consumed the side yard.

My memories of Aunt Maude are less vivid, but I do recall assisting her in the fall on several occasions, as she liked to make homemade applesauce from a backyard apple tree. Aunt Maude occasionally attended a movie with Esther and me; *Some Like It Hot* was one we saw together. We also saw a summer stock production of *The Music Man* at the Valley Forge Music Fair, starring Gig Young.

After I went off to college, I saw less and less of the Quinns, and to my disappointment, I do not know how their lives played out.

57

BETHLEHEM PLANT PICNICS

On three or four occasions when I was elementary school age, J. T., Esther, and I would drive to Bethlehem, Pennsylvania, in our 1956 green Chevrolet for a summer picnic held by the employees of Fuller Typesetting's Bethlehem plant. As general manager of the company, J. T. felt an obligation to attend. The drive from Lansdowne to the picnic took all of two hours, but it seemed so much longer driving to the event than it did returning home.

We rarely picnicked as a family (J. T. and Esther were not outdoor enthusiasts), so I greatly anticipated these events. The picnic was held at the same location every year: a small, rural, forested park complete with picnic shelter, permanent grills, picnic tables, a volleyball net, athletic field, gravel parking lot, and even a small pond for fishing. My memories are sketchy except for delicious aromas emanating from the grills, tasty and plentiful food, and the unique opportunity to play volleyball (very poorly) with the adults on a few occasions.

I befriended some peers, played Wiffle ball, participated in some organized kids' games, and explored the park. Strangely, I also remember an excessive number of frogs, which would leap from the pond's bank to safety in the water as my new buddies and I neared while circling the pond.

After five to six hours of major picnicking, I was dirty, sweaty, sticky, mosquito-bitten, in need of a Band-Aid or two, probably cranky, and most certainly very, very tired. Unquestionably, I slept with a peaceful and fulfilled smile on my face on the rides home. I'll bet as well that these were rare occasions when Esther did not demand my taking a bath when we arrived home. Why spoil a perfect day?

58

BILL

William Floyd Bingham was born on July 25, 1938, in Philadelphia, Pennsylvania, eleven months after J. T. and Esther's wedding in Elk Rapids, Michigan. Bill was my only sibling and ten years my senior. Like me, he had blond hair as small child, the color changing to brown during his elementary school days. Even as a teenager, college student, and adult professional, Bill always wore his hair short. Bill was lighter and smaller framed than I, and in many ways we did not physically look like brothers. A sharp difference in personalities, intellectual abilities, interests, and temperaments was soon evident between us as well.

Unlike my history of basically growing up in one town and one school district, Bill spent kindergarten in Pensacola, Florida, and his early elementary school years at Oak Park Elementary in Traverse City because of J. T.'s military call-up. His late elementary school years were split between one year at a Catholic grade school in West Philadelphia and his remaining grade school years at Blessed Virgin Mary School in Darby. Why J. T. and Esther switched to Catholic school midstream is a mystery, although it could have been because Bill was frequently targeted by bullies. Perhaps Catholic School was thought to be a safer and better disciplined setting. When we moved to Lansdowne in 1950, Bill spent all of his junior and senior high school years at Lansdowne-Aldan.

Bill quickly set himself above his peers by his intelligence and maturity. He was one of those rare students who easily, almost effortlessly, outpaced his classmates. He was extremely intelligent and knew it. Socially, he was somewhat awkward.

During my childhood and teen years, Bill never embraced the role of brother. We rarely did things together, as the ten-year separation in ages was an understandable obstacle. He did teach me to tie my shoes and ride a bike. We also attended an occasional movie together. We both enjoyed watching *Sgt. Bilko* and *Victory at Sea* on TV, but those instances were rare and far apart.

Regrettably, I remember Bill as self-absorbed, disinterested, condescending, and distant, and I seemed to serve more as an annoyance or novelty to him, depending upon the circumstances. It is also striking to me that when I recall holidays, birthdays, and other special family events, Bill is not in the picture. It's as if he didn't exist. On many levels, my life seemed to resemble that of an only child rather than a child having an older brother.

Bill was valedictorian at Lansdowne-Aldan in 1956, earning a full academic scholarship to Franklin & Marshall in Lancaster, Pennsylvania. J. T. and Esther could not have been prouder. Bill also ran track at LAHS, wrote for school publications, studied at times in the bathtub, and had a small circle of misfit male friends. He also began dating classmate Tish Henderson, whom he eventually married in April of 1961.

Bill, or "Floyd" as we sometimes needled him, excelled academically at F&M in pre-med courses (especially chemistry). Surprisingly, he pledged to a jock fraternity and was captain of the Diplomats' track team, setting a school record for all-time points scored. Again, J. T. and Esther beamed. Bill rarely came home during the college year, but when he did, he primarily spent time at the University of Pennsylvania, attending parties and other functions with Tish.

J. T. had a definitive, private conversation with me as a seventh-grader upon Bill's return home for his first year of medical school at Jefferson Medical College. He cautioned me that I needed to be especially quiet and respectful of Bill, whose room was next to mine, because of the challenging demands of medical school. An irony here is that despite this purposeful buildup from J. T. about all the study time Bill would require, I might have studied longer and harder as a junior high student than Bill did during his initial year of medical school.

Bill was that smart. He simply grasped and understood principles, theories, and formulas more quickly and more thoroughly than his classmates, and he did so with a modicum of effort. He was accomplished in all sciences and all levels of mathematics. I cannot imagine a field of study that he could not have mastered, were it law, engineering, economics, etc. Bill was, in all measures, the poster child for superior intelligence—and the smartest human being I ever knew.

Bill's marriage in 1961 increased the chasm between us as brothers, and during my high school years, we saw little of him, as medical and family demands replaced his immediate family. He attended one varsity football game during my junior year, and I remember how he railed on me for dropping a touchdown pass. Despite our high school football championship and an undefeated season in 1965, Bill did not attend a single game. Likewise, he did not attend my high school, college, or graduate school graduations.

In spite of the great personal distance between us, Bill did something that surprised me when I went off to college. He gave me his 1955 Volkswagen. This gesture still causes me to smile, but I also ponder it, as it was so sharply outside of his character.

59

ALLERGIES

During my middle elementary school years, Esther began volunteering at the US naval hospital in South Philadelphia a few days a week. She worked primarily for an internist/allergist by the name of John Suess. Dr. Suess eventually became a family friend and moved to Clarksburg, West Virginia, in the late 1960s when his navy stint was up.

Through conversations with my mother, Dr. Suess was convinced that I was suffering from a series of allergies related to my frequent bouts with strep throat and the multiple surgeries I'd had for adenoids and polyps. At about age ten, I was tested for sixty to eighty substances.

Allergy testing was in its infancy at this time. The testing had to be done in two sessions at the naval hospital. This relatively painless process involved a nurse or technician pricking the skin with a needle, allowing a small sample of a specific allergen to penetrate the skin. Approximately twenty separate allergens were applied to my upper arm. When this process was completed, I waited for twenty to thirty minutes before Dr. Suess read the results. The sites where the allergens were introduced felt and looked like mosquito bites, and if I was allergic to a specific substance, the site swelled and reddened.

Based on my physical history, Dr. Suess had speculated that my most heightened responses would be to tobacco, dust, molds, trees, and grasses. He was dead right. My worst reaction was to tobacco, where my score was at the highest grade, so now it was very evident that my parents' heavy smoking was an irritant and strong complication to my personal health.

The next step was to begin a regular, ongoing regimen of allergy shots with a serum specifically created for my major allergies. Throughout late grade school, junior high, and high school, I received regular allergy shots at a local allergy clinic or at Dr. Wallace's Lansdowne office. It is important to note that my ENT symptoms did not improve while I was receiving allergy shots. I continued to experience frequent bouts of strep throat, and in the fifth and ninth grades, Dr. Wallace surgically removed returning adenoids. During junior and senior high and college, Dr. Wallace performed numerous polypectomies in his office. Throughout all of this, Esther and J. T. continued to smoke cigarettes in the home, with business as usual.

Out of frustration, I stopped receiving allergy shots in college, as I felt they were doing no good, not to mention being an unnecessary expense. All in all, I believe the total eight-to-ten-year experience was a monumental waste of time, energy, and especially money.

60

BASEBALL CARDS

Collecting and trading baseball cards was a major hobby during my early childhood. I squandered a fair amount of coinage on their purchase during my elementary school years. The majority of cards was purchased at the Windermere Delicatessen, Van De Boe's Hardware, Westie's, and Coffman's Drug Store.

Fleer and Topps brand cards were the desired draw during my collection period. A package cost five cents and was eventually elevated to ten cents a pack before I stopped collecting. I usually bought a quarter's worth, which for many years was my weekly allowance. Much of the money I received on my birthday (April 8) was spent on baseball cards for the recently launched season.

I also collected a series of Bowman cards, which was very unique. Apparently, in an effort to be strikingly unique, the Bowman '55 series featured players' photos that appeared within a frame resembling a television screen.

Baseball card photo quality was poor. Photos were in color and were more fuzzy and grainy than clear. The back of the card listed personal data and career stats and sometimes a trivia question. I enjoyed finding out where players grew up, since hometown information was usually listed along with the player's height, weight, birth date, and so on.

A single pack of cards included about six cards and a small, rectangular stick of bubble gum, which was good for one major chew. An individual pack typically included a wasted card, such as a check-off card or team photo. This was pretty much worthless in my opinion, since one could barely identify the players on the team card because of poor photo quality. My collecting peers would most likely agree that there was nothing quite like opening a pack of fresh baseball cards to get that first initial whiff, that jolting rush of bubble-gum aroma. As that initial bubble-gum high quickly faded, it was time to learn which new cards—and unfortunately, which duplicates—we had purchased.

Being a die-hard Phillies fan, I naturally looked for red-capped Phillies players first when I examined my newly purchased pack. It was always a disappointment when my pack was dominated by American League players, whom I barely followed. Next to the Phillies, my favorite National League teams were the Cubs and Reds.

The baseball card companies were shrewd and deliberate in their release and distribution of cards, and an individual player's card might not be released until July or August. A diminished profit would have existed for the baseball card companies if we had been able to complete our team rosters by June. Unfortunately, cards were released in timed series, so if you bought a quarter's worth of cards in May, you likely had many repeat cards in your purchase. This was good if the duplicate cards were of Roberto Clemente or Richie Ashburn, but it was bad if they were of relatively unknown players such as the Dodgers' infielder Frank Kellert or Tigers' pitcher Jim Stump. I was always angered when my new packs included primarily American League players, as I did not know or care about the vast majority of them. I truly hit the jackpot when a Del Ennis, Rip Repulski, or Willie Jones was included in a pack.

When buying baseball cards, I even resorted to riding my bike to Drexel Hill or Yeadon or Stonehurst in the hopes that distant stores would supply me with different released sets of cards. Wrong. The distribution process was well calculated and well timed so that a person couldn't purchase a Stan Musial or Frank Robinson card until well into the baseball season. This plan assured the companies that impulsive kids like me would continue to waste their money and buy cards throughout the summer.

A marvelous component to collecting baseball cards was the trading. This was how a person could obtain that Vada Pinson card that had eluded him all summer. Now, he might have to give up a duplicate Gil Hodges card to make it work, but that was where duplicates were valuable. The negative aspect to collecting and trading was the slug cards. They included information like the .208 lifetime hitter for the Milwaukee Braves, or the journeyman pitcher for the Cardinals who had a career mark of eighteen wins and fifty-five losses. I traded regularly with Andy Thompson and other peers. I also had my cards alphabetized, organized by team, and rubber-banded so that I could quickly check stock.

I collected cards well into sixth grade. I had hundreds and hundreds of cards covering five to six seasons. When my family relocated from our home on Marshall Road to our apartment on North Lansdowne Avenue, I was naturally part of the moving process. I recall one day transporting hundreds of then loosely organized baseball cards in a red wagon the short distance between residences. While crossing the busy intersection of Lansdowne Avenue and Marshall Road, my wagon tipped over, and hundreds of cards tumbled onto the highway. Despite the major traffic flow, I totally ignored any interest in physical safety, as there simply existed no other option. I had to recover my treasured baseball cards. Fortunately, a caring motorist stopped to assist me, and we gathered my bounty back into the wagon.

My collection of cards was unintentionally discarded by Esther or me. The set would certainly hold minimal value today, as there were no Honus Wagner or Christie Mathewson cards within the mix. I do wish that I had saved my Phillies cards, since that was the team I lived and died with as a child growing up in the late '50s. But I will always retain the memory of eager anticipation as I opened a new set of baseball cards, checking which Phillies' players were absent from my collection, and honing my negotiation skills on the back porch of a friend's house as we "wheeled and dealed" our cards. These childhood memories are far more valuable than the cards themselves, then or now.

61

BEERS, GASOLINE, AND RAILROADS

When I was a child, summer vacations were not really vacations at all. My family did not travel to New England or the Virginia Blue Ridge or the Jersey Shore. We visited relatives. The destinations included Louisville and Traverse City/Drummond Island, Michigan.

Whether we traveled on the Pennsylvania and Ohio turnpikes or on two-lane state highways, travel was an ordeal for all of us, a real grind. Speed limits were reduced, bypasses did not exist, fast-food had yet to be invented, and it was rare to avoid a flat tire or overheated radiator during the journey. Bill skillfully avoided most of these trips once he had entered college, so with J. T. driving and Esther sharing the front seat, I was exiled to the backseat of a cramped, non–air-conditioned Chevrolet. Our AM radio provided little, if any, relief. A small child could only read or crayon or doodle so much.

Most likely at J. T.'s suggestion, I began keeping lists in a spiral notebook. The lists pertained to beers, gasoline brands, and railroads. I soon learned by observation that beer brands were commonly related to particular cities or regions, so what I saw advertised in Philadelphia might not be popular in Wheeling or Grand Rapids. Long before the days of Budweiser and Miller dominating the American beer industry, most large- and medium-sized cities sported local breweries, which produced indigenous brands of beer. Philadelphia boasted local brews such as Ortleib's, Esslinger, and Schmidt's. New Jersey–based beers, such as Piel's and Ballantine, were also popular in the Philadelphia area.

In traveling by car in Pennsylvania, West Virginia, Ohio, Kentucky, Indiana, and Michigan, I soon learned that dozens of local beers were produced throughout the states traveled. Here are some examples.

Pittsburgh
- Iron City
- Rolling Rock (actually from Latrobe, Pennsylvania)
- Old German
- Olde Frothingslosh
- Duquesne

Cincinnati
- Burger
- Hudepohl

Louisville
- Fall City
- Fehr's
- Oertel's 92

Detroit
- Old Detroit
- Stroh's
- Goebel
- Pfeiffer

I learned much while compiling my lists from billboards and other signage encountered on our travels. For certain, I learned that German-Americans sure loved their beer. And how can one not smile when envisioning a tired Pittsburgh steelworker ordering a tall, frosty Olde Frothingslosh after completing his shift?

The gasoline list was not nearly as exotic. I learned that some companies were national in scope, such as Texaco and Mobil. I also discovered gasoline brands that were not found in the Philadelphia area where Atlantic and Gulf were dominant companies. An incomplete list of the gasoline companies common to the states we traveled in the Midwest and upper South included Skelly, Ashland, Pure, Marathon, DX, Sohio, Conoco, Shell, Sinclair, Admiral, Clark, and Leonard.

In the 1960s, Conrail had yet to be introduced, and the country then relied on hundreds of freight railroads. Some of these lines included Detroit, Lansing, and Lake Michigan; Dayton and Cincinnati; Huron and Eastern; Illinois Western; and even the Traverse City Railroad. The majority of these lines were regional, and some were very small. While the limited interstates we drove avoided railroad crossings because of an intentionally designed system of underpasses and overpasses, no such advantage existed on state and county highways.

All-day road travel on state and county highways in the 1960s included expected delays due to train crossings. While the initial game was to count the number of freight cars in the train, I soon became focused on the names and lettering on the cars. What did Frisco, Monon, and Grand Trunk mean? And what were all of those initials about: L&N, TP&W, C&NW, and NYC?

J. T. was an enthusiastic support, as were numerous, tattered state highway maps. He and I developed a game where he would help me figure out the abbreviations. I specifically recall seeing the lettering "T, P, & W" on a freight car. J. T. told me the T stood for Toledo, but I had to find the city in Illinois represented by the P. Eventually I discovered that the mystery rail company was Toledo, Peoria, and Western. My father was rarely stumped, but on occasion he did not recognize an abbreviated lettering, and the inquiry would have to wait until our return to Lansdowne.

Certainly these are nerdy little games by today's standards, but they did creatively help pass the time, and much to J. T.'s pleasure, I learned a great deal about American geography, history, and local culture during summer travels in hot Chevrolets.

62

FAVORITE TV SHOWS

Favorite National TV Shows

Paul Winchell (Jerry Mahoney, Knucklehead Smith)
Howdy Doody
Soupy Sales
Winky Dink
Rocky and Bullwinkle
Sky King
Lone Ranger
Victory at Sea
Roy Rogers
Mr. Wizard
Have Gun, Will Travel
The Twilight Zone
Red Skelton
Captain Midnight
The Cisco Kid
Sgt. Bilko
The Honeymooners

Favorite Local TV Shows

Pete's Gang (hosted by Peter Boyle's father)
Bertie the Bunyip (Just what is a Bunyip anyway?)
Chief Halftown
Willie the Worm
Sally Starr
Little Rascals
Laurel and Hardy
Three Stooges (no Shemp episodes, please)
American Bandstand
Phillies baseball
What in the World?
Fabiano's Mat Time
Shock Theater with Roland

63

FRANKLIN & MARSHALL

Because of my brother's excellent grades in high school (he was valedictorian of the 1956 Lansdowne-Aldan class), he could have attended any university in the country. I know that some Ivy League schools were in the running (Penn and Princeton), as was Tufts College in Boston, but Bill chose Franklin & Marshall College located in Lancaster, Pennsylvania. Founded in 1787, which made it one of the oldest colleges/universities in the country, F&M was a small, private, all-male, highly respected liberal arts college with an outstanding pre-med reputation.

Even at the age of eighteen, Bill was already focused on becoming a surgeon. The strong pre-med emphasis, plus the generous scholarship package provided, were, no doubt, key factors influencing Bill's choice of F&M. Unlike his younger brother, Bill never had any aspirations to follow in J. T.'s steps at the naval academy.

Bill's years at F&M were productive and full. He majored in chemistry and aced every science course offered. He graduated with high honors in 1960. During his four years at F&M, he also ran track (hurdles, pole vault, long jump, high jump), and when he graduated, he had become F&M's all-time points-scoring leader in track and field. Bill also captained the track team in his senior year.

I remember a phone call my parents received in the fall of 1956 when Bill was a college freshman. He informed my parents that he was pledging a fraternity, Phi Kappa Psi, known as a jock fraternity within the F&M Greek system. I still recall my complete befuddlement, even at age eight, at this concept. What was a fraternity, what did Phi Kappa Psi mean, and what was "pledging"? I eventually got a handle on it. For most of Bill's college career, he lived in the Phi Kappa Psi fraternity house adjacent to campus with roommate Charlie Gorenberg of Ridley, Pennsylvania, a shot-putter on the track squad.

Bill did experience a bump in the road while pledging his freshman year, as he was briefly detained by Lancaster police on one occasion in connection with a Halloween prank that startled some female townies. Certainly J. T. and Esther were not happy with that development, but no charges were filed. I believe my father may have had to make a hurried trip to Lancaster on the evening of the incident.

Bill dated Leticia Henderson, his future wife and a fellow LAHS '56 classmate, during his four years at F&M. Tish attended Penn, and there were occasional weekend trips back and forth by train between the campuses for them both. (Cars on campus were a luxury at that time.) My parents and I usually drove to Lancaster for parents' weekend in the fall and for some spring track meets. Throughout his life, Bill was always very positive about and appreciative of his years at F&M. His will even included a handsome gift to the school's chemistry department.

64

PEPPER'S

Pepper's was the neighborhood pharmacy that my family adopted after the major falling-out with Nate Coffman. Pepper's was located on Plumstead Avenue near Wycombe Avenue in Lansdowne and is still in business today.

Unlike many of Lansdowne's pharmacies, Pepper's was newer and a little larger. It was extremely clean, conveniently organized, modern, and brightly lit. In the summer, the store was an icebox. At one time it operated a soda fountain, and I remember my parents treating me there for ice cream at the fountain after Sunday Mass. We had a charge account at Pepper's, and we were frequent and loyal customers. My parents and I were on a first-name basis with Mr. Pepper, the other pharmacists, and the store manager, Dillard Jordan, who repeatedly attempted to employ me there as teenager. I even knew Mr. Jordan's kids from the town, since the family lived only a few blocks from the store. Esther used Pepper's right up until her relocation to Drummond Island in 1980.

I made many bike and car runs to Pepper's to pick up a prescription, buy over-the-counter medicines, purchase a last-minute greeting card, select some Russell Stover holiday chocolates for Esther, or request the inevitable mixed carton of cigarettes. Pepper's never challenged me regarding the cigarettes, since regulations prohibiting teen purchase were rarely enforced. And they knew Esther, J. T., and me so well that they never questioned the integrity of the sale. Personally, I bought a lot of candy, baseball cards, and ice cream at Pepper's, and of course, the college football magazines and copies of *Sports Illustrated.*

Pepper's eventually ditched the soda fountain—probably in the late '50s or early '60s, as did other pharmacies—and expanded to include medical equipment such as walkers, crutches, portable toilets, etc., in a backroom.

I question how the store remains in business today with such corporate competition from CVS, Walgreen's, and the like. Whenever I'm in Lansdowne, I try to pay Pepper's a ceremonial visit, not so much for a purchase but more in homage and appreciation to a business and employees that were very good and kind to my family and me many years ago.

65

BUS TRIP TO TRAVERSE CITY

It is impossible for me to recall the exact year of the bus trip to Traverse City, but I will go with 1958 or 1959. I have no recall of who came up with the idea, and it may well have been me, but during one of these summers, I traveled unescorted from Philadelphia to Traverse City by Greyhound bus. The trip took almost twenty-four hours and covered over nine hundred miles. The intent was for me to spend a special week with my maternal grandparents, Floyd and Lenora Pitcher, later to be joined by my parents, who would travel from Lansdowne by car.

Once we were at the bus station, my father befriended an adult passenger and slipped him some cash to look after to me on the ride to Detroit. While I hold no physical description of this gentleman, I recall that he worked for GM. His job was to ferry new school buses from the GM plant in Michigan to the school customer and then return by bus, train, or plane to Michigan. The man slept nearly the entire travel time to Detroit.

The bus ride to Detroit seemed to last a week. My bus departed Philadelphia in early evening while it was still light. Looking back, and somewhat to my surprise, I had no meltdown in leaving my parents as I embarked on this great adventure. I was equipped with a suitcase and a brown bag filled with sandwiches, treats, and some cash. The bus stopped at major cities like Harrisburg, Pittsburgh, Cleveland, Toledo, etc., which lengthened the journey considerably. I do recall that I found most of the bus stations and some of their inhabitants pretty creepy, so I soon learned to infrequently leave the bus during scheduled stops. I discovered it impossible to sleep or even read, so I was pretty much awake all night, bored to death, while my GM guardian slept soundly next to me.

My bus made it to Detroit early to midmorning, and there I transferred to a more local service for the ride to Traverse City. I don't recall the route of the cities we passed through in Michigan, but the cities were smaller, and the bus stations were less threatening. Stops were also more frequent but not as elaborate.

I was quite tired when I arrived in Traverse City prior to dinner, and my maternal grandparents both met me at the bus station. They were delighted to see me, and after a home-cooked dinner, I was in bed by early evening. I enjoyed a wonderful, fun week with my grandparents, which included fishing for yellow perch in Lake Michigan, swimming, playing catch with Grandpa Pitcher in the side lot, and visiting the Traverse City Zoo. My parents joined us a week later.

Today I look back on this experience with mixed feelings. Even though we view the world more cynically today, this was still an odd proposition in the late '50s, considering my age. However, J. T. and Esther and my maternal grandparents apparently were fine with the travel plan at the time. Maybe, in viewing the experience through a less traditional lens, one might conclude that the decision to let me travel by Greyhound was a trust issue and a testament to my maturity and intelligence. This is possibly so, but I believe today that the more telling piece was expense with both train and airline travel considered too costly.

66

ESTHER'S PIANO

During my childhood and adolescence, our house or apartment was furnished with a piano. It was a dark-brown, lacquered spinet piano manufactured by the Baldwin Piano Company. I know no purchase or acquisition history except that this same piano is seen in the background of photos taken at our home in Darby, so I am speculating that it was acquired in the late 1940s.

At our Marshall Road home, the piano assumed a cramped position at the foot of the stairway to the second floor. On Lansdowne Avenue, it sat in roomier quarters at the east end of our large living room. On Essex Avenue, it was snuggled into a small, crowded living room next to J. T.'s olive-green armchair.

This was Esther's piano. As a child and teenager growing up in Traverse City, she took piano lessons into high school. I have no knowledge of her playing the piano at school, church, or recreational/community events, and to my recollection and surprise, she never played outside our homes in Lansdowne. Bill took lessons from her for a while, and I believe Esther may even have taught beginning piano to young children in our Marshall Road home in the early '50s. Even I took lessons from her for a while, but I was a whiny, disinterested piano student who would much rather be outside at play. No doubt, I complained so much that my mother quickly abandoned the cause.

Esther naturally read sheet music and was a quick learner, but much of her playing was by ear and from memory and improvisation. She especially liked popular classics and tunes from Broadway shows and the movies. I recall "Out of my Dreams" from *Oklahoma*, "Some Enchanted Evening" from *South Pacific*, "Edelweiss" from *The Sound of Music*, and "One Hand, One Heart" from *West Side Story* as being her particular favorites. She frequently played popular songs of the time, such as "Friendly Persuasion," "Good night, Irene," "Born Free," "Moon River," and "I Left My Heart in San Francisco." She could play some light classical (parts of "Claire de Lune," for example), some folk songs ("Jimmy Crack Corn" and "On Top of Old Smoky" were frequent requests of mine as a small child), and even a little ragtime. Not only talented, Esther was diversified as well.

Christmas songs were an accomplished genre too, and she knew all of the popular Christmas songs and carols by heart. In my adolescent years on Essex Avenue, it was not unusual for Esther to enthusiastically invite carolers into our home at Christmastime for an impromptu concert where she would provide accompaniment on the piano. I recall one noteworthy time when a trumpeter joined the assemblage as well. As carolers exited, Esther would share Russell Stover chocolates or cookies with them as a gesture of holiday gratitude and good will.

As an adolescent, I discovered that Esther appreciated the gift of sheet music to a popular song of the day. She especially liked "Lara's Theme" from the movie *Dr. Zhivago*, which was the first sheet music I ever bought for her. A frustrating irony to me was that Esther would instantly "consume" the purchased sheet music in one playing. After the initial effort, she no longer needed any written prompt, because it was already filed away in her musical memory vault. Regardless, Esther rarely used sheet music. In most instances, all she needed was to do some mild experimentation and humming, and within a short minute or two, she had the melody mastered.

How often did Esther play? It's hard to say. It was probably daily during her middle adulthood as I was growing up. When I was in grade school, it was not uncommon for me to return home from school or play to find Esther lost in a song at her piano. Esther and J. T. occasionally harmonized on sentimental songs that she played, which is another fond memory for me. They were a cute duo. Esther's piano interest waned considerably when she began working full-time after I entered junior high school.

My hunch is that Esther enjoyed playing more when she was alone, almost as a form of escape or therapy. A warm memory for me now is to visualize Esther playing a favorite tune on her piano without the benefit of sheet music—her eyes closed, head tilted back, with a soft smile on her face, totally enthralled and lost in the melody.

67

FAMILY FRUITCAKE

My hunch is that my family did not do much together as a unit because of the ten-year age span between Bill and me. When I was eight years old and just starting to get an understanding of things, Bill was off to college and was gone nine months out of the year. However, Bill would concur that an annual undertaking for us as a family was the ritualized preparing, baking, wrapping, addressing, and mailing of Christmas fruitcakes to family relatives and out-of-state friends on a Saturday or two prior to Christmas. Bill tried to skirt the duty, but J. T. would have none of that. During Bill's college years at F&M, J. T. intentionally scheduled the exercise in clear conjunction with Bill's return home during Christmas break. I recollect this holiday activity at all three of our Lansdowne residences—the same process but in different settings.

With military precision, J. T. directed the assignments, even though the bulk of the work fell to Esther. My mother, loving her sleep and never being an early riser, was up very early on those designated Saturdays. Fueled by multiple cups of black coffee, Esther carefully assembled massive amounts of a complex batter that included either bourbon or brandy as a liquid ingredient. Bill's role was to wrap the five-by-nine-inch loaves after minimal cooling. J. T. addressed the packages, the vast majority of which were bound out of state, and directly assisted Esther in the kitchen. I have no recollection of my specific duties. Perhaps I helped open those jars of horrid candied fruit. And throughout the many hours of monotonous kitchen labor, Esther, always in control, never broke a sweat or lost her cool.

All of us washed, rinsed, and dried the assorted pans used for baking. Remember, there was no dishwasher at our disposal. There was naturally downtime too, since the loaves took at least an hour to bake. Once all twelve to fifteen loaves were baked, wrapped, addressed, and checked off J. T.'s list, J. T. and I were off to the Lansdowne post office to mail them.

To be fair, Bill and I never gave Esther's fruitcake a fighting chance. Any adult who tasted it gave my mother's fruitcake the highest grade. Of course, this was fifty to sixty years ago when people actually liked fruitcake. To this day, I am disappointed that I cannot come up with better support for my dislike of fruitcake. In honesty, the process was fun. We worked as a team, and when Esther finally hung up her apron, we all felt accomplishment and some family pride as well.

On second thought, I'm pretty certain that it was the slimy candied fruit …

68

THE MARLYN

Located in a long, rectangular building at 23 North Lansdowne Avenue, the Marlyn was as close to a local, small-town restaurant as was available within the borough. The Marlyn's only downtown competition was the Horn and Hardart restaurant located on Baltimore Pike at Owen Avenue. During my childhood, it was not unusual for my family to eat at the Marlyn for dinner several times a year. Meals were reasonably priced, and customers ordered from a traditional and bland menu.

The Marlyn was owned and operated by the Boccelli family, and I remember an attentive adult brother-sister team frequently seating customers. I believe the man's name was Freddy, and he was well known and well liked by the regular customers, of which there were many. I can never recall a time when the restaurant was not busy, as it served a faithful and appreciative clientele.

The Marlyn clearly catered to repeat customers. Tables were small, accommodating two to four customers. Seating capacity grew to 170, and I recall a major remodeling that took place during my senior year in high school. Primarily an older crowd, couples, and single seniors regularly dined there. My first-grade teacher, Dibby Koller, regularly ate dinner there by herself. The Marlyn also served lunch, but the restaurant's prime emphasis was always dinner.

Looking back from today, the Marlyn seems very sterile, homogenous, and black and white – no Technicolor. The crowd was exclusively white, with few minority customers, but Lansdowne's minority population in the 1960s was small. The Marlyn was not a family restaurant either, as few parents brought their children there for dinner. It seemed to specifically target an adult clientele by design. The restaurant maintained a friendly air, and there was frequent socializing and common visiting between tables as customers took and left their seats at dinner.

In many ways, the restaurant served as a welcome gathering spot for many town residents, where they could eat a solid meal in comfortable surroundings and mix with acquaintances, old and new. It was not uncommon for my parents to run into adults they knew primarily through the local school system. I even knew fellow LAHS students who worked there as busboys. The one who most easily comes to mind is Paul Hampel, whom I knew from high school football and track. My guess is that Paul worked there as a busboy throughout his high school years. Tom Speers, three years my senior, also bussed tables at the Marlyn.

The highlight for me at the Marlyn was always the dessert, the Marlyn Special, of which I was a major fan. The Marlyn Special was served in a small, chilled ice-cream-sundae glass with vanilla pudding loaded in the bottom of the glass and topped by a small scoop of vanilla ice cream and drizzled with chocolate syrup. That was good stuff. Many times I have thought of replicating "the Special" as a holiday dessert.

69

THE BURNING OF THE GREENS

This was a special event, a tradition unique and native to Lansdowne, as far as I can recall. During the '50s and '60s, artificial trees either didn't exist or were in their infancy. Most families celebrated with natural Christmas trees, which resulted in a disposal dilemma for many families and communities after the holiday season had ended.

Lansdowne had a unique plan. The borough would pick up residents' Christmas trees at curbside, free of charge, in early January. Pickup date(s) were well publicized, and once the hundreds and hundreds of tress were collected, borough personnel transported them to Ardmore Avenue School and deposited them in a large mound in the center of the school's athletic field. It seemed that the pile could be as high as forty to fifty feet.

On the designated January Saturday around 5:00 p.m., townspeople assembled at the field for the annual "Burning of the Greens." With the Lansdowne Fire Department in full presence, a contest was sponsored among local Boys Scout troops to ignite the trees by primitive tools of flint and rock. Eventually a boy succeeded, and the largest bonfire one could ever imagine was lit. The entire pile was quickly engulfed in roaring, crackling flames that seemed to extend eighty to ninety feet in the air. The heat was intense, and the crowd, which probably numbered a thousand or more in attendance, quickly retreated to the field's bordering streets for protection.

After ten minutes or so, the Lansdowne Fire Department swooped in and doused the smoldering remains for several minutes with fire truck water cannons. In a half hour or so, the event was over, and local citizens quickly shuffled home to warmer environs. An aftereffect of the event was that the field was often covered with ice the next morning, with some enterprising children and their parents attempting to ice skate on a rough and uneven surface.

I usually attended the Burning of the Greens, meeting school classmates at a designated time and place. As much as anything, I remember the height of the flames when the bonfire was at its summit, the intense heat, and the fact that the Saturday chosen for the event typically seemed to be the coldest day of the year.

I remember attending most often when we lived on North Lansdowne Avenue, as I had a quick four-to-five-block walk to the field and back home. On one occasion when my brother was home for a weekend from Franklin and Marshall, Bill slyly commented on my return home that I had returned from "the pagan ritual." I had no idea what he was talking about, so I quickly consulted a dictionary. After consulting the dictionary, I still had no idea what he was talking about.

70

THE HENDERSONS

When Bill was a senior in high school, he began dating Letitia Henderson, a fellow LAHS 1956 classmate. "Tish" lived with her parents, maternal grandmother, and younger twin brothers, Chad and Jim, in a large, stately, brown-and-yellow house on Plumstead Avenue, half a block west of Lansdowne Avenue. The house had a wonderful wraparound porch that accented the front and sides of the house. I always considered the Hendersons' house one of the finest in Lansdowne.

Our family got to know the Hendersons reasonably well as Bill and Tish's relationship deepened during their college years. Tish attended the University of Pennsylvania, and I believe she majored in English. Charlie Henderson, Tish's father, was an executive at Insurance Company of North America, and he commuted to and from work in center city Philadelphia on the Media local. Charlie may originally have been from upstate New York, as the family frequently vacationed at Lake George during the summer. Charlie's hobbies included sailing and HO model railroading. He held the rank of captain in the naval reserves.

Virginia Henderson, Tish's mother, was dean of women at the University of Pennsylvania. Ginnie was a delight, a petite, pretty woman with short salt-and-pepper hair. She was a splendid conversationalist, always positive and pleasant. I liked her a lot, and she was always very kind to me.

Bill and Tish married after Bill completed his first year of medical school at Jefferson Medical College in Philadelphia in April of 1961.

I got to know Chad and Jim well, especially when we lived on North Lansdowne Avenue from 1956 to 1960. They were two years older than I was, and in a neighborhood void of Green Avenue classmates, they were my main contacts after school and on weekends. The Henderson twins liked sports, and I spent a fair amount of time at their home, shooting hoops and especially playing football in a side lot. I was also mesmerized by Charlie's expansive HO railroad layout in the basement, although I was never allowed to operate it.

The Hendersons had a wonderful tradition that I always looked forward to. They held an open house on New Year's Day at their home. It was heavily attended, and my parents and I usually frequented it through my college years. Drinks and light refreshments were served, while women chatted and men watched televised football bowl games, which were typically reserved for New Year's Day. I met Navy's football captain Ned Oldham at this event, which was a big thrill. Ned dated Karen Anderson, an Olympic javelin thrower and fellow LAHS classmate of Bill and Tish.

When Bill and Tish left the Philadelphia area in the mid '60s, J. T. and Esther's contacts with the Hendersons grew less frequent.

71

LETTER TO TIME MAGAZINE

In the late 1950s TV westerns flooded the airwaves. Programs such as *Gunsmoke*, *Have Gun Will Travel*, *Maverick*, *Bonanza*, and *Wyatt Earp* dominated television programming during evening hours. The pattern was similar to today's television audience's fascination with crime shows. I was hooked on TV westerns, just like the bulk of America was. One of my favorite shows was *Wyatt Earp*, starring Hugh O'Brien. I effortlessly remember the chorus lyrics to the theme song:

Wyatt Earp, Wyatt Earp,
Brave, courageous, and bold,
Long live his life, and long live his glory,
And long may his story be told.

America's obsession with TV westerns was well chronicled by the electronic and print media at the time. In early April of 1959, *Time* magazine ran a cover story on the subject, an article that I read with spirited interest. In one reference, the article mentioned that Hugh O'Brien, who portrayed Wyatt Earp, wore two Buntline specials, a customized handgun characterized by a long, extended barrel.

I was horrified, appalled, and aghast. Hugh O'Brien wore *one* Buntline special on the show, not two! Any fool knew that. I expressed my outrage to journalist J. T., and his initial efforts to mollify me were of no help. I was beside myself. What was I to do? What could I do regarding this injustice, this unspeakable faux pas of contemporary American journalism?

J. T. suggested that I write a letter to the editor. A letter to the editor? What was my father getting at here? He explained the concept and process, and I subsequently jumped at the opportunity. On a small, portable, black-and-white Corona typewriter at a vestibule desk, I pecked out a short and polite letter to *Time*, challenging the discrepancy in the article. J. T. proofed it, and even though my initial draft was only four to five sentences in length, he trimmed it some, claiming that magazine editors did not like to receive long letters. I specifically recall the last line of the letter: "Please look into this matter."

I retyped the letter and ran the finished copy by both J. T. and Esther, who gave it their blessing. J. T. determined the address for me to include on the envelope. I asked for a stamp, and not wishing the matter to be further delayed, stamped and sealed my letter and personally walked the envelope to a postal box (former President Truman had nothing on me) located in the nearby Marshall Road commercial district. I most likely grabbed a candy bar for the walk back home. After that, I felt better.

Approximately a week later on a Saturday morning, I received a telegram at our 278 North Lansdowne Avenue address. Now, understand that nobody received telegrams anymore. That was a form of communication reserved for the movies, being more common to the 1930s and 1940s. Telegrams were intended for adults, not a kid who had only recently turned eleven. I looked at J. T. for direction as to what was happening, and he encouraged me to open the telegram.

The telegram had come from *Time* magazine and indicated that an excerpt ("Pop, what's an excerpt?") of my letter would appear in an upcoming edition of *Time*. We were all astonished, probably J. T. and Esther even more than I.

The letter did appear in the April 20, 1959, edition of *Time* that had a portrait of the Dalai Lama on the front cover.

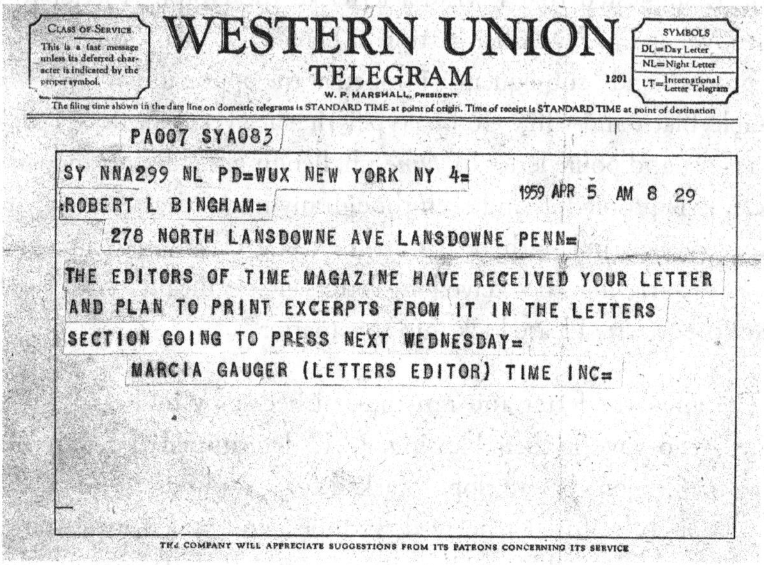

CLASS OF SERVICE
This is a fast message unless its deferred character is indicated by the proper symbol.

WESTERN UNION
TELEGRAM
W. P. MARSHALL, PRESIDENT

SYMBOLS
DL=Day Letter
NL=Night Letter
LT=International Letter Telegram

1201

The filing time shown in the date line on domestic telegrams is STANDARD TIME at point of origin. Time of receipt is STANDARD TIME at point of destination

PA007 SYA083

SY NNA299 NL PD=WUX NEW YORK NY 4=

1959 APR 5 AM 8 29

ROBERT L BINGHAM=

278 NORTH LANSDOWNE AVE LANSDOWNE PENN=

THE EDITORS OF TIME MAGAZINE HAVE RECEIVED YOUR LETTER AND PLAN TO PRINT EXCERPTS FROM IT IN THE LETTERS SECTION GOING TO PRESS NEXT WEDNESDAY=

MARCIA GAUGER (LETTERS EDITOR) TIME INC=

THE COMPANY WILL APPRECIATE SUGGESTIONS FROM ITS PATRONS CONCERNING ITS SERVICE

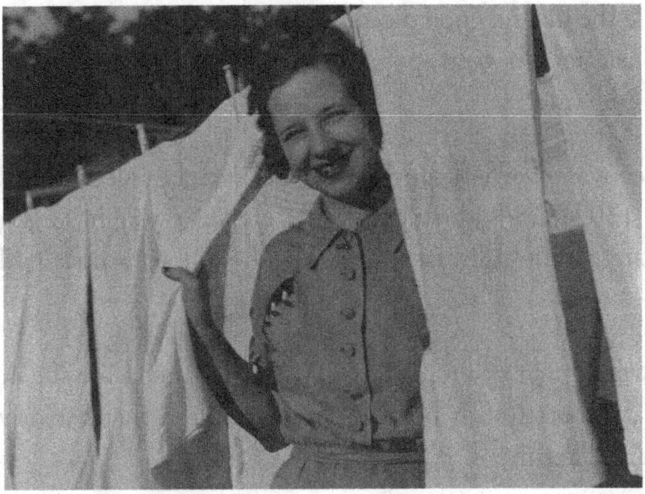

Esther and the laundry, circa 1940

72

ESTHER'S HEALTH

Esther experienced a number of medical issues during her lifetime, with the majority of them being manageable.

She never exercised, and not surprisingly, she did not have much stamina walking, climbing stairs, and so on. Certainly her lifetime of heavy smoking did not help.

Esther's diet was unremarkable. She was an extremely light eater, as food simply was not that important to her. She was an avid drinker of black coffee in the morning, probably having four to six cups by 10:00 a.m. She liked half a grapefruit for breakfast. She also enjoyed grilled cheese sandwiches and tongue sandwiches.

While she liked a good piece of candy now and then, she was not a heavy consumer of sweets, pop, or snack foods. She rarely snacked and never pigged out.

Esther was five foot three, with her weight fluctuating between 110 and 130 pounds during her lifetime. Her weight was generally appropriate, although in the early '60s, she did get a little pudgy for a few years.

She wore prescription reading glasses, and late in life she developed macular degeneration. It became serious enough that her driving was restricted to daytime.

Esther's greatest medical issues were periodic migraine headaches, which totally debilitated her. Migraines were most prominent during her forties and fifties.

Like many adults of her era, she wore false teeth. Esther had severe allergies to the materials used in constructing dentures. She hopped from dentist to dentist for years until she found a dentist who devised the correct nonallergenic formula for her dentures.

In her forties, Esther began taking daily thyroid medication in the morning. I don't recall if her thyroid was overactive or underactive.

Esther had a lump removed from her breast while in her forties. It proved to be nonmalignant. I can recall no major surgeries other than a hysterectomy, which she also experienced in her forties.

For several decades, she regularly visited Dr. Pete Leaness, podiatrist, for corns and calluses on both feet.

Esther avoided direct sunlight, because she said she was allergic to heavy sun exposure.

While living on Marshall Road, she was exposed to a furnace explosion, which burned her face and both hands. However, she suffered no permanent damage. Her hands were bandaged for several days after the incident.

Esther seldom suffered from colds or flu. She occasionally experienced mild heartburn.

In her late thirties, Esther contracted a very serious case of the mumps, which almost caused her to be hospitalized. She became ill on one of our summer trips to Michigan, with the trip being cut short because of her illness. I recall that J. T., Bill, and I drove nonstop back to Lansdowne with Esther in the backseat, sweating and shivering under a blanket in ninety-degree heat.

She also developed osteoporosis, for which she took medication. She was extremely thin and frail in her final years.

The Lansdowne Theater

73

THE LANSDOWNE THEATER

The Lansdowne Theater—or simply "The Lansdowne," as we called it—is very likely to be a warm childhood memory for any Lansdowner within my generation. I seemed to grow up there, attending dozens and dozens of shows at the Lansdowne during my youth and adolescence.

The theater is located in downtown Lansdowne at 31 North Lansdowne Avenue. Two commercial stores, which were part of the actual theater building, flanked the main entrance/ticket booth during my childhood, one being a dry-cleaning store on the left, and the other being the long-standing Lansdowne Pharmacy to the right.

The theater opened in 1927 with a main-floor seating capacity of 1,381 seats. The Lansdowne did not have a balcony. The architecture of the building reflects a Spanish mission style. One Internet reference claimed the Lansdowne Theater to be "an ornate movie palace inspired by romantic Spain." The lobby and foyer were painted in soft colors: cream and pink and maybe some light blue. Spacious and outdated restrooms were located in the basement.

Unlike so many movie houses of its era, the Lansdowne did not have a concession stand. Instead, it housed several vending machines that served ten-cent popcorn, ten-cent soft drinks (small cup, no ice), and five-cent candy. A favorite mix for me was a bag of popcorn and root-beer-barrel candy.

The Lansdowne was graced by a massive maroon curtain and an elaborate chandelier, which would have served any *Phantom of the Opera* production extremely well. Theater seats were soft and plushy in a maroon color.

My first exposure to the Lansdowne Theater was not a good one. Esther, Susan Bartlett, Susan's mother, and I attended a viewing of *The Wizard of Oz* on a Saturday afternoon. It was my first time attending a movie in a theater, and I was about three at the time. I did not handle the movie well at all. Early in the movie, I freaked out—*really* freaked out—and cried hysterically, especially when Toto was snatched away from Dorothy by Miss Gulch.

I was so out of sorts that Esther and I quickly retreated to a sofa in the lobby where we could still hear and see much of the movie through an archway. This was hardly the needed respite. Despite being in the safety of Esther's reassuring arms, I was doing no better. Now I had a flying witch to deal with, a mean-sounding and intimidating wizard, all those little Munchkins, flying monkeys, and so on. My only thought was, *Get me outta this place!*

I was never comfortable watching the movie until adulthood because of childhood trauma, and that's the truth. *The Wizard of Oz* is most definitely not a movie for small children.

As I matured, I began attending regular Saturday matinees with my classmates and neighborhood friends. Twenty-five cents paid for admission, and I usually carried another quarter for candy and popcorn. These were glory years. Usually five or six Warner Brothers cartoons were shown for starters, and then came the main feature, a movie considered especially suited for children, usually a horror or science fiction movie, war movie, comedy (Abbott and Costello), western, action flick, or Tarzan epic.

Yes, it's true: when the bad guy finally got what he deserved at the movie's end, we all clapped and cheered as good rightfully triumphed over evil. By the way, Saturday matinee attendance was all gender specific: guys sat with guys, girls with girls. However, peppering the girls with peashooters was fair game and well within the code.

Saturday matinees were frequently accented by peashooters (often bought at Westie's immediately prior to the show), rolled marbles, and even exploding torpedo fireworks. And who can forget those memorable Halloween Saturdays when a monster flick was scheduled for the main feature as we attended in our trick-or-treat costumes?

Sometime in seventh grade, a highly memorable incident occurred during an unremarkable Saturday matinee at the Lansdowne. Highland Avenue School had a bully, Jack Samuels,[2] that nobody liked. Samuels was a true pariah at the school, though we didn't yet know the meaning of the word. He shook down kids for cafeteria money, intimidated and slapped younger kids for no reason, made idle threats, and so on. Nowadays he reminds me a lot of a heavier version of yellow-toothed Scut Farkus from *A Christmas Story*.

During this particular show, many of us observed Samuels in the audience. This was unusual, since he was not a matinee regular at the Lansdowne. We kept our eye on him, hoping that he would bother others. Well into the main feature, we heard a blood-curdling scream

[2] Name has been changed to protect individual's privacy.

emanating from the concession area. The shriek was legitimate and constant. As this was too good to miss, many of us dashed out of our seats to the concession area to find Samuels on his knees, writhing in pain, begging for mercy, with his hand caught in an inner mechanism of the popcorn machine. Samuels had apparently attempted to trigger a free release of popcorn, but instead his hand was trapped and being chewed up by the inner workings of the popcorn machine.

A theater employee quickly intervened and rescued Samuels, but not before his hand was coated with blood. Our crowd showed no empathy toward our antagonist. It was his just desserts in our minds. Oddly enough, that was the last time I ever saw or heard of Jack Samuels.

Junior high included making our first pathetic efforts at asking girls out for dates. A Friday or Saturday night movie at the Lansdowne was a likely happening for us seventh- and eighth-graders, with many first kisses stolen there.

For high schoolers, the Lansdowne took on additional importance, as many of us now had steady girlfriends. As older teenagers, we recognized that we had spent hundreds of hours there in this safe and familiar movie house. Within its confines, we had been entertained, had flirted with and romanced our dates, and perhaps had even fallen in love.

I saw some epic films at the Lansdowne over the years. My attendance there extended into college and beyond, but like the majority of early twentieth-century movie houses, the Lansdowne fell on hard times, a victim to the sterile, cookie-cutter mall movie theaters that are now the current standard. The Lansdowne eventually became a "dollar theater" in the mid '80s. It closed its doors for good as a theater in 1987, the last screened movie being *Beverly Hills Cop II*. Ironically, that same year, the Lansdowne Theater was placed on the National Register of Historic Places.

The excellent news is that the Lansdowne will soon reopen as a result of the outstanding preservation efforts of the nonprofit Historic Lansdowne Theater Corporation and its CEO, Matt Schultz. One day, I will return with my wife, and when the lights from that glorious chandelier dim, I will steal one more kiss "as time goes by."

74

DR. WILLIAM "PETE" LEANESS

Esther had terrible feet. She was cursed with corns and calluses for most of her adult life, and for years while living in Philadelphia, Darby, and Lansdowne, she scheduled monthly appointments with a West Philadelphia podiatrist, Dr. Pete Leaness. My hunch is that Esther began seeing Dr. Leaness in the late 1940s when J. T., Esther, and Bill lived briefly in a West Philadelphia high-rise apartment, Walnut Park, located at 63rd and Walnut.

As it was with the forays to visit Mr. Richards, her hairstylist, I frequently accompanied Esther on these trips, but I sense that it was because Dr. Leaness's basement office was located in a deteriorating neighborhood. Unlike the trips to Mr. Richards, I did not mind visiting Dr. Leaness.

Dr. Leaness was Jewish. He was really my first exposure to a Jewish person, and I had a wonderful first impression. He was a knowledgeable and skilled professional, educated in podiatry at Temple University. He was short and dark-complexioned with thinning black hair, and he wore black-rimmed glasses while he worked. He was not only an excellent podiatrist but a consummate gentleman with superb social skills. He took an interest in me as well. During my late elementary years, I learned that he was also the men's soccer coach at Temple University, which opened up a whole new world for me.

Esther's initial response at appointments was pretty standard. She would turn away from Dr. Leaness, who afforded her privacy as she removed her shoes and nylons. Once in the examination chair, Dr. Leaness would lightly spray Esther's feet with treated water. Then he would proceed to skillfully remove her painful corns and calluses with chisels and corn knives. Once all skin was removed, he applied a brown liquid medication and padded bandages to the treated areas. Esther always claimed that the improvement was dramatic and 100 percent—like she had "new feet."

I was a patient as well during the years of junior and senior high school when I suffered from several ingrown toenails (thank you, Susie Willis). During my sophomore year at football camp, I developed severe blisters from assigned football shoes that did not fit. Upon my returning home from football camp, Esther arranged for an emergency Monday morning appointment with Dr. Leaness, who was angered at what he found. Infection would likely have set in had I not been treated. He was so irritated that he threatened to call Head Coach Spafford, but he eventually backed down. I saw Dr. Leaness a second time later that week, at which time my blistered heals had much improved.

In researching for this chapter, I gained major background on "Dr. Pete's" athletic background and coaching career. He was an All-America soccer player at Temple in 1929. He was also an exceptional baseball player and could have played professionally. He served as head coach of the Temple soccer team for forty-one years from 1930 to 1971, producing thirty-six all-American players and five Olympic players. Temple was the NCAA soccer champion in 1951 and 1953. Dr. Pete was inducted into both the National Soccer Coaches Hall of Fame and the Philadelphia Jewish Sports Hall of Fame.

Dr. Pete was a warm and caring guy. Since I had only distant uncles, he would have been a superb local substitute.

75

RANDOM REMEMBRANCES III

Birthday recognition and celebration was fairly typical for the times. Yes, we celebrated, had a cake, and received presents, but most times we did not go out for dinner. Usually Esther prepared a special, requested dinner for J. T., Bill, and me. My most common request was for roast pork, mashed potatoes, and homemade gravy as the main meal. Since J. T. was not accomplished in the kitchen, Esther's birthday was the exception, with the Marlyn most likely getting the call.

Like most families during that era, we had home milk delivery service. We used Turner and Wescott and then Wawa. A uniformed milkman delivered milk, which came in glass bottles, several times a week to our front porch. This service died out in the late '60s and early '70s.

The old Lansdowne Library was located on Lansdowne Avenue just south of the train station. It was small and compact, with the children's section being on the second floor. I visited the Lansdowne Library a lot as a sixth-grader, mainly checking out Landmark and Tarzan books. Nothing was computerized. We used a card catalog to find books or research a topic. The attendant handstamped the books with the return date. I believe the loan period was two weeks in length. As much as anything, I recall the distinct smell of the library as I first entered. It always smelled of books, old books. The new, larger Lansdowne Library, which I have never visited, is located a few blocks south of the former site.

My interest in model trains began with Jackie Pruitt's basement Lionel set when I lived on Marshall Road. Jackie had a permanent layout in his basement, to which I eventually earned engineer honors. He actually had a locomotive that spewed real smoke generated by smoke pellets that he could drop into the engine's smokestack.

Tish Henderson, Bill's first wife, lived nearby on Plumstead Avenue, and as a child living on North Lansdowne Avenue, I befriended her younger twin brothers, Chad and Jim. Tish, Chad, and Jim's father, Charlie Henderson, had constructed an elaborate, unfinished, multitrack HO layout in his basement. The Henderson HO layout, had it ever been fully electrified and landscaped, would have been worthy of a model-railroad magazine-photo layout. I could not play as freely at the Hendersons' house as I could at the Pruitts' house, but what a layout!

Through Charlie Henderson, I got to know a retired man down the street on Plumstead Avenue, who had built a very handsome HO layout in his basement. He was a real mentor and taught me a lot about model trains.

The first Lionel train set (1954) included:

- New York Central steam engine and tender
- Silver Western Pacific boxcar
- Green Railway Express reefer
- Gray hopper (Soo Line?)
- Black Lionel gondola
- Silver Sunoco tank car
- New York Central caboose
- Two New York Central lighted passenger cars

The first HO train set (1958) included:

- Baltimore and Ohio F7 diesel engine (A and B units)

- Blue Wabash boxcar
- Green Elgin, Joliet, and Eastern (EJ&E) gondola
- Brown Missouri Pacific cattle car
- Silver tank car (Shell?)
- Gray Monon hopper
- Red Baltimore and Ohio caboose

I forget the time of year, but Green Avenue School had an annual weekend fair held on the school's playground. It was a fundraiser, and Esther was always active in some capacity. I recollect that she staffed a table selling donated books during one fair. While the Green Avenue Fair was actually a small event, it was gigantic to a grade schooler. Some small, carnival-like amusement rides and food trailers were on site at the school. The highlight that I best remember was the wonderful pizza made by Marilyn Della Porta's mother. Pizza was in its infancy, but still, this was good stuff.

Despite not having a sophisticated, well-stocked workshop, J. T. was a decent carpenter. While living on Weymouth Road in Darby, J. T. built a small bookcase, which included latched doors. This white bookcase is seen in the background of many black-and-white photos taken in the 1950s. The bookcase now occupies my basement office. J. T. also built a simple desk for me while I was in junior high school, which I used through graduate school.

Within the Marshall Road commercial district was a tiny, family-owned-and-operated hardware store, Van de Boe's, located on the Drexel Hill side of Marshall Road. I was a frequent customer for school supplies, rubber balls, baseball cards, balsa flying airplanes, and model airplanes. I bought a lot of Revel model airplane kits at Van de Boe's, including kits for such World War II classic airplanes as Spitfire, Messerschmitt 109, Hellcat, P-38, and Zero. I had a bad habit of trying to assemble the model without first reading the directions, believing that I didn't require such basic guidance (big mistake). I was sloppy with the glue as well. You could also purchase television tubes at Van de Boe's, as they had a tube tester available to customers. Oddly, I do not recall any individual staff who worked there.

Generally, few activities were scheduled when we visited Kentucky relatives. I always anticipated a boring time off by myself while adults sat around and smoked and talked and smoked some more. Bill and I sometimes took a bus to and from downtown Louisville to attend the movies. On one eventful occasion, I was exposed to my first Three Stooges short, a 3D film where they worked as car mechanics. Look out for that flying wrench!

On summer vacation in Louisville one year, Bill and I were surprised to learn that an outing had been scheduled to an amusement park located in, of all places, Santa Claus, Indiana. With the park located midway between Louisville and Morganfield, our Bingham/Drury relatives from Morganfield met us there for a day of picnicking, amusement rides, and swimming.

Upon arriving at the park, Bill was ecstatic to learn that a zip line had been installed between two towers. At its low point, the line allowed users to drop into the lake during descent. Bill seemed to be active on the zip line all day long. I had fun that day with same-age third-cousin Judy Drury. I recall one memorable incident where Judy and I were both flying high on a swing set when an adult relative discovered a three-to-four-foot, nonpoisonous snake beneath us. To my knowledge, the FBI was not alerted, but you would have thought so, considering the hysteria raised. Judy and I just laughed it off and kept swinging, unharmed. The snake suffered a crueler fate.

Our family dentist during my childhood was Dr. Kotanchik. How and why he was selected remains a mystery. Dr. Kotanchik was of Russian ancestry, a short man with a wide and forced smile who always squinted when he smiled. His compact office was located in the 69th Street area, so I was usually driven to and from his office by Esther. In the 1950s, dentistry was extremely primitive by today's standards. Aside from a receptionist, Dr. Kotanchik did everything, working without an assistant, which was a familiar dental practice in those days.

For some reason, my baby teeth did not lose their roots, so most of them had to be extracted. Local anesthesia was rarely used, but the extraction was quick and not that painful. High-speed water drills had yet to be invented, so for cavities, a slower-RPM drill was used. It had a horrible grinding sound that one immediately linked with pain. Dr. Kotanchik only gave local anesthesia as a last resort, and in those days, an oral injection was far more painful a process than it is today. A frequent retort of his was something like, "You probably won't need anything for this small filling." Easy for him to say.

I recall the dental office as always very cold. The waiting room, which was the size of a tiny living room, included a full wall mural of a Rocky Mountain lake and a small aquarium to help lessen patient anxiety.

A notable characteristic of Dr. Kotanchik was his short, stubby fingers. They were made even more memorable by the fact that his favorite hobby was masonry, so they were always extremely rough, like sandpaper. Good call on the hobby, Dr. K.

As I entered junior high school, my parents switched dentists. I do not recall their reasoning or justification for the change

These were my favorite toys as a child:

- Bicycle
- Lincoln Logs
- View-Master
- Model trains
- Building blocks (pre-Lego)
- Microscope
- Baseball cards
- Football
- Baseball gear
- Model airplanes
- Comic books
- Slinky

I was never into yo-yos, which periodically were popular.

After spending six years at Green Avenue Elementary, I attended sixth grade at Highland Avenue School, the former high school building originally constructed around 1900. Highland Avenue was a dump—a huge disappointment after attending a modern elementary school like Green Avenue. The fact that we were blended with unfamiliar, new students was not as much a negative factor as the facility and grounds.

Highland Avenue Elementary was located on Highland Avenue near Baltimore Pike. The playground, which provided adequate space, was covered with macadam and concrete and no grass, a major step down from Green Avenue. Kickball was a major sport at recess and lunchtime.

The school itself was old in every sense. The hallways were dark, with antiquated light fixtures hanging from high ceilings. A plus was that the classrooms were good size, with high ceilings and large windows that could be opened in warm weather. The basement gymnasium was not just old; it was ancient and resembled a set from a 1930s horror movie. Highland Avenue also had a permanent musty smell, which suggested that fresh air died immediately upon entering the building.

I did like the cafeteria, which was a new twist for former Green Avenue students. I bought my lunch and especially looked forward to the macaroni and cheese.

My teacher was Mr. Habecker, my first male teacher. He was strict in the classroom, but I did like the fact that he played kickball with us at recess.

Highland Avenue proved to be my first major exposure to black students, who lived on Lansdowne's south end. I especially recall getting to know Brad Dickerson, whom you definitely wanted on your kickball team, and Hubert Barnes, students with whom I would go through high school.

At LAHS Lansdowne kids walked to school, as did East Lansdowne students. Aldan students were bused to and from LAHS by contracted Red Arrow busses. All elementary school children in Lansdowne walked to and from school.

Collecting bottles was a childhood exercise we frequently used during desperate times when we needed a replacement pink ball or pimple ball. Carbonated soft drinks—or "soda," as it was called in the area—were primarily sold in returnable glass bottles. Standard soda bottles netted two cents when returned at a local grocery or deli, with the larger, quart-sized bottles bringing a nickel. Favorite haunts for finding returnable bottles were the high school athletic fields and Ardmore Avenue playground. A superb time to hit these areas was the day after the Fourth of July prior to clean up. I never saw bottle collecting as degrading, as it was an accepted response during childhood when we needed some spending change.

I can never recall any family outings to museums, either locally or on summer trips. I suppose J. T. and Esther relied on school field trips to meet that exposure.

Norman Rockwell, the legendary American illustrator, gained much fame during his career for the magazine covers he painted for *The Saturday Evening Post*, a popular weekly magazine midcentury. *The Post*, as it was known, was a Curtis publication, the company for which J. T. worked for sixteen years from 1934 to 1940 and 1946 to 1956. Due to the Curtis connection, J. T. met Norman Rockwell on some occasions in a business capacity. Norman Rockwell gave J. T. an autographed copy of the 1946 Arthur Guptill text, *Norman Rockwell: Illustrator*, which remains in the family today.

As best I can determine, my uneasiness, if not fear, of the water is based upon an incident that occurred at the naval swimming pool located on the grounds of the US naval base in South Philadelphia. Our family had a pool pass because of my father's reserve status in the navy, and Bill agreed, with Esther's blessing, to take me there for a day's outing in the summer of 1955. Bill had turned seventeen that summer and was approaching his senior year in high school.

At age seven, I did not know how to swim, a surprising retrospection in light of Esther's expertise in the water. I had received neither formal lessons nor any impromptu instruction from any family members. Bill had agreed to begin teaching me, but he chose an unorthodox and questionable method.

After my begging for reassurance that nothing bad would happen, that Bill would protect and take care of me, the lesson began in earnest. With Bill standing on the side of the crowded pool's deep end, I lowered myself into the water, keeping full grasp of the pool's edge. After much coaxing, I allowed Bill to hold both of my hands while he extended me further away from the safety of the pool's side. While crouched but still holding both of my hands, he proceeded to pull my body straight up and down in a series of dips into the water. He continued to pull me up and down in the water with the intent to eventually lower my head into the water. To the best of my recall, I was okay with all of this so far, but on one of the deeper dips in the water, Bill intentionally let go. This was no accident.

I immediately panicked and naturally failed in my attempt to reach the edge of the pool. I took in several gulps of water and sank to the bottom of the pool. I remember my feet barely touching, but that is all. I have no memory of who retrieved or revived me. What I do remember is crying, coughing, and spitting up water as I lay by the side of the pool, looking up at a lifeguard, Bill, and total strangers.

I am somewhat surprised that I remember as much of this event as I do, but I have no memory of the ride home, Bill's explanation, or my parents' response. I was not close to drowning; that wasn't the issue. But how could someone so bright and reportedly mature explain such reckless behavior? Was an awkward wedge implanted between Bill and me on that summer day? I think so. I am convinced that my lifelong discomfort with swimming and all aquatics is directly tied to this event.

Lansdowne's primary waterway is Darby Creek, a stream that rises in Chester County and Radnor in Delaware County. It separates Lansdowne on the west from Upper Darby Township, Clifton Heights, and Aldan. As children we often walked or rode our bikes to the Creek to patrol its banks and the limited woods surrounding it. Children and adults attempted to fish it, especially near the five-foot falls on the Clifton Heights side under the railroad trestle, but Darby Creek was badly polluted at that time. I still recall on many occasions seeing foaming soapsuds several feet high, created by kids at the base of the falls. We saw some limited aquatic wildlife along Darby Creek, namely turtles, frogs, and muskrats. I never attempted fishing it because of the severe pollution.

When I was in late grade school, I was introduced to classical music, courtesy of Acme Markets. Acme offered famous classical record albums at a great discount (ninety-nine cents, I believe) as part of our grocery purchase. I learned to like several of the LPs that were offered, including Edvard Grieg's *Peer Gynt Suite* and Joseph Haydn's *Surprise Symphony #94*. Good stuff.

Largely a result of collecting over thirty million S&H Green Stamps, I obtained a very crude set of golf clubs in sixth grade. Classmates Dave Minnich and Larry Jennings and I began playing golf. We would take the bus to the 69th Street Terminal and then walk with our clubs to the nearby Cobbs Creek Golf Course in Philadelphia to play. This pattern lasted for about two months, until we ran out of money and lost interest because of our inept play.

I received an allowance, probably starting at age six, and I earned it. I had some standard chores to complete: unloading the dishwasher (when we had one), emptying and washing ashtrays, picking up dog poop in the yard, taking out the trash, picking up my clothes, keeping my room neat, etc. I also made countless, pre-dinner runs to the Marshall Road stores over a six-year period to buy items that Esther needed for dinner. In my older years, I was also responsible for cutting the grass, raking leaves, and shoveling snow. My first weekly allowance was twenty-five cents. I forget what it bottomed out at during my senior year of high school.

During my elementary school years, Esther and J. T. had a practice of inviting my teacher to our house during the school week for dinner.

Teachers were free to bring their spouse, if married. While this practice would be frowned upon today, it was a harmless gesture of gratitude reflective of J. T. and Esther's small-town roots. The act was a tangible, simple way of saying thank you, nothing more. When Esther was elected to the school board in 1960, the practice naturally stopped.

A favorite recipe that Esther often prepared for these dinners was a dish known as "Hungarian Chicken." For some reason, I could not pronounce *Hungarian* as a small child. I casually referred to the meal as "pink chicken," the color reference signaled by the healthy presence of paprika in the sauce.

When our family made periodic summer visits to Traverse City, I looked forward to visiting the Traverse City Zoo. This small municipal zoo specifically housed animals and fish native to Michigan. The initial highlight was to ride the miniature steam-powered train around the zoo property. After that short ride ended, a leisurely stroll through the zoo's buildings and grounds was completed in less than an hour. The deer, badger, coyote, and wolf were popular attractions.

Urged on by Esther, I had read a fair amount about wolverines and had even done a school report on the animal. I learned that wolverines were extremely aggressive and dangerous mammals that could kill an animal as large as a deer. I also knew that they did not adapt well to captivity.

On one Michigan visit when I was about eight, my paternal grandfather informed me that one of the few wolverines in captivity was housed at the Traverse City Zoo. I was naturally intrigued but also somewhat anxious about viewing this aggressive predator, even from safe proximity within the zoo. My grandfather escorted me to the zoo on the day I was to observe my first wolverine in captivity. I was scared, and I tightly grasped my grandfather's hand as we neared the smelly small-animal building. What we encountered was not what I had expected. We observed a single male wolverine, oblivious to the public, propped up with his back to the wall, licking his genitals.

This was it? No snarling? No gnashing of teeth? No aggressive greeting? No charging of the steel mesh fencing? This was it?

On the contrary, it was just a lonely male wolverine calmly giving his privates a bath.

76

SPUTNIK I

On Saturday morning, October 4, 1957, I retrieved the family's delivered edition of the morning paper, *The Philadelphia Inquirer*, and promptly gave it to J. T. as he was eating breakfast. The headline immediately got his attention.

The previous day, the Soviet Union had launched a small satellite known as Sputnik I, the first artificial satellite rocketed into orbit by man. As a nine-year-old, I had no grasp of the significance of the event, but the launch precipitated a major governmental reaction and the official onset of the space race with the Soviets. I recall J. T. mumbling under his breath to the likes of "Boy, things are sure going to change now."

As was frequently the case, J. T. was right. For several evenings, Americans raced to their backyards with binoculars in hand to observe the satellite's passing at determined times. Sputnik I was small, only fifty-eight centimeters, and it was barely visible in the evening sky. Shortwave-radio operators also listened for the orb's beep as it passed over the country at eighteen thousand miles per hour, circling the earth every ninety-six minutes.

The biggest and most immediate impact was a change in our math curriculum the next year at school. We were suddenly exposed to Yale math, which I suppose was an Ivy League improvement over non-Yale math. Yale math was more challenging and nontraditional in its presentation of the subject. It was also different in that our textbooks were now soft-covered.

On the national scene, a more aggressive emphasis on science and technology was instantly generated. American citizenry was genuinely nervous about the Russians' scientific superiority to the West. The federal government invested heavily in science and technology research in an aggressive attempt to catch and surpass the USSR's clear advances. NASA was created in November, the following month. A palpable sense of urgency existed to fuel the evolution of an inspired generation of scientists committed to gaining and maintaining American superiority in space.

77

WORLD WAR II COMIC BOOKS

In fifth and sixth grades, I went through a period where I was fascinated with World War II comic books. Boy, was I ever into them. There were several comics produced by DC Comics that I read and collected. The series I best remember are: *Our Army at War*, *Sgt. Rock*, *G. I. Combat*, and *Our Fighting Forces*. I especially liked the stories that featured submarines, destroyers, aircraft carriers, fighter planes, and secret missions.

Why the interest? I was very aware of my father's service in World War II, and perhaps it was an unconscious attempt to get closer to him. Bill and I both enjoyed watching *Victory at Sea* on television, as reruns of that series aired frequently. Finally, the movie serials of the '40s and '50s (*Don Winslow of the Navy* instantly comes to mind) frequently had a World War II theme.

The DC war comic books that I devoured came out ten times a year, usually at the same time of the month. The cost was ten cents per comic. Lansdowne's Braddock Avenue Pharmacy, another small neighborhood drug store, carried a complete lineup of DC comics, and I soon became one of their best customers. I must have inquired of a pharmacy employee as to the specific date/time of delivery, because on that highly anticipated date, I would ride my bike to the pharmacy after school with fifty cents in my pocket for another major purchase. Sometimes I was so excited that I couldn't delay gratification until my arrival home. I would then complete a cursory review of my purchase while seated on the store's front steps.

The DC comics I read had a complete World War II focus, which was what I wanted. Stories were split between European and Pacific theatres. Our guys always won, and the publishers responsibly protected their readership from extremely graphic and gory images within the stories' frames. Never did we see a wounded or dead serviceman's face. Instead a lifeless hand, a bullet-pierced helmet, or the like were routinely employed as subtle substitutes.

Certainly I was attracted to the heroic stories that I could easily understand even as a ten-year-old, but I loved the depictions of military equipment—ships and tanks and planes—and I still do to this day. I spent many an hour trying to copy those images with paper and pencil.

Why did my interest suddenly subside in junior high school? I think hormones and other forms of publications had a lot to do with it.

78

THE NORTHWEST PAPER COMPANY

I stumbled across the impetus for this essay during a deep cleaning of the basement last year, and what rekindled the memory were three scratch pads that I discovered. They were dated 1959 from the Northwest Paper Company of Cloquet, Minnesota. The Northwest Paper Company was an international supplier of paper to printing and graphic-arts companies such as Fuller Typesetting where J. T. worked as company general manager.

Even though the Northwest Paper Company was based near Duluth, Minnesota, the company drew heavily upon the historical imagery of the Canadian Royal Mounted Police in its marketing and advertising plans. Northwest commissioned an American illustrator and painter, Arnold Friberg (1913–2010), to compose over two hundred oil paintings, which evolved into calendar scenes of Canadian Mounties for Northwest Paper. These calendars became both desirable and famous because of Friberg's superbly structured, visually impressive scenes of Mounties working assorted duties in the Canadian wilderness.

Friberg attended the Chicago Academy of Fine Arts as a young man, also doing commercial work for local printers while he attended school. This work included calendar assignments for Northwest Paper where his paintings became legendary, literally becoming the face of Northwest Paper around the world. His Mountie paintings became so renowned that Friberg became the only American ever to be made an honorary member of the Royal Canadian Mounted Police. Despite his Mountie association, Friberg may be best known for his 1975 painting, "The Prayer at Valley Forge," which portrays General Washington in a solemn, snow-covered scene during the Revolutionary War.

Mountie illustrations were rugged, colorful, and typically involved Mountie interactions with settlers, prospectors, trappers, Canadian Indians, and wild animals. There was a strong patriotic flare to the paintings. They displayed the same handsome, respectful, good-willed Mountie who was usually, weather allowing, decked in a stunning red jacket, blue trousers, boots, and flat-brimmed Mountie hat/trapper hat as he attended to his diverse tasks in the wilderness.

A welcome treat for me prior to the December holidays was J. T.'s delivery of the upcoming year's Northwest Paper calendar. It came in a hard cardboard tube, and after inspecting the next year's twelve new paintings, the calendar was subjected to flattening under a rug or mattress for several weeks. When I eventually retrieved it, I displayed it proudly on my bedroom bulletin board or closet door for the course of the current year. This pattern lasted through my high school days. On hundreds of occasions (while doing homework comes to mind), I became immersed in the romance and nostalgia of the calendar's vivid scenes while speculating as to the Mountie's next exploits.

I mentioned the three scratch pads earlier; all three contained Mountie scenes on their small front covers, one with a trapper and one with native Indians. The third scene is the most dramatic, the most memorable, and one that perfectly sums up the series. It depicts the tired and snow-covered Mountie plodding through a winter blizzard on his trusted horse. In his arms he holds a lost or abandoned fawn considered unlikely to survive the storm. Without a doubt, the Mountie and the fawn will soon escape any degree of harm or danger, for a warm, furnished log cabin, complete with fire blazing in the hearth, is just over the next hill.

79

"THE LOUISE CHEST"

Sometime in the mid to late 1950s, a Bingham family relative and his wife relocated to Lansdowne and lived briefly in a large, second-floor apartment near Baltimore Pike. This couple, Dee and Louise Greenwell, had some Morganfield roots. The couple was middle-aged and childless. Dee was a naval officer in his midforties, briefly assigned to the US naval base in South Philadelphia. I recall that he had thinning hair swept straight back, and he wore a Boston Blackie–type mustache. Louise was a full-figured, matronly type of woman, whom I suspect was a few years older than Dee.

I had limited contact with them both, but my parents attended regular dinners at their apartment and ours. Aunt Louise, as I was to call her, never seemed comfortable in Lansdowne; she was very southern and proper in dress and appearance, giving the impression of being more suited for Kentucky plantation life as opposed to living on the east coast in the mid-twentieth century. Despite Dee's somewhat creepy mustache, I got along with them both, but as they were childless, I was an awkward addition to our scheduled meetings. The relative connection was with Dee, not Louise.

Aunt Louise and Uncle Dee's time in Lansdowne was short-lived, and in only a few years, Uncle Dee received new orders. I was never to see them again, but when they left, our family inherited a massive piece of furniture from them, which became known within our family as "the Louise chest."

How it was moved from the Greenwell's third-floor apartment to our second-floor apartment remains a twentieth-century miracle of engineering, as the chest of drawers was approximately 5' x 5' x 3' in size and extremely heavy. The chest housed two small drawers up top, with three deep drawers located beneath. The large drawers were opened by tugging on two inscribed-bronze, looped handles, which proved difficult to pull because of the weight of the drawers, even without contents. As a child, I wasn't strong or agile enough to open the main drawers, always relying on Esther or J. T. for help.

In our North Lansdowne Avenue apartment, the chest was housed in our large living room. At East Essex Avenue, it stood in our small dining room, dominating and crowding the room because of its immense size. It housed a variety of objects over the years, including important legal and financial documents, linens, tablecloths, candles, silverware, china, serving dishes, crystal, carving knives, playing cards, poker chips, photo albums, scrapbooks, phone books, World War II memorabilia, magnifying glasses, and a host of lesser items.

I have no idea as to the types of wood used in construction, but "the Louise chest" regularly provided a woody aroma when we opened the drawers. It was one solid, handsome, and very heavy piece of furniture. It was painted light tan, with a large, hand-painted floral design dominating the main drawers. It is an example of a furniture piece that might well be featured today on *Antiques Roadshow*, even though I have no reliable knowledge as to its actual value.

I do not remember the chest's moving to our apartment on North Lansdowne Avenue, but I well recollect how difficult it was to move from our apartment to our new home on Essex Avenue. This hernia-worthy piece of furniture required three or four movers, much time, careful attention, and frequent rest stops because of its weight and bulk.

When Esther moved to Drummond Island in 1980, "the Louise chest" remained behind with the new owner on East Essex Avenue. Would I have preferred for this major family artifact to have remained within the family? Absolutely. But then again, retaining it and moving it were two totally separate issues.

80

PETE PETRELIUS

A few years after Andy Thompson and his siblings moved to Newtown Square, a new friend moved onto Albemarle Avenue. His name was Pete Petrelius, and he was a year older than I. Ironically, Pete moved into the home previously owned and occupied by Andy's grandmother, Mum Mum.

I don't recall where Pete and his family moved from, but his background was unusual. He was an only child, and you would never suspect him of having any Greek heritage, because Pete was fair skinned and crew-cut blond like me. His mother was Swedish, while his merchant-marine-captain father was Greek. Both of Pete's parents were older than the typical norm.

I only met Mr. Petrelius a few times, as he was most often away from home and at sea, but he made an impression on me just the same. Mr. Petrelius had a shaved head (this was a real rarity in 1956–58), and he spoke with a foreign accent, which was initially difficult for me to understand. He impressed me as being rugged and strong, despite his relatively medium stature. Looking back, I certainly can see him in the role of a ship's captain.

For a few years, and despite the fact that Pete attended a private school, we were good friends. Albemarle Avenue was our playground, with Indian ball and stickball being our major activities during spring and summer months. The side yard to Pete's house served as our football field. Pete was a very good athlete, far better than I, and his presence for those few years helped fill the enormous void of Andy Thompson leaving town.

Mrs. Petrelius was in her late forties or early fifties, about ten years younger than her husband. She was very pleasant, kind, blonde, and attractive, always well-coiffed and tastefully dressed. On one occasion, and upon invitation, my mother and I drove to the Germantown section of Philadelphia with Pete and his mother a few days prior to Christmas to attend a Swedish Christmas celebration. I had no clue what we were attending, but I did as I was told.

The church was very old and relatively small. Esther and I sat in a side balcony with Pete and his mother. What we attended was a four-hundred-year-old tradition known as the Feast of St. Lucia. In a church now totally devoid of electric light, girls dressed in white gowns, carrying candles and wearing lit candles in their hair, slowly entered the small sanctuary while singing a traditional Swedish Christmas carol to the accompaniment of the church organ. The procession was visually stunning and gloriously accented by the angelic voices of "the maids of St. Lucia." With the church illuminated only by candlelight, there was a short concert followed by the girls exiting the church to a final hymn, most likely "Silent Night."

While I have viewed this beautiful tradition on video numerous times, I only saw it live on that one memorable 1950s evening in Germantown. I have Mrs. Petrelius to thank for the beautiful and lasting imprint.

St. Philomena Catholic Church

81

ST. PHILOMENA CATHOLIC CHURCH

I was raised Catholic until the sixth or seventh grade. My father grew up in the Catholic faith in western Kentucky. However, he attended public school in Morganfield, Kentucky, due to fiscal limitations within his fatherless, six-sibling family. In those days Catholics could only wed Catholics, so my mother had converted to Catholicism from her Congregational/Quaker roots to marry my father in a Catholic church in Elk Rapids, Michigan, in 1937.

Upon moving to Lansdowne, my parents began attending St. Philomena Catholic Church, the town's sole Catholic church, located on the corner of Highland Avenue and Baltimore Pike in downtown Lansdowne.

As I attended public school, it was necessary for me to attend catechism classes after school one day a week during the school year. Enrollment in these classes was a requirement for public school kids to receive their first Holy Communion and confirmation. Routinely for several years, my fellow Catholics in Green Avenue School (Lorraine Nasuti, Judy Jackson, Denise Kane) and I would regularly trudge four or five blocks from Green Avenue to St. Philomena School for weekly instruction. Summer instruction was held as well, but I am unclear on the format.

The catechism environment was not friendly. It was near frightening at times. The message I recall receiving was that public school Catholics were not "true" Catholics, as they did not attend Catholic school. We were taught by nuns wearing full habit. I cannot state that our teachers were openly hostile, but they were certainly not friendly or engaging. As was their reputation, nuns were no-nonsense and humorless. No effort was exerted to make Catholic instruction appealing or fun.

Much of catechism was rote memorization. I still recall the first question ever asked of our class: who is God? Answer: God is the Father, Son, and Holy Ghost.

Lorraine, Judy, Denise, and I somehow survived catechism and received our first Holy Communion. However, it was in late sixth grade or early seventh grade when my family's relationship with St. Philomena drastically and unalterably changed.

Father Lambert was the head priest, and he typically served the eleven-o'clock, Sunday morning Mass that J. T., Esther, and I attended. Father Lambert was a short, rotund, gray-haired man who had a reputation for being no nonsense. J. T. and Esther liked their sleep, and

11:00 a.m. was the last Mass that we could attend on a Sunday morning. We typically sat up front in the second row, center section.

At this time, Esther's desire to run for the school board had been announced and was no secret. Knowing full well of my mother's attendance and seat location in the church, Father Lambert went on a tirade one Sunday morning, his sermon zeroing in on Catholic parents who did not fully embrace Catholicism but rather supported their children's attendance at public schools. From his gestures and body language, Father Lambert's rant was directed personally toward Esther.

In the midst of Father Lambert's diatribe, J. T. and Esther exchanged whispered messages, which originated with my mother. My father then nudged me, and in full view of several hundred parishioners, my parents and I stoically walked out of the church in mid service, never to return to St. Philomena or any Catholic church. Without question, this event is one of the most dramatic moments within my childhood. At the time, I was oblivious as to why we were abruptly leaving church, but I did understand that something had gone terribly haywire.

Any formal religious upbringing for me now ended, as my parents did not seek a Protestant alternative. I have no knowledge of the basis of their decision, although the Congregational church, which my mother attended as a youth, was not prevalent in the Philadelphia suburbs. Were congregationalism an active faith in the area, my parents' decision might have been different.

82

MR. RICHARDS'S

Esther and I ran a lot of errands together: ACME, department stores, doctor/dental appointments, and so on. Unfortunately, this list included trips to her hairstylist, Mr. Richards,[3] whose salon was located nearby in Drexel Hill next to the Red Arrow trolley tracks.

I despised the trips to Mr. Richards's, and I did everything imaginable to avoid them. Unfortunately, Esther was crafty in scheduling her hair appointments, usually linking them to a department store trip (because I needed pants), or a visit to receive my allergy shots, etc. I dreaded these outings, because it meant ninety minutes of pure boredom.

Mr. Richards's was typical for hair salons of the day, including the bank of hair dryers, three or four chairs, sinks for washing hair, and a small waiting area. The magazines in the waiting area were all dated and pertained solely to women's themes. The aged, near-death potted plants in the salon's front window begged for water, and the smell—the smell upon entering the salon was sickening.

I typically brought homework or a book to read, but I was always bored out of my mind. On some occasions, if the weather accommodated, I even took brief walks around the neighborhood—anything to get away

[3] Name has been changed to protect individual's privacy.

from that disgusting smell. There were no distractions such as a TV, a current newspaper, a complimentary bottle of Coke, or a misplaced *Sports Illustrated*. There was only total boredom and the soft, shallow smiles offered from patrons as I anxiously waited, and waited, and waited.

Mr. Richards and his wife were the primary stylists, and Esther typically scheduled appointments with tall, salt-and-peppered, wavy-haired, creepy Mr. Richards. He was always dressed in uniformed stylist's attire of the day. Esther soaked up the phony attention he awarded her, and even as a child, I saw through his act. He was equally gooey with me, with his eyes tightly squinting as he smiled.

I believe Esther continued to have her hair cut and treated at this salon until she moved to Drummond Island in 1980. My final recollection of Mr. Richards's salon is an occasion of ushering Esther to and from an appointment while her car was being serviced, as I was home during summer break from college. Mr. Richards's hair was now silver, and he was not as tall and upright as I remembered him, but he still wore the same shoes designed for people constantly on their feet.

Little had changed within the salon in ten years, including some of the same tired and neglected plants somehow surviving—sans any signs of growth—in the salon's ignored and dusty front window. And yes, Mr. Richards was still creepy.

J. T.'s office

83

LANCE CRACKERS

For most of my growing-up years, J. T. worked in downtown Philadelphia. J. T.'s Fuller Typesetting/Creative Litho office, if you could call it an office, was located in an ugly and forgettable office building situated just north of 8th and Market Streets. The neighborhood was grungy and dirty as it approached Skid Row about three blocks to the east. Small storefront businesses lined 8th Street, both north and south of Market street: a jewelry store, two working-men's clothing stores, a camera store, some small sandwich shops, a wig shop, a watch store, etc. The neighborhood got decidedly tougher and more dangerous at night.

The men's clothing stores were particularly memorable, as they usually included salespersons strategically stationed at the stores' entrances. These "hawkers," as J. T. called them, would attempt to entice passersby (teenage boys were especially susceptible) to patronize with ludicrous claims as to savings and quality of merchandise.

The building housing the Creative Litho plant, J. T.'s office, and numerous other businesses was solid and uninspired, reinforced by thick concrete walls; high ceilings; hard, drab stairwells; and concrete, gray-painted flooring. Flooring had to be extremely strong to carry the weight of two dozen or so heavy and noisy linotype machines, which were in near-constant operation. A rickety, slow-moving elevator transported employees and visitors to and from the fifth-floor office/plant. There was absolutely no glamour or allure to the building or Creative Litho's surroundings.

Outside of the small office area, the lighting in the plant was poor, except for gooseneck operator lights stationed at the clickety linotype machines. The few windows were drab and dirty. Air was musty, tobacco flavored, and poorly circulated. The plant was not air-conditioned in the summer, which made the environs a furnace in July and August, and the plant was chilly and drafty in the wintertime. Printing plants are loud and dirty, which was the case at Creative Litho. Large black trash drums were heavily stuffed with excess, used paper. The employee restrooms were small, dated, and in need of more regular cleaning.

Even then, when visiting the plant on rare occasions as a child or teenager, I thought the environment colorless (a lot of gray and black) and depressing. Who would want to work here, either in the plant or the office area under these conditions?

J. T. did not have an individual office, even though he was responsible for running this plant and several other Fuller sites. His metal desk was located in a slightly recessed section of the main office in close proximity to his assistant and other administrative employees.

I recall two vending machines located between the office and plant: a red, lever-mechanized Coca-Cola machine that only dispensed 6.5 ounce bottles of Coke, and an aged Lance Crackers machine. For several years, J. T. would bring home packages of Lance crackers and cookies. Initially, I enjoyed the novelty, but even as a child, I eventually deciphered that the packages were dated, stale, unwanted leftovers.

As a company, Lance Crackers is still around today. You can buy their products at convenience stores, gas stations, and supermarkets. Their website informs that the company is over one hundred years old. But whenever I see their products on a store shelf, I am drawn back to 125 North 8th Street in Philadelphia and the dingy and completely unremarkable locale where J. T. quietly and steadfastly labored for over a decade. Through it all—including a daily, monotonous, almost hour-long commute to and from work—I never heard J. T. complain once. He was simply doing his part to support his family.

84

FAVORITE ENTERTAINERS

J. T.'s favorite entertainers:

Lawrence Welk
Jack Benny
Jackie Gleason/Art Carney ("The Honeymooners")
Red Skelton
Perry Como
Dean Martin
Jack Paar
Jonathan Winters
Florence Henderson
Minnie Pearl
Dolly Parton
Flip Wilson (especially as Geraldine)
Johnny Cash
Phil Silvers as Sgt. Bilko
Phyllis Diller
George Gobel
Nat King Cole
Buddy Hackett
Victor Borge
Johnny Carson

Tennessee Ernie Ford
Joan Rivers
Engelbert Humperdink

Esther's favorite entertainers:

Grace Kelly
Dan Duryea
Florence Henderson
Phyllis Diller
Perry Como
Dorothy MaGuire
Phil Silvers as Sgt. Bilko
Julie Andrews
Bishop Fulton J. Sheen
Pearl Bailey
Joan Rivers
Victor Borge
Patti Page
Jean Simmons
Jack Paar
Art Carney

PART IV

29 East Essex Avenue

85

29 EAST ESSEX AVENUE

My family moved to a three-bedroom Dutch Colonial house at 29 East Essex Avenue in summer of 1960. The house was slightly smaller than our home on Marshall Road, but it was adequate for my parents and me. Bill lived with us during the majority of his first year in medical school, until he and Letitia Henderson were married on April 8, 1961 (my thirteenth birthday). Purchase price of the East Essex home in June of 1960 was $16,500. Our new beagle puppy, Eloise, actually attended the closing and supposedly stole the show at the real-estate office.

This home, which I most identify with my childhood, was of stone construction with white clapboard comprising the second floor. The house was trimmed in forest green and was shingled with a dark-green, almost-black roof. A separate two-car garage stood at the end of the driveway.

Upon our moving in, and without any prompting from me, J. T. installed a basketball backboard, hoop, and net on the garage, which proved enormously popular to neighborhood and school friends during my junior and senior high school years. Again, on his own, J. T. dramatically took the backyard basketball court one step further by rigging a floodlight on our back porch so that my friends and I could play at night. Cyclone fencing confined a backyard that was small and unremarkable. A Norway maple and a mature, tall sycamore dominated the backyard to such an extent that attempts at growing flowers were routinely hampered by poor sunlight.

Like our home on Marshall Road, this home featured a front porch that was never used. The front door granted entry to a small living room that was complete with a woodburning fireplace. The living room also contained a small upright piano, which my mother irregularly played whenever the spirit moved her. The living room flowed into a cramped dining room where we ate our evening meals at a large, cherry dining table. A major drawback to the house was a small, narrow kitchen that included a tiny dining area for two people. There was no room for a dishwasher, so all plates, bowls, silverware, glasses, pots, pans, etc., were washed by hand. Despite the kitchen's multiple weaknesses, Esther smoothly maximized use of the limited space and tight quarters.

The second floor included three bedrooms and a showerless bathtub for most of my parents' years at the residence. Closet space for homes of this era, including ours, was small and inadequate. My bedroom included a single bed; a small night table and lamp; a homemade desk/chair; a small, aged sofa salvaged when my parents bought a new one for the living room; a large bulletin board; and a maple dresser. My bedroom had the largest closet, so Esther and I shared closet space.

Our home had hardwood floors throughout, with large area rugs used in all rooms except the kitchen and bathroom. A large attic was unheated and unsuitable for any use other than storage. The basement was unfinished, as many were at this time and era, and included an oil-fed furnace, washer/dryer/washtub station, a workbench for my father, and a crude one-seat toilet, which was only used in dire emergencies.

Initially our home was only air-conditioned in the living room by a large window unit, but Esther quickly changed all that by eventually adding window air-conditioning units in all second-floor bedrooms. In summertime my mother preferred the living room and master bedroom bordering on frigid.

In touring the home in 1996—thanks to the kindness of the current owner, Larry Contrisciano—our Essex Avenue home struck me as exceedingly small and confined by today's standards. When I lived there in the '60s, I never fully appreciated the home's limited space—except for my parents' complete unwillingness to surrender the living room on date nights.

For an active teenage boy growing up, the 29 East Essex Avenue location was ideal. Our home was situated on the busiest street contiguous to the high school. The high school's main athletic field (Stewart Field), stadium, and track were in easy view across Essex Avenue from our home.

In warmer months, and especially during summer vacation, I spent hundreds of hours camped out alone or with friends—Jimmy Bower, Billy Skinner, Jerry Carothers, Andy Willis, etc.—on our front-porch steps, observing the comings and goings around the high school. Especially during my high school years, 29 East Essex became a popular gathering place for my peers because of its visibility and strategic location. The backyard basketball hoop helped as well. Esther equated major foot traffic in our house with her younger son's popularity, when in reality, it was all about our home's visibility and central location.

Esther lived in the house for twenty years until 1980 when she moved to Drummond Island, Michigan.

Stewart Field

86

STEWART FIELD

Stewart Field was the main athletic field for men's sports at LAHS. It was located adjacent to and west of the high school and was bordered on the north by Essex Avenue. The site is especially significant to me because it was almost directly across the street from our home at 29 East Essex Avenue.

From 1960 to 1966 during my junior and senior high years, it served as an extended front yard for me. It was there where I played football and ran track. Stewart Field served as a gathering point during weekends and summer months where I participated in touch football, baseball, softball, and golf. To say that it holds special memories for me is an understatement.

Historical records indicate that Stewart Field was created in 1902. I found no reference suggesting what the field looked like when it was first developed, when the track was installed, etc. The former Lansdowne High School that became LAHS was designed in the late 1920s, and it was natural for the new high school to be constructed immediately adjacent to Stewart Field. The new concrete football stands were dedicated on Thanksgiving Day of 1950 at halftime of the annual Lansdowne-Swarthmore football game. These standards were 10 rows deep and stood between the 20 yard lines. A memorial is engraved on the stands at the 50 yard line honoring the 57 Lansdowne residents who died during World War II; the inscription reads: "They never fail who die in a great cause."

A genuine problem for LAHS was the lack of practice fields and physical education grounds. Because of this shortage, poor Stewart Field was unfortunately used for nearly everything, including seventh- and eighth-grade football, ninth-grade football, JV and varsity football (not only all home games but preseason varsity practice and some practices during the season), and even youth league football on Sundays. Competition for use of the field for football and baseball practice was a real problem. Stewart Field was also used during warmer months for junior and senior high gym classes of both genders.

As if that wasn't enough, Stewart Field doubled as an inadequate, if not dangerous, baseball field for junior and senior high teams. The baseball infield was situated on the southern end of the football field. This created an intriguing set of ground rules because of trees overhanging into the field of play along the left-field foul line, permanent football stands in left-center and center field (which complicated umpire calls on ground-rule doubles and home runs), the running track (which literally cut through shallow left field), and so on. Because of its overuse and difficulty in sustaining permanent grass, the baseball infield was a disaster and rarely yielded clean hops. My exposure to the baseball field in general was limited to a deep, multiyear history of participating in lengthy weekend pickup practices directed by a former minor-league pitcher ("Pro," as we called him) and one highly unproductive year of Lansdowne Boys Club baseball.

Because of its overuse, the football field was more dirt than grass by mid season. The only permanent grass existed from the end zones to about the twenty-yard lines and along some sidelines. I learned from my association with two LAHS custodians, Big John and Tattoo Al, that chickweed was actually planted on the football field as opposed to grass, as it was easier to grow and more durable than standard grass. To this day, whenever I see an occasional growth of chickweed, I think of Stewart Field.

The football field could also be extremely hard, and it no doubt assisted in players receiving concussions and other injuries. During my senior year, I developed a blood clot on the underside of one of my forearms below the elbow. According to the team physician, the injury was definitely irritated by the hardness of the playing surface. A major drought during the fall of my senior year made Stewart Field so dry and dusty that the Lansdowne Fire Department was summoned to hose down the field midweek and prior to some Saturday home football games.

The track was an inferior model as well. It included six lanes, not eight. However, what was most noteworthy about the track was that it was not a quarter mile in length; it was one fifth of a mile in length, which thoroughly complicated middle- and long-distance races, since most high school tracks were a quarter mile in circumference. This design flaw was dictated by limited physical space and perhaps finances, but the model meant that a mile run included close to five laps being run, not four; and the two-mile run included ten laps, not eight. While this unique configuration may appear to be a mild inconvenience, it was a significant and annoying consideration for visiting distance runners and their coaches.

The track was a tired cinder track that was rarely rolled. Footing was loose, which meant disappointing times for sprinters. I believe the best time I ever ran in the hundred-yard dash on this track was 10.3 seconds. More typically I ran a 10.6 or 10.7, which was a poor time for the era when compared to times run on evolving rubberized surfaces.

Another negative of the one-fifth-mile track was that it cut into the corners of the football field's end zones. On all four corners of the field, the end zones extended a few yards onto the track, creating a potentially hazardous condition for players, especially receivers and defensive backs. As a receiver, I was always aware of this shortcoming, especially when running corner patterns into the end zone.

Stewart Field technically also included a small outdoor basketball court where competitive summer-evening games were played, even drawing players from surrounding communities. Also featured were a wading pool and four tennis courts, which were creatively scheduled to accommodate both boys' and girls' high school tennis teams. The tennis courts were enthusiastically used by community residents on evenings and weekends during more temperate months.

Because of the limitations and challenges that Stewart Field presented, I silently looked forward to away athletic events at other venues simply because those grounds and facilities were usually superior to those available at LAHS. The best example was when LAHS and Swarthmore played each other in the final football game of the year, the traditional Thanksgiving-morning game. When Thanksgiving games were played at Swarthmore, they were played at the Swarthmore College Field, which was the best football field on which LAHS ever played.

I also knew Stewart Field from another perspective. During my college years, I worked summer maintenance for the school system at LAHS and some elementary schools. For assorted assignments at Stewart Field, I cut grass, pulled weeds, trimmed bushes, pruned trees, painted fencing, repaired bleachers, and collected trash on the day after the Fourth-of-July fireworks.

I am probably being too hard and too negative in my assessment of Stewart Field. In retrospect, the high school administration did as best they could with limited resources and an imperfect model. Despite what the grounds or facilities lacked, so much of my childhood remains anchored to that piece of community property. In many ways, I grew up as much on Stewart Field as I did at 29 East Essex Avenue.

After graduating from high school, Stewart Field proved to be a quiet, desired sanctuary for me, preferably in the early morning and late at night. I did a lot of heavy thinking there. I also visited the site on numerous occasions when life was unsettling or when heavy issues were prominent: going off to college, a failed romance, my parents' deaths and burials at Arlington Cemetery in Drexel Hill, a new job, and so on.

During my occasional returns to Lansdowne, Stewart Field is always an automatic stop. After parking the car in front of my old home, I usually stroll around the track for at least one lap. I may even eat a hoagie or a cheese steak in the home football stands or on the Essex Avenue gate steps.

I recognize these examples as my private, respectful homage to a distant time and a framework of experiences that helped mold me as a man, husband, and father. I owe much to Stewart Field that goes far beyond football, track, and baseball.

87

SANDLER'S

Downtown Lansdowne in the early to mid '60s had three drugstores. Two of them were located catty-corner from each other at the intersection of Lansdowne Avenue and Baltimore Pike. Sandler's was the largest, nicest, and most modern of the three downtown drugstores and was located on the intersection's northwest corner adjacent to Keller's Record Shop. Sandler's had an attractive layout with easy-to-find items, was brightly lit, and carried a more complete inventory of products than its competitors. It was the only downtown pharmacy of the three that operated a soda fountain.

My memory suggests that Sandler's did not serve sandwiches, just ice cream and fountain drinks. One of the unique fountain drinks they served was known as a Rickey. Rickeys were non-carbonated fruit drinks served in cool, tall glasses and sipped through a straw. They came in a variety of flavors, and I remember preferring the orange- and lime-flavored Rickeys. They were pricier than a standard Coke or 7 Up, so one had to be frugal in choosing when to buy one.

Rickeys were not sold everywhere. They were somewhat of an exclusive novelty drink, so one made due note of which stores offered them and which did not. They could not be purchased in bottled form from stores or machines. They were only sold at soda fountains, which added to their allure. I believe Rickeys were unique and exclusive to Sandler's within the borders of Lansdowne.

Sandler's was the site of a bellwether, plaque-deserving event that occurred during my early adolescence. Several of my immediate friends and I were drinking Rickeys at the soda fountain one Saturday afternoon when we were joined by a classmate typically outside of our normal crowd. The boy's name was Richard Goetz,[4] and he only attended LAHS during our junior high years.

Richard boasted that he had a unique talent. He could take a sip of his Rickey from a straw and then instantaneously shoot the consumed liquid back out through his nose. The challenge was on. Under our disbelieving and watchful eyes, Richard performed his talent as claimed, and a local folk hero was born. Richard's social status within our male crowd instantly skyrocketed. He achieved immediate celebrity, and the next school day, he was invited to our lunch table for a repeat performance.

Unfortunately, Richard's talent was nontransferable and limited to non-carbonated fountain drinks. His follow-up demonstration in the LAHS cafeteria with milk produced ugly and disappointing results, especially for Richard. Unfortunately for him, the viscosity upgrade from Rickey to cafeteria carton milk proved insurmountable.

Fame is both fickle and fleeting. Richard Goetz's rock-star status lasted less than seventy-two hours. It was his one and only requested presence at our lunch table. We were a tough crowd. You either produced or you didn't. There were no second chances.

[4] Name has been changed to protect individual's privacy.

88

69TH STREET

Sixty-ninth Street remains a major transportation center in Upper Darby to this day because of the presence of the 69th Street terminal where the Market Street–Frankford subway/elevated line has its western terminal. Numerous trolley and bus routes from the western suburbs and city also terminate there. J. T. began his rail commute to Philadelphia for years through the 69th Street terminal.

During my childhood and teen years, 69th Street served as a major commercial district anchored by three well-established department stores: JCPenney, Lit Brothers, and Gimbels. These department stores were all located on 69th Street, with smaller clothing, electronic, variety, and specialty stores sandwiched between on a long, ascending block primarily from Market to Chestnut Street. Esther would drive to this area for shopping and would typically park in a public or store-operated lot. Esther's most frequent visits to 69th Street were for school clothes and Christmas shopping.

When I was a small child, a frequent stop was Tiny Town, a children's clothing store located on the 69th Street hill that operated on ground- and basement-floor levels. Tiny Town's unique feature was a long playground-like slide connecting the ground and basement floors, which kids could play on while their mothers shopped. It was always a treat to visit Tiny Town to use the slide.

During our periodic trips to 69th Street, Esther usually frequented the J.C. Penney store and almost always visited the candy counter in the center of the store. I naturally was delighted with this ritual. Esther knew the white-haired woman who operated the candy counter, but I never knew the actual connection. By the way, the multicolored, candy-coated bridge mix was excellent.

As reported by Esther, she and I supposedly met J.C. Penney one day while he was visiting the store to mingle with the customers and staff. I was too young to remember the historic meeting.

In junior and senior high school, my friends and I would occasionally walk the two-plus miles to 69th Street from Lansdowne to attend a movie at one of the locale's three movie theaters, or to shop at music or sporting goods stores. There was also a model train store that I enjoyed walking through. An obligatory stop on the walk home was S. S. Kresge's variety store (the forerunner of Kmart) at the top of the hill, where we could purchase a cup of Rosati's water ice. Lemon and cherry were my standard favorites.

89

DR. WILLIAM NUGENT

When we moved to Essex Avenue, William Nugent became our veterinarian. Dr. Nugent lived about five blocks away at the corner of Essex and Crawford in a row home. His small office was located in the basement, and within a very confined space, there was a small examining room (everything was small) that doubled as an operating room, a waiting room with five or six chairs, and a tiny, cramped kennel where dogs and cats were boarded.

I recall that Dr. Nugent attended veterinary school at Cornell University, and during the day he inoculated and treated cattle in Delaware, Chester, and Lancaster counties for the Department of Agriculture. His private-practice hours were confined to evenings and Saturdays. Dr. Nugent knew his trade, but his office maintained little of the equipment or diagnostic/treatment refinements of today. He was direct and to the point, kind, and extremely knowledgeable. His care was guided by sound veterinary training, experience, and instinct. I can never recall him being stumped or in error with a diagnosis. Dr. Nugent suffered from hearing loss, and he wore a clunky hearing aid, which was only partially effective.

He treated our cats—Cassandra, Carolina, and Ophelia—but he primarily cared for our overweight beagle, Eloise, who suffered from chronic ear infections. He also monitored Eloise during her two pregnancies, and her sixteen puppies after they were born. Donna Nugent, Dr. Nugent's daughter, was a few years ahead of me at LAHS, and Donna and Dr. Nugent's wife often assisted with the practice. Donna actually helped Eloise deliver her first litter of puppies at our house.

Eloise was a very reluctant patient, and she somehow knew when we were physically proximate to Dr. Nugent's office in our car. She grew extremely anxious and began shaking when transported for her appointments. She also groaned under her breath at this point, a type of guttural resentment. Upon arrival, we could not lead Eloise into the office on a leash. She had to be carried, which, due to her obesity, was no easy task. However, on the examining table, Eloise was a lady, never snappy or difficult.

Dr. Nugent was a class act, and I remember him with respect, admiration, and gratitude. His fees were reasonable and much lower than his competition. My sense is that he offered his veterinary services at reduced rates simply as a service to his community and fellow neighbors.

90

J. T.'S PERSONALITY CHARACTERISTICS

- Kind
- Hardworking
- Intelligent
- Humble
- Quiet/private
- Loyal
- Ethical/principled
- Faithful
- Steady
- Unapologetic

91

THE DIME DANCE

I recall the "dime dances" occurring when I was in junior high school. They were held in the Green Avenue Elementary School auditorium/multipurpose room during the summer recess. I believe they were on Tuesday evenings, probably beginning around 7:00 p.m. while it was still light, and ending around 8:30–9:00 p.m. I don't recall who sponsored or organized the dances. There may have been an age limit, as I cannot recollect high schoolers in attendance. I also believe the dime-dance crowd consisted mainly of local kids in their early teens.

Yes, admission was a dime, ten cents. Popular rock-and-roll tunes of the day and some oldies, a combination of up-tempo and ballads, were served over the auditorium's public address system. On the fast, up-tempo tunes, girls primarily danced with girls, with a few exceptions. The slow dances were reserved for boy-and-girl couples.

Many of my classmates attended. It was fun to see them, since we no longer regularly saw each other because of summer recess. What was memorable about these dances was that our peers who attended Catholic school frequented these dances as well. This was somewhat awkward to the public schoolers, since we viewed the school as our domain. I still recall Matty DeMaria's sister, a parochial schooler, enthusiastically dancing to Bobby Lewis' 1961 hit, "Tossin' and Turnin'."

While my memories of these dances are not deep, they are fond and positive. What I do recall was the heat and humidity, since the school was not air-conditioned. I remember these dances being heavily attended, but again the room was small. There were no fights, just some mild tension between the Catholic teens and the public schoolers. Most importantly, the dime dances served as an innocent respite from summer boredom.

92

SLEDDING

Sledding during winter fell into two distinct time frames and locales. When I was younger and lived on Marshall Road and North Lansdowne Avenue, an Upper Darby golf course bordered on the north by Marshall Road was within easy walking distance from both of my homes. My golf course sledding partners included Susan Bartlett, the Thompson kids, Sally Cheeseman, and other neighborhood and school friends. On occasion even Bill and neighbor Jackie Pruitt would join us at the golf course.

The hill really was not that substantial, but as it became worn and glazed from use, our assaults on the hill picked up, as did the likelihood of flying into shallow Naylor's Run. Bill actually taught me a useful maneuver. Should my sled ever approach Naylor's Run, I was to quickly roll off my trusty Radio Flyer and freely allow the sled to crash into the water, since retrieving it from the shallow creek would not be a problem.

As we approached our early teen years, I grew tired of the golf course and its lame hill and craved a more daring adventure. It was probably through my new Highland Avenue classmates that I learned of better sledding available on runs adjacent to Pennock Terrace and Lansdowne Court. This new locale was situated in a hilly section of hardwood trees in south Lansdowne.

To get there meant a half-mile hike through the recent snowfall, but it was worth it. Classmates Steve Paxson and John Echternach lived in this neighborhood, and they taught us the runs, many of which simply crossed backyards as we sped toward Darby Creek below. On some of the runs, we actually went airborne like a snowboarder, and there were few who avoided at least minor bumps and bruises. While we didn't consider the conditions dangerous, they probably were, in hindsight. I do recall one unknown boy breaking his leg while sledding at this site. I sledded at this location well into high school.

Prior to our high school years, the roughest part was walking home, sometimes in the dark. We were like wounded warriors—tired, beat-up, wet, cold, red-cheeked, snotty-nosed, and very hungry. Even after a hot bath, a home-cooked meal prepared by Esther, and lengthier sleep than usual, I was typically sore and slower moving the next day.

93

BOXBALL

During the warmer months, boxball was a popular game for me from about the fifth to ninth grade. I cannot say that it was unique to Lansdowne, since there was evidence of it being played in the city and other Philly suburbs, but I never heard of it being played outside of the Philadelphia area. It required only two people to play and minimal equipment.

Ardmore Avenue and Green Avenue school playgrounds were my prime playing sites. Standard equipment was a small athletic ball that could be purchased at a five-and-dime or hardware store. Varieties included pink balls, pimple balls, and tennis balls. Ten-cent pink and pimple balls were not that durable (the pink balls frequently split in half upon solid impact of the bat). Tennis balls were preferred, but they were more expensive. As I lived near the town's only tennis courts, and in order to beef up my supply of equipment, I occasionally would patrol the grassy areas contiguous to the courts, attempting to salvage misplayed and lost tennis balls. More times than not, I was successful.

Bats were typically one-inch dowels, with the length determined by the age and specifications of the owner. Most bats were thirty to thirty-four inches in length. Boxball players frequently customized their bats' grips with tape, and some bats were even painted. Bats never broke, but they took a severe beating by being tossed or thrown on the playgrounds' hard surfaces. Pitchers could wear a baseball glove in the field if they preferred.

A key component to the game was the "chalking" or sketching of a strike zone or "box" on the bricks and mortar of a school's exterior wall. The strike zone was drawn by chalk and was typically very big, as much as 30" x 36". It was also a high strike zone extending from above the batter's knee to the neck. Some school walls actually had multiple strike zones to accommodate different ages and sizes of players. I never heard school officials complain about our modifications to the schools' exteriors, as the chalk would eventually wash off from exposure to rain and wind, causing no permanent damage. I recall on one occasion at Green Avenue during summer recess when I actually went into my old school to fetch some chalk to enhance the lines of the strike zone, as it had grown faded and indistinct.

The game involved a pitcher and batter and was nine innings in length. Many standard baseball rules applied, but there was no base running. The pitcher called balls and strikes so the integrity of the pitcher could occasionally be called into question. The goal was to strike out the batter or cause a ground ball or pop up cleanly fielded by the pitcher. A bungled ground ball or dropped pop up was a single. A double play could be executed by the pitcher fielding a ground ball (one out) and then firing a strike to negate an on-base runner. However, this was a risky process, because failing to throw a strike allowed both runners to be safe.

The distance of a line drive or long fly ball determined, by prearranged ground rules, the value of the hit (single, double, triple, or home run). Ground rules varied from one field to the next, and they could be tricky and prone to the interpretation of the pre- and early-adolescent mind. For example, at Ardmore Avenue a home run had to clear a very low brick wall, whereas at Green Avenue, all hits were totally judged by distance into a grassy field.

A curse of boxball was the high pop-up behind the batter. This play typically caused the ball to land on the Green Avenue school's multipurpose-room roof, never to return, with the end result being that the game was over. At Ardmore Avenue, a pop-up had to travel a higher distance, with balls potentially caught by a gutter serving the school's slate-shingled roof. Again, it was the same result. It was game over, unless a backup ball was available.

My main opponents in junior high school were Andy Willis and Billy Skinner. Andy and I were pretty much dead even as to talent. Billy, who later went on to play varsity baseball, was always my superior, and he usually won the contests.

I recollect a memorable doubleheader one summer day at Ardmore Avenue, where I actually split games with Danny McMullen, a talented Ardmore Avenue–playground mainstay two years my junior. Despite the age difference, I actually won a game from a superior player. In the highly competitive world of 1960s Lansdowne boxball, this triumph serves as a special memory.

94

VIRGINIA DONUTS

This chapter was clearly one of the easiest to write. Any Lansdowne male within five years of my birth—younger or older, it didn't matter—knew about Virginia Donuts. The factory and retail store was located on the north side of Baltimore Pike between Highland and Wycombe Avenues immediately east of St. Philomena Catholic Church. Unbeknownst to me as a child, Virginia Donuts baked doughnuts for several major grocery chains in the Philadelphia area.

As boys growing up in the town, our sole focus at Virginia Donuts was the ten-cent bag of cut-up, day-old doughnuts, which were on sale at the retail store. In my dozens of trips into that store, I doubt if I ever once bought a whole doughnut; it was always the ten-cent bag that my peers and I sought. And it seemed like it was always the same Virginia Donuts employee who waited on us: an indifferent, smileless, middle-aged woman whose prematurely white hair was poorly cradled by a frumpy, brown hairnet.

The ten-cent bags were composed generally of a mix of powdered sugar, cinnamon, glazed, and jelly doughnuts. On occasion, perhaps another random type was thrown in (I always hoped for chocolate-covered), but the standards were generally the expectation. While the doughnuts were wonderful enough in their own right, I well recall the semi-spiritual process of unfolding the creases of the waxed bags to savor the first smell of the contents. It was pure heavenly bliss. Instantly, all troubles and problems disappeared by way of sugary avalanche. Many excursions to downtown Lansdowne were fittingly accompanied at their conclusion by a pilgrimage to Virginia Donuts. It seemed like the respectful thing to do. After all, we needed closure.

A word of caution: the contents of the ten-cent bag were messy. Many was the time that powdered sugar, glazed coating, or raspberry jam found its way to my shirt, jacket, or pants before I arrived home. I even recall one time when Esther suggested that I wash my face, as my lips were accented with powdered sugar.

For many of my peers and me, Virginia Donuts remains a sweet and savory part of our Lansdowne youth. Sadly, the landmark ceased operation decades ago—to the dismay of local dentists.

Oh, and it wasn't just a guy thing. Girls were in the loop as well.

95

LOCAL MOVIE THEATERS

While the beloved Lansdowne Theater dominated my childhood and adolescent attention, I also frequented other suburban theaters, depending on what was playing. During the '50s and '60s when I was a child, most theaters ran a special Saturday matinee where a movie suitable for children would be shown without the primary, first-run feature. Unlike feature presentations, Saturday matinees were not necessarily current movies and could be several years old.

If a matinee movie was on my Saturday agenda, I would scour the movie listings in the newspaper, not only for the Lansdowne but for other movie theaters within walking distance. I typically would encourage classmates to join me, but if that option fell through, I was comfortable going by myself. Most times I would walk, take Red Arrow to 69th Street, or rely on my parents to shuttle me to and from the theater. I never biked to any of these theaters, as I recall.

The more memorable theaters are described below, in no particular order.

The Yeadon

After the Lansdowne, this was the theater I attended most often. Bill used to frequent the Yeadon a lot as well. The walk from home was about three miles one way. The theater was small and compact, with art-deco styling and a tiny lobby. It was located on Church Lane in the heart of Yeadon's tiny commercial district, across from the fire station. One immediately met the concession stand upon entering the theater. I recall the theater having very soft-colored interior lighting and curtains that opened and closed with each presentation.

A middle-aged woman seemed to run everything: tickets, concessions, etc. She was most likely the projectionist as well. Research determined that this woman-of-all-trades was Rhea Perelman Friedman, the owner who took over operation of the theater in 1954 when her husband died.

The Yeadon was always affordable, and Mrs. Friedman was a memorable and likeable lady. Late in its existence, the Yeadon became a bargain theater—with one-dollar admission—showing movies recently taken out of first-run circulation. The theater was demolished in 2006 after a fire, an event that saddens me to this day.

The following is from Rhea Perelman Friedman's obituary in 2005:

> Rhea Perelman Friedman, 98, the former owner of the Yeadon Theater who treated movie patrons like family, died Wednesday at Arden Court in Warminster. Mrs. Friedman operated the Yeadon Theater from 1954 until she sold it in 1984. She furnished the lobby like a living room, with photo displays of her grandchildren, her daughter Janet Lazrow said, and, in motherly fashion, posted signs reminding moviegoers not to forget umbrellas, gloves, and eyeglasses. She served free cookies and coffee to adults and distributed Popsicles

to children during Saturday matinees. When customers were stranded at the theater by bad weather, Lazrow said, her mother—who hated to drive—gave them a ride home. During the 30 years Mrs. Friedman operated the theater, admission was never more than a dollar—with discounts for children and senior citizens.

The Tower

The 69th Street commercial district supported three theaters, with the Tower being the largest by far. Built in 1927 as a movie/vaudeville house, it was much larger than the Lansdowne, and it included a balcony. It was easily identified by a major tower that displayed "TOWER" lettering rising skyward from the building's second-floor roof. It also featured a large, curved marquis above the theater's entrance.

It included an extensive concession stand like none other. I recall seeing *Moby Dick* and *Twenty Thousand Leagues under the Sea* at the Tower. I didn't care for their cartoon selections—Tom and Jerry, and Woody Woodpecker—as I was a Warner Brothers fan.

In the early '70s, the Tower became exclusively a music venue for Philadelphia. One Philadelphia newspaper reporter claimed in 1972 that "Philly finally had a Fillmore." Pop and rock musicians who have played the Tower include Jerry Garcia, David Bowie, Peter Gabriel, Jackson Browne, Lou Reed, Steve Miller, Moody Blues, Hall and Oates, Bonnie Raitt, Grateful Dead, Paul Simon, Kelly Clarkson, Bruce Springsteen, and the Rolling Stones (yes, the Rolling Stones).

The Tower remains operational today as a popular musical venue.

The Terminal

The Terminal was aptly named, since it adjoined the 69th Street terminal. The theater was small and unremarkable, and it entertained some of the less savory patrons, including drunks who were sleeping it off and transients. The Terminal had a creepy feeling to it at times, and I rarely visited it unless the movie was very special. I recall seeing Steve McQueen in the forgettable 1958 sci-fi flick, *The Blob*, at the Terminal.

What was most memorable to me about the Terminal was its proximity to Red Arrow trolley tracks, which were located just outside the rear of the theater. Every five or six minutes, or less, you could count on hearing and feeling the rumbling of Red Arrow trolleys pass by.

The Terminal closed in the late 1980s and was last reported to be a Rite-Aid pharmacy.

The 69th Street

This was the last of the 69th Street area movie theaters. It was medium-sized, between the sizes of the Tower and the Terminal. It opened in 1921 and closed in 1965. I may have attended four or five movies there, so I do not hold any deep memories compared to other movie houses. The building is now occupied by a Christ-based nonprofit agency. I usually walked to and from the 69th Street area theaters, unless bad weather encouraged me to take a Red Arrow bus to and from the theater.

The Waverly

Located in Drexel Hill on Burmont Road, the Waverly was an easy walk to and from Lansdowne. It was a very large theater for a suburban movie house, seating over 1,500 customers. It opened in the 1920s and closed in the 1980s. I did not attend many, if any, Saturday matinees at the Waverly; I saw more feature presentations at night. I recall seeing *Gone with the Wind* there when I was in junior high. Perhaps the most memorable feature of the Waverly was that the concession stand sold chocolate-covered, vanilla-ice-cream bonbons, three to a package. Delicious.

The Waverly ceased operation in the 1980s. The building is now a bar and beer distributor.

The Stonehurst

Along with the Yeadon, this was the movie house outside of Lansdowne that I attended the most. This theater served primarily Stonehurst and East Lansdowne residents and was located on busy Long Lane in the heart of Stonehurst's business district just up the street from one of DelRoy Pruitt's five-and-ten stores. Built immediately prior to the Depression, the Stonehurst was a true community movie house, with most patrons walking to the movie house from their homes or apartments.

Bill liked the Stonehurst as well, since it was one of the few theaters that showed serials, which he and I both enjoyed. Research shows that the Stonehurst opened in 1929 with the theater having 1,200 seats; however, I recall it being smaller for some reason. I believe the Stonehurst also had a balcony. The Stonehurst was an easy walk from home, and like the Yeadon, it was a very viable option if I was not attending a show at the Lansdowne.

The Stonehurst closed in the late 1970s and was eventually converted to a bowling alley and then a thrift shop. The building was demolished in the 1980s.

The Brookline

The Brookline was a situated a good four miles from home, so it was not walkable—or was it? I only attended the Brookline a few times. It was a small, neighborhood movie house nestled in a quiet Havertown neighborhood. When I was seven and a half years old, Jackie Pruitt, a former neighbor, was babysitting me, and we went to an evening double feature at the Brookline. While the first show was appropriate, the second movie was *Man with the Golden Arm*, a very controversial movie at the time because of its theme of narcotics and drug abuse. Esther knew we were going to the movies, and she strictly, emphatically forbade me from seeing *Man with the Golden Arm*. She could not have been more clear, and I got the point.

The deal I had with Jackie was that we would leave the Brookline after the first movie had ended. Jack reneged on the agreement, most likely because he was intrigued by the forbidden subject matter of *Man with the Golden Arm*. Despite my protests, Jackie would not budge. I told him I would walk home if he didn't change his mind. Jackie called my bluff. So I walked home in midwinter, leaving the Brookline around 9:00 p.m.

I was adequately dressed for the season, but I walked fast. I eventually crossed West Chester Pike and Township Line Road and then began a spooky walk past the Har Jehuda Cemetery. I didn't walk at this point; I ran. Then came the familiar Acme store at Lansdowne and State, and a trudge up the hill past the Dairy Queen. But now there was an additional obstacle, another cemetery: Arlington. I ran past Arlington on the other side of the street, feeling more comfortable closer to Upper Darby High School. Then I journeyed down the hill by Delaware County Hospital and past Bonner and Prendergast high schools. I crossed over the Red Arrow trolley tracks and Garrett Road, and in another one third of a mile, I was home—a little chilled but no worse for the wear. I used the front-door key that was hidden under the welcome mat, went inside, and immediately went to bed. My guess is that I covered the route in a little more than an hour.

Shortly thereafter, my parents came home, naturally very surprised about what had transpired. They really did not know what to say, as I had followed Esther's directive to the letter. They called the Pruitts and told them my saga, as Jackie had yet to return from the Brookline. Jackie got into major trouble for his actions, and while our two families remained close, my relationship with Jackie was never quite the same.

96

LANSDOWNE SWIM CLUB

The Lansdowne Swim Club opened in 1959 when I was eleven years old. It was located at the intersection of Baltimore Pike and Shadeland Avenue.

As I entered junior high school, I started to hear a lot about the Swim Club, especially in summer months. Some of my friends were members, so I naturally asked my parents if we could join. This lobbying effort continued unsuccessfully for a few years. I can never remember receiving a straight answer, but in retrospect, I think we did not join for multiple reasons.

First, Esther and J. T. were not big swimmers or beach people. Perhaps J. T. had seen enough water in the navy. Esther claimed that she had a sun allergy, and she was always prone to stay out of the sun at all costs. I can only recall one trip to the Jersey Shore for us as a family, and that was the eventful time of Bill's mishap with the stingray. Also, it is hard for me to imagine my parents fitting in with the swim club's social scene. That just wasn't their thing.

Second, I believe they viewed membership as a poor investment. I was a horrible swimmer, and while they could have viewed it as an opportunity for my swimming skills to improve with lessons, they didn't.

If I'd had siblings who also could have benefitted from membership, perhaps their response would have been different, but I think not.

As much as anything, it came down to money, and a membership to the Lansdowne Swim Club simply was not in the budget. Esther and J. T. never made that admission, but I believe I am correct in this conclusion decades later.

My exclusion from the swim club bothered me throughout junior and senior high school. Both Aldan and Lansdowne had swim clubs, so many of my friends regularly attended when the facility was open. The Lansdowne and Aldan Clubs were major social attractions during summer months for my peers who were members, and it was difficult being on the outside.

Occasionally, both the Aldan and Lansdowne swim clubs had "open" days/nights when nonmembers could attend upon the invitation of a member, but I never attended.

A saving grace for me was that the vast majority of my close friends were not members either, so the sting was not that fierce. However, I do recall one time when a friend or two and I found a clandestine, elevated viewing perch behind the Gladstone Pharmacy (Saul's) and watched the Lansdowne Swim Club during a hot and sunny summer's day. There they all were—Harry Gicking, Jack Nalbandian, Joan Dale, Sandy Devenney, Beth Dunkle, etc.—all having a grand time in the refreshing confines of the Lansdowne Swim Club.

In retrospect, I think J. T. and Esther were right. It would have been a poor investment.

97

SLAM BOOKS

My junior high classmates will remember slam books. Anyone could create them, but they were primarily developed and circulated by girls. One simply took a spiral notebook and developed a registry on the first page. There, fellow students would sign in next to an identifying number. A series of one-page benign questions would follow, such as "Who is your favorite singer?" or "What do you like on your pizza?" or "What is your favorite movie?" You get the idea.

The juicier questions, the questions that everyone really cared about, were sprinkled in with the benign questions. These questions naturally received the most attention, as they dealt with relationships and issues, which were of burning, exaggerated interest to young, socially conscious teenagers. Examples of these questions might be "Who is the best-dressed girl?" or "Who is the hottest eighth-grade boy?" or "Who is the best dancer?" or "Who is the cutest couple?"

All one needed to do was answer the question on that page and then write in the identifying registry number under the answer. Sometimes some answers received multiple numbers. Students soon learned to be careful, intentional, and politically correct (even though the term did not yet exist) with their answers, or major fallout could spiral out of control. Yes, relationship breakups could be traced to slam-book answers. However, new romances were also spawned within these pages. Some questions could subtly, or even intentionally, call for disparaging and cruel responses, and such was the ugly side to the activity.

I remember that the more popular students dominated the registry, so it was imperative that one registered, but it was also important that results were reviewed. Slam books were passed around with great regularity at LAHS and were of keen interest. It was not unusual for multiple slambooks to be in circulation. Plus, registration was more highly valued with some books than it was with others, most likely dependent upon the social status of the book's owner.

The presence and circulation of slam books seemed to go in spurts, since teachers and school administration frowned upon the related activity, rightfully viewing the focus as a distraction and nuisance. Teachers were extremely mindful to detect and confiscate them during study halls—no demerits, no detention. You just lost your slam book, and it was never returned.

Slam book interest waned as the "more mature" high school years approached.

98

LAMB

LAMB stood for Lansdowne Aldan Music Box. It was a Saturday night dance that was held at the Aldan Elementary School in seventh grade. In my memory, Suzie Lord's parents were the adults linked to the organization and running of the event. They were fun and enthusiastic hosts in that role. Admission cost was minimal, but what was memorable about LAMB dances was that the event was held in a "foreign country" known as Aldan, a town barely contiguous to Lansdowne, which I never gave any thought to until junior high school.

I remember attending several of these dances with Mark Gilbert, Ronnie Townsend, and other classmates. Parents would alternate driving to and from the school to drop us off or pick us up. We would call for a ride home after the dance from a phone booth located at an Aldan stop on the Sharon Hill trolley route.

The event was fun and engaging, as we started to get to know the seventh-grade girls from Aldan. The dances were held in the school's small gym, and I recall the room being dimly lit. The chaperoning parents, who also served as DJs, played forty-fives over the gym's loudspeaker system. True to form, girls sat exclusively in folding chairs on one side of the gym, boys on the other. If you bravely crossed the room to ask a girl to dance, you sent a considerable message, as everyone in the room observed your intention. The same response occurred when an occasional "ladies choice" brought girls over to the boys' side to pick a partner. Oh, and yeah, the girls danced with each other during up-tempo songs. Boys only danced with girls to ballads.

These dances were very innocent, the earliest example of an instance where romantic interest could be demonstrated. I attended five or six LAMB dances. I readily recall winning a George Chakiris album in a raffle. I remember I didn't even know who George Chakiris was, but the girls in attendance quickly enlightened me as to his starring role in the movie *West Side Story*. Having no interest in either *West Side Story* or George Chakiris, I gallantly gave the album away to Marjorie Spencer, a fellow Lansdowner and sixth-grade classmate from Highland Avenue School, as I knew she was a major fan of the musical.

99

BURNING LEAVES

A memorable quality of Lansdowne, past and present, is that it boasts many tall and stately hardwoods. They are primarily located in the older parts of town where I was raised. Oaks, maples, sycamores, elms, beech, and an occasional linden are the primary hardwoods that line many of the town's streets. If you lived there, you took them for granted. However, during my childhood and adolescent years, raking leaves was a familiar activity in Lansdowne during the autumn months.

Sure, some residents bagged their leaves and left them for curbside pickup in trash cans, paper bags, or plastic bags, but an alternate method of disposal was to burn raked leaves curbside to your house. At the time, there was no borough ordinance banning the practice, and there was no concern about polluting the air. My recall suggests that the majority of residents who lived on properties that included large hardwoods would burn their leaves in the street after raking them together. My family was no exception, as we burned collected piles of sycamore and Norway maple leaves.

Weather played a role in the practice as well, since the leaves needed to be dry. Unwanted moisture brought on by steady rain would postpone the process for several days, as would high winds. Once the leaves were collected, one ensured that the piles were a safe distance from any parked vehicles on the street. The leaves could be lit by matches or lighters. Some industrious types would strategically position newspaper scraps in the pile to guarantee prompt and balanced burning.

Providing that leaves were dry, the pile was quickly consumed in flames, which soon dissipated after only a minute or two, depending on the pile's size and content. During the fire's short life, tenders needed to carefully reposition leaves with their rakes to assure a complete burn, and one had to be careful so as not to have their wood or plastic rake catch fire. What resulted was a smoldering pile of ashes, which, after cooling, could easily be swept up the following day.

Curb fires seemed to be lit most frequently in mid to late afternoon and on weekends. On autumn days—when ideal conditions existed—many Lansdowne neighborhoods were accented by the soft aroma of burned leaves and lingering, light layers of smoky haze in the air.

Nowhere is this memory more vibrant for me than at football practice, especially at the Green Avenue practice field, which was used for varsity and junior varsity football practice. This practice field was immediately adjacent to numerous older homes situated to the south on Greenwood Avenue. Many of these Victorian-era homes were sixty to eighty years old at the time, and their lawns were handsomely adorned with stately oaks, maples, and sycamores. If you owned one of these homes, you had a lot of leaves to bag or burn, come fall.

The delicious aroma common to this neighborhood seemed to be an almost permanent scent at football practice during the latter weeks of the season leading up to the Thanksgiving Day game against Swarthmore. When I think of high school football, I instantly recall that sweet smell and the occasional layer of thin smoke that quietly blanketed the field as we labored at practice.

100

WESTIE'S

Westie's was a strange little store in downtown Lansdowne situated on Lansdowne Avenue next to Holmes Colonial Flower Shop. Westie was seemingly the owner and the only employee I ever saw in the store. He was a short man in his early fifties. His appearance was distinguished and memorable, as he wore a black visor like the one worn by railroad ticket agents or poker-playing Sgt. Bilko.

Westie's was unique in that it sold primarily ice skates, hockey equipment, and other sporting goods. Also sold were cap guns, HO trains, kites, peashooters (frequently purchased in advance of a Saturday matinee at the Lansdowne Theater), and plastic model kits, as Westie's was a store geared toward boys. I know I bought some HO freight cars there, including a powder-blue New Haven boxcar with large white and black lettering.

The store was small, as practically all stores were in downtown Lansdowne. It also had few patrons, and especially now I wonder how Westie ever made a living. Whenever I visited Westie's, I was typically the only patron in the store. However, fellow Lansdowner Peter Pitts claims that Westie's did get crowded when sales were posted for cap guns or sports equipment. I also remember the store as very dark and poorly lit. Westie's wasn't big on signage either, so you did a lot of hunting around to get what you wanted.

Westie frequently occupied himself in a back room, and when I entered the store, he appeared to greet and serve me. He was always personable and accommodating. Again, I never found the store busy, as there were only so many ice skates and hockey sticks that one could buy in our community. And what was the visor all about?

101

ELOISE

Eloise, a fifteen-inch Maryland variety beagle pup, joined our family when we moved to Essex Avenue in the summer of 1960. She came from excellent lineage as the offspring of the field and show champions of Maryland. As was standard for the Maryland variety of the breed, Eloise had a black saddle across her back, with white and tan coloring elsewhere. She was a true tricolor beagle. I believe my parents purchased her from a Mennonite family from Berks County.

Esther had grown up with beagles, so she was exceptionally pleased to be reunited with the breed. Beagles have a strong tendency to roam, and we soon learned that Eloise was no exception. Above anything else, Eloise was a hunter, pure and simple, with that gene being deeply engrained in her beagle DNA. "Weezie" was larger than life, a *bona fide* character. She roamed freely about our neighborhood, which was not an uncommon practice for dogs of that era.

Classmates who dropped by our house became major fans. She was popular with both neighbors and strangers. Unlike Dixie, Eloise was very independent and occasionally stubborn. She was poorly disciplined, almost delinquent. She was warm and affable to nearly everyone, but when she was irritated by another dog, cat, or circumstance not to her liking, her hair rose on her back, and you knew from her bark and howl that she was perturbed.

Despite her impressive bloodline, Eloise did not have good points. She was barrel-chested with a stout frame. Part of Eloise's heaviness was a result of the network of neighbors she routinely visited for handouts. One elderly woman actually made Eloise peanut-butter-and-jelly sandwiches with the crusts cut off when Eloise paid a call. What a con artist! (Eloise, not the neighbor.)

My parents decided to breed Eloise when she was two years old. She was mated twice with Brainerd's Bantam, a handsome, champion stud from New England. In an elaborate schedule, the owners of Brainerd's Bantam would fly him to the Philadelphia airport from Boston, where my father and I picked him up and transported him to a farm in Newtown Square for the supervised mating. Esther separately transported Eloise. When the mating process was completed, my father and I then returned Brainerd's Bantam on the same day to the freight depot at the Philadelphia airport for his return flight to Boston.

Eloise had two litters of eight pups each, with a ninth pup from the second litter not surviving birth. She actually gave birth to her first puppy in an armchair in our living room. I was present for the birth of all pups, and it was an amazing experience to witness firsthand as a young teenager. J. T. and I temporarily converted Bill's bedroom into a nursery, using old wooden screens as dividers. Weezie was a proud and attentive mother, and she was undisturbed by numerous classmates of mine, boys and girls, who visited to ogle her pups.

My parents advertised in a Philadelphia newspaper and had no difficulty selling the pups—$35 for males and $50 for females. Today, beagle pups of this lineage would cost more than $1,000 apiece, so our customers enjoyed a real bargain. For Esther and J. T., it was never about the money. It was all about the experience, including the process of securing good homes for the pups once they were weaned.

Eloise's most pronounced trait was her marked ability to roam solo far from home as she trailed rabbits. She usually ran north or west from Lansdowne toward more open country. Her early travels found her in nearby Drexel Hill on the property of the Bond family farm. She followed what little open land remained along creek beds to pursue rabbits. Then we started to get phone calls from Springfield, easily double the distance to Drexel Hill, then Media, seven miles from Lansdowne. In one of her final sojourns, Eloise was picked up by a family living in Newtown Square, setting her all-time, one-way distance record of twelve miles.

Eloise would be absent during her hunting escapades for two to three days. We naturally always worried that she may have been hit by a car, but like Dixie, Eloise was smart and crafty around vehicles and traffic. Upon earning my driver's license, I would generally be the one to retrieve her, and when I did, Eloise was always dirty, foul-smelling, "burred up" (as Esther used to call it), hungry, and very, very tired. Despite the time of year (Eloise's hunting exploits were usually reserved for warmer months), she usually received a bath from me upon returning home and a full brushing afterward. She would then eat a hearty meal, lap half a bowl of water, and retreat to a makeshift bed in a cool corner of the basement where she was prone to remain for twenty-four hours or more in a deep sleep, totally exhausted.

Eloise's most celebrated adventure was easily the time when she found her way into a neighbor's house on a balmy Thanksgiving afternoon. Tempted by aromas coming from the dining room—and while family photographs were being taken in another room prior to the family's sitting down for Thanksgiving dinner—Eloise yanked the tablecloth enough for the holiday turkey to crash to the floor. Another version recalls that this incident occurred when Eloise accessed the table from a nearby chair and dragged the turkey carcass to the floor. An irate neighbor called our house in an X-rated frenzy, lambasting everything and anything Bingham. Our obnoxious beagle had ruined their Thanksgiving.

Esther, exhibiting the coolness-under-fire demeanor for which she was famous, quickly soothed, apologized, and suggested to the angry neighbor that we hold a joint Thanksgiving feast at our house, since we had more than enough food to feed both families. This was the only time I ate Thanksgiving dinner on the steps to our second floor, but years later, both families chuckled about the incident.

As for related discipline, Eloise was banned to the basement for the rest of the day by an inflamed Esther, who, with accentuating index finger, sternly reprimanded a shrinking Eloise: "Bad beagle, *bad* beagle."

Eloise lived to be eight years of age. During my sophomore year of college, she died from a heart attack on nearby Congress Avenue, a favorite haunt of hers for handouts.

102

"THE ASHTON"

During my late junior high and high school days, I discovered a favorite hoagie/cheese steak venue: the Ashton Market off of Marshall Road in the Beverly Hills section of Upper Darby. Before we got our driver's licenses, we generally walked to the Ashton Market—or as we dubbed it, simply "the Ashton." We became even more frequent customers when cars were available.

The Ashton was a small community grocery, really the forerunner of today's convenience store and less than a mile walk from my house. It was locally owned and operated, but I did not forge any relationships with the owners or full-time employees. Most of the teenagers working there part-time likely attended Monsignor Bonner or Upper Darby High School and not LAHS. Just imagine a large neighborhood convenience store that also made sandwiches, and that was the Ashton.

The hoagies were huge, at least twelve inches long, well stuffed, and delicious. I credit the Ashton with introducing me to the cheese steak, and these sandwiches too were large, loaded, and incredibly good eating. So the dilemma frequently arose: hoagie or cheese steak? On a few, insane occasions in my later high school years when my pockets were heavy with money from cutting lawns or shoveling snow, I bought a hoagie *and* a cheese steak, and to my credit, I downed them both. How did I do it? To this day, I have no idea.

LAHS classmates Jerry Carothers, Jimmy Bower, and especially Billy Skinner often accompanied me on frequent trips to the Ashton. I recall that there were no dining tables at the store, so we frequently took our hoagies/cheese steaks elsewhere to eat, including the high school athletic field or my house. Frank's orange or black-cherry Wishniak soda was typically my choice to serve as a drink. By the way, we were clueless as to the mysterious Wishniak reference.

We're not done. Growing up when and where I did, it was considered almost sacrilegious not to end one's meal without a Tastykake item for dessert. My favorites then were chocolate Tasty-Takes and buttercream-iced chocolate cupcakes.

We're easily talking a two-thousand-plus-calorie intake here, with hoagie/cheese steak, soda, and Tastykake.

103

RANDOM REMEMBRANCES IV

Upon moving to our Essex Avenue home in June of 1960, I began mowing neighbors' lawns that summer. J. T. had broken down and bought a gas-powered lawn mower, which I was allowed to use for my business, providing I paid for the gas.

The business started small, with customers close to home on Essex, Albemarle, and Wayne Avenues. My lowest charge was two dollars per lawn; my highest was five dollars for a double lot, which took two hours to cut. I went through three or four lawn mowers in six years. J. T. and I split the cost of new purchases, which only seemed fair. At my busiest, I was doing eight to ten yards per week, with customers as far away as West Essex and Greenwood Avenues.

I still recall the last names of many customers: Bowman (my first customer), Allen, Giardella, and Ogden. I even mowed for Philadelphia Eagle great and NFL Hall of Famer Steve Van Buren, who lived on East Plumstead Avenue for some time.

What greatly complicated my lawn-cutting business was varsity football. Even in preseason, I could keep up cutting lawns on weekends, even though I really wanted to rest and take it easy. I could do three to four lawns each on Saturday and Sunday and stay current. Despite my sophomore hand injury, I still cut yards, but more slowly. Junior and senior years were much tougher, especially in the fall when we played a

Saturday afternoon away football game, as I then had to cram all of my lawn jobs on Sunday, which made for an extremely long day.

I had loyal customers because I was reliable and did good work. In those warmer months, I was never short of money for movies and dates, albums, hoagies, cheese steaks, soda, and the occasional Tastykake.

As a seventh- and eighth-grader, I used to climb the Dormons' gingko tree next door. When I got near the top of the tree, I could see the William Penn statue adorning the top of Philadelphia City Hall.

We had a nasty basement toilet on Essex Avenue. It was always the backup toilet of last resort. It was intended for family emergency use only. We didn't have the nerve to allow visitors or guests to use the basement "crapper," as Bill referred to it. The unpainted wooden stall was extremely small (2.5' x 3.0') and was located at the bottom of the basement steps. There was no lighting, so when the stall door was closed, it was extremely dark, with only limited light coming in from a small window above, located on the ground floor. The site was always musty and humid in the summer and cold in the winter. Another joy to the spot was the abundance of spiders. I have no phobia about spiders, and never have, but those guys were everywhere and were of multiple varieties. There was no way you could sit and do your business without being visited by at least one or two spiders.

When we moved to our Essex Avenue home, I quickly became friends with Andy Willis, a neighborhood kid living on nearby Wayne Avenue. Andy was a year younger than I, but we quickly bonded through our mutual interest in sports. Andy was a middle child, having an older brother, Pete, and younger sister, Suzie.

Especially during our summer junior high years, Andy and I were frequent companions. I got to know Andy's parents and siblings well—especially Pete, whom I looked up to as a role model two years my senior.

Major activities included stepball at my house, boxball at Green Avenue, and especially epic Wiffle-ball games in the Willises' backyard, with their attractive, short, left-field hedge that invited home runs. Andy and I would pitch into a pitcher's practice net, which was marked for balls and strikes. His team was the Orioles, and mine was the Cubs. We announced lineups like an actual professional announcer would have, kept stats and standings, and even played doubleheaders. This was serious stuff.

Wayne Avenue was also the site of impromptu touch-football games that included participation from Pete and his friends. In many ways for me, Wayne Avenue briefly became the new Albemarle. In a few short years, however, the Willis family moved to nearby Swarthmore, thus ending the greatest Wiffle-ball rivalry in borough history.

Bill married Letitia K. Henderson, LAHS '56, on April 8, 1961, at St. John's Episcopal Church in Lansdowne, with Reverend Francis Davis officiating. The wedding was held on my thirteenth birthday. I recall little about the wedding or the reception that followed at a suburban country club.

Bill and Tish then lived for three years in the Strafford Arms Apartments in Lansdowne while Bill finished medical school at Jefferson Medical College. During this time, Tish worked as a proofreader at the *TV Guide* offices in Radnor.

My major complaint about Lansdowne as a youth was its lack of open space. The town was already congested in the 1950s with few vacant lots. A major section of the eastern end of the borough was dominated by row homes with tiny front yards. Many separately standing homes also had small yards. Certainly there were some exceptions in the oldest sections of Lansdowne, but the largest lots in the town, which were few and far between, were only one half acre in size.

There was only one park in town, and that was the tiny and insignificant Shrigley Park, inconveniently located on Scottdale Road. Youth played in their yards, in the street, or at Stewart Field/Green Avenue playground and Ardmore Avenue playground and field. That was it.

There were no dirt roads, forested parks, ponds, lakes, or open fields. The only fishing locale was the ignored and polluted Darby Creek, the area seeming like wilderness to a small child.

The absence of open space—for which we can only hold long-deceased, negligent public officials accountable—was in part a certain factor for many Lansdowners relocating to Media, Newtown Square, and beyond in recent decades for more spacious, less-developed surroundings.

Our Essex Avenue property was graced by two trees (a very tall sycamore and a mature Norway maple) in the backyard, so the north side of the lot was a poor site for flower and vegetable gardening. Sunlight was sparse except for the front yard. Wearing an old short-sleeved shirt, faded jeans (the only time he wore them), and old business shoes, J. T. planted zinnias and marigolds in flower beds bordering the front porch in late spring. These flowers did reasonably well throughout the summer. He also made certain that he had a strong supply of mint for his iced tea, which he grew on the east side of the house near the outside water faucet.

Favorite evening snacks for J. T. were freshly popped and buttered popcorn or homemade oatmeal-raisin cookies.

When I was in early junior high school, Esther began working for an Upper Darby–based urologist, Dr. Edward Kavjian. Esther's decision to work was twofold; another paycheck would definitely help the family finances, and Esther had grown tired of being a full-time housewife as I grew more independent as a young teenager.

Initially, she worked for Dr. Kavjian part-time, but in less than a year, she was working full-time as office manager and personal assistant. Esther loved the job. She had found her niche. She checked in patients, roomed them, took vitals, processed billing, ordered supplies, made referrals, worked the phone, and even assisted in minor surgeries such as vasectomies. Esther threw herself into the job, frequently working uncompensated hours to stay current.

Dr. Kavjian was a major fan of hers, and patients loved her as well. Esther worked for Dr. Kavjian for almost twenty years, only retiring at age sixty-four when she relocated to Michigan.

I recall one funny story. After undergoing a successful vasectomy in Dr. Kavjian's office, a Georgia truck driver was being checked out by Esther. The truck driver was instructed to rest comfortably for several days and to avoid sitting, lifting, or engaging in any strenuous activity. Totally ignoring Esther's advice, the truck driver respectfully responded when leaving the office, "Well, thank you, ma'am, but I've got a load of pig iron to haul to Alabama. My truck's outside running. I've got my doughnut."

When I was a high school sophomore, Esther eventually started working on Thursday evenings as part of her weekly schedule, thus creating a void for Thursday dinner. J. T., never a talent within the kitchen, was left with a dilemma. His initial plan was to heat up Morton's chicken pot pies. This response eventually proved tiresome, so J. T. and I started going out for dinner. The chosen restaurants were affordable and uneventful—the Marlyn in Lansdowne and a few haunts that J. T. knew in Drexel Hill and Havertown. These Thursday evening dinners proved valuable, because J. T. and I were guaranteed some regular time together, one on one.

I learned more than I wanted to know about the printing/graphic arts industry, but more importantly, we drew somewhat closer as father and son. Some of the awkwardness that J. T. had exhibited toward me during my earlier years started to wane. He liked to talk about his days in Annapolis, which had been a happy and productive time for him.

We had five lunch periods at LAHS: periods A through E. Periods A and B were typically reserved for junior high students, with lunch A beginning at about 11:10 a.m. We really had it made when we were scheduled for the elite D or E sections, since we were then juniors or seniors, but oftentimes it was hard to wait 'til way after noon to eat. We were slotted about twenty minutes to gobble down lunch.

I rarely took my lunch. I usually ordered "the Federal," the government-sponsored meal that cost thirty-five cents. Students naturally complained about the food, but I don't recall the food being that bad.

We consumed lunch in the basement cafeteria. Boys ate with boys; girls ate with girls. There was little socializing between the genders in the cafeteria. Table seating got very cliquey, especially in our junior and senior years. There were no fights that I can recall.

In the early 1960s, a new and novel shopping destination opened in neighboring Clifton Heights. It was called the Bazaar of All Nations. It was an enclosed, indoor shopping mall with two long central hallways housing dozens of small, open stores within the building. The Bazaar consisted of clothing stores, wig shops, watch and jewelry stores, electronics shops, shoe stores, gift shops, a major sporting-goods store, a record store, and other novelty shops.

The Bazaar was basically a collection of cheap, junky stores. Nothing of real value was sold there, with the possible exception of the sporting goods. The Bazaar was another walkable destination, although it was almost a three-mile hike from Lansdowne. Usually we drove to the Bazaar once we were of driving age.

The Bazaar also sold all the junk food known to the Western World, including pizza, burgers, fries, soft drinks, cotton candy, popcorn, assorted candy, ice cream, Italian-water ice, hoagies, etc. The dazzling menu of cholesterol-laden food, plus the thick cigarette smoke, created a memorable aroma that instantly assaulted our senses when one entered the building.

I especially recall one time when Jerry Carothers and I went to the sporting-goods store when famed Baltimore Colts quarterback Johnny Unitas was scheduled to make an appearance. When Jerry and I arrived, the store was near empty, and Johnny was just passing time, casually sitting on a store counter as he conversed with store employees. Rather than take advantage of this unique opportunity, Jerry and I froze, staying out in the hallway, mesmerized and semi-paralyzed from afar by the NFL Hall of Famer.

LAHS was constructed in 1927. The architect was Joseph Linden Heacock, and the builder was John McShain, who subsequently was contracted as the builder for the Jefferson Monument, the Pentagon, and the Kennedy Center. The architectural style of the school was Italian Renaissance, and the exterior of the building was tan brick. At its time of construction, the former Lansdowne High School was cited as one of the finest high schools the country. Now it is one of the oldest.

From 1928 to 1953, the school was known as Lansdowne High School, but in 1953 a merger with neighboring Aldan changed the name to Lansdowne-Aldan High School. I attended both junior high (seventh to ninth grades) and senior high (tenth to twelfth grades) at this building located at Green and Essex Avenues.

In 1950 a second story was added to the south wing. In 1957 and 1958 a major addition costing $1,225,000 was constructed. It included a new gymnasium, locker rooms, music and band rooms, health classrooms, and facilities for art and homemaking classes.

In the early 1980s, another merger was enacted with school districts representing Yeadon and Darby-Colwyn. The new high school was named Penn Wood High School.

At present the former LAHS building provides instruction to eleventh- and twelfth-grade students attending from the Penn Wood school district's six communities: Lansdowne, Aldan, East Lansdowne, Yeadon, Darby, and Colwyn. School colors are now red and blue, with Patriots being the Penn Wood mascot.

I suspect that I speak for the majority of LAHS alumni when I mourn our high school's closing. I despise admitting that my old high school no longer exists. I also suspect that Yeadon and Darby-Colwyn grads feel the same way about the similar demise of their high schools more than thirty years ago. Obviously finances dictated consolidation, but it is a result that will never feel right with me.

During my youth and adolescence, J. T. and Esther belonged to a nearby club in Drexel Hill known as Drexelbrook. The club offered dining and dancing and also included a swimming pool and tennis courts, but no golf course. Occasionally we would dine there on special occasions. I believe the dancing opportunity was the main attraction for J. T. and Esther. Esther was light and athletic; J. T. was accomplished as well. They appeared especially happy as a couple on the dance floor.

Lansdowne did not have a pool hall, which was in total concurrence with its Quaker heritage.

A favorite restaurant of my family's was the Lamb Tavern in Springfield. It still exists today despite numerous remodelings and changes in ownership. I vividly recall seeing my first lobster tank at the Lamb Tavern. I also recall a major meltdown when I learned that lobsters from the tank were actually an offering on the menu.

104

THE BIG STORE

Most likely I learned about the Big Store from an upperclassman at LAHS. The Big Store was located in Darby, a good six-mile, round-trip hike from Lansdowne, straight south on Lansdowne Avenue past the Fitzgerald-Mercy Hospital, where I was born, and the Blessed Virgin Mary Church, where I was baptized. The Big Store was situated in downtown Darby in a deteriorating commercial district, and it more resembled a store one might find in questionable locales in downtown Philadelphia. A PTC trolley ran to and from Philadelphia and down Darby's main street on which the Big Store was housed.

The Big Store sold clothing: work shirts and pants, jeans, jackets, gloves, boots, sneakers, hats, etc., and it catered to blue-collar customers, of which there were many in Darby and surrounding communities. The Big Store also sold imperfect, remnant high school gym shirts, which were collected from all across the country. For one dollar, we could purchase three gym shirts, typically representing unknown and distant American high schools and towns.

The most valued shirts also included a picture of the school mascot. Also esteemed were unusual school names, mascot images, and bold color schemes, i.e., a bright-orange shirt with black lettering or a maroon shirt with orange and yellow ticking. Lettering was sometimes blurred or too lightly/too heavily inked, but any imperfections simply added to the shirt's mystique. One did not worry that one sleeve might be slightly shorter than the other or that the lettering was incomplete or a word was misspelled.

During our anticipated visits to the Big Store, we usually bought three shirts. But if the Big Store boasted an unusually large and valued inventory, we might splurge and buy six shirts for a total expense of two dollars.

One of the clerks was very memorable for his good nature. He always belittled us as we entered the store, exclaiming, "What do you drecks want?" or "Are you drecks back again?" As we exited, he would kindly profess, "Hey, you drecks, see you next time."

Shirts from the Big Store served as standard casual attire during junior high and high school days, and they saw a lot of football practices. Many simply deteriorated from overuse. Our girlfriends were not amused by them and considered them childish. Esther thought the Big Store T-shirts were horrid and unworthy of my wearing them, but her protests were futile as she encouraged me to wear something more "normal" and becoming. Because of his knowledge of American geography, J. T. took spirited interest in some of the T-shirts' locales. He would challenge me to determine where Clare or Bellingham was, so the family atlas got some work.

During our non-driving years, the round-trip hike to the Big Store was pretty much a half-day commitment. I remember Jerry Carothers, Jimmy Bower, Don Petrosa, and Billy Skinner as frequent companions. Harry Gicking, John Echternach, and Chris Greening were also into the Big Store inventory. Visits were monthly during summer months to allow the Big Store to refresh its inventory. Virginia Donuts on the return traverse through downtown Lansdowne was likely an expected stop. There's nothing like mixing remnant, "seconds" T-shirts with day-old donuts.

And my most highly valued T-shirt, you ask? Without question, it was the Tonopah Muckers. What's a mucker, anyway?

105

ADELINE

For about fifteen years, my parents enlisted the services of a housecleaner: Adeline Collins. Adeline worked for our neighbors, the Pruitts, for years in this capacity, and thus her connection to our family. Adeline was a full-time domestic, and she labored every weekday, cleaning houses in Lansdowne and Drexel Hill. She commuted daily from her home in West Philadelphia via the Market Street/Frankford "el" and Red Arrow bus or trolley.

Adeline was in her forties and fifties when she worked for us. Adeline was born and raised in the rural South. She never married and had no children. The only family member I ever heard her speak of was a sister who lived near her in West Philadelphia. Adeline was very religious, attending church services regularly on Sundays and some weekday evenings, and singing in the church choir. An unusual characteristic of hers was that she sang while she worked—always a gospel tune or spiritual. She never sang the complete song but joyfully kept repeating a favorite verse, series of lines, or chorus. She was short, stout, and walked with a slight limp. Her eyesight required glasses with strong lenses. She was also hard of hearing, and a frequent Adeline retort was, "Say what?"

Because Adeline cleaned our house every two weeks during my childhood and adolescence, my exposure to her was generally limited to summer months and holiday breaks during the school year. I don't recall how it began, but I occasionally started eating lunch with Adeline at our small kitchen table, just the two of us. It was during these lunches that I started to better understand her country dialect, her staunch commitment to her faith, and her common decency.

She talked in brisk, mumbled phrases, as opposed to complete sentences. She had a lovely laugh, which I attempted to evoke as much as possible. Adeline was very likeable, kind, and funny. She never voiced a hard or unkind word toward anyone. The only irritation I associated with her had to do with Eloise, our pet beagle, whom she viewed as a nuisance and complication to her cleaning duties.

Our conversations were always safe and practical. So much of our contact was during the early and mid sixties when race relations were tense, as civil-rights developments dominated the headlines. Adeline was too respectful to ever broach anything controversial.

During my summers home from college, I had a seasonal job that allowed me to be home on workdays by 4:00 p.m. For some long-lost reason, I began driving Adeline to the 69th Street terminal to catch the "el" home on days when she worked for us. These occasional trips evolved into my driving her to her home in West Philadelphia near 60th and Vine, which only extended my drive by a few minutes. My motive here was part gratitude and part admiration. Adeline worked incredibly hard, and at the day's end, her limp was noticeably more prominent and more painful.

While the differences in our ages and backgrounds were sizeable, Adeline taught me much about work ethic, discipline, respect, and dependability. She was genuine. She was solid. She was the real deal. Nothing about her was presumptuous or phony. Esther repeatedly referred to Adeline as "a sweetheart," and she was absolutely correct.

Especially in Adeline's later years, as she physically slowed down and as I approached early adulthood, I finally started to appreciate and value her full character and integrity. Decades later, I continue to benefit from her quiet example.

Esther was right, but Adeline Collins was much more than a sweetheart. To this day, she remains the most decent and honorable person I have ever known.

106

KELLER'S RECORD SHOP

Keller's Record Shop was located on Lansdowne Avenue just north of Sandler's Drug Store on the northwest corner of Baltimore Pike and Lansdowne Avenue. It was a frequent destination for me in junior high school as I sought to examine forty-fives and LPs, which were on display for sale. Keller's was a walk-in store with limited street parking.

Like so many stores in downtown Lansdowne, Keller's was extremely small, absurdly tiny by today's standards, with two very short aisles and a basic and very modest inventory. Remember that in these days all music was promoted through AM radio. There were really only two popular teen genres of the day: mainstream rock 'n' roll and urban pop, which had a following more linked to African-Americans and urban whites. Country and western music existed, but it had next to no following in urban and suburban settings.

Keller's was mainstream in every sense of the word. Rock 'n' roll and even some easy-listening artists were featured, like Frank Sinatra and Doris Day. Folk music, as the genre's popularity grew, was mildly in evidence on the shelves as well. The owner was very hospitable and used to talk about popular music with anyone who would listen. Jerry Carothers, a close friend throughout junior and senior high school, frequently accompanied me when I visited the store. It was not unusual at Keller's to run into a classmate or at least someone you recognized from school.

The vast majority of records I purchased in junior high school and into high school were bought at Keller's. I mainly bought popular songs, top-forty forty-fives, and I clearly recall that my first purchased records ever were two forty-fives at Keller's: Del Shannon's *Runaway* and Joey Dee and the Starlighters' *Peppermint Twist.* The first album I ever bought was also bought at Keller's: *Joan Baez in Concert, Part II.*

In the early '60s, forty-fives generally cost less than a dollar, frequently between sixty-nine and eighty-nine cents per forty-five. Albums cost close to three dollars. They were an affordable and well-received birthday or Christmas gift for male friends and girlfriends. My lawn-cutting and snow-shoveling earnings bought a lot of forty-fives and LPs at Keller's in the early 1960s.

Keller's also sold some small record players and needles. I know: what's a needle?

107

MONONUCLEOSIS

During the fall of eighth grade, I contracted mononucleosis. I remember that the glands in my throat and neck were swollen, which is a standard, anticipated symptom of the disease. I was also overly tired and fatigued for no apparent reason. I give Dr. Whitman, our family physician, a lot of credit here, because I was so prone to throat infections that this could simply have been another one. A blood test confirmed Dr. Whitman's suspicion of mono.

In the early stages, I only missed a few days of school until they figured out what was wrong. The greatest impact on me was related to physical activity. I was not allowed to take gym class or participate in junior high track during the spring of 1962. I was to especially avoid all contact sports in and outside of school. Even bike riding was banned because of the potential for a fall. I learned later that the contact issues were related to the spleen being especially vulnerable during the course of the disease.

This was a very unhappy time for me. I would sit in the bleachers during gym class, pining for good health to return. For that horrible semester, my interactions with both male and female classmates drastically declined. I was even cruelly labeled "queer" by a female classmate and childhood friend because of my inability to take gym.

Through junior and senior high school, I knew several students who contracted the disease, and I learned that there were different intensities and qualities to mono. My form was not intense, but it was long lasting; it took seemingly forever to shake. Some kids, like friend Billy Skinner, had an intense, disabling variety that was short-lived.

After the first week of diagnosis, I felt reasonably normal most of the time, although I did require more sleep. What I especially recall were about a half-dozen episodes of extreme fatigue that immobilized me for several hours. There was no pattern to them, no obvious link. When they occurred, I was so weak that I couldn't get up, almost as if I were drugged. As was the case with Esther's migraines, if the house had been burning down during one of these episodes, I doubt that I could have raised myself to flee to safety.

Even today there is little treatment for mono (the disease is known as "self-limiting"), but in those days, family friend and physician John Suess recommended that I receive regular injections of crude-liver extract as a preventive measure, since the liver was thought to be particularly vulnerable to the disease. Dr. Whitman did not object, and because of my proximity, my ENT doctor, Joseph Wallace, agreed to give me crude-liver injections every two weeks.

The story does not end there. The injections were brutal. The syringe was long and thick, much bigger than I was familiar with when receiving penicillin. I received the injections in my butt, and poor Dr. Wallace pretty much had to stab me with the needle. I also recall that the actual passage of the crude-liver extract was a sustained, painful burn. It is no exaggeration to state that I sat very purposefully at my school desk on the day following these injections.

Finally, during late spring of 1962, a blood test confirmed that the disease was no longer active. After six months of mono, life returned to normal—which was much overdue in my mind.

Fourth of July parade car

108

FOURTH OF JULY

The Fourth of July was a holiday—a celebration—that Lansdowne really got right during my childhood.

My memories of this holiday are vivid. In the '60s my family lived right on the parade route and immediately across the street from Stewart Field where the fireworks and other celebratory events were held.

The day was dominated by the parade, footraces held on Stewart Field after the parade, a youth baseball game held at Ardmore Avenue field, a picnic in our backyard before the fireworks entertainment at Stewart Field, and of course, the grand finale: the fireworks.

Preparations for the picnic started many days earlier and included lawn-cutting and yard-grooming. It was also my job to hose down and wash all tables and chairs. I most certainly accompanied Esther to the local Acme to buy food and supplies. We cleaned the house, paying special paid to our only bathroom on the second floor. Esther started food preparation very early on the morning of July 4, and she saw little of the parade.

The parade began around 10:00 a.m., with all participants assembling somewhere in downtown Lansdowne—a task that must have been challenging to orchestrate because of downtown Lansdowne's compact design. I never knew exactly where or how this was accomplished, because I was always back home helping out with preparations.

One of the prime advantages of living where we did on East Essex Avenue was the fact that my family and I had a superb vantage point from which to view the parade. Watching from our front yard, the parade literally passed right before our eyes. As I remember it, the parade included the following actors and components, not necessarily in this order: children on decorated bikes; decorated wagons; pets; Lansdowne Boys Club teams and managers; Boy Scout and Girl Scout troops; cars escorting the mayor (really the burgess) and other elected officials, a much-reduced summer version of the Lansdowne-Aldan High School band; another unknown band staffed by older men wearing white police-officer-type hats, white shirts, black pants, black ties, and black shoes; and police, fire, and emergency vehicles. No doubt I missed a component or two, but you get the gist of it.

The parade lasted about forty minutes and covered a half-mile parade route that extended north on Lansdowne Avenue, making a right turn onto Essex Avenue on its way to Stewart Field. It was always delayed at points en route by something or other—like when an eager, inexperienced four-year-old smashed his training-wheeled bicycle into another bike or wagon, which resulted in tears, mild injury, and/or major meltdown. Let's just say that crashes were frequent and expected. The elected officials and political supporters frequently threw wrapped hard candy, bubble gum, or Tootsie Rolls from parade cars, to the delight of the juvenile spectators who sat on the curb. The fire trucks were always a big hit with the children. There may have been a float or two thrown in there at some times.

On one occasion in the early '60s, Eloise, our legendary beagle, had recently given birth in late spring to a litter of eight AKC-registered puppies with outstanding pedigree. J. T., always attempting to seize an opportunity, penned the puppies in a makeshift, screened enclosure on our front lawn in hopes of actually selling a pup or two. It actually worked, as two puppies were sold at the ridiculously low price of thirty-five dollars for a male and fifty dollars for a female.

The parade somehow dispersed at Stewart Field, at which time the Union Athletic Association officials attempted to monitor footraces for children. These races were divided by age groups and lasted perhaps a half hour. Participants earned ribbons if they won their group race. I especially remember that cheating was rampant at the starts of the races. I doubt that I ever saw a clean start.

When the races were over, there was a lull in activities until the afternoon baseball game between the Lansdowne Boys Club and the visiting Springfield Boys Club. I never participated in the game, as I was not on a traveling squad, but I remember that many of my friends played: Eddie Cope, Jimmy Bower, and others. Despite the game being played on Ardmore Avenue's raggedy diamond, the outing drew a large and enthusiastic crowd.

After the baseball game, I hurried home to help with preparations for our backyard picnic. Bill rarely attended, so it was typically my parents hosting Maude and Harry Quinn, Jean and DelRoy Pruitt, Helen and Eddie Bartlett, Ginny and Charlie Henderson, Ed and Gladys Berman, and possibly even my father's boss, Vince Fuller, and his wife, Gladys. I also believe that my first grade teacher, Dibby Koller, attended a year or two, as did Dr. John Suess and numerous others. It was not unusual for the guest list to approach the mid to high teens, and by 5:30 p.m., our driveway was clogged with cars.

While J. T. and I helped with assorted preparations, Esther was in complete control of the kitchen. This was likely because of the skills she'd learned in association with J. T.'s public-relations duties while stationed at the naval air station in Pensacola from 1941 to 1944. She had this marvelous organizational sense when it came to entertaining. Everything was meticulously set and timed in her head. She relied very little on anyone else to prepare the food, and that was the style she preferred. She definitely had a system, and when the meal was finally presented, all food was well prepared, delicious, and at the proper temperature. And what was additionally impressive about Esther's culinary performance was that she accomplished it all in a tiny, cramped kitchen, which more resembled a submarine's galley than an efficient kitchen. She relied on no written lists; everything was in her head.

A large picnic table and card tables displayed the food that Esther had been preparing since early morning. The typical menu was half fried/half baked chicken, homemade baked beans, homemade potato salad, corn on the cob, deviled eggs, tossed salad, Waldorf salad, watermelon, warmed Italian bread, iced tea, and Esther's homemade apple pie with Breyer's vanilla ice cream for dessert. There was no beer or wine, only mixed drinks, which were plentiful. People ate their food from china plates (no paper plates for Esther) in their lawn chairs, as there was no table seating. Sometimes if the weather was inclement, guests ate in our house, which was air-conditioned.

Bringing a dish to share was not requested or encouraged, as Esther prepared the entire Independence Day feast pretty much by herself. She was calm and collected throughout the entire process, always in control, never agitated, never breaking a sweat, and always the perfect hostess. To this day, I marvel at how she did it.

After everyone had gorged themselves on Esther's assorted dishes, the assemblage moved with their lawn chairs to the front yard to ready themselves for the fireworks that would evolve in about two hours. Even by 6:00 p.m.—and certainly by 7:00—folks were spreading their blankets and coolers on Stewart Field in anticipation of the Union Athletic Association sponsored fireworks show, which attracted visitors not just from Lansdowne but from many nearby suburbs. Stewart Field's concrete bleachers were always packed, since they offered an excellent vantage point for viewing the fireworks. Some pre-fireworks family entertainment was routinely provided on a flatbed truck in front of the home bleachers. I recall accordion players, tap dancers, magicians, singers, some lame comedians, and a local TV personality, Chief Halftown, all performing during these shows at one time or another.

By 9:00 p.m. Stewart Field was completely covered with blankets, strollers, coolers, and fireworks enthusiasts. Parents attempted as best they could to control and quiet their weary, impatient small children. Teenage couples flirted on blankets under darkened skies. Anticipation was as thick as the gathered population, which extended to the sidewalks along Essex Avenue. And finally, the first aerial firework burst into the Lansdowne sky, and the town's regaled fireworks show was underway. The display included both ground and aerial fireworks. The ground fireworks could not be seen from our front yard, but no one paid much attention to them anyway.

For thirty to forty minutes, the skies over Stewart Field were alive with exploding colors and loud bangs, to the delight of an energized crowd. While most in attendance were happy and captivated by the display, some small children, not surprisingly, took offense at the loud bursts caused by the aerial fireworks, requiring comfort and major reassurance from their parents. The Lansdowne Fire Department usually parked a truck across the street from our house to control any potential sparks landing on the Whiteheads' garage, which was dangerously proximate to the staging site.

With the air clogged with thick smoke, the fireworks always ended with a furious finale that thoroughly delighted the thousands in attendance. And to the delight of Eloise, who howled and shivered under my parents' bed during these shows, it was all over. The masses gathered their belongings—which included hundreds of tired, sticky, whiney children—and the slow trudge from Stewart Field to parked cars on clogged streets began. By 11:00 p.m., our neighborhood and a trashed Stewart Field had returned to quiet normalcy.

After all guests had departed and Eloise had cautiously removed herself from underneath my parents' bed, the cleanup began in our kitchen. This design and process had military roots as well. With J. T. and me fully involved, all pots, roasting pans, serving dishes, plates, glasses, and cutlery were washed, dried, and stored—after trash and any leftovers were secured. While the reorganizing of the backyard would wait until the next day, the house was returned to order, so that when we all woke on July 5, there was no semblance of any special event having been held the previous evening.

J. T. as a reporter/editor for *Country Gentleman* magazine

109

J. T.'S HEALTH

J. T. was almost thirty-seven and a half years old when I was born. He was not the rough-and-tumble father expected of a small boy, because he had two deteriorating discs in his lower back. I have no memory of the cause or whether it was linked to athletics or military service during World War II. One incident underscored this condition more than any other on a winter weekend on Marshall Road.

As a family, we often enjoyed a weekend fire in the living room fireplace. As J. T. lowered himself to add a log to the fire, he screamed in pain and fell to his hands and knees as if paralyzed and locked into position. As a child of four or five, I was petrified. I had thoughts of my father dying before me. I had no comprehension of what was wrong or what was happening.

Our family physician, Ben Whitman, was summoned, and he made an emergency house call about a half hour later. At this time, J. T. was still on his hands and knees, still paralyzed by the pain, unable to move. Bill was ordered to usher me elsewhere in the house, as I was only complicating matters by my questions and emotions. I have no knowledge of how J. T. got to his feet, but I speculate that Dr. Whitman gave him a shot in his lower back to ease the pain enough for him to stand and limp off to bed. This remains an all-too-vivid memory for me.

Occasional back troubles flared during his forties and fifties, but nothing even closely resembled the fireplace incident. J. T. was always very cautious and deliberate with body movements. Esther was highly protective as well; she would frequently warn me to "watch your father's back" if I got too playful with him.

J. T. also had food allergies and a touchy stomach. There were numerous foods that he could not eat, especially some types of fruit and seafood. His response was predictable; he would generally vomit ten to fifteen minutes after eating the suspect food. The strange thing was that he loved some foods so muchfresh peaches, for example—that he would eat them anyway, fully knowing the result. J. T. vomited so frequently that it was not a big event for him. I remember a time as a teenager when we were watching TV together, and in the midst of the program, he calmly left the living room and returned five minutes later after having vomited in the bathroom. It was no big deal.

I learned from reading saved correspondence that J. T.'s gastrointestinal symptoms were very severe in the 1940s, and he had numerous appointments scheduled with personal medical specialists, the US naval hospital in Pensacola, and VA physicians associated with the Philadelphia naval hospital. He even underwent exploratory surgery in February of 1944, but the results proved inconclusive. Ironically, correspondence suggests that J. T.'s gastrointestinal misery actually lessened somewhat during his time at sea in the Pacific.

J. T. fared no better after the war, until allergists were consulted in the mid-1950s: doctors Leland and Elizabeth Brown. Through a series of skin and dietary tests as well as laboratory examinations, it was determined that J. T.'s condition was caused by acute abdominal angioedema (hives on the wall of the stomach), a condition induced by food allergies. A restricted diet and periodic vaccine shots produced significant results and marked physical improvement.

Esther was adamant that J. T.'s accelerated gastrointestinal issues upon returning to civilian life were a result of his direct exposure to nuclear fallout in Japan at the close of World War II. Not surprisingly, the VA took an indifferent, hands-off approach to his claims for medical disability.

A serious condition impacted J. T. three or four times during my youth. He contracted cellulitis, a local skin infection caused by a break or cut in the skin that allows disease-causing bacteria to enter the body. It is most commonly contracted on the lower legs. Mosquitoes and spiders can carry the bacteria, and J. T.'s theory was that he was infected with the disease, always during the summer months, from a mosquito bite. Symptoms include pinkness/redness of the skin in the infected area, local swelling, pain, clammy/warm skin, and a possible fever.

Treatment for cellulitis in the mid to late '50s and early '60s included a two-week course of penicillin and bed rest so as to keep the infected area elevated. J. T. was a good patient because he needed to be; unchecked cellulitis can lead to a potentially life-threatening condition that necessitates hospitalization and IV-administered antibiotics.

J. T. rarely contracted a cold or flu. He did wear bifocal glasses for eyesight problems developed while he was a midshipman at the naval academy. He took no regular, daily medications, although he suffered regularly from heartburn, especially at nighttime. J. T.'s remedy was to access a box of baking soda he kept in the bathroom, and mix a teaspoon of it with a small glass of water.

In his middle-adult years, J. T. stood six feet tall and weighed in at about 210 pounds.

110

DOMINIC'S OR DOMINICK'S

Dominic's (or was it Dominick's?) approached iconic status in Lansdowne in the 1960s. The 1940s-era cream-colored ice cream truck with dark lettering was a frequent sight at the high school and Ardmore Avenue school playground/athletic field during the warmer months of the year.

When junior and senior high school were dismissed in the spring and fall months, one would frequently find the Dominic's truck parked on Clover Avenue under the sweet gum and gingko trees near "the Monument." In September and October, my teammates and I would typically pass it as we trudged onward to football practice at the Green Avenue School field. Occasionally Dominic's might make a special visit to the high school campus for a scheduled event, such as the Delco track meet or the Fourth of July celebration, splitting time between LAHS and the Ardmore Avenue Field. One very predictable thing about Dominic's at the high school was that it was always parked in the same location on Clover Avenue near "the Monument."

The Ardmore Avenue School playground and athletic field seemed to be the major draw for the Dominic's truck during the summer months. I recollect the truck frequently being parked on West Essex Avenue near third base on the main baseball field. I suspect that Dominic's was especially popular with basketball players who frequented the popular Ardmore Avenue School courts.

An odd observation about the Dominic's truck was that I can never recall seeing it driven through the town. Somehow the truck just seemingly appeared and disappeared at its parked locations. I am bothered to say that I cannot recall anything memorable about the drivers who waited on us.

The Dominic's truck was memorable because it was very old—probably a 1940s model—with big, black tires and an unusually high counter that few kids could reach. Unlike Good Humor trucks, which did not operate in Lansdowne (probably due to licensing or zoning restrictions), Dominic's patrons were served by the truck's driver, who remained inside the vehicle as he sold and distributed ice cream treats. No gimmicks such as bells, horns, or recorded music were associated with Dominic's—just ice cream and frozen treats that were reasonably priced.

Dominic's ice cream treats were basic: Popsicles (orange and cherry were the mainstays, and occasionally lime and grape were available), Creamsicles, Fudgsicles, ice cream sandwiches, chocolate-covered ice cream bars, etc.,—all of which were Popsicle brand products. They may have also sold vanilla/chocolate ice cream Dixie Cups. If my memory serves me correctly, a listing of items for sale was posted on the side of the truck near the counter.

Surprisingly, I did not frequent Dominic's often, as anything they sold could be purchased in a drugstore or neighborhood grocery. Their menu by my standards was uninspired. (I was spoiled by Good Humor treats while living on Marshall Road.) But after two hours of a hotly contested baseball, football, or boxball game on a hot and humid August Saturday, nothing tasted better than a purchase from Dominic's.

Who was Dominic, anyway? Or was it Dominick? I haven't a clue.

111

LANSDOWNE-ALDAN HIGH SCHOOL INTERSCHOLASTIC SPORTS

Lansdowne-Aldan High School offered interscholastic sports to its students. Boys' sports included football, wrestling, basketball, track, baseball, and tennis. Sports offerings for girls included field hockey, basketball, lacrosse, and tennis.

The school did not offer soccer, cross country, gymnastics, swimming/diving, volleyball, or golf for either boys or girls. There was also no lacrosse for boys and no track or softball for girls.

Sports offerings were dictated by finances, grounds, and facilities. Soccer was typically only offered at larger high schools. LAHS had no high school pool, which eliminated swimming/diving as an option. Lansdowne had no open space that would allow a cross-country course. Golf was not yet popular with adolescents, and Lansdowne had no golf courses, public or private.

Lansdowne Methodist Church

112

CHURCHES OF LANSDOWNE

Being that Lansdowne had strong Quaker roots, it was not surprising that the borough's first religious building was the Friends Meeting House constructed in 1831. The current meeting house and school are located on the northwest corner property at Stewart and Lansdowne Avenues. Despite the church and school presence, I knew no one who attended either institution.

During my childhood, the major churches endorsed the following faiths: Catholic, Presbyterian, Episcopal, Methodist, Lutheran, and Baptist.

The Catholic church, St. Philomena, is referenced in another essay, but it was the church where I attended hundreds of Sunday Masses with my parents. When I occasionally pay a nostalgic visit back home, I am struck by its size. It seemed very serious and hugely imposing to me as a child, but now it appears average in size.

Possibly the church of greatest prominence in Lansdowne was the First Presbyterian Church located on the southwest corner of Greenwood and Lansdowne Avenues. It was first known as the First Church of Lansdowne and was originally chartered in 1887. The current church-school building was constructed in 1928. Many of Lansdowne's more influential families attended First Presbyterian, and in 1955 membership totaled 1,825. First Presbyterian is located in Lansdowne's prettiest section. The church is of stone construction, strongly accented by traditional stained-glass windows. The sanctuary is dark, somber, and very Presbyterian. I was only in attendance there on one occasion when I was required to meet with a Presbyterian minister to gain a reference letter supporting my application to Davidson College.

St. John the Evangelist Episcopal Church was located in downtown Lansdowne at 19 West Baltimore Avenue. It first held services in 1881 but at a different location. In 1888 the cornerstone of the current chapel was laid at the present site. Membership in the late 1960s totaled over 1,100 congregates. I was only in the sanctuary once in association with Bill and Tish's wedding there on April 8, 1961. St. John's is of stone construction and is very consistent with traditional Episcopal church design. By my account, the sanctuary was dark, staid, and aesthetically reassuring. Reverend Francis P. Davis married Bill and Tish. His son, Frank, was a 1966 LAHS classmate.

The Methodist Church first organized in Lansdowne in 1891. The current site at the northwest corner of Lansdowne and Stratford Avenues was secured in 1894 when Lansdowne's population approximated two thousand residents. As Lansdowne grew, so did the Methodist Church, and in 1950, with membership numbered at about 1,100, plans called for a new sanctuary to be constructed, with the new church being dedicated in 1955.

Many of my LAHS classmates attended Lansdowne Methodist Church, including Beth Dunkle, Jerry Carothers, Dick Witmeyer, Billy Poole, Susan Packer, Gail Wiggins, Sandy Flinterman, and Bob Vincent. I was only present in the church on one occasion, the ever-so-sad day of LAHS classmate Bob Vincent's funeral. As far as the design of the 1955 church and sanctuary, I will keep this simple: I was never a fan. The church membership deserved better.

The borough also had a Lutheran church on Plumstead Avenue, which I passed for years walking to and from Green Avenue Elementary. I recall as a youngster buying Esther an African violet plant at a Lutheran church bazaar. It cost ten cents. Esther loved that plant and kept it near a second-floor-landing windowsill at our Essex Avenue home for close to twenty years, claiming that it was the "best ten cents" that I ever spent.

The Baptist church was located in downtown Lansdowne, but I was never in the sanctuary. I only visited the building for Boy Scouts as a seventh-grader.

There was also an impressive-looking Church of Christian Science located on the northwest corner of Owen and Stratford Avenues.

I certainly have left out some smaller churches, including a predominately African- American church located in the extreme southeast corner of Lansdowne that served both Lansdowne and Yeadon populations. During my child and adolescent years, Lansdowne did not house a synagogue or mosque.

A common problem for many Lansdowne churches was the lack of lot parking. The majority of church attendants in the town were forced to rely on street parking, which certainly did not enhance church attendance, especially during inclement weather.

113

"HALF WINSTONS, HALF SALEMS"

As was not surprising for adults of their era, both of my parents were heavy smokers throughout their adult lives. I am unclear as to when they started to smoke, but I am assuming Esther started in high school. My dad probably started smoking in earnest after he graduated from the naval academy. I also doubt that he had the money for such a luxury when growing up poor in small-town Kentucky.

Like many servicemen, J. T. was an especially heavy, nonstop smoker when at sea in the Pacific during World War II. He was not alone, since smoking was the social norm, an almost expected diversion and comforting reminder of life back home. It cut into the boredom and terror for Americans at war. I asked J. T. once how many packs he smoked a day when at sea. He said four, and he freely admitted that it was not uncommon for him, in the same motion, to snuff out an old cigarette while lighting up a new one. During battle, he smoked nonstop.

Filtered cigarettes did not arrive on the scene until the 1950s. Prior to filtered cigarettes, both my parents smoked unfiltered Chesterfields. Possibly in response to some preliminary health concerns, my parents switched to filtered cigarettes sometime in the mid-1950s, with J. T. smoking Winstons and Esther opting for mentholated Salems. In his early fifties, J. T. occasionally smoked small, wood-tipped Hav-A-Tampa Jewels. I hate to say this, but Hav-A-Tampa Jewels have a wonderful aroma, and they proved to be a pleasant alternative to standard cigarette smoke. J. T. generally smoked these cigars when alone and at leisure.

Unfortunately, my childhood and adolescent years were dominated by my parents' habit and its ramifications. Smoking was a most acceptable, almost expected pastime for adults of the mid-twentieth century. J. T. smoked while he shaved in the morning, and as a small child, I recall the routine smell of tobacco on his breath when he kissed me good night. Cigarettes were always smoked after meals. Our living room typically featured floating layers of cigarette smoke, as both Esther and J. T. smoked while watching television. Disgustingly, one of my daily chores was to empty assorted ashtrays about the house and to wash them once a week. I can recall the frequent click of my father opening and closing his metal lighter to this day.

During my upbringing, there was no ban or restriction on smoking in hotels or motels, restaurants, stores, public transportation, airplanes and trains, movie theaters, arenas, stadiums, businesses, colleges and universities, public buildings, etc. Even hospitals allowed smoking in designated areas.

As I've referenced in other chapters, I was sickly as a small child, frequently having strep throat and sinus infections, with an occasional asthma bout thrown in as well. I missed a lot of school days and nearly had to repeat the first grade because of excessive absence. I was in the fifth grade when I was first tested for allergies, and out of the assorted allergies detected, I was found to be highly allergic to tobacco.

I challenged this finding only once as a junior high schooler when I attempted to smoke a cigarette behind our garage. Once was enough, as my eyes quickly watered with my throat getting raw and scratchy. As most of my friends were athletes, none of them smoked, to my knowledge. None of my girlfriends in high school smoked either. This is not to say that teenagers of the times didn't smoke, because they did—just not in my peer group.

While smoking was surely eliminated for me, there was little I could do to consistently avoid the secondhand smoke that was ever lingering in our home. Decades later, it is now very clear to me that tobacco smoke was a major contributing factor to my frequent health issues as a child and teenager. J. T. and Esther simply ignored or downplayed the connection.

Ironically, I was a principle procurer of cigarettes for my parents at Pepper's Drug Store. Frequently J. T. would make the request: "Say, Bob, could you run up to Pepper's and get us a carton of cigarettes—half Winstons, half Salems? Put it on the charge." As the dutiful son, I would promptly hop on my bicycle or drive the Corvair to Pepper's to fulfill the task. We were frequent and loyal customers at Pepper's, and the staff never questioned my request despite my age. The majority of Pepper's employees knew our family well and must have determined that I was a safe risk and not inclined to smoke.

I can never recall any instance or effort when either J. T. or Esther attempted to stop smoking. Both my parents eventually paid the price for their addiction to tobacco. My mother's death certificate lists respiratory failure/idiopathic pulmonary thrombosis as the immediate cause of her death. Emphysema was a major contributing factor to J. T.s death. A sad memory for me is one of actually lighting a cigarette for my father during the last week of his life. J. T. immediately picked up on my reluctance, and he justified the act, stating: "It's one of the few pleasures I have left."

114

DRUMMOND ISLAND

First of all, this essay is a major rewrite. I shared the original draft with my cousin, Jill McConnell-Wirth, and I was very surprised to learn that what had been verbally handed down to me about Drummond Island's place in Pitcher family lore was largely inaccurate.

Drummond Island is located in Lake Huron at the extreme eastern tip of Michigan's Upper Peninsula. It is technically within the border of Chippewa County and is separated from the mainland by the St. Mary's River channel. This island consists of 249 square miles and is primarily undeveloped woodlands. It is the only island within the Canadian Manitoulin Island chain that is American soil, resulting from an early-nineteenth-century surveying error.

I had always been led to believe that Grandfather Pitcher had discovered Drummond Island prior to World War II as a base for deer hunting. I was dead wrong. Our family's link to Drummond Island is directly tied to Melvin McConnell, husband to Esther's younger sister, Jan. Perhaps Uncle Mel learned about Drummond Island from a Grand Rapids friend or neighbor, but he first visited Drummond in the late 1940s, somewhat as a respite for his hay fever. He soon fell in love with the island, and in 1950 he and Jan honeymooned there after their wedding.

My maternal grandparents, Floyd and Lenora Pitcher, bought a house known as the "creosote log cabin" and spent many summers on Drummond Island during their retirement years. This is the home that I remember during summer vacation visits. My Aunt Jan and Uncle Mel actually owned and lived in three different houses on Drummond, even formally retiring there from 1980 to 1983 until Mel's passing from a heart attack.

So much of Drummond Island as I knew it growing up revolved around accessing the ferry to and from the island via the mainland dock in DeTour. Much island history, folklore, and local color is linked to the Drummond Island ferry.

Drummond Island's permanent county population in the 1960s was about six hundred residents. Well-established families on the island were the Baileys, the Fairchilds, and the Seamans. The major Drummond Island industry was the dolomite mine and businesses linked to tourism, the marina, cabin rentals, etc.

Two small groceries existed on the island: Suny's and H&H. Grocery prices were outlandish, clearly designed to take advantage of visiting vacationers and tourists. The TeePee served soft ice-cream treats. Drummond had one flashing light, as I recall it, where Drummond Road (MI 134) intersected with Bailey Road. The island had one gas station, a small airport with a grass runway, and several marinas.

A small medical/dental clinic provided limited hours during the week. The closest hospital was War Memorial Hospital in Sault Ste. Marie, a ferry ride and minimum sixty-mile drive one way from DeTour. If you wanted to attend a sit-down movie theater or visit Kmart, you needed to drive to Sault Ste. Marie. The closest affordable grocery was Red Owl in Cedarville, a ferry ride and twenty-five-mile drive one way from DeTour.

I am unclear about law enforcement presence, but my guess is that a Chippewa County sheriff's deputy was assigned to the island. Island children attended elementary school on the island, further isolating them from the rest of the Upper Peninsula. Middle school and high school students were bussed off the island to mainland schools.

Unfortunately, the summer weather was frequently overcast and chilly in the morning and evening. Lake Huron's water temperature, even in August, was generally cold and not supportive of swimming for more than a few minutes.

Here are some select memories:

- Negotiating ferry parking—as an anxious sixteen-year-old driver—while driving Eloise to and from a veterinarian in Cedarville for emergency treatment of multiple bee stings

- Swimming with cousins MariJo and Jill, while their English springer spaniel, Music, continually swam around us for protection

- Sitting outside at night with Grandfather Pitcher as we listened to coyote howls

- Taking trash to the dump in the hope of seeing a black bear

- Deer, deer, and more deer, including my being confronted by a mature, six- to eight-point buck as I exited the sauna shack one morning

- Grandmother Pitcher serving me oatmeal for breakfast in August

- Bingo at the elementary school

- Some of the brightest evening skies I have ever seen, with hundreds of stars everywhere

- Hearing distant explosions from the dolomite mine
- Hearing sonic booms from military jet aircraft based at the US air force base near Kincheloe
- Fishing with Grandpa Pitcher

Charlie's

115

CHARLIE'S

I started going to Charlie's in ninth grade. I cannot recall who introduced me, but my hunch is that I caught rides there with Pete Willis and/or Pete's friends who had their driver's licenses. Charlie's was originally located in nearby Springfield at the intersection of Baltimore Pike and PA 420, about four miles from Lansdowne, straight down Baltimore Pike. While Charlie's relocated to nearby Folsom in 1986 to make way for a car dealership, my references are of the Springfield site.

Charlie's décor was very basic, mainly stools and counter tops from which to eat. Blue and white were the interior colors. The shop oozed a greasy ambience from the moment one entered the store. Charlie's was small in square footage, and during peak hours it was very crowded. (On Saturdays during the school year, it was letter-jacket city from area high schools.) Many times there was nowhere to sit and eat, so we requested our order to go and ate in our cars in their small parking lot. Charlie's was open six days a week and closed on Tuesdays, a reality that has both angered and disappointed me on more than one occasion during my return, out-of-state visits to the Folsom location.

Charlie's was and remains a working-man's eatery, and during my teen years, it was rare to see female customers. The predominantly male staff mostly wore white T-shirts and small, folded, white aprons in front. Hair nets? Not in the old days, and maybe not even now. The menu was very basic: hamburgers, cheeseburgers, and hot dogs—and either soda or phenomenal milkshakes. There were no fries on the menu in the old days, as I recall.

When I started to frequent Charlie's, I actually rehearsed my order in advance, as the place was intimidating to a fourteen-year-old. Charlie's was no nonsense, all business. You'd better know your order, since anxious, hungry customers were typically behind you in line. A standard greeting from the order taker was "What'll it be?" Warning: this was not a time to be undecided, to ponder, to debate. If you ordered cheeseburgers or hamburgers, the next question was "Loaded?" Research was required. You needed to know the definition of "loaded" at Charlie's, which was ketchup, chopped onion, relish, and pickle.

Employees were direct, efficient, and even a little curt—again, all business. Charlie's had a definitive division of labor. Positions included grill man (the top of the staff's food chain, usually a senior employee), order taker/cashier, and the milkshake specialist (usually a fledgling employee). Another lower-level employee performed trash pickup and counter cleanup. The restaurant also had a strange payment protocol for a hamburger joint. You paid when you left as you turned in your plate.

A memorable activity was to watch the grill man slap the uncooked meat onto the seasoned grill from a plate of prepared patties. Phenomenal, deadly accurate wrist action was the norm. The grill-toasted rolls were lined up in systematic fashion in anticipation of meeting their burgers.

The adding of condiments was sloppily conducted with a long plastic or metal spoon from assorted metal containers in lightning fashion by whoever was available.

The cheeseburgers were divine, heavenly. While they were not especially big, they were extremely flavorful, a little crusty on the edges, and like none other anywhere. My speculation is that Velveeta-type cheese graced the cheeseburgers. There were lots of theories as to what made them so good: the veteran grill (did it actually make the physical move from Springfield to Folsom?), the hamburger mix, which was rumored to include some horsemeat, special seasoning, etc. Milkshakes were a highlight—very thick, large servings made with real, hand-dipped ice cream.

My typical order was three cheese, ketchup and tomato only, and a "thin" vanilla shake. The latter was foolish thinking on my part, since "thin" was not part of Charlie's vernacular.

When I occasionally return to Philly, Charlie's is always a mainstay. Just don't screw up and travel to Philly on a Tuesday.

At present, Charlie's is now open seven days a week—including Tuesdays.

116

RANDOM REMEMBRANCES V

The school motto for Lansdowne High School and eventually LAHS is inscribed over the front entrance to the high school: "To Teach the Art of Living Well (Seneca)."

Esther and J. T. typically voted Republican, although they voted for Lyndon Johnson, not Barry Goldwater, in the 1964 presidential election.

Math was my clear nemesis in junior and senior high school. Arithmetic came easily for me in grade school, but I started to have significant trouble with concepts and theorems as the subject grew more complex in junior high. I attended tutoring after school as my schedule allowed. I even sought out J. T.'s help, which in the long run was a mistake. The subject came so easily for J. T. that he could not transition it well to my level. A few sessions at the dining room table ended very teary-eyed for me. Part of J. T.'s frustration was linked to his comparing me with Bill, who probably could have taught J. T. some lessons. The disappointment for J. T. was likely a matter of wondering how two offspring could be so different in skill level.

To my knowledge, Pennsylvania has never held a state fair. Bummer.

Once we met minimum requirements and passed a driver's education course offered in high school, we could apply at age sixteen for our "Cinderella" driver's license. This process included a written exam followed by completing a road course accompanied by a Pennsylvania state policeman. I was so nervous during the driver's test (for starters, while parked up a hill, I released the parking brake prior to starting the car) that I thought I'd surely failed, even though I had handled many of the officer's commands very well. To my surprise, I passed.

American Bandstand, the teenage-dance TV program, originally aired from WFIL Channel 6 studios at 46th and Market Streets in West Philadelphia. Bob Horn hosted the show from 1952 to 1956, but *American Bandstand* went to a higher level, eventually going national in 1957, one year after legendary Dick Clark began hosting the program.

American Bandstand aired daily in a thirty-minute time slot, mid to late afternoon, Monday through Friday. This live show consisted of several segments. Teenagers danced to popular hit songs, and a guest performer lip-synched a current hit record. For "Rate-A-Record," two teen dancers rated a new record on a scale from thirty-five to ninety-eight. During roll call, a line of students took turns telling Dick Clark their first names and where they went to high school, e.g., "Theresa, West Catholic" or "Danny, South Philly." My recall is that the show may have been extended to a sixty-minute format when it was aired from Philadelphia.

The teen regulars on the show, most of whom were kids from Philly, became very popular, received fan mail, and even had fan clubs organized in their honor. Norm Smith, LAHS '64, was an occasional *Bandstand* attendee in the early '60s. I believe neighborhood friend Pete Willis may have attended a show or two as well. Dick Clark became a local, then national, icon as the show's popularity soared. Rumor had it that Dick Clark lived in adjacent Drexel Hill, and Dick Clark sightings in our area were not unusual.

In 1967 the lure of California moved *Bandstand* from WFIL studios to Los Angeles, and the show solidified its presence as a popular, longstanding Saturday afternoon fixture for teenage America.

A lengthy railroad trestle connected Lansdowne and Clifton Heights as it towered over Scottsdale Road and Darby Creek. This trestle serviced the Media local and was approximately one hundred feet tall and two hundred-plus feet long. A rite of passage for Lansdowne youth was to run the trestle to the Clifton Heights side and back. This effort was not that dangerous compared to the scene in the popular movie, *Stand by Me*, since the commuter line ran on two tracks. This left us with the built-in safety of the neighboring track 99 percent of the time. I ran the trestle several times with friends and probably by myself on occasion. I never cared to walk close to the edge, even on a dare, because that was really dangerous, as there was no railing or fence. My first run came in sixth grade.

On two or three occasions during my early elementary school years, and on a school holiday, J. T. took me to Washington, DC, via Pennsylvania Railroad as part of a business trip. We never stayed overnight, but we left Philadelphia early in the morning and arrived back home late at night, exhausted. We had breakfast on the train in the dining car, and upon reaching DC, I accompanied J. T. on some short business stops, commuting by cab. While J. T. kept his various appointments, I sat patiently in the lobby, reading or coloring. I was the perfect little boy and always got high marks from the secretarial personnel who kept an eye on me. We capped the day by having dinner in the dining car during the two-and-a-half-hour return trip to Philadelphia.

Sixty years later, I still don't know what prompted the trips, but they remain a tasty memory—especially the thrill of eating meals on real china with real silverware in the dining car. These unique opportunities with J. T. made me feel special, since few, if any, of my friends or classmates shared this experience with their fathers.

Playtown Park was a small and very lame amusement park that operated during the summer months on Baltimore Pike in Springfield near Marra's Pizza. Playtown certainly was no Six Flags or Great America, but it was all we had for the time. It operated a Ferris wheel, small train, merry-go-round, Tilt-A-Whirl, and assorted other rides. It also included a Skee-Ball, pinball, and arcade area and the standard amusement park foods: popcorn, cotton candy, soft drinks, soft-serve ice cream, etc. By today's standards, Playtown Park resembled a small traveling carnival, save for the train ride or what one might find on the boardwalk at the Jersey Shore. It was a common and affordable stop with peers in summer during childhood and adolescence.

The Tilt-A-Whirl was not kind to me during one junior high visit. On the return drive home, Pete Willis wisely pulled over the Willises' Ford station wagon, allowing me to barf my guts out onto Baltimore Pike. Lesson learned: the soft-serve ice cream–Tilt-A-Whirl combination was a dangerous mix.

I failed to make the National Honor Society my junior year in high school because of a regrettable incident that occurred in an assembly while seated next to Chris Greening. This was a major disappointment for me. Chris had forgotten his glasses, and I had attempted to interpret some text that had been projected on a screen as part of the assembly presentation. We both got silly, and Mrs. Mary Bailey, our homeroom teacher, tossed us from the assembly. Chris and I both received two demerits and after-school detention. As I had received a formal disciplinary action from the school, I was ruled ineligible for the National Honor Society that year.

As if the exclusion from NHS wasn't enough, the after-school detention was awful, as I was primarily sharing space with the school's delinquent population. I slunk into the designated classroom after school dismissal—to the surprise of many, including the faculty proctor. I recall the disbelieving eyes from my fellow students and such cutting comments as: "Well, look who's here!" or "Boy, never expected to see you here." I spoke to no one, promptly did my homework, and exited as quickly as possible once my sentence had been served.

Esther and J. T. were not beer or wine drinkers. They preferred the hard stuff, as did their circle of friends. J. T. was a martini drinker, while Esther drank a bourbon mist, bourbon served over cracked ice. During my teenage years, it was routine for them to have a drink or two before dinner. I sometimes played bartender.

Even in the 1960s, solicitors sometimes came to our front door. The two offered services that I recall were knife sharpening and address stenciling. Address stenciling involved painting white numbers corresponding to one's numbered street address through a stencil onto the curb in front of one's house. This was a common practice during my Lansdowne youth, and upon my last trip to Lansdowne, I still observed homes sporting recent address stenciling.

Esther and J. T. were music lovers. They primarily liked big-band sounds from the '30s and '40s and Broadway show tunes. They also liked aspects of the 1960s folk revival. Music was rarely played in our household, save for Esther at the piano. On rare occasions, J. T. listened to AM radio while working at his basement workbench. He primarily listened to country music stations.

Friends of Esther who I remember were Janet Greening, Ruth Hough, Helen Bartlett, Jean Pruitt, Dibby Koller (my first-grade teacher), Ruth Pitts, and especially Dot Langley, with whom she served on the Lansdowne-Aldan School Board.

I don't know if my male jock friends in high school ever felt the same as me, but I was always jealous of the playing field used by the girls' field hockey and lacrosse teams. It was simply called "the hockey field." It was located directly across from the high school on Green Avenue. The hockey field's surface was flat, smooth, and well turfed with thick, green grass. I know this because the hockey field was the preferred touch-football site during summer evenings as we prepared for the start of varsity practice.

It is interesting to note in retrospect that at a time when girls' high school sports always played second fiddle to the boys' sports, the LAHS Lassies had a superb high school playing surface for field hockey and lacrosse. Good for the Lassies, despite the shortcomings of Stewart Field.

For several years in the time before snowblowers, classmate Billy Skinner and I shoveled snow when we had a decent accumulation, which might be three or four times per winter. Lansdowne had an ordinance wherein homeowners had to clear their sidewalks (most homes had sidewalks in front of the property) within twenty-four hours after a storm. Technically, homeowners could be fined if they did not clear their walks within the twenty-four-hour window.

Billy and I had about six to eight regular customers (many of my lawn-cutting customers) plus some new ones. We would service these customers first, and then if we had the time and energy, we would solicit our services to homeowners as they began to dig out. Sometimes we would be hailed down by a homeowner: "Hey, how much do you boys charge?" Our fees were reasonable, and we shoveled the entire width of the sidewalk and the walkway to the front door. I do not recall our ever doing a driveway.

Saturdays and Sundays were not a problem, as we did not have school as a conflict. However, if the snow fell on a school night, Billy and I got started early—sometimes as early as 4:00 the next morning. We shoveled like maniacs, like real John Henrys, and in three or four hours, we completed our work, sometimes collecting our pay later in the day. With shoveling completed, Billy and I limped to school, exhausted and sore, hoping that P.E. was not on our schedule for the day. If schools were closed, we kept shoveling until day's end.

Snow removal was not as lucrative as my lawn-cutting business, but it certainly helped at a time of year when Christmas checks from Louisville and Traverse City had been exhausted.

J. T. was an iced-tea fanatic. As soon as the warmer summer months arrived, so did his massive consumption of freshly brewed iced tea. Either Esther or J. T. would daily brew the tea from standard teabags. J. T. had a small collection of thirty-two-ounce glasses, which he would rotate for use. When one of these glasses was accidentally broken, it was a major event, with the broken glass to be replaced by a newly bought substitute within seventy-two hours. It was not unusual for J. T. to consume two of these large glasses of iced tea at dinner, and even a third one later in the evening.

J. T. liked his iced tea freshly brewed, heavily iced and sugared, and accented with fresh mint pulled from his mint patch next to the outdoor driveway faucet. A frequent refrain at the summer dinner table during my teen years was, "More iced tea, Bob, please, with a fresh sprig of mint." At restaurants, J. T. demonstrated his iced-tea snobbery. If the tea was not freshly brewed, he sought an alternative beverage.

In the early '60s two comedy albums proved hugely popular. In 1960 a live album, *The Button-Down Mind of Bob Newhart* was released. It currently ranks as the twentieth most popular album of all time. It was that good and that funny, with some incredibly memorable bits such as "The Driving Instructor" and "Abe Lincoln vs. Madison Avenue." Also, Vaughn Meader, a relatively unknown comedian/impersonator from Maine, released a 1962 parody album of the Kennedy White House known as *The First Family*. It too proved extremely popular. However, Meader returned to obscurity after the assassination of President Kennedy in November of 1963.

Friends and I repeatedly listened to these albums, along with a second Bob Newhart album, at Andy and Pete Willis's house. I still consider *The Button-Down Mind of Bob Newhart* to be the greatest comedy album ever produced. I am not alone in my estimation.

My passion for college football magazines goes back to junior high school days when I first started collecting these publications. I remember primarily buying them at Pepper's Pharmacy. The college football magazine standard for years was *Street & Smith's*, a publication no longer in print. And, yes, I still have some copies of those early-1960s editions.

As a child, I kept a wooden toy chest in my room. It is still within the family, though for years was seemingly lost and forgotten. It measures 25 x 15 x 14 inches, is crudely built, and is of mixed wood construction. My hunch is that it was handed down from the Pitcher side of the family and may have been acquired when Esther and Bill lived in Traverse City during later World War II.

This unremarkable piece of furniture held my treasures, essential toys, and other assorted items for me, such as baseball cards, View-Master, baseballs and baseball glove, rubber/pimple balls, pre-Lego construction blocks, Lincoln Logs, my piggy bank, postcards, letters, foreign coins, and perhaps even some money and candy.

Never to be confused with a phenomenal find on *Antiques Roadshow*, this mundane piece of furniture is all about sentiment and passed-on tradition.

Bicycles died in elementary school. As junior high students, we relied on our parents for transport, or we walked. I remember a lot of walking: to 69th Street, the Big Store, the Bazaar of All Nations, movie theaters, favorite hoagie/cheese steak haunts, etc. This all changed once we received our driver's licenses at age sixteen.

On a few occasions, J. T. and I would go on a road trip to Annapolis, just the two of us. J. T. was very active in the Naval Academy Athletic Association, and I suspect these trips were tied to some association-related duties or commitments. On one occasion after he had completed his business, he shocked me by taking me sailing on Chesapeake Bay. This was a first: J. T. sailing? Really?

Even though J. T. had never once suggested that he knew how to sail, I was enthused about the prospect. Sailing had never been a family activity. Despite my expectation of a limited and rusty understanding of sailing, J. T.'s skills proved to be the opposite. In a small, rented dinghy from the naval academy, we effortlessly glided across Chesapeake Bay for an hour, with J. T. demonstrating himself to be a competent navigator and tactician.

When we had completed our foray and returned to land, I naturally had to ask where J. T. had learned his sailing skills. He looked at me quizzically and announced, "Here." He went on to inform me that a requirement for all midshipmen during their stay at Annapolis was to learn to sail. This requirement was deeply rooted in naval tradition and was to be maintained.

I never ice-skated or snow-skied as a youth. I only participated in some very limited and unsuccessful roller-skating in the basement of the Methodist Church.

117

THE MEDIA LOCAL

For approximately one hundred years, Lansdowne has been a stop on a commuter rail line known as the Media local. At one time service extended all the way to West Chester, but the current line now ends one stop past Media in Elwyn. Scheduled stops along the route were serviced by stations where patrons could buy advance tickets indoors at the station's ticket window, or they could buy tickets from the train's conductor, preferably during hours when the ticket offices were closed (evenings and weekends). Conductors collected passengers' tickets between stations and clicked them with a personalized punch. The Lansdowne station is located one block south of Baltimore Pike on Lansdowne Avenue. The two railroad tracks are cleared by an overpass on Lansdowne Avenue.

Stops along the Media local, going west to east, included:

- Elwyn
- Media
- Moylan–Rose Valley
- Wallingford
- Swarthmore
- Morton
- Secane

- Primos
- Clifton-Aldan
- Gladstone (in Lansdowne)
- Lansdowne (main station)
- Fernwood–Yeadon
- Angora
- 49th Street
- 30th Street Station
- Suburban Station

Today the Media local route extends to a Market Street station (the old Reading terminal), finally terminating at Temple University in North Philadelphia.

For almost sixty years until being retired in 1980–1981, Philadelphia's original Pennsylvania Railroad commuter routes were serviced by electric multiple-car units known as MP54 cars. These units were originally unpowered coach cars first built in 1915, but as the potential for electrified commuter service was realized, these units were converted to motorized cars that drew electricity from overhead power lines through pantographs housed on the cars' roofs.

The MP54s started their movement in a slow grind and gradually gained adequate speed—although it always seemed a struggle. Budd M1 and Pioneer III silver cars eventually replaced the retiring MP54s. These units had superior pickup and overall power when compared to their predecessors. Overall, almost five hundred MP54 units were converted to be used throughout the Pennsylvania Railroad's northeast corridor. Maximum speed for these units was sixty-five miles per hour on very unremarkable roadbed.

One could never categorize a ride on the Media local as a smooth ride. The ungainly MP54s were painted a drab garnet color scheme and were appropriately regarded as "red rattlers." Some later versions were painted in equally unattractive olive green.

Originally the Media local and several other commuter lines, including the popular and heavily used Paoli local, were operated by the Pennsylvania Railroad (then Penn Central) after the merger with the New York Central, and later by SEPTA (Southeast Pennsylvania Transit Authority), the current operator.

For many Lansdowners, "taking the train" to their workplace in Philadelphia was the logical commute. However, the other option was the Red Arrow bus connection at the 69th Street terminal for the Market Street subway. It was totally impractical for J. T. to take the train, since his office was located almost ten blocks from Suburban Station where the Media local then terminated its run to center city Philadelphia. The Market Street subway dropped him off one block from his office. I always thought there was a "snoot appeal" about taking the train. It certainly was faster and more efficient than the Red Arrow–Market Street subway combination, but it was also more expensive.

Bill traveled by train for four years from Lansdowne to Jefferson Medical College while he was a student there. Bill's father-in-law, Charlie Henderson, was also an avid train taker, as was neighbor Bill Dormon.

A familiar scene then and now in downtown Lansdowne is that of hundreds of daily train passengers scurrying to the station in the morning to catch their respective trains to Philadelphia. The reverse process is similar—from 5:00 to 7:00 p.m.—as Media local patrons return to Lansdowne for their walk or ride home.

Lansdowne-Aldan High School or alternative photo

118

LANSDOWNE-ALDAN HIGH SCHOOL ALMA MATER

Though we roam the wide world over,
Though from home afar we stray,
We shall ne'er forget our school days,
'Neath the Garnet and the Gray.
And our classmates we'll remember
As the years go swiftly by,
And no matter where we wander,
We'll remember L-A High.
We'll be true to thee, dear high school,
And our thoughts will ever stray
To our school days spent at Lansdowne
'Neath the Garnet and the Gray.

119

FAMILY CARS

An Internet inquiry was necessary for this topic. Four family vehicles were active during my childhood and adolescence. Interestingly enough, they were all Chevrolet models, cars that were consistent with our family's income.

Until my college years, our family owned one car, an arrangement that was true for most families in the '50s and '60s. J. T. took public transportation to and from work in center city Philadelphia. Esther used the car during the day for shopping and other errands. The only void in the list is from 1948 to 1950, so I do not know the make, model, or year of the family car that brought me home from the hospital in April 1948.

Here is the list:

- 1950 black Chevrolet sedan (manual transmission)
- 1954 green Chevrolet sedan (manual transmission)
- 1960 gray Chevrolet sedan (automatic transmission)
- 1964 black Chevrolet Corvair (automatic transmission)

I barely remember the 1950 black Chevrolet sedan.

Other than running around Lansdowne and other nearby suburbs, I mostly associate the 1954 green Chevrolet sedan with the epic summer trips we took to visit relatives in Kentucky and Michigan. None of the above cars were air-conditioned, which made long-distance summer driving hot, sticky, and generally uncomfortable. Air-conditioning did not become a standard feature in American and foreign cars until decades later.

Our '54 Chevy had a push-button AM radio with five settings, and a roomy and comfortable backseat. During one of these marathon forays to visit relatives, I left some crayons on the ledge behind the backseat. They melted and left a memorable beauty mark for the life of the vehicle.

The 1960 gray Chevrolet sedan was our first car with automatic transmission and power steering. J. T. and Esther bought the car from a Chevrolet dealership in Pilgrim Gardens. Our salesperson was Gus Flamo. (How could anyone possibly forget that name?) Esther loved the car's automatic transmission and power steering, since she did most of the driving. The car had a very powerful engine and was more stylish than any of our other models to date. This car was active during my junior high school years, and as I approached driving age, my parents made a conscious decision to trade it in for a smaller vehicle with a less commanding engine. I never truly understood this decision, but I concur that our 1960 Chevrolet sedan was the most powerful car my parents ever owned.

Compact cars were introduced in the early '60s, and the 1964 black Corvair was Chevrolet's offering in that style. Corvairs were small, which was reinforced to me in the summer of 1965 when we visited southern states (Virginia, North Carolina, and Tennessee) for college interviews. I sat crammed in a tiny backseat while my parents did the majority of the driving. Around town the Corvair was generally fine, and it was adequate as I dated through high school, but long-distance travel was not its forte, with its just-adequate engine, cramped seating, and poor trunk space.

In compiling this essay, I learned a surprising fact. Not once during my childhood can I recall any family member being involved in a traffic accident. Esther was an especially attentive and careful driver. J. T. typically drove only on weekends, and generally on short excursions. Though it was uncharacteristic for our gender and ages, Bill and I never endured any accidents. I never received any speeding tickets as a high schooler either. That distinction had to wait until college.

One final thought: J. T. and Esther were very generous about letting me use the car for dating. They rarely went out on Friday or Saturday evenings, and if they did, I simply got creative in how I got around. They never ragged on me about gas money either, for which I was always grateful.

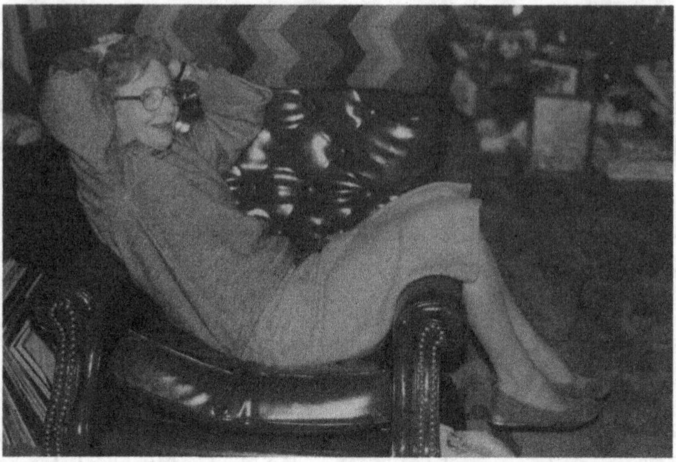

Esther in retirement

120

ESTHER'S PERSONALITY TRAITS

- Kind
- Unselfish
- Outgoing
- Opinionated
- Faithful
- Supportive
- Unfulfilled
- Altruistic
- Socially adept
- Unapologetic

121

LANSDOWNE-ALDAN HIGH SCHOOL DRESS CODE

While I attended LAHS from 1960 to 1966, a school dress code was enforced and reasonably well followed.

Boys were to wear collared shirts, slacks, and any shoe which was not classified as a sneaker or athletic shoe. Boys could not wear T-shirts or jeans. Typical attire for boys was a sport shirt (shirts were to be tucked in at all times), khakis, socks, and desert boots or loafers.

Girls wore blouses or sweaters with skirts, which were to break no higher than the top of the knee. Girls did not wear slacks, as that was not popular or accepted school attire in those days. Typical dress for a girl was a Peter Pan–collared blouse, skirt, knee socks, and loafers. Girls could wear open-toed sandals in the warmer months.

I doubt that the LAHS dress code was much different from dress codes established at other suburban public high schools in the Philadelphia area during the era. Dress codes for students attending parochial or Catholic high schools included a dress shirt and tie for boys, and girls frequently wore a plaid jumper uniform, which was customized by color and design for the specific high school.

I cannot recall any serious or controversial infractions pertaining to the dress code or its interpretation, but there must have been some instances where limits were challenged. Boys hated the no-sneakers rule, but that was simply not going to change.

An irony is that LAHS actually sponsored a student-inspired "dress-up day" roughly once a month during my senior high days. On those occasions boys might wear a tie with their shirt, and girls would simply wear fancier outfits. Participation was totally voluntary.

My dress complied with the school code at all times, but I did provide a strange twist during warmer months when I wore white slacks. I have no recollection as to what inspired my interest, and I certainly set no trend. I caught a fair amount of grief from fellow students, including classmate George Patton, who affectionately referred to me as "Mr. Softee."

By the way, male teachers always wore ties and coats, and female teachers dressed in appropriate business attire.

122

ITALIAN SPECIAL HOAGIES

Hoagies are indigenous to the Philadelphia area, and I am certain I ate hundreds of them during my adolescent years. I was not very discriminating as a teenager, and I went to a variety of hoagie/cheese steak shops near Lansdowne. (Again, Lansdowne did not have any legitimate hoagie/cheese steak shops in the early to mid-1960s). Most of these shops were located in the nearby Drexel Hill, Beverly Hills, and Stonehurst sections of Upper Darby.

Standard hoagies (less of an emphasis on Italian lunch meats) were always an option, as were American ham/cheese, roast beef, and even tuna hoagies. As a teenager, I gravitated toward the Italian version, which was immortalized during my early-adult years by *The Italian Kitchen* on Baltimore Pike in East Lansdowne.

The keys to a truly memorable hoagie rest with the roll and the lunch meats/cheese. Unavailability of these essentials dooms hoagie legitimacy from the onset. If you live in the Philadelphia area, it is pretty much a given that your hoagie or cheese-steak roll will be from Amoroso's bakery, which originated in South Philadelphia in 1904.

I am uncertain as to why Amoroso's rolls are so special, but they do not taste like the typical hoagie roll baked anywhere else in the country.

There seems to be a sweetness and a sponginess, even a softness, to the roll. It is very important too that rolls be fresh—the fresher the better. Nothing is worse than a hoagie on a crusty, hard roll. A hoagie made without an Amoroso roll, even if it has proper lunch meats, is pretty much worthless.

For an "Italian Special" hoagie, you need the following lunch meats, cheese, and ingredients: Genoa salami, pepperoni, capicola (ham), provolone cheese, and prosciutto (optional).

The horizontally cut roll is typically prepared with a light application of pure olive oil. (Trust me, you do not want a soggy hoagie roll.) Then you generously layer in your meats and provolone. (Do not bastardize your hoagie with any other cheeses.) Follow next with your standard acceptable garnishes, which include shaved iceberg lettuce, tomatoes, and sliced white onion. Some folks also add green peppers, banana peppers, and pickles. Spices are last: salt, pepper, and the all-important oregano.

Be sure to cut that hoagie in half. That makes it much easier to handle and prevents carpal tunnel injury.

Now, *mangia*, *mangia*!

123

FOLK MUSIC

Musically, I never followed the crowd. This tendency first surfaced when I was in sixth grade. I recall my brother having a Kingston Trio album, the first folk group to achieve major commercial success in the United States when the folk revival started to take hold in the late '50s and early '60s. I admired and looked up to my brother in many ways, so I decided to give the Kingston Trio's initial album a play while Bill was out of town. I liked it, and my interest in this emerging genre was spawned.

As folk music's popularity increased in the early '60s, in large part due to the Kingston Trio's success, ABC developed and broadcast a TV show called *Hootenanny*, which was aired on a Friday or Saturday evening. Jack Linkletter hosted the show, which was recorded at a different college campus every week. The show introduced to the general public veterans and emerging folk acts such as Judy Collins, the New Christie Minstrels, the Smothers Brothers, Theodore Bikel, the Simon Sisters (Carly being one), the Chad Mitchell Trio, the Serendipity Singers, the Limelighters, and Ian and Sylvia, for starters. After viewing a few shows, I was hooked. Not only did I enjoy many of the assorted acts, but I liked the fact that the show aired from different college campuses every week.

What evolved early on for me was a major interest in old English/Scottish/Irish ballads such as "Jackeroe," "Geordie," "Fennario," "Matty Groves," and "The House Carpenter" (my all-time favorite), which was so beautifully performed by Joan Baez. How I became a fan of Joan Baez is lost in my memory, but it struck me early in junior high school. The folk revival also introduced me to the traditional mountain and bluegrass music indigenous to southern Appalachia, which continues to be a favorite niche for me today.

Not all folk performers appeared on *Hootenanny*. In protest, major headliners like Joan Baez, Bob Dylan, and Peter, Paul, and Mary refused to appear in response to folk icon Pete Seeger being blacklisted by the television and radio industries. To my disappointment, the Kingston Trio did not appear either, possibly because of their success in appearing in more mainstream TV shows such as *The Ed Sullivan Show*. *Hootenanny* lasted only two seasons, but it introduced me to several musical acts that are favorites to this day: the Chad Mitchell Trio, Judy Collins, and Ian and Sylvia.

During that same time, I also liked and collected more contemporary music, such as doo-wop, Motown, and the Beach Boys, but my heart was really connected to folk music. I was a musical outcast and received a fair amount of ribbing from peers. However, during my senior year in high school, I was vindicated somewhat when our English class addressed a brief unit on ballads of the British Isles. An assignment was to bring a recorded example of a British/Irish/Scottish ballad for playing in class. Suddenly my record collection and I became very popular.

To this day, my favorites from this era include Ian and Sylvia, Chad Mitchell Trio, Doc Watson, Joan Baez, Gordon Lightfoot (whom I discovered in college), Tom Rush, Judy Collins, Pozo Seco Singers, Joni Mitchell (early years), and Peter, Paul, and Mary. How fitting it is that I am listening to Gordon Lightfoot's *Marie Christine* on my iPod as I finish this writing.

124

THE GLADSTONE PHARMACY [SAUL'S]

Before the likes of CVS and Walgreens, Lansdowne had any number of small neighborhood pharmacies. There were actually three in downtown Lansdowne within a football field's distance of one another.

The Gladstone Pharmacy—or Saul's, as it was known by the locals—was located at 210 West Baltimore Avenue across from the Gladstone Manor neighborhood in southwest Lansdowne. Located in a small commercial strip of stores, all of which contained second-floor apartments, Saul's was a small (practically everything in Lansdowne was small in those days) neighborhood pharmacy with a tiny soda fountain that served soft drinks and ice cream.

The location of Saul's was not prone to attract me, since it was located in an area of Lansdowne that I visited infrequently. I likely learned about Saul's from LAHS classmates Harry Gicking or Ray Shockley. I believe I paid my first visit to Saul's in my early teens.

The main attraction to Saul's for me was the store's legendary milkshakes. I'm sure I had them all: vanilla, chocolate, black/white. Saul's used either Breyer's or Hershey's ice cream, with milkshakes served in tall, chilled glasses. They were delicious, pure perfection, as good as it gets.

Saul was the store's proprietor and principle pharmacist, and while others claim that his son also worked the store, I only remember Saul. He was a highly memorable figure. With his thinning black hair combed straight back, a thin mustache, and a protruding lower lip, Saul moved like a snail. He also had poor peripheral vision, as he always stared, slightly bent over, straight ahead. He never craned his neck; he craned his whole body. Saul had a permanently dull effect and was not personable or conversant, but he was never mean. To Saul, it was all about the milkshake, and he was all business.

Most memorable was Saul's quasi mantra as he worked the milkshake to eventual conclusion. While slightly nodding his head to keep time, Saul would mumble a weak, groaning hum as he poured the shake into the glass and then stirred it a few times with a long metal spoon. Total credit is awarded to classmate Ray Shockley's imitation of Saul's milkshake routine, which he totally nailed. Harry Gicking's mimic was solid too.

Another commanding interest at Saul's was the magazine rack on the right side of the store as you entered. Sharing space with *Sports Illustrated* and *Time* was a worthy assortment of men's magazines, which were a considerable draw to a fourteen-year-old male. A trip to Saul's was simply not complete without a hurried ("Is Saul looking?"), thirty-second thumbing through of *Playboy* or its cheaper, inferior imitators.

125

THE NIXON POSTER

In the early 1960s, J. T. served as president of the Philadelphia Typographers Association. For their annual banquet, the association invited former US vice president and 1960 Republican candidate for president, Richard M. Nixon, as their speaker. J. T. emceed this black-tie event in Philadelphia, and Esther also attended. As a young high school student, I was apparently very unmoved by the event, despite a gift I found the following morning.

When I came down to breakfast, I found a large poster of Richard Nixon resting on the dining room table. It had been personally signed by Richard Nixon in black magic marker: "To Bobby—Warmest regards, Richard M. Nixon"

I was so unimpressed that I rolled up the poster, rubber-banded it, and stashed it in my bedroom closet for over a dozen years. I doubt if I even mentioned the event to any of my classmates, although I did thank my father for securing it for me. Despite my parents' Republican leanings, I was a Kennedy supporter. As a young, naive high school student, I failed miserably in understanding the significance and value of the gift. At the time, Richard M. Nixon, the political figure, meant little to me, as did his personally signed message and signature.

The clock ticked forward to 1974. Because of his knowledge and involvement in the Watergate cover-up, then President Richard M. Nixon was publically disgraced and forced to resign from office, ending "America's long nightmare."

Fast forward to 1976. I had recently earned my MSW, had a new job, and was soon to be married. I discovered the Richard M. Nixon poster while emptying my former bedroom closet, cursed at the man, and ripped up the poster.

Big, big, *big* mistake. I learned a year later that my former Richard M. Nixon poster had been extremely valuable because it was (1) poster size, (2) personalized, and (3) definitely hand-signed by the man himself.

Estimated political-memorabilia value for the poster in 1977 was $7,000. *Antiques Road Show* (2015) estimated the value between $20,000 and $30,000.

Damned Republicans!

126

GOLDFINGER

The third film in the James Bond series, *Goldfinger*, was released in late December of 1964 when I was a junior in high school. Most of my male high school friends had seen the first two James Bond movies, *Dr. No* and *From Russia with Love,* and we were mutually enthralled with everything about the series. We especially idolized Sean Connery, who was for us the ultimate male role model: athletic, intelligent, suave, and so sophisticated with the ladies. We also loved the series' high-energy action, gadgetry, music, cinematography, and leading ladies.

As Christmas had come and gone, several of us, wishing to make the best of our Christmas break, decided to take the commuter train to Philadelphia to attend the movie. In those days, recently released movies were first shown at the major movie houses in downtown Philadelphia. Had we waited, *Goldfinger* would not have arrived at the suburban theaters until well into January or even February, as the movie was extremely popular having received rave reviews. Knowing that we couldn't possibly wait, and with testosterone fully engaged, three or four classmates and I traveled to downtown Philadelphia to attend a daytime viewing of *Goldfinger*. In our collective sixteen-year-old minds, this was a major outing.

The movie ran continuously, so the theater was not cleared out when the feature ended. We were so captivated by the first viewing that we decided to stay for a second showing, and then a third. A close friend, Billy Skinner, would have stayed for a fourth time, and perhaps even more, but we eventually convinced Billy to leave with the rest of us. On the train ride home, we naturally dissected the movie from beginning to end. We loved Odd Job, the numerous beauties who graced the film, and of course, Sean Connery, who could not have been more cool as the leading man.

Billy was quick to pick up dialogue and accents, and he recalled, much to our delight, a memorable line from the film as James Bond was about to be dissected at the crotch by a laser beam.

James Bond: "Do you expect me to talk?"

Auric Goldfinger: "No, Mr. Bond, I expect you to die."

Billy mimicked Goldfinger's foreign accent to a tee as we howled for encores.

127

THE LANSDOWNE-ALDAN SCHOOL BOARD

The best I can tell, Esther was a member of the Lansdowne-Aldan school board from 1961 to 1967. The Lansdowne-Aldan school board included almost two dozen members and had only a few female members. Elected membership included representatives from the district's three participating communities: Lansdowne, Aldan, and East Lansdowne. As demonstrated by high school yearbook photos during Esther's term, the board was all white, with no participating minority membership.

When we lived on Lansdowne Avenue in the late 1950s, Esther hosted several meetings in our apartment's large living room, with typically ten to twelve adults in attendance. There was a sense of importance, almost a degree of urgency, to these meetings from my naïve perspective, and I was instructed to stay in my room for their duration, only exiting to use the bathroom. My parents even bought me a small, black-and-white, portable TV that I could watch in my bedroom during these evening gatherings.

During these meetings, Esther went to uncommon lengths in serving coffee/tea and small pastries in our dining room. However, much to my displeasure, I could only sample the remaining goodies the following morning, as the meetings continued after my bedtime. J. T.

worked late on most of the meeting nights and was not in attendance that I recall. In retrospect, I believe these meetings were called to help direct and support Esther's candidacy for the school board.

Esther ran as a Republican, which certainly was a safe decision in conservative Lansdowne. She might have even run unsuccessfully for the school board before 1961, as I know she was an open critic of the school board's decision to build a new gym as opposed to a swimming pool when a major school expansion plan was devised in the mid-1950s. I was always proud of my mother's statement to the local newspaper about her choice (paraphrasing): "No one ever saved a life by playing basketball."

My mother's school-board responsibilities were of no interest to me as an adolescent, but I can never recall her throwing her weight around or abusing her position to somehow gain any advantage for me. I also recollect no references from any of my teachers as to her status or any display of preferred attention. For one, I really didn't need or favor any assistance, and secondly, that wasn't Esther's style. I especially recollect one instance where Esther showed remarkable restraint.

During my sophomore year of football, I wore an unsanitized football helmet during the first weeks of preseason practice. From the untreated helmet, I suffered a severe rash across my forehead, including numerous bumps and pimples, and I assure you that this was not standard teenage acne. Evidence of the condition is displayed in my tenth-grade class photo. The rash was severe enough that I attended weekly treatments with Dr. Levy, a Lansdowne dermatologist, during much of the season. My understanding is that Esther did report the development to the coaching staff, but the matter ended there. My further understanding is that my parents assumed full expense for my visits to Dr. Levy, which included numerous exams, ultraviolet treatments, and topical medications.

Esther took her school-board role seriously. The school district struggled with funding issues during her six years of service, since Lansdowne, Aldan, and East Lansdowne had no meaningful industrial/corporate tax base and relied near solely on local property taxes to administer and operate the schools. In the early 1950s, J. T. and Esther chose Lansdowne as their new home community because of the excellent public schools, but any edge that Lansdowne-Aldan schools had had at one time started to wane in the 1960s. Esther saw this issue clearly and was one of the few board members open to considering further consolidation with contiguous communities.

During her school-board years, Esther respected and highly regarded Superintendent Carlton Abbott and was particularly fond of school-board president Bob Stevens. She also gained a close personal friend in fellow board member Dot Langley.

128

TO KILL A MOCKINGBIRD

To Kill a Mockingbird was first the book (1960) and then the movie (1962). I was exposed to the story in reverse order. The movie was released on Christmas Day 1962, and like the book, it became an immediate hit with the public. I recall my parents talking about the movie at the dinner table and announcing their desire to see it. Sometime in early January 1963 after the holidays had passed, my parents and I attended a screening of the movie at the City Line Center movie theater on City Line Avenue. The theater was crowded, and I recall it was a Friday evening, since my father was still in business attire, wearing his customary suit and tie to the show.

What was highly unusual about the event was that my parents rarely attended the movies. Even more surprising was the fact that we attended it as a family (minus Bill, who was married and attending medical school at Jefferson). This was the only time during my childhood that I attended a movie with both of my parents. Their action that winter evening was very intentional. To their credit, they saw the value of the story and wanted me directly exposed to the lessons taught within the film. Even before the movie began, I knew this movie was going to be special.

I immediately liked the characters, but I only partially understood the story. I was confused by the alleged attack and rape of Mayella Ewell and who was responsible. I instantly related to Jem and Scout and to their relationship with their older father. An early scene in both the book and the movie instantly resonated with me: where Jem climbs and sulks in a tree in protest of Atticus's "refusal to play football for the Methodists." Gregory Peck's physical resemblance to my father was also evident, including his quiet and dignified manner. I know I left the theater strongly impacted by the story and the injustices displayed. I most certainly asked question after question on the short ride home from the movie house.

My reading of the book followed, and I read it on my own. I loved it and read it in two to three days. It was later assigned as required reading sometime during my high school years. The book answered some of my questions, but more importantly, it exposed me to exceptional writing, the quality of which I recognized even as a young teenager. There are still passages I treasure, like this one from chapter 1:

> Maycomb was an old town, but it was a tired old town when I first knew it. In rainy weather the streets turned to red slop; grass grew on the sidewalks, the courthouse sagged in the square. Somehow, it was hotter then: a black dog suffered on a summer's day; bony mules hitched to Hoover carts flicked flies in the sweltering shade of the live oaks on the square. Men's stiff collars wilted by nine in the morning. Ladies bathed before noon, after their three-o'clock naps, and by nightfall were like soft teacakes with frostings of sweat and sweet talcum.

Understand that *To Kill a Mockingbird*, as both a novel and a movie, was released in the early '60s during stressful and ugly times as the nation's Civil Rights Movement was gaining momentum. The book and movie helped raise the country's consciousness by graphically exposing the painful impact of ignorance and bigotry. The brilliant irony is that the tragic storyline is actually conveyed within a multilayered love story: the love between father and children, and the distant and unrecognized love generated by Boo Radley toward Jem and Scout.

I cannot tell you that *To Kill a Mockingbird* was the direct cause of my career choice, because it wasn't. My goal in high school was to become a journalist, but I felt the story's influence immediately in my job as a naïve and fledgling juvenile probation officer back in 1970. Why? Because in a few short months on the job, I was directly exposed to similar forms of the poverty, ignorance, violence, and racism so masterfully portrayed in both the novel and movie. Within eight weeks on the job, I knew that probation would be my lifelong vocation, and in my own small way, I wanted to make a contribution in righting so many wrongs that continued to cruelly and predictably impact disadvantaged people.

Teenagers especially are in need of role models and heroes to help them determine values and career direction. Outside of family members, we often turn to athletes, historical figures, literary characters, entertainers, etc., to emulate. I cite Atticus Finch as a past and current hero of mine, and I know I am not alone, since the American Film Institute listed Gregory Peck's portrayal of Atticus Finch as the number-one movie hero of all time. Millions of Americans, especially of my generation, would concur with my choice.

I have read *To Kill a Mockingbird* at least half a dozen times, and I plan on reading it several more times. I know the movie nearly by heart. There are still times when I predictably smile and even tear up when I watch it.

To Kill a Mockingbird certainly influenced my decision to seek a career in a helping profession. It clarified the importance of personal values, and provided a simple formula to treat *all* people, regardless of circumstance, and at *all* times—with common decency, dignity, and respect. To that extent, both the book and movie have had a profound and lasting impact on me both personally and professionally. And again, I certainly am not alone in that pronouncement.

Now if all of us could be a little more like Atticus…he made it look so easy.

129

FOOTBALL CAMP

Part of the Lansdowne-Aldan High School football heritage, when I played from 1963 to 1965, was a week-long, preseason football camp spent at YMCA Camp Conrad Weiser near Wernersville, Pennsylvania, just west of Reading. As I recall, football camp was scheduled in late August after about a week of preseason practices in Lansdowne. I don't recall the exact cost, but I believe it was around fifty dollars that parents needed to contribute in order for their sons to attend.

Camp Conrad Weiser was located in the rolling hills and forested stands of eastern Pennsylvania. It was extremely rural by suburban Lansdowne standards. During our week stay here, five or six other high schools were in attendance as well (Central Bucks, Conshohocken) but none from Delaware County. None of these other high school teams would we play during the regular season.

There was a lot of culture and folklore associated with football camp. The seniors played it up as to how horrible it was, and as sophomores (freshmen could not play varsity ball), we were all scared to death. Whenever seniors or juniors spoke of the experience, we sophomores dropped what we were doing and listened intently.

The Camp Conrad Weiser complex consisted of several residential camps scattered throughout the main grounds. Varsity coaches stayed in a cabin surrounded by about eight canvassed platform tents, which individually housed six players. Practice fields were scattered throughout the complex. All schools utilized a central shower location and a main dining hall. There was a swimming pool as well, which I believe we were allowed to frequent once a week as a rare reward during our stay.

Attending players and coaches gathered at the high school late Sunday morning. Chartered buses were scheduled, since players needed to bring clothing, personal items, equipment, and junk food—not to mention the equipment the coaches brought: dummies, balls, backup equipment, shoes, medical gear, etc. Back then the bus ride to Wernersville took about two hours, with a brief thirty-five- to fifty-mile stretch spent on the Pennsylvania Turnpike. I recall the bus rides to Camp Conrad Weiser being unusually quiet, bordering on gloomy in anticipation of what the forthcoming week had in store.

We had three practices a day: morning, afternoon, and evening. Morning and afternoon sessions were in full pads. Evening practice required only helmets and shoes and was utilized to introduce offensive plays. As I recall it, we had contact every day and a scrimmage with another school on Wednesday and on Saturday morning before we left. LAHS was one of the smaller high schools scheduled for our week at beloved Camp Conrad Weiser.

Practices were tough, especially the afternoon session because of the heat and humidity. The practice regimen consisted of unit drills on both offense and defense, installation of offensive and defensive teams, and conditioning, including sprints up a hill in the dreaded cow pasture practice field, if we drew that practice area. The week at football camp had much to do with who would start on both offense and defense, so competition was high. Injuries were fairly common, with injured players receiving minor medical treatment from the coaches. I recall assistant coach Seaman being especially busy in this department. Our team physician, Dr. Patton, was also in attendance during part of camp. A few players quit during camp and were transported home by summoned parents.

While I survived three exposures to football camp, I ran into injuries. The shoes I had been fitted with as a sophomore were too small, and by midweek I had major blisters on the backs of my heals that oozed and bled. They were so bad that I could not wear shoes or even sneakers. By Thursday and Friday, I actually practiced in my socks. My junior year was uneventful, but in my senior year, I suffered a bruised shoulder midweek, courtesy of Steve Paxson's helmet in a blocking drill. I could still practice but without contact for two to three days.

As players, we naturally complained a lot about the intensity and frequency of the practices; our physical aches and pains; the food, which included "big juice," a local version of Kool-Aid; our living conditions; mosquitoes; the weather; and our practice equipment and clothing, which never dried. But the experience definitely bonded, toughened, and advanced us as a football team. There was limited adolescent goofing off; we were simply too tired and too sore. Sleep was a much-anticipated respite. While the coaches drove us hard, they were never mean-spirited or over the top.

There was some mild hazing in evidence, but the coaches kept it under control. Each sophomore was assigned a senior, and I fortunately drew neighbor friend Pete Willis, who was very easy on me. Mail call was big, as we all awaited letters and even packages from our girlfriends. I remember the coaches having a field day one summer when a player actually received a box of cupcakes from his girlfriend. What little spare time we had was spent resting on our bunks, eating and drinking our junk food (Hawaiian Punch was a favorite), talking guy talk, and listening to a local Reading AM radio station. Major camp songs that I especially recall during our football camp summers were: "My Boyfriend's Back" by the Angels, "Bread and Butter" by the

Newbeats—including Billy Skinner's version and "I Can't Help Myself" by the Four Tops.

Football camp was a grueling week and something of a rite of passage for adolescent male athletes at LAHS. After our Saturday morning scrimmage, we could not wait to see those beautiful chartered buses arriving around 1:00 p.m. on the gravel road servicing our camp for the short ride home. At last we had a few days without football, with the toughest part of preseason now completed.

130

HOPPING CARS

Perhaps hopping cars was indigenous to the Philadelphia area and the era in which I was raised, but I think not. It was a common activity during winter months when packed snow covered the side streets for several days after a snowstorm. Cars temporarily slowing at stop signs and slower-moving vehicles were particularly vulnerable. Elderly drivers were easy targets, as they generally did not pick up on what was happening. To the best of my recollection, hopping was exclusively a male activity. It was particularly popular after high school dismissal as an opportunity to impress one's peers.

The intent was to hitch a ride on the back of a slow-moving car by crouching down to grab the back bumper while your boots served as skis. The act was intended to be surreptitious so the driver was unaware of events. Hopping, therefore, had two joys: (1) fooling the driver and (2) the ride itself, which generally was measured in yards and lasted less than a block. Hopping was typically performed by one youth or by two youths in tandem.

Esther abhorred the practice, as she thought it extremely dangerous. Having been raised in snowy Traverse City, Esther had no patience, no tolerance for suburban Philadelphians who could not responsibly handle periodic snowfalls. There were obvious dangers to the practice: a sudden stop could throw the rider under the vehicle, and disengaging from the car had to be carefully planned as to not cast oneself into oncoming traffic. Hopping was clearly illegal, but I cannot recall anyone arrested for the practice. I also do not recall anyone seriously injured by the act.

Esther was an excellent driver, and she was confident and experienced in driving on snow. She always had an eye out for anyone attempting to hop, and this generally mild-mannered lady would even role down the car window, angrily wag her finger, and admonish youth on the street to not even consider the practice on her vehicle. She also referred to car-hoppers as "hoodlums, nothing but hoodlums."

I never car-hopped. Not a chance. I clearly saw the dangers, and I doubted that I had either the skill or nerve for the activity. And Esther would have killed me; or if not killed, I would have been grounded for life or sent off to military school. Some of my friends and neighbors hopped occasionally, but the practice simply was not worth the potential for severe parental penalty.

131

J. T.'S FAVORITE COUNTRY SONGS

- "For the Good Times" by Ray Price
- "Ring of Fire" by Johnny Cash
- "Snowbird" by Anne Murray
- "El Paso" by Marty Robbins
- "Scarlet Ribbons" by The Browns
- "Little Bitty Tear" by Burl Ives
- "He'll Have to Go" by Jim Reeves
- "Jolene" by Dolly Parton
- "By the Time I Get to Phoenix" by Glen Campbell
- "Crazy" by Patsy Cline
- "Make the World Go Away" by Eddy Arnold
- "A Boy Named Sue" by Johnny Cash
- "Little Jimmy Brown" by The Browns
- "Behind Closed Doors" by Charlie Rich
- "Kisses Sweeter Than Wine" by Jimmie Rogers
- "Do Not Forsake Me, Oh My Darlin'" by Tex Ritter
- "Sixteen Tons" by Tennessee Ernie Ford
- "I Fall to Pieces" by Patsy Cline

132

RANDOM REMEMBRANCES VI

Beginning in 1920, Lansdowne had a long-standing tradition of playing Swarthmore High School in football on the morning of Thanksgiving Day. What I especially liked about the tradition, even long before I played varsity high school football, was the community response. Regardless of LAHS's record, many Lansdowners attended the game, even if they only attended one game during the season. As a small child, I recollect instances of attending this game with J. T. and next-door neighbor, DelRoy Pruitt. On one occasion or two, we even traveled to Swarthmore when it was an away contest. The LAHS-Swarthmore rivalry survived until 1972 when it was discontinued. Swarthmore won the final meeting, seven to six.

A Philadelphia area tradition during my childhood was "Mischief Night," the night prior to Halloween. On this occasion, youth played neighborhood pranks, such as soaping windows, shooting shaving cream into unlocked cars, lighting brown paper bags of dog poop on someone's door mat, and possibly even committing minor theft/vandalism. You get the picture. And yes, I was a participant.

Letter sweaters and letter jackets were popular attire in high school but more so for boys. Letter jackets were garnet in color with gray sleeves. The "LA" varsity letter (copying the Los Angeles Dodgers "LA" design) was worn on front with a small cloth icon designating the sport for which it was earned. Pins were added to designate multiple letters earned. "Lansdowne-Aldan" was displayed on the back of the jacket.

Letter sweaters were white with long sleeves and were buttoned up the front. Gray and garnet stripes, indicating the school colors, were included on one of the sweater's arms. The "LA" varsity letter was worn in the same manner and style as the letter jacket. It was very common for athletes to have both a letter sweater and a letter jacket in their wardrobes.

Favorite AM radio stations during my youth were WIBG and WFIL. Popular disc jockeys for the era were Hy Litt, Joe Niagara, and George Michael. Another popular radio personality was the legendary Jerry Blavat, a Philadelphia icon known as "the geater with the heater" and "the boss with the hot sauce." Blavat was heard on various Philadelphia stations starting in 1961. Popular R&B stations were WDAS and WHAT.

Pinball was a popular arcade pastime during my childhood and adolescence. This was well prior to electronic games such as Pac-Man and Donkey Kong taking over. It was not unusual to see pinball machines displayed in bars, sandwich shops, neighborhood markets, gas stations, pizza/hoagie shops, transportation terminals, etc. I was never a fan, as I lacked even minimal talent.

John Facenda, the voice of NFL films, was the evening anchor for WCAU Channel 10, the CBS affiliate in Philadelphia for over twenty years. He had an articulate, deep, dignified voice (one Philadelphia newspaper reporter dubbed Facenda "the voice of God"), and for many Philadelphians, he was the overwhelmingly preferred choice for local TV news. He started his TV broadcasts with a familiar, "Hello there." He concluded them with the comforting "Have a good night tonight, and a good day tomorrow … good night all." Our family preferred NBC for national news, but like the local majority, we chose John Facenda for local news over the weak competition from channels 3

(NBC) and 6 (ABC). For years Facenda was joined on his broadcasts by Herb Clark for weather and former Philadelphia Eagle defensive back Tommy Brookshier for sports.

The LAHS mascot for boys' teams was "Lords." For girls' teams, it was "Lassies."

As a family, we never went camping. J. T. and Esther camping? Are you serious?

The 69th Street shopping district hosted a year-long farmer's market that attracted farmers from counties west and northwest of Delaware County. Many of the vendors were of German heritage and Mennonite faith. The 69th Street Farmer's Market was open all day Saturday throughout the year, plus one full day during the week (Wednesday or Thursday). It occupied a permanent, air-conditioned building close to the 69th Street terminal.

J. T. liked to visit the farmer's market on Saturday mornings when he had the opportunity, and I was a usual visitor with him. He especially liked buying homemade beef sausage. A stop at a bakery stall was standard procedure as well. J. T. enjoyed visiting the farmer's market because it linked him to his reporter/writer days at *Country Gentleman*, as it was standard behavior for him to talk shop with local farmers when visiting.

The 69th Street Farmer's Market offered numerous butcher shops, bakeries, and produce stands (operating in season). Summer months were clearly the busiest and best attended. At many of the stalls, elementary school-age children and teenagers worked shifts, helping their parents by taking and bagging orders, collecting money, preparing and hauling produce, etc. Parents and children worked long, hard hours at the farmer's market, plus there was the early-morning preparation back at the farm, the tedious travel to and from Upper Darby, the clean up, and so on.

The farmer's market even operated a small restaurant. On one rare occasion, J. T. treated me to breakfast there, which was a major, unexpected treat. However, the meal quality could in no way match the delicious aroma of meats and cheeses that greeted customers as they entered the building. What a rush! The memorable aroma was certainly on par with the Windermere Delicatessen.

In tenth grade I had a leaf collection project assigned in biology class. I was on top of the project and pulled it together over a weekend. While my collection was adequate, J. T. took an unusual interest and announced that "we" could do better. All of a sudden, we were in the car patrolling Lansdowne and other adjacent suburbs on a Sunday afternoon for lesser-known species. Possibly because of his many years with *Country Gentleman* magazine, J. T. knew a lot about trees, and by his personal observation, he recalled where some species rare to our region were planted. We went as far as the Swarthmore College campus to collect one leaf.

I stayed up later than usual that Sunday evening because of the additional leaves collected and the related work they entailed. I received an A on the project, and my teacher, Miss Strout, informed me by written comment that I had the most diverse collection within her classes. When J. T. received news of my grade, he beamed, having proved that we could truly do better.

Marley's was a popular soda shop that sprang up in downtown Lansdowne just north of the train station in the early 1960s. My best estimate is that it operated for two years when I was in junior high school. It was the place to grab a hamburger and Coke on a Friday or Saturday night after a movie or basketball game. During the day it operated as a sandwich shop and small restaurant. I patronized it on several occasions, but the older teens dominated the customer base, making junior high kids like myself feel out of place.

For years our family had a very antiquated refrigerator. I failed in my research to determine the year and model, but it was a white Frigidaire. What bothered me the most was its inadequate freezer space;

it was so small that it could only hold pint boxes of ice cream—*pints.* This was not acceptable for an ice cream lover.

J. T. was a bottomless reservoir of jokes and quotes. He was responsible for a humor column in *Country Gentleman* for years, so he reviewed hundreds of jokes annually. Some of them were appropriate for airing with family, and some were not. I recall that he shared a lot of "private" material with DelRoy Pruitt.

J. T.'s diverse quote vault was developed over time. He had dozens and dozens of quotes memorized, ranging from Shakespeare to Minnie Pearl to General Douglas MacArthur. He utilized them during timely situations for emphasis. Often he would recite the quote and ask if I knew the author, book, or play that was the source. One quote I directly attribute to J. T.: "There is value to our mistakes if we learn from them."

Esther was an extrovert, and J. T. was an introvert. J. T. was comfortable and accomplished in social situations, but he did not seek them out. He much preferred time alone or simply with family. J. T. was quiet, soft-spoken, and comfortable being alone and by himself, whereas Esther desired more contact with people.

About twice a year, Esther would travel to nearby Sellersville, Pennsylvania, to shop at a Pendleton outlet store that was located within the factory. Esther loved Pendleton jackets, and she bought several jackets over the years for J. T., Bill, and me. Note: I am wearing a Pendleton jacket in my first-grade class photo.

The Philadelphia area—as was true with major US urban settings during my childhood—was serviced by a local soft-drink company, Frank's. If you went to buy "soda," Frank's products would be in the display case or refrigerated section along with Coke, Pepsi, and Canada Dry items at local neighborhood stores and retail grocers. Frank's produced traditional flavors but also some unique flavored sodas, like cream soda and my all-time favorite, black-cherry wishniak.

By the way, what is *wishniak* anyway? I never knew the history as a youth, but wishniak is actually an Eastern European, vodka-based, black-cherry liqueur. Rumor has it that Frank's black-cherry soda received its "wishniak" tag from Philadelphia's Eastern European neighborhood influence. Today, Frank's and Canada Dry both produce a black-cherry-wishniak-flavored soft drink.

The principle Philadelphia department stores daring my youth were Snellenberger's, Strawbridge and Clothier, and John Wanamaker's. All three stores were located in center city Philadelphia on Market Street east of Broad Street. Snellenberger's ceased to operate late in my childhood, allowing Strawbridge's and Wanamaker's to monopolize major department-store trade in downtown Philadelphia well into my adulthood.

Wanamaker's is the department store most associated with Philadelphia, including its tea room, elaborate holiday light and music show, and the frequently suggested directive to "meet me at the eagle," a large, bronze statue on Wanamaker's ground floor, where it was considered good luck to touch the eagle's beak. All three department stores are now distant memories because of buyouts and consolidation.

My first exposure to fast-food was in late junior high school at an Arby's restaurant on Baltimore Pike in Clifton Heights. I was likely with Pete Willis, two years my senior, who was licensed to drive. The roast beef was actually sliced in full view of the customers. Drive-through windows came several years later.

There were times on weekends or holidays when J. T. and I would play Scrabble. I do not recall who initiated our playing together, but it was always J. T. and me, as Esther had no interest. These matches began in late grade school and went past my high school years. Games were played in the living room on the card table, with J. T. positioned comfortably in his olive-green armchair and me sitting on Esther's piano bench. Many times we played these games while watching television.

J. T. never really cared about the scoring. To him, the game was about using the most letters and coming up with the most exotic or clever words. Sometimes he would use "xray" or "jabber" on a triple-word score and be pleased, and because he had a broad vocabulary, he introduced me to dozens of new words. During my high school years—and especially when I was desperate to rid myself of some challenging consonants, I would make up words. I would claim that "ijam" was a species of African antelope or "jiosk" was a fish common to Norwegian fjords.

We shared a lot of laughs over my silly efforts. I still recall one game when he used all seven letters on his rack to play the word *dribble*, linking the word to an available *s*. While he didn't score that heavily, the important accomplishment to J. T. was that he had exhausted all his letters.

Esther was known to send flowers through a florist, since grocery stores did not sell flowers at the time. In this activity, she was very loyal to Holmes Colonial Flower Shop in downtown Lansdowne and its handsome proprietor, Fred Holmes. In the 1960s Mr. Holmes was close to retirement age, was white-haired, and wore black-rimmed glasses. I knew him from placing or picking up orders for Esther at his store, which was near Westie's and the Marlyn restaurant. Mr. Holmes predictably wore a white shirt and tie, and he was always pleasant, friendly, and efficient. Esther claimed that no one was better with cut flowers than Fred Holmes.

Like all junior and senior high schools, LAHS typically had assemblies scheduled every few weeks. Assemblies were held during first period in the morning, necessitating the remaining periods to be reduced in length to forty-two minutes from the standard length of fifty-one minutes. Usually the high school auditorium was used for this purpose, but sometimes the new gym was used.

Assemblies could be devoted to musical presentations, pep rallies, awards, guest speakers, elections, movies, etc. I recall on at least two occasions a memorable assembly where a speaker showed homemade movies of his canoe trips into the Canadian wilderness. However, the most recollected assembly ever was the "birds of prey" assembly where a biologist lectured on large, carnivorous birds—while hawks, eagles, and condors rested on perches on the auditorium's stage. At one point he actually released a large bird, which circled around the auditorium on several trips as many students shrieked and ducked for cover.

I had a crush on Patty Townsend, an LAHS student one year my junior, for years in high school. I never announced this to the world until now. I didn't have the nerve to ask her out on a date. I wasn't worthy and was too intimidated.

133

ESTHER'S MIGRAINES

These were no joke. They were awful. I recall these attacks peaking for my mother in her forties when I was in late grade school and/or junior/senior high school.

Esther would suffer these severe headache attacks two to three times a year. Because of their frequency, they developed an all-too-familiar pattern. When my mother anticipated a migraine coming on and was already too ill to go out, our family physician, Ben Whitman, would be contacted by phone. Dr. Whitman would make a timely house call to my mother, who would already be isolated in the darkened master bedroom. Esther would receive an injection of morphine (nothing else could dull the pain) and then try her best to sleep through the pain, a process lasting two to three days. Her major enemies at this time were light (all blinds were fully drawn) and sound. She typically vomited a great deal during the early stages of these episodes, which further exacerbated the pain.

J. T. moved to Bill's bedroom out of necessity during these attacks. Esther drank and ate very little during these spells, fearful that anything she ate or drank would naturally be rejected. Occasionally she would go to the bathroom, but for two or three days after the injection, she was generally confined to bed (no bathing, no brushing of teeth or combing of hair, etc.). She would lie there, pathetic and disabled, with her hands sadly clutching a heating pad to her forehead. Her illness was so drastic, so paralyzing, that she did not possess the wherewithal or strength to exit the house on her own, even in the event of a home emergency.

One day when I was in seventh or eighth grade, J. T. directed me to stay home from school to care for Esther during an especially trying attack. He called the school and explained the circumstances, since he did not trust leaving her alone. Certainly as a grade schooler and even into junior high, these episodes were very upsetting to me. All I could really do was quietly enter her bedroom and ask if she needed anything, empty the aluminum bowl known as the "vomit bowl," and offer words of consolation: "I'm here if you need me, Mom" or "Let's hope the worst is over."

I was always relieved when J. T. returned home from work at the end of the day during Esther's migraines. He demonstrated a warm and supportive quality toward Esther during these challenging days, which no doubt comforted her to a large extent. In a quiet, darkened room, he patiently sat by her side and reassuringly held and stroked her hand as she toughed it out.

Eventually the pain would subside, and my mother would rejoin the world. Predictably, she was weak and unstable at first, as she had been through a highly challenging physical ordeal. Her appetite would eventually return, but most certainly she lost three to four pounds or more with every migraine. I never felt that she was truly back to normal for almost a week after the migraine had subsided.

When I went off to college, her migraine episodes gradually decreased in frequency. In Esther's final twenty years, migraine headaches were no longer the threatening menace that had haunted her in earlier life. So perhaps there is something to the idea of outgrowing an illness.

134

NOVEMBER 22, 1963

November 22, 1963, was a Friday. I was a carefree sophomore at Lansdowne-Aldan High School. Thanksgiving was nearing, and the football team was continuing its preparations to play the traditional holiday game the following Thursday against Swarthmore High School at the Swarthmore College Field.

On November 22, 1963, around 1:00 p.m., I was on a hall pass while walking through the new gym section of the high school. Carol Sticklin, a fellow sophomore and a girl I had dated briefly in junior high school, suddenly appeared, running from the opposite end of the hallway. She was crying and emotionally distraught. She ran toward me, a familiar face, sobbing. "They shot him. Someone shot President Kennedy." Carol longed for consolation, and we briefly hugged in the hallway as she continued to sob, shake her head, and repeat the shocking news. Offering awkward support as best I could, I escorted Carol to wherever she was going and then returned to my classroom.

Very shortly thereafter, there was an announcement over the school's intercom system that President Kennedy had been shot and killed during a scheduled trip to Dallas earlier that afternoon. No adult, teenager, or child was prepared to hear such unthinkable news on that late November Friday. As high school students, we were bewildered, shocked, angered, and frightened by such horrible events. Millions of Americans uttered the same unanswerable question: "How could this have happened? How?"

Immediately after school, Coach Spafford canceled football practice and told us all to go home. The funeral was scheduled for Monday, November 25th, and school was canceled on that day out of respect for Americans observing the funeral and mourning the untimely passing of our president.

J. T. and Esther both worked on that Monday of the funeral, and in their absence I remained home alone to watch NBC's coverage on our living room's small black-and-white television. On that day, first lady Jacqueline Kennedy taught the world the meaning of courage, dignity, and personal sacrifice. In the midst of one of the ugliest occurrences in American history, her quiet and ennobling resolve was something I will always remember and hold comforting. Unashamedly, I cried several times throughout the broadcast.

I buried my parents many years ago. While that process was naturally difficult and an expected rite of passage, I am not alone when I admit that the grieving process for President Kennedy will last within me until my own passing. It was the pivotal event of my adolescence, and much of the hurt and anger remains. Our country's innocence vanished that November Friday. As teenagers, we all had to grow up a bit more quickly—more cynical and more distrusting.

By the way, Lansdowne-Aldan lost to Swarthmore, twenty-seven to eighteen, on that Thanksgiving morning in 1963—as if it even mattered, then or now.

135

"101"

During the summer between my sophomore and junior years in high school (1964), I came to the conclusion that I did not want to be a career naval officer and thus did not wish to attend the naval academy. As J. T. and I had discussed this possibility for years, it was only fair that I inform him of my decision—and soon. This was not a talk that I looked forward to, but it had to be done.

My decision had everything to do with the curriculum at the naval academy, which was extremely heavy on math and science in those days—not exactly my strong suit academically. I suspected that I would have struggled in the classroom at Annapolis and most likely would have been grossly unhappy. Navy was interested in my playing football there, but the mix of challenging academics, football (I doubt that I would have played much, since Navy, in those days of Roger Staubach, was nationally ranked), and the demanding military regimen would have been a poor match for me. The decision had nothing to do with the Viet Nam War, which was brewing in Southeast Asia.

I summoned up my courage and was very straightforward with J. T. at the dining room table one Saturday morning. To my surprise, he graciously took the news and did not offer any attempt to counter my decision. In retrospect, I think he saw Annapolis as a stretch for me academically, so perhaps he was relieved as well. He said he was glad that I had reached the decision then and not *after* I had been accepted and enrolled. He had done some preliminary work for me, and my chances of gaining a political appointment to Annapolis were very high because of my legacy status. He also told me that I needed to get focused on colleges I might wish to attend.

This Saturday morning conversation was somewhat of a watershed moment for J. T. and me. The discussion was honest and direct. He surprised me with his reaction and was highly supportive of a college choice other than the naval academy. He also surprised me in that he was supportive of my attending a college distant from Pennsylvania and the Philadelphia area. Not once did he mention college tuition and costs as a deciding factor.

Based on his suggestion, I consulted a recent edition of *Webster's Collegiate Dictionary*, as it contained a section at the very end of the text, which listed all American colleges and universities. I then began a slow, methodical, and somewhat boring listing of schools that held some interest to me, using next to no criteria. I did look at location, founding year, and of course, the exoticness of the name (I seemed to like hyphenated names). I ran some of my preliminary selections by my father, and he made such telling comments as "good school," "beautiful campus," "tough winters," etc.

After the list was drawn up, I began the tedious process of typing individual postcard inquiries to the 101 schools on the list. The text read something like this:

Dear Sir:

> Please send me a current college catalog and related materials about application for admission to ____________________. Thank you very much.
>
> Sincerely yours,
> Robert L. Bingham

I was very busy that summer, typing about ten postcards per day on a portable Smith Corona typewriter. Our local mailman was not happy with me, since colleges and universities at that time freely distributed thick college catalogs to prospective students.

What evolved was a list that primarily included small- to medium-size colleges and universities located in the Midwest and South. I avoided large state universities simply because I felt the size to be intimidating. Of the 101 inquiries, I narrowed the list down to twenty schools, then to twelve, and then to six, which I visited and made application to in the summer of 1965.

Ironically, I addressed my Wake Forest postcard to Winston-Salem, Virginia, as opposed to Winston-Salem, North Carolina. Wake was in the final batch of postcards to go out, as I went through an alphabetical listing of the schools. I recall debating whether or not to actually type a 102nd postcard, but to be true to the process, I did address and mail a second postcard to Wake Forest College in Winston-Salem, North Carolina.

Some schools on the 101-list that I did not apply to were UNC, Duke, Baylor, Wabash College in Crawfordsville, Indiana, and Knox College in Galesburg, Illinois.

The final cut included William and Mary, Davidson, Virginia, Washington and Lee, Vanderbilt, and Wake Forest. After visiting and interviewing at all six schools during the summer of 1965, I applied to all six and was accepted at Wake Forest, Vanderbilt, William and Mary, and Washington and Lee. I was rejected at Virginia because of heightened out-of-state admission requirements where I fell short. I believe that Davidson, a Presbyterian-affiliated college, did not accept me because I did not have any Presbyterian ties.

I rejected Vanderbilt because of the distance and Nashville's seeming dependence on country music—and, unfortunately, because I visited the school on a stormy and ugly summer's day. I ruled out Washington and Lee, because I saw it as a money school where I would be less likely to fit in—and it was an all-male school at the time. I disregarded William and Mary primarily because I felt like I would be attending college in a tourist Mecca (colonial Williamsburg), which in hindsight was a foolish reason.

There was nothing about Wake that I initially did not like. It seemed the best fit for me, and ironically it was one of the cheapest schools on my list at $700 for tuition per semester. As any Wake Forest alum would say, "How times have changed."

136

CONNIE MACK STADIUM

Connie Mack Stadium, the nation's first concrete-and-steel baseball stadium, opened in 1909 as the baseball home of the Philadelphia Athletics. Original field dimensions were 515 feet to center, 378 feet down the left-field line, and 340 feet down the right-field line—hardly a home-run hitter's paradise. Then, the site was known as Shibe Park, named after the principle owner of the Athletics at the time. Shibe Park eventually became Connie Mack Stadium out of respect for the legendary Hall of Fame manager of the Athletics: Connie Mack. From 1938 to 1954, Connie Mack Stadium was home to both the Athletics and the Phillies.

The first professional baseball game I ever saw was in Connie Mack Stadium between the Athletics and the Boston Red Sox, because Esther wanted to see Ted Williams play in person. All I remember from the outing was my uneasiness, if not fear, over the steep concrete steps in the upper deck. I tightly clutched J. T.'s hand as we traversed the steps up and down.

The Athletics relocated to Kansas City after the 1954 season, allowing the Phillies to be sole occupants through the 1970 season. Beginning in the 1971 season, the Phillies would play in the new, sterile, doughnut-shaped Veterans Stadium in South Philadelphia.

From the outside, Connie Mack did not resemble a baseball stadium. Some say it more resembled a church with its French Renaissance architecture. It was located in North Philadelphia at 21st and Lehigh Avenues in a declining neighborhood of residential row homes when I attended games there in the late 1950s and 1960s.

As a baseball park, Connie Mack had a comfortable and intimate feel to it, with unusually good acoustics on the field and in the stands. Hall of Fame Phillies outfielder and long-time Phillies broadcaster Richie Ashburn commented, "It looked like a ballpark. It smelled like a ballpark. It had a feeling and heartbeat, a personality that was all baseball." From a fan's perspective, I couldn't agree more.

Fans were close to the field. Lower and upper-deck seats ran from the left-field line to deep center field. Hitting a home run over the left-field bleachers was a Herculean feat accomplished by very few. A thirty-four-foot-tall, corrugated right-field wall was divided in right-center field by a massive Ballantine Beer scoreboard topped by a Longines clock. Billboard advertising was in evidence on the outfield walls and left-field roof. Some familiar advertisers were Alpo dog food, MAB paints, Foremost hot dogs, Ferraro Cadillac, and Goldenberg's Peanut Chews.

Playing field dimensions during my years of attendance were 334 feet to left field, 447 feet to dead center, and 327 feet to right. Due to its spacious dimensions, Connie Mack witnessed a lot of triples and more inside-the-park home runs than most of its counterparts.

I annually attended a Phillies games on chartered Red Arrow buses with the Lansdowne Boys Club, and we were always quarantined in the left-field bleachers. Occasionally, I attended a game with a reluctant J. T. He was most definitely not a baseball fan, as he found the game boring and slow. The vast majority of my visits to Connie Mack were with high school classmates (Jimmy Bower, Billy Skinner, and Andy Willis) or solo. During my junior high and high school days, if no friend was willing or available, it was not unusual for me to attend a game on my own, taking a sack lunch and commuting by Red Arrow bus and two subways to get to the park, typically for Sunday doubleheaders. I frequently sat in the upper deck directly behind home plate for a $2.25 ticket. The only foul ball I ever caught was in this section, hit by Giants first baseman Willie McCovey—or was it Orlando Cepeda?

Most years during my youth, the Phillies were a lackluster club, so getting tickets the day or evening of the game at the stadium was not a concern. The primary food offerings at Connie Mack were primitive by today's standards—hotdogs, popcorn, ice cream, soda, and beer and were purchased from tiny concession stands or strolling vendors. Oh, and seemingly everyone smoked, producing a visible haze that drifted over the field once night had fallen.

One of my most memorable trips to Connie Mack was to a Sunday doubleheader with the San Francisco Giants. For some reason, I wound up with a lower level, will-call seat in the midst of a large outing from a black AME church. The church members hollered hysterically on each occasion when the legendary Willie Mays ran into the dugout from the outfield at the end of an inning. Through their constant encouragement, they demanded that Willie tip his cap, which he always did, further prompting the church crowd to erupt into joyous applause.

Because of the questionable neighborhood, J. T. had a rule that if I was attending a rare night game, I was only to leave the stadium with the crowd at game's end. Billy Skinner and I attended a rain-delayed, twilight doubleheader between the Phillies and the Cardinals, with the second game going extra innings. It got very late as the game dragged on in a stalemate. I called J. T. and asked him what we should do. He said to stay until game's end and then "leave with the crowd." I was to call him from the 69th Street terminal after Billy and I had commuted back from the ballpark. J. T. got my call after 2:00 a.m., thus ending my attendance at twilight doubleheaders.

When the Phillies were soon to relocate to the new Veterans Stadium in 1970, I was one of the fans not excited about the move. It was true that Connie Mack had numerous shortcomings: the commute, the neighborhood, the obstructed-view seats, terrible parking, and the crowded ramps and corridors. It had hard wooden seats. It was dirty and grimy, which necessitated my taking an immediate bath upon my return home. However, the stadium had charm, class, history, and character that the cookie-cutter, symmetrical ballparks of the future could never deliver.

There is no more wondrous memory of my childhood than attending a Phillies game at Connie Mack. And my favorite pitch from a vendor, whom we dubbed Bob Hope because of a physical resemblance, was "Hot dawg … hot dawg sandwich!"

137

THE JEW STORE

(Please note that the title of this essay is included for purposes of local accuracy. In no manner is any racist association endorsed by the author.)

I frequented the Jew Store as an adolescent in the '60s because it had the distinction of being the only neighborhood store proximate to Steward Field and LAHS. It was housed on North Wycombe Avenue within a four-block walk of the high school and Green Avenue School. I have no recollection as to why it was tagged the "Jew Store," but it conveyed an ugly stereotype.

As a neighborhood store, the Jew Store sold candy, gum, ice cream, soda pop, Tastykakes, chips, milk, bread, some boxed and canned foodstuffs, newspapers, magazines, limited over-the-counter medicines, nail clippers, Chapstick—you get the picture. The Jew Store did not sell hoagies or any other sandwiches.

The store was dark and dirty and was not air-conditioned. Flies were frequently more common than customers in summer months. It was as basic as it came for a neighborhood store. I primarily visited the store during the summer after playing boxball at Green Avenue or touch football on the hockey field during summer evenings. My summer school classmates and I also hurriedly visited the store during midmorning breaks from the American History course we took in 1964.

The main proprietor was memorable. He was a short, stout man in his late forties or early fifties with a gruff exterior. He usually looked like he needed to shave, take a shower, and change his clothes. I don't recall his name, but some kids simply referred to him as "the Jew." The irony here, as if it mattered, is that I doubt that he was Jewish. More likely, he was Italian. (Imagine Pauly from the *Rocky* movies). We immediately got the impression that he didn't like his job, the store, or demanding, irritating children and teenagers. A woman, who I assumed was his wife, also worked the store, but I remember little about her.

Unfortunately, some of my peers had targeted the Jew Store for shoplifting. Usually this was not an issue when I was with a friend or two, but when a crowd of six to eight young people entered the store, I had a sense of what would happen. On these occasions, I did something strange and outside of adolescent character: I did not join the crowd. I stayed outside, much to the disapproval of many peers, and waited until my peers exited before I entered the store to make my purchase.

Initially, I caught some grief about my decision, since the peer pressure to participate was extremely strong, and I wanted to be liked and accepted like any teenager. I was called out several times, but I stood by my conviction that I would not participate in something that wasn't right. I wasn't so much criticizing or judging others, and I wasn't preaching or proselytizing. They just had to accept my decision not to participate, even though my stance uncomfortably underscored with the crowd that what they were doing was wrong. Again, the stance was more about me than them.

While I was definitely not perfect or consistently law-abiding as an adolescent, shoplifting was never, ever on my agenda. Credit J. T. and Esther for nurturing that principle in me.

138

MONTBARD BAKERY

I discovered this gem during my high school years. Most likely, credit for this rests with Mark Gilbert, an LAHS classmate who lived in that neighborhood. The Montbard Bakery was located in a small string of retail stores known as the Montbard Shopping Area on Shadeland Avenue between Berkley and Drexel Avenues. Besides the bakery situated within the retail area, there was a very small grocery and Paul Revere Pizza, which, at last inquiry, is still in business.

The Montbard Bakery was typical for the era and locale as to its offerings: cakes, cookies, rolls and breads, breakfast items such as Danish and cinnamon rolls, and doughnuts. It was a small store with the actual kitchen/ovens located on-site. Items were always very fresh, usually baked a few hours prior to purchase.

For $1.60 one could purchase a dozen fresh doughnuts of multiple varieties. All types were very good, but to this day, I cannot recall a better cream-filled doughnut than the ones sold at Montbard. J. T. especially liked the nut-covered variety, and upon suggestion, he was an easy mark to quickly offer up two dollar bills for me to make a Saturday or Sunday morning run to Montbard. I always quickly obliged.

Again, a better cream-filled doughnut was not to be had. Sadly, the Montbard Bakery is no longer in operation.

The Monument

139

THE MONUMENT

Anyone who attended LAHS in the 1960s recognized and understood this reference well. "The Monument" was a World War I memorial located on the southern grounds of the high school at the merging of Green and Clover Avenues. According to the publication, *Lansdowne, 1893–1968: 75th Anniversary*, this memorial was originally located on the grounds of the Lansdowne School at Highland Avenue and Baltimore Pike. It was subsequently transferred to the grounds of LAHS and became a cultural fixture on the campus.

The Monument was approximately nine feet tall, a cylindrical concrete shaft that cradled a world globe at the top. It stood on a concrete pedestal, which was often used for seating, and thus made the site a convenient gathering spot. A short, concave stone wall flanked the Monument on two sides, as did some shrubbery, which, in tandem with sweet gum and gingko trees, provided some limited privacy.

Inscribed on the memorial are the names of twelve Lansdowne residents who sacrificed their lives in the World War I conflict. The inscription reads, "To the honor of the men from Lansdowne who entered the Great World War, 1914–1918. This monument is dedicated by their fellow townsmen in token of sorrow for their loss, of pride in their valor, and in the full assurance that the memory of their heroism in life and death will inspire the future youth of Lansdowne with the same courage and devotion."

While the intent of the memorial was not totally lost on the junior and senior high schoolers who attended the school, the Monument was a recognized appendage to the high school, a permanent meeting site on campus. It was a popular gathering place after school. Students might meet there before or after a football game, an open house, or some special event held at the high school.

For Lansdowne students, the Monument did double duty on weekends and summer months as a meeting site. It provided a good view of anyone cruising the south side of the high school, and if you drove past the Monument in a car, you automatically glanced to see who might be present.

The Dominic's ice cream truck frequently parked adjacent to the Monument, and what better place to sit and enjoy one's summer or after-school ice cream or Popsicle than the pedestal at the Monument.

The Monument held an even deeper meaning for many. It was a semi-private locale where some serious and important discussions were held about relationships, life, and future plans. No doubt, many "going steady" and "no longer going steady" talks took place there. Hands were held. Kisses were stolen. Rings were shared and returned. Cigarettes were dared to be smoked. No doubt, there were some life-changing talks about going off to college, family relocation, employment and careers, an unplanned pregnancy, joining the service and perhaps serving in Viet Nam, etc. Some initial wedding plans may have evolved there as well.

Oh, and yes, the Monument occasionally took on a Dodge City flavor as male high school rivals arranged for their disputes to be physically resolved "after school at the Monument"—although I cannot recall a single resulting fight.

The Monument was as much a part of my six years at LAHS as the old gym, the auditorium, the hallways, the classrooms, and the locker rooms. During my infrequent returns to Lansdowne, I routinely visit it for purely nostalgic purposes, and I'm always glad I take time for the visit.

140

RANDOM REMEMBRANCES VII

Esther and J. T. were major advocates and enforcers of good manners with Bill and me. I suppose this emphasis was a combination of Quaker influence on Esther's side and J. T.'s naval academy background. "Yes, sir; yes, ma'am; no, sir; and no, ma'am" were expected of Bill and me within the household and elsewhere.

Profane language was not tolerated, and Esther and J. T. were exemplary models. The roughest words I ever heard from them were *damn* and *hell*. They didn't proselytize the point; they merely lived the example. Think about that: they never spoke the *s*-word or the *f*-word, and they never took the Lord's name in vain. I tried to live up to their example throughout my childhood and adolescence.

In late grade school, I recall a classmate challenging me because I never used foul language. I simply responded that I didn't have to. I still recall J. T.'s statement that resorting to it simply degrades your intelligence by displaying your lack of self-control and limited creativity with the English language.

During my upbringing, there were no automatic car washes. You washed your car in the driveway with a sponge, soap, and a bucket full of water drawn from the outside faucet. You dried the car with old towels saved for this purpose.

The Family Drive-In movie theater was not located in Lansdowne but in nearby, adjacent Clifton Heights. Surprisingly, I never attended a movie there in high school or college. Years later, I have no explanation as to why. My memory recalls that it was not a popular destination for my high school crowd. Perhaps this was because we thought ourselves more creative in our pursuit of romance. Perhaps we also feared that the common Family Drive-In reference might come true: "Go to the Family, make a family."

During my junior and senior high years, I frequently listened to the half-hour NBC national news show at 6:30 p.m. known as *The Huntley-Brinkley Report*. I became somewhat enamored with the news profession, and for several years I desired to follow my father into the newspaper-magazine industry or even to pursue television. I especially recall following the 1960s Civil Rights Movement with marked concern.

Very few of my high school classmates wore braces. Everyone had a regular dentist, but orthodontics as we know it today was in its infancy in the 1960s. The need was not yet there, nor was the money available in a community such as Lansdowne.

While the Phillies were definitely my favorite professional sports team as a youth, I was also an Eagles fan. I especially liked wide receiver Tommy McDonald, number "25." A conflict for me in 1960 was that I was also a long-time Packers fan years before they were the mega team of the 1960s. I was very torn in the 1960 championship game played between the Eagles and the Packers, a game the Eagles won, 17–13, at Franklin Field in Philadelphia. The Packers went on to shut out the New York Giants, 37–0, in the 1961 NFL championship game. This would be the first of five NFL championships won by the Packers during a seven-year span.

Billy Skinner and his father treated me to my only Eagles game at Franklin Field in the early 1960s, in which the Eagles defeated the Pittsburgh Steelers.

In the mid-1960s for approximately a year, we had two beagles. A male, Louisiana-bred beagle started hanging around Eloise. This duo became very attached, to the point where Spot (not our choice of name) refused to go home. We subsequently learned that Spot was owned by Steve Van Buren, the ex-Eagle NFL Hall of Famer who lived a long block from us up on Plumstead Avenue. Eloise had puppies at the time, and J. T. and Steve Van Buren cut a deal whereby Spot would be swapped for one of Eloise's puppies.

The Louisiana-bred beagles are different in stature and color from the Maryland variety, which was Eloise's background. Spot was taller and more long-legged, a very handsome pedigreed beagle. Esther said they were bred that way in order to hunt deer in the Louisiana swamps. Spot did not have a black saddle like Eloise, and his coat was primarily white with black and tan blotches.

Spot was only with us about a year, and then he disappeared. Esther's theory was that he got snatched by an admiring adult. Despite their bond and near inseparability, Eloise appeared unfazed by her partner's sudden absence.

For the record, J. T. and Bill were the true track athletes. J. T. set a naval academy high-jump record of six feet, two and seven-eighths inches during his senior year, with the record standing for over twenty years. Legend has it that he set the mark against Army, contributing toward Navy's victory against the Cadets in the 1934 meet. J. T. also ran hurdles and long-jumped.

Bill captained the track team at Franklin & Marshall his senior year, becoming F&M's all-time point scorer in track and field. Bill participated in five events: pole vault, low and high hurdles, the high jump, and the long jump.

Then there was me. I won only one event during my entire freshman track season at Wake Forest: a first-place finish in the hundred-yard dash in freezing rain against Virginia Tech in Blacksburg.

When you own a property and you wish to landscape and add trees, be careful. If you dare to select a ginkgo tree, make certain it is a male tree. My advice is fueled by teenage memories of collecting the fallen fruit from a female ginkgo tree that bordered our East Essex Avenue home. Ginkgo trees are an attractive, almost prehistoric species with fan-like leaves, but unfortunately its most distinctive feature may be the foul-smelling fruit that the female trees drop in mid-autumn. The putrid smell is so strong that any boots or shoes worn while collecting the fruit must be discarded.

J. T. experimented with numerous ineffective methods of collecting ginkgo fruits. He tried collecting them with a canvas tarp, but the tarp blocked the sun and killed the grass. He tried collecting with plastic covers, but the weighty mass of the ginkgo balls ripped the plastic. He tried to ignore the problem, but then the grass would certainly die.

The eventual solution was actually the original response: collecting the dropped balls by rake. Even with gentle raking, the grass took a beating. The crop was usually plentiful, and once the fruit was collected in a small pile, we raked it onto the blade of a snow shovel and carefully deposited it in a trash-bag-lined garbage can. A key here is that we were forced to use multiple cans because of the weight of the balls, since our trashman was not keen on heavily-loaded trash cans. Once this delightful process was completed, which always seemed to fall on a rainy and raw November Sunday, J. T. and I would remove our footwear on our small back porch. Esther supervised and ensured the ceremonial discarding of contaminated shoes or boots into a waiting trash can.

A wonderful aspect to life in Lansdowne in the 1950s and 1960s was the lack of crime. The borough (yes, Lansdowne was a borough, not a town) had a small professional police force that patrolled regularly. We knew many police officers by name. They were decent officers, and I can never recall being hassled by any of them as a youth. We were naturally not privy to police radio at the time, but assuredly the Lansdowne police had their share of calls for domestic issues. Home break-ins were rare, as were other major crimes. I cannot recall a single homicide, and I only know of one suicide.

An exception to this pattern was a time in sixth grade when a man occasionally exposed himself to school children from his car. These incidents occurred over several weeks, and school kids were alerted as to what to do if they had any encounter. The offender, known as "the man in the yellow shirt," was eventually arrested, prosecuted, convicted, and sentenced to prison.

While Lansdowne employed a professional police force, its fire response team was staffed by volunteers. Several LAHS students were heavily involved in volunteering at the fire station: Arnold Moore, Glenn Weiss, Paul Bailey, and LeRoy Wallace, to name a few. Despite its volunteer status, equipment was well-maintained, and the cadre of volunteers provided a good response. Lansdowne's one firehouse was inconveniently located in downtown Lansdowne on East Baltimore Pike.

I purchased a Wilson, Glenn Beckert-model baseball glove in the summer of 1962 at Rath's Sporting Goods in Drexel Hill. The cost was less than twenty dollars. That glove is now fifty-three years old, and it has been through the wars, including being lost and left out in the rain for forty-eight hours, fielding beautifully in dozens of adult softball games, protecting me during youth baseball batting practices, and defending me while in attendance at numerous major- and minor-league baseball stadiums. Ironically, close friend Jim Bower had the exact same model, and we spent innumerable hours playing catch in my front yard as high school students—Glenn Beckert to Glenn Beckert. My Glenn Beckert glove received some minor surgery two summers ago, but it is still in service as needed.

LAHS had several dances scheduled throughout the school year. There was the Harvest Moon Ball in autumn, complete with a Harvest Moon Ball queen and her court. The Sadie Hawkins turn-around dance was held in late winter. Freshman, sophomore, and junior classes had proms designated throughout the school year. All dances were held in the old gym, and I always pitied the decorating committees, because it was next to impossible to spruce up that drab and tired gymnasium.

The senior prom was a formal event held at a Philadelphia hotel and was the only dance held off-site.

Through his naval academy education and military service, J. T. had been trained in the use of firearms. He never discussed guns of any kind. He was never a hunter. He was never a gun owner. The only gun in our house was an old, inoperative shotgun that Grandpa Pitcher once used for rabbit hunting.

Main corridor stairways at LAHS were designated for "up" or "down" passage during class changes, and students were allowed three minutes to pass from one class to another. Stairwells at the ends of the high school were not so restricted.

In junior high school, a number of house parties, some of which I attended, got out of hand. Some basements were mildly trashed, food was thrown, toilets were clogged, etc., but it was nothing really serious. However, word spread quickly among the parents, and with the exception of birthday parties, teenage parties pretty much became taboo. Unfortunately, this moratorium continued well through high school.

Class rings were popular. Most LAHS seniors purchased them after being fitted for them during the spring of their junior year. They were a popular symbol exchanged between a boy and girl to indicate that the couple was going steady. Girls typically "waxed" their boyfriends' rings to reduce the ring size so they could wear them on their fingers.

The 1966 *Lahian* includes a supportive advertisement for Lansdowne Hardware, but I always referred to it as a five-and-dime. It was located at 24 North Lansdowne Avenue, and unlike many downtown Lansdowne business, it was a big store. The store anchored Lansdowne's downtown commercial district.

Entering Lansdowne Hardware was a major step back in time. The store had dark hardwood floors and inadequate overhead globe lighting. With just a few minor modifications, the store looked as it probably did twenty-thirty years earlier. The back of the store, which I rarely visited, was devoted to hardware, and I recall paint cans, tools, shovels, rakes, etc., in evidence. One part of the store included a sewing section, where cloth could be cut to the desired specifications. I was mainly concerned with the front of the store where candy, baseball cards, comic books, balsa airplanes, rubber balls, and school supplies were located.

Many items were not individually packaged or available on wall displays. Instead, items were available in flat display cases, separated by interlocking glass panels, allowing easy inspection and access by customers. Looking back now, the store was a shoplifter's delight because of the poor lighting, large space, and limited sales force.

The store also specialized in seasonal items for such events as the Fourth of July, Halloween, and Christmas.

These small-town hardware stores served as the forerunners of today's Walmart and Target stores.

141

J. T., PREJUDICE, AND UNCLE VINCE

J. T. was born in western Kentucky in 1910, only forty-five years after the end of the American Civil War. Kentucky fought for the Confederacy, and a great-grandfather on the Bingham-Drury side of the family soldiered for the South in the war. Many decades later, family folklore recalls that this distant relative proudly rode on horseback in Morganfield's annual Fourth of July parade dressed in full Confederate uniform. Were I to speculate, I think it likely that some of my ancestors on the Bingham-Drury side were slave owners, as farming was a major occupation within both families.

From 1882 to 1930, 118 lynchings were recorded in Kentucky, the majority of the victims being African-American men innocent of any crime. Lynchings required little, if any, justification or foundation during this despicable time in American history. In 1911, when J. T. was one year old, a notorious event known as "The Livermore Lynching" took place in Green County, Kentucky.

Such was the culture and history to which my father and his five siblings were exposed in the first decades of the twentieth century. Morganfield and Union County, Kentucky, were 90 percent white, and J. T. and his siblings assuredly attended segregated schools. Without question, J. T.'s home on Spaulding Street in Morganfield was in an all-white neighborhood. J. T.'s youthful employment at *The Union County Advocate* and a local coal mine may have exposed him to some black coworkers and possibly some customers at the newspaper, but his 1934 class at the US Naval Academy did not include one African-American midshipman.

One might think that J. T. carried much of the racial hatred and intolerance that surrounded him in his upbringing. Despite the fact that his mother and three older sisters were openly racist, J. T. was not. Even on the supposedly more liberal and accepting east coast, the *n*-word was typically used behind closed doors and within all-white company. However, to their total credit, I never heard any racial slurs mentioned by either J. T. or Esther.

When I visited Louisville, Kentucky, as a child, the word *nigger*—and eventually the supposedly less offensive *nigra*—was a common slur, frequently referenced by my female relatives, who were decidedly afraid of African-American men. To my limited recall, J. T. never openly challenged his mother and older sisters about such usage, but keep in mind that I was a child, and there was much adult conversation to which I was not privy.

I found this language in Louisville to be more objectionable and troublesome upon my graduation from high school, and during one brief summer visit to Louisville as a college student, I had had enough. I mustered up the courage and political correctness during an evening meal to clearly and respectfully state that I found their "*n*" references objectionable. I wanted them to stop.

Death-like silence followed. I departed the following day as scheduled, with the atmosphere at 1703 Bonnycastle Avenue decidedly chilly and reserved. When I returned home to Lansdowne, I explained the circumstances to J. T. He was accepting of my act, seemingly untroubled by any potential family rift, and appreciative that I had been tactful and respectful with my words.

J. T. set a memorable example for me regarding racial bias and prejudice. Where had the amazing twist to his position on racial issues come from? He was clearly not like his mother and sisters, but what had canceled and negated the hate? What events or people had redirected his mind and heart to reject the ignorant bigotry of his upbringing?

Sadly, I don't have an answer here. I never fully understood or grasped this realization until long after J. T.'s death in 1977. When racial violence was ripping the country apart in the early to mid-1960s, J. T. watched the television news coverage with keen interest, although he rarely commented, which was simply his style.

So, again, from where or whom did this enlightenment come? A key might be Uncle Vince. For years I had heard J. T. and his sisters fondly reference Uncle Vince, and I had mistakenly assumed that he was a family relative I had yet to meet. While I was in college, I learned that Uncle Vince was actually a black sharecropper who lived on a Drury family farm that my father frequently visited.

Uncle Vince and his wife were childless, but they smothered J. T. with love and attention as he was growing up. Maybe the strong connection was because J. T. needed a father and Uncle Vince and his wife needed a son. J. T. was highly impressionable during those early years, and he spent a lot of time with Uncle Vince and his wife at their small cabin. J. T.'s sister Connie remarked that a frequent scene was that of J. T. sitting on Uncle Vince's lap as the two rocked in Uncle Vince's rocking chair and sang songs together.

Kindly disregard that previous statement about not having the answer.

#83, Barry Drake, Head Coach Spafford,
Coach Cornman, and Coach Seaman

142

FAVORITE HIGH SCHOOL COACHES

It surprises me somewhat that all my favorite high school coaches were football coaches. I introduce them here in no particular order.

Ed Kolodgie

Ed Kolodgie was my ninth-grade football coach. Ninth grade was the first season in which I started on both offense and defense. Coach Kolodgie was a tough and knowledgeable coach who also coached high school JV baseball. He was short and stocky with a blond flattop. Somehow he had earned the moniker "Easy Ed," which absolutely did not reflect his personality. Coach Kolodgie was demanding and hard to please. When he got especially irritated and angry, he reversed his baseball hat and ordered the team to "take a lap."

Coach Kolodgie worked the roof at our home varsity games and was a good scout, relaying useful information down to the sidelines by phone. He taught business, and I never had him as a teacher. He was kind and responsive to me throughout high school, frequently greeting me with a smile and a "Hey, Bingham" in the hallways or locker room. Easy Ed frequently worked home basketball games and open houses, where he was a familiar figure storming the boys' locker room to catch any students foolish enough to smoke.

Coach Kolodgie and his family lived in Lansdowne on the corner of Berkley and Windermere Avenues adjacent to the Ardmore Avenue athletic field, so Coach Kolodgie was one of the few high school faculty members with whom I might have contact in the community outside of school.

Don Cornman

Coach Don Cornman was my physical education teacher in my latter years of elementary school. He too wore a flattop, and he eventually moved on to teach physical education at the high school. Coach Cornman was knowledgeable, friendly, levelheaded, respected, and not easily excitable. He also had a somewhat understated sense of humor and a warm, easy smile. He coached both the offensive and defensive backs, and he also coached baseball in the spring as the varsity head coach. Even if you screwed up big-time in practice or a game, Coach Cornman took the time to help you learn from your mistake. He treated all players with common decency and respect. He succeeded Ray Spafford at LAHS as head coach in the 1970s.

Ray Spafford

Coach Ray Spafford was my head coach for three years. He was a native Vermonter who played quarterback at West Chester State College in Pennsylvania. Coach Spafford had a deep knowledge of football, especially offensive football, and he knew well how to mold the offense to his liking. He was fond of me, and he routinely made fun of my inability to play defense.

Coach Spafford showed a lot of fire when we practiced poorly or underperformed, and he was not opposed to chewing out a player in practice or during a game, but he never crossed the line. His criticisms were always well intentioned, accurate, and needed. Like the other coaches, he simply wanted us to play to the best of our abilities. He could be overly dramatic at times in an effort to motivate us, and his admonitions to defeat Interboro at all costs were legendary. However, he also liked to joke and tease with players, and if he caught us in the hallway being overly friendly with a girlfriend, the needling went on for weeks.

After our epic victory against Chichester my senior year, he quietly took me aside after the game in the locker room to congratulate me on the best game he had ever seen me play. I know it was only high school, but that moment remains special with me.

Nort Seaman

Norton Seaman was a part-time coach for me. He was the line coach, and sometimes I ran drills with the linemen and sometimes with the receivers under my position coach, Tom Jenkins. Coach Seaman was the real deal. He was an accomplished high school football player from central Pennsylvania who had earned second-team all-state honors in Pennsylvania, playing several different positions. He was also a starting lineman and placekicker at the University of Pittsburgh where he played with NFL Hall of Famer Mike Ditka in the late 1950s. What was especially notable about Coach Seaman was his humility, as he never mentioned where he went to college, the Mike Ditka connection, and so on.

Interestingly, Coach Seaman was Indian and had been raised in that country until age eleven, at which time he and his family moved to central Pennsylvania. He had no discernible accent. We knew nothing of his ethnic heritage, nor would it have mattered if we did.

Coach Seaman was one of the more memorable adults I encountered during my adolescence. I never had him as a teacher, as he taught elementary physical education, but he made a major mark upon me—more as an individual than as a coach. He certainly knew his football, no doubt about that, but I learned so much more from him about how one should interact with and treat people, and especially how adults in authoritative positions should relate to youth. He was a superb model for anyone who might wish to teach, coach, or work with adolescents.

I observed him closely at practices and marveled at how easily he interacted with not only his position players but all players on the team. I always wanted to hear what he had to say, regardless of the situation. When we screwed up, he let us know it, but not in a demoralizing or insulting manner. He might call you a knucklehead, but he got his point across in a supportive, "you're better than that" style. By the way, I attribute my use of the term *knucklehead* toward small children to Coach Seaman.

Coach Seaman was an active, attentive listener. He genuinely wanted to know what we had to say. When we talked with him, he shut out the world and gave us his undivided attention. He frequently injected humor into his coaching efforts. He handed out a lot of nicknames. He called me Les Bingaman after a famous Chicago Bears lineman. His easygoing personal style made him extremely popular with players, who grew fiercely loyal to him.

By example, Coach Seaman taught me the value of dignity and respect. He taught me the value of really listening to people and giving a damn about their circumstances. And he also demonstrated that it was okay to inject levity into situations as a way to help motivate.

When I return periodically to Philadelphia, I try to meet up with Coach Seaman for a cheese steak. He is well into his seventies. He has long since retired from teaching, school administration, and coaching, and he lives in Glen Mills, Pennsylvania.

I doubt that Nort Seaman can fathom the phenomenal impact that he had on the lives of so many children and adolescents during his teaching, coaching, and administrative career. In his humble way, he would downplay his significance and quietly deflect his value. What is true and certain is that he remains an inspiration, a mentor, an example, a hero, and a forever bright light in my life. If anyone ever got it right, it was Nort Seaman.

143

FUNERALS

Vincent B. Fuller, J. T.'s boss for close to twenty years, saw his network of printing/graphic arts businesses expand greatly during my father's years as general manager.

Fuller plants were located in downtown Philadelphia, Havertown, Radnor, Broomall, and Bethlehem, Pennsylvania. Payroll expanded to several hundred employees in the early 1970s, and I credit my hard-working father, as much as anyone, for the company's expansion and success. I think Vince Fuller agreed with that opinion as well.

Some of the roles usually assumed by a company's owner fell intentionally to my father. J. T. signed hundreds of weekly payroll checks every Thursday night while seated in the living room in his worn, olive-green armchair at the portable card table. Vince Fuller did not believe in signature stamps, but he also did not want to be bothered by the annoying, repetitive task of signing payroll every Thursday. Another assignment frequently delegated to J.T. was attending funerals of current or past employees and their family members, especially if they lived in Philadelphia or nearby suburbs.

J. T. wasn't averse to this duty, but he was not particularly enthusiastic about the role either, especially upon arriving home after 6:00 p.m. and a hard day's work. It meant freshening up immediately upon arriving home, skipping dinner, and driving directly to the funeral home for the evening visitation. However, J. T. understood the value and importance of employers paying their respects in response to these sad events.

I don't recall precisely how my accompanying J. T. on these funeral visits first evolved, but I joined him on a dozen or so of these excursions. It possibly could have been at his suggestion "to take a ride," but more than likely it was because I was not overwhelmed by homework or a summertime commitment, and I had available time on my hands. It was an odd and unique way for a father and teenage son to be together. Sometimes I would do homework on the rides to and from the funeral homes, and sometimes not.

Upon my asking, or his volunteering, J. T. would comment about the departed and identify him or her as a current or past Fuller employee. We also talked about a variety of other topics, but I never viewed this as deliberate father-son "check in" time on his part. J. T. was never a great conversationalist with me. I always sensed that these occasional bites of time were somewhat awkward for him, so I usually guided the talks to more familiar and comfortable topics: his job, his college days at Annapolis (always safe and well-received turf), and his early naval career. Until much later in life, J. T. was not at ease in discussing his childhood. He was also never comfortable in detailing his experiences at sea during World War II, a response so common to servicemen of his generation.

When we arrived at the funeral home, I remained in the car, or J. T. flipped me a dollar or two to grab something to eat if there was a fast-food restaurant in the area. More typically, I stayed in the car and completed homework, read, listened to the radio, or ate a sandwich.

J. T. never stayed more than fifteen to twenty minutes. He paid his respects and quickly left. Regarding this role, he did impart one significant pearl of wisdom, which I have never forgotten. He told me on more than one occasion that family members, the majority of whom he had never met, were more comforted by his taking the time to pay respects than they were by any verbal condolences. The grieving family valued and remembered "presence" rather than the content or quality of spoken word.

During my professional career, I attended several hundred funerals that were job-related. I learned this sensitivity as much from J. T. as anyone. An irony to this topic is the fact that, to this day, I remember that my boss at the time, Paul Gesregan, attended J. T.'s funeral in December 1977 in Drexel Hill. Even though I was a relatively new employee, Paul and some of his administrative staff took almost half a workday to convey their condolences in person during visitation held at the funeral home. I will forever remember such kindness.

Again, it was more about presence than spoken word.

144

GEORGE IGNATIUS DRURY

George Ignatius Drury was J. T.'s cousin on his mother's side. These cousins, both born in 1910, were in some ways more brothers than cousins. George Ignatius, more commonly known as "Snats" by family and friends, was unquestionably my favorite Bingham relative and one of the more memorable people I have ever met. To say that "Uncle Snats" was a character is doing him a disservice.

J. T. and Snats (source of the nickname is unknown) grew up together but under very different circumstances. They both graduated from Morganfield High School in 1928, with Uncle Snats being the class valedictorian of a small graduating class. They were also teammates on the Morganfield High School basketball squad.

The Drury side of the Bingham family produced several lawyers, including Uncle Snats's father, George Lucien Drury, and his uncle, William Drury. This side was also active in local and state politics. Uncle Snats attended the University of Kentucky for his undergraduate degree, and he subsequently graduated from Catholic University in Washington, DC, with a law degree. An irony here is that despite earning a law degree, Uncle Snats never actively practiced law. He likened himself as more of a gentleman farmer and investor.

Outside of college and law school, Uncle Snats never left Morganfield. He married a local woman, Bertha Ann Greenwell, and fathered four children: Peggy Jo, George, Julia (Judy), and Mary Dee.

Uncle Snats owned over four hundred acres of prime farmland in northern Union County. He primarily produced popcorn and raised beef cattle. Just as important, he also owned mineral rights to the land, which was rich in oil. His property was dotted with active oil well pumpers, which continually produced oil.

I got to know Uncle Snats through summer visits to Morganfield while I was in junior and senior high school and even in college. His daughter Judy and I were the same age and remained in contact until Judy's untimely death in 1984.

For some reason, Uncle Snats took a major liking to me, and whenever we visited Morganfield, he made it a priority to show me the town and his farm properties.

The stories abound. Here are just a few of them.

Peek Brothers Bar-Be-Que was one of Uncle Snats's favorite restaurants. On one of my visits as a young teenager, he took me to Peek's in nearby Waverly and purposely bought me a "hot" barbeque plate. He also requested a pitcher of ice water, which he set in the middle of the table. He quietly sat there grinning and chewing on his cigar while I sampled the barbeque. As my mouth caught on fire, Uncle Snats poured me a glass of ice water and chuckled, knowing that the water would only make things worse.

I had never smelled oil wells up close, and their odor is plain nasty. While touring one of Uncle Snats's farms, I commented with something like "Boy, do those oil wells stink," to which he responded, "Yeah, but they stink dollars and cents to me."

Uncle Snats drove a white Thunderbird convertible, and on one trip he allowed me to drive his car—even as a newly licensed driver—to and from his farms. At one point when we were leaving one of his properties and approaching a county highway, I slowed down to honor the stop sign. He loudly protested and directed me to drive through the stop sign. Once on the county blacktop, I angrily challenged him: "Why'd you make me do that? I could have gotten a ticket." His smart response was, "I just got the car washed. I didn't want the dust to settle on it."

Uncle Snats routinely drove the wrong way down a one-way street in Morganfield so that he could better access a mailbox at the post office from the driver's side of the car.

Uncle Snats allowed a disabled World War II veteran and high school classmate, Peanuts Brown, to permanently keep his trailer on Drury-owned land that bordered the Ohio River. One of Peanuts's means of support was "jugging for cats" in the Ohio. The catfish he caught were then sold to local restaurants. Peanuts lived on the property rent-free. Uncle Snats's only requirement was that Peanuts produce two catfish a week for Drury Sunday dinner.

Uncle Snats routinely parked his car on the site of the old Morganfield High School beginning at 11:55 a.m., Monday through Friday. This site was one of the higher elevations in the county and thus allowed Uncle Snats the best radio reception for the noon stock report.

As a middle-aged man, Uncle Snats underwent a colostomy. He hated the inconvenience and embarrassment of his medical condition, and when the colostomy bag gurgled, he would loudly pound the site and scold it: "God damn bag … God damn bag!" He would provide this animated response anywhere, including the dining room table.

We visited Morganfield during the summer when the television program *The Fugitive* was reaching its eventful conclusion. My cousin Judy, her boyfriend, and I decided to stay home to watch the final episode. Uncle Snats did not understand our interest and gruffly left for a favorite haunt, the city's pool hall. Approximately forty-five minutes later, he returned in a huff. "Say, what the hell is this *Fugitive* shit all about? The pool hall's deserted. Everyone went home to watch this *Fugitive* shit." Now interested in the show, he watched the final episode, constantly interrupting the dialogue so as to get up to speed on the main characters and story line.

Uncle Snats was a gambler, especially of college football. His daughter Judy was married in Itasca, Illinois, in the fall of 1980. My wife, infant son, and I attended the wedding and reception held at a local resort. Aunt Bertha Ann instructed me to look after Uncle Snats and keep an eye on him at the reception, as she knew he had major money placed on several college football games. As the traditional father-daughter dance approached, Uncle Snats could not be found, and Bertha Ann implored me to find him. I discovered that Uncle Snats was not in his hotel room but had moved down the hall because of the poor TV reception in his original room. When I found him, he was lying somewhat dejectedly on the bed with his tuxedo tie and pants loosened, watching college football, paying close attention to the game score updates running at the bottom of the screen. I mildly reprimanded him and pressed him to reassemble his tuxedo and return to the reception hall for his dance with Judy. On the return walk to the reception hall, he repeatedly mumbled, "God damn Syracuse ... God damn Syracuse. Those assholes cost me two hundred dollars ... two hundred dollars!"

Uncle Snats died in 1982. My last direct contact with him was in 1980 at Judy's wedding.

145

MARRA'S

Marra's Restaurant and Pizzeria was located at 313 Baltimore Pike in Springfield in the general vicinity of Playtown Park, a local amusement park, and in proximity to the original Charlie's Hamburgers. It was about a fifteen-minute ride from Lansdowne, depending on the traffic through congested Clifton Heights where Baltimore Pike (US 1) ran only two lanes. It was a recurrent gathering point on weekends for high school students from any number of suburban schools. While this type of restaurant is now taken for granted, it was in its infancy in the 1960s. At the time, Marra's had little local competition.

Marra's was a good-sized, sit-down restaurant with era décor right out of *Ozzie and Harriett* or *Leave It to Beaver.* When our crowd frequented the place, we always ordered pizza and soft drinks. Either the guys attended as a group, or we would take dates. The pizza was very good, and with several of us splitting the cost, no one got gouged financially. I now feel sorry for the waitresses, since we were not known as gracious tippers. I also recall a memorable waitress whom we lovingly referred to as "the Bulldog," Harry Gicking's favorite.

My memory suggests that we seemed to patronize Marra's more frequently during football season, especially in our senior year when we went undefeated. My teammates and I all wore our letter jackets on these junkets, and it was a glorious feeling to saunter into Marra's with your best girl by your side in full view of your suburban rivals.

Long since demolished, I still look for Marra's on Baltimore Pike during infrequent returns home. Marra's Restaurant and Pizzeria surely deserved a better fate.

146

THE LAWRENCE WELK SHOW

Without any question, without any doubt, *The Lawrence Welk Show* was J. T.'s favorite television program. It first aired on ABC in 1955 and ran until 1982 when it went into syndication. There were 1,065 episodes in all, and I'll bet J. T. saw the majority of them. J. T. was hooked from the original broadcasts in 1955 as a middle-aged groupie. Esther liked the show as well, but J. T. faithfully watched the show without fail—typically on Saturday evenings—until his death in 1977. Reruns of the show continue to be aired on PBS to this day, a tribute to the show's ongoing popularity.

The Lawrence Welk Show was the first television show *ever* where I was allowed, if not directed, to pivot our black-and-white console TV around for viewing from the dinner table.

J. T. was not alone in his adoration. *The Lawrence Welk Show*, which attracted a large and loyal television following and high ratings, was a one-hour musical variety show that featured the Lawrence Welk orchestra and a permanent cast of attractive male and female singers, many of whom also danced. Sometimes members of the band would also perform as singers. Welk often referred to his musicians and singers as his "musical family." During musical numbers, audience members were allowed to dance on a studio dance floor. Welk would frequently dance with female audience members during at least one song in the show, hamming it up for the TV camera and loving every minute of it.

The show's theme song was "Bubbles in the Wine," which became an iconic, easily identified American instrumental. The weekly show usually had a patriotic, seasonal, or holiday theme and was very conservative in content. Welk, a native North Dakotan, was a veteran accordionist and big band leader prior to the show's first airing. He was of German descent, and he still carried a mild German accent. His introduction of musical numbers was awkward and even comical at times because of his frequent mispronunciations. Regardless, the show was directed toward the World War II generation and was highly successful, having a monumental twenty-seven-year run.

The Welk musicians and singers performed classics from the big band era and the first half of the twentieth century. Welk particularly like contemporary composers like Hoagy Carmichael and Cole Porter. Popular Broadway numbers were also performed. Welk's audience was clearly older white Americans, and the presentation of his musical selections was always safe and squeaky clean. He eventually even allowed some country and pop music to be performed, as long as it was done in his champagne style. Welk even had a popular instrumental, *Calcutta*, released on AM radio in 1960.

Most members of the "musical family" had specific, well-defined roles and were bound by a strict set of professional ethics dictated by Welk. One of the more prominent positions within the cast was the "champagne lady," who typically sang a ballad or religious solo number near the end of the broadcast. I recall only two champaign ladies: Alice Lon and Norma Zimmer.

J. T. had several favorites over the years: the Lennon Sisters (America literally watched them grow up before their eyes on television), deep-voiced Larry Hooper, accordionist Myron Floren, violinist and singer Aladdin, singer/dancer Bobby Burgess (an original Walt Disney

Mouseketeer), and Jimmy Roberts, who hailed from western Kentucky like J. T.

During my teen years, I was usually readying for a Saturday night date while J. T. watched *Lawrence Welk* from his olive-green armchair in our small living room. So many times I recall J. T. bellowing, "Esther, Esther … *Lawrence Welk* is on." For all practical purposes the house could have been on fire at the time, or I could have been carrying a case of beer out the front door; J. T. would not have noticed or cared. He was that focused; he was that happy.

When I occasionally stumble across a *Lawrence Welk* rerun on PBS, I usually watch the show for a few minutes out of respect and warmly think of J. T., knowing that he likely saw the same episode.

Good for J. T.

147

THE NAYLOR'S RUN TROLLEY TRESTLE

Two Red Arrow trolley routes (Sharon Hill and Media) run through Drexel Hill just north of Lansdowne along Garrett Road. They split further west in Drexel Hill from their common trackage. This line was a good half mile or more from my home on Essex Avenue. As these trolleys left a neighborhood known as Beverly Hills, they traversed a long trestle that was constructed to cross a shallow creek known as Naylor's Run. The creek was only a few feet wide, but the trestle was considerable in height and length, as it had to span the creek and an infrequently used railroad spur and a narrow road.

Despite my Essex Avenue neighborhood's distance from this trestle, I could frequently hear trolleys for a few short seconds as they clickety-clacked across this long stretch of elevated trestle track. The sound was even more evident at my previous home on Marshall Road. Certainly the wind and other variables had to be correct, as they frequently were, and this distant calling was always a welcomed distraction to me.

To my dismay, we rarely, if ever, heard train whistles where we lived, but the Red Arrow trolley rumblings over the Naylor's Run trestle warmly echo for me even now. So many times it served as a backdrop as I dragged my hot and sticky self home after summer-evening touch-football games on the hockey field, or as I deposited a letter at the

Highland Avenue mail box, or as I walked a date to my house after an open house. That sound could sometimes be heard as frequently as every five to ten minutes.

For some odd reason, certain sounds and effects penetrate us more than we initially recognize. We may not know it at the time, but they are part of the molding process that composes our formative years. I always turn a soft smile when I think of that distant clickety-clack and the hundreds of times that it called to me, most poignantly on hot summer evenings, always issuing comfort and reassurance without my asking.

Even now, that distant sound causes me to think about what I was doing on those long-ago occasions and perhaps about who accompanied me. The sound instantly transports me to simpler and better days. Upon my rare returns to Lansdowne, I always hope to hear its greeting—its sweet, haunting sound as I slowly walk familiar streets to reconnect with an earlier life.

148

SUMMER SCHOOL

In some local school districts at the time, summer school was reserved for struggling students who had failed courses during the main school year. Possibly Lansdowne-Aldan's system was not unique, but it also offered courses to assist students in taking intensive six-week specialty courses or a major course scheduled for the upcoming school year.

At my parents' encouragement, I took a typing course in junior high, and American History prior to my junior year. I should have taken biology the summer prior to my sophomore year as well, but I missed the registration date. Big mistake.

Our typing course was taught by a student teacher from Temple University. Casting absolutely no blame whatsoever on our instructor, I was a poor typist. I struggled. I was slow. I made lots of mistakes. My fingers didn't work very well under pressure. I improved little during the course and probably maxed out at thirty words per minute with no mistakes. On the contrary, classmate Beth Dunkle was a whiz and easily doubled, possibly even tripled, my output per minute.

Despite being a disappointing student, I greatly benefited from the course, as I typed assorted class notes and all assigned papers in high school and college from that point onward. Who can ever forget home row? "A-S-D-F … J-K-L-; now repeat."

I took American History between my sophomore and junior years. American History class proved to be the total opposite of typing class. Regina Stretch was our instructor. She was a respected veteran teacher of LAHS social studies/history who made the course both informative and fun. Class was held in a first-floor, non–air-conditioned high school classroom at LAHS for six weeks from approximately 8:00 a.m. to noon, with a midmorning fifteen-minute break. From my limited recall, some of my classmates included Mary Ann Vella, Jo Ellen Franz, Barbara Miller, Jack Nalbandian, Alex Deveney, and Beth Dunkle. Taking the course greatly relaxed academic requirements for me during my junior year.

I experienced an eventful eighth-grade math class with Grace Straley, a mainstay of the LAHS mathematics faculty and somewhat of a legend with students. Miss Straley was also a family friend, having taught my older brother with far different results. Even though I struggled with course content, which included after-school tutoring and frequent homework sessions with my father, I received an legitimate B in the course at year's end.

Despite my grade, my parents accurately sensed that my confidence had been rattled, and they thought it wise for me to enroll in a remedial class during summer school. I did enroll in the summer of 1961, and this time I aced the course, which was no surprise or distinguished accomplishment. My fellow classmates in this summer school course had all failed eighth-grade math the previous school year, and they often asked me, "What are you doing here?" However, this bold experiment did little for my confidence, and I continued to struggle with math even more in tenth and eleventh grades, as geometry and algebra were offered.

149

VINCENT B. FULLER

Vincent B. Fuller was J. T.'s boss for almost twenty years, starting in 1956. Mr. Fuller was a native of Otego, New York, a town of one thousand people located on the Susquehanna River about thirty miles northeast of Binghamton. Having learned the printing trade well as a young man, and with J. T.'s careful and pragmatic direction, Vince Fuller developed a printing network of half a dozen plants in the Philadelphia area.

I have no knowledge of how Mr. Fuller found his way to suburban Philadelphia, but the first plant he owned and operated was in Havertown, the same suburb in which he lived with his wife, Gladys. When J. T. joined the organization, the small Havertown plant was in operation, as was the much larger plant in Philadelphia at which J. T. worked in center city Philadelphia for almost a dozen years.

Vince Fuller was a short, stout man with thinning gray hair and rosy cheeks. He wore dark-rimmed glasses, and while he was not physically imposing, he was a tough and demanding employer. While I learned much from my father about managing employees, I learned a lot from Vince Fuller too, much of it firsthand.

Fuller Typesetting, as the parent company was known, was a diverse graphic arts company whose bread and butter was typesetting—not the actual printing—of a number of magazines. The most profitable account the Fuller company held was setting all the type for the dozens of east-coast editions of *TV Guide*, a popular weekly publication that came out long before the days of cable television. Fuller built a plant near the Radnor offices of *TV Guide* in the late '50s to accommodate this huge volume. Fuller plants also printed greeting cards for Norcross, another big account.

While Vince Fuller was sole owner of the company, he did not run it. That job was entrusted to J. T., who gave his heart and soul to the company and consulted with "Vince" as needed. There existed an admirable trust factor between these two men, which I respect to this day.

Fuller Typesetting was a non-union shop at a time in Philadelphia when most graphic arts companies were unionized. Mr. Fuller maintained a very simple philosophy as an employer: if you treated employees fairly and paid them a competitive wage, there was no need for a union. Understand that Mr. Fuller worked his people hard, but they were well compensated and well treated.

In 1966 I worked a summer job at the Radnor plant, running copy back and forth to the Radnor *TV Guide* plant, melting pig iron, crushing cardboard, sweeping floors, collecting trash, cleaning bathrooms, stacking paper, assisting pressmen with repairs, packing and loading skids onto trucks, etc. While Mr. Fuller was visiting the Radnor plant one morning, a call came in from Norcross in north Jersey that a recent job needed to be reprinted. The order had not been properly banded on the skid, and hundreds of sheets of cards had been tossed all over the tractor trailer and ruined. Mr. Fuller was furious, and he went on a mission to determine the employee at fault. Only three employees banded skids, and I was one of them. However, on the date of shipment,

I had been doing other duties. I witnessed Mr. Fuller fire a nineteen-year-old employee firsthand, and it wasn't pretty.

Yes, he was hard-nosed and demanding (a frequent catchphrase from Mr. Fuller was "What the hell?"), but Vince Fuller had a marked humane side as well. There were several instances where he extended medical leave, paid excessive medical bills, helped pay an overdue mortgage, and even advanced paychecks. He would inform employees of his assistance in private, with the instruction that they were not to mention his response to anyone. Oh, and if any bills were paid or money extended, Mr. Fuller did not wish to be repaid. That was the way he wanted it.

The greatest example of Vince Fuller's generosity came one year as Christmas fast approached. While attending a Christmas party at the Radnor plant on December 23, an employee's car trunk was broken into, and all the family Christmas gifts were stolen. The theft was not discovered until late Christmas Eve. Somehow, word got to Mr. Fuller, who, on Christmas Eve, contacted a family acquaintance who happened to be a manager at Kiddee City, the major toy store in the area. J. T. met with the affected employee and the store manager at Kiddee City around 2:00 on Christmas morning in order for the employee to select Christmas toys for his children. Mr. Fuller also instructed J. T. to write checks for one hundred dollars to both the employee and his wife. The store manager was also compensated for his efforts.

The lesson learned here was to treat employees fairly and pay them a decent wage. This workplace philosophy produced loyal and hard-working employees.

150

THE ARMY-NAVY GAME

While my father was not big on attending collegiate or professional sporting events, the Army-Navy football game, traditionally played in Philadelphia because of the city's proximity to Annapolis and West Point, was an annual exception. During my youth, the Army-Navy game was always played on a Saturday afternoon in late November or early December at Memorial Stadium (later named John F. Kennedy Stadium) in South Philadelphia. I eagerly attended games with my father from early grade school through my senior year of high school. We would always sit in a reserved section with classmates of his naval academy class of 1934. On a few occasions, Esther attended, as did Bill.

Cold, uninspired Memorial Stadium held more than one hundred thousand spectators, and in those days, both Army and Navy fielded highly competitive teams that could hold their own against the country's best college teams. The weather was usually cold, with rain and/or snow occurring on occasion, but the hard wooden bleacher seats made it seem even colder. Poor weather deterred or discouraged no one, because this was Army-Navy.

The pageantry began well prior to game time, with the pregame march-on and formation of the West Point cadets and the midshipmen from Annapolis on the Memorial Stadium turf. This tradition lasted about an hour, and regardless of one's political persuasion, the solemn, dignified procession always impressed and reassured.

I was fortunate to see several all-Americans and three Heisman Trophy winners at play—Pete Dawkins from Army, and Joe Bellino and Roger Staubach for Navy—during my years of attendance. To this day, I still regard Roger Staubach's play as a sophomore quarterback during the 1962 Army-Navy game as the best individual performance I've ever witnessed at a college football game. "Roger the Dodger," as he was known, frustrated Army all afternoon with his scrambling, passing, and open field runs. Staubach was totally unstoppable that day.

J. T. and I would drive to the stadium a few hours prior to the kickoff in order to witness the march-on. We would typically park on the Philadelphia naval base's golf course and then make our way to the stadium less than a mile away. Our early arrival gave J. T. ample opportunity to reconnect with his classmates. He naturally introduced me to his Annapolis buddies, and this pregame socializing was highly anticipated by my father. While the liquor surely helped, I cannot recall an event outside of the family where J. T. appeared more animated and alive.

I fondly recall a time pregame when I met J. T.'s Annapolis buddy, Fred "Buzz" Borries, a fellow Kentuckian who starred at halfback for Navy in the early '30s. Borries was eventually elected to the College Football Hall of Fame and was best known for his touchdown run against Notre Dame in 1933, which secured a rare Navy victory over the Irish. That meeting remains very special to me. Buzz Borries proved to be an accomplished naval aviator during World War II, and he may have served with J. T. on escort aircraft carriers in the South Pacific.

Navy won most of the games I attended, which suited J. T. just fine, since Navy did not win a single game against Army during his four years as a midshipman. The rivalry between these two schools is like nothing in college football, and it exists all year long. The enthusiasm is deeply embedded in both academies, because a victory against the archrival relaxes military and disciplinary demands for the winning school and establishes bragging rights for an entire year. Military service interest in the game is far-reaching, with the game being broadcast around the world to foreign military bases, ships at sea, etc. During my years of attendance at the Army-Navy game, the president of the United States frequently attended the game, and as tradition dictated, the Commander in Chief sat for one half on the Army side and the other half on the Navy side so as not to show preference.

The head coach during Navy's highly successful days in the early '60s was Wayne Hardin. Hardin was an innovator, and he enjoyed adding twists and wrinkles to confuse his opponents. On one occasion, Navy had "Beat Army" printed on their jerseys in Chinese, a reference to Army's head coach, Paul Dietzel, who had developed a "Chinese Bandits" defensive scheme when he was head coach at LSU.

Hardin's craziest scam ever involved Navy's eligible receivers wearing fluorescent pink/orange helmets during the 1961 Army-Navy game. The Navy players wearing these helmets were eligible receivers, and Hardin wanted them to be easily identified, since both Army and Navy wore gold helmets. I believe this tactic, while allowed for that game, may have prompted an NCAA rules change disallowing the practice.

I only saw my father under the influence of alcohol once in my life, and it was at the 1964 Army-Navy game. Knowing that he had no business driving home, he wisely flung the car keys to me after the game's conclusion and stated that I was to drive home. Most probably, it was no big deal, but I had only had my license for a few weeks, and the traffic leaving the stadium area was brutal, with demanding Philadelphia traffic cops impatiently gesturing directions. Somehow we survived the frenzied maze of traffic and my first drive over a major bridge, the Penrose Avenue Bridge, which led us to Island Avenue and eventually into Colwyn, Yeadon, and then on to Lansdowne.

An artifact associated with the Army-Navy game was a massive game program that cost several dollars. I would devour that program during the weeks following the game, reading every single page and learning as much about the players, coaches, traditions, and the game's unique history as possible.

My bucket list includes at least one more Army-Navy game in Philadelphia. I believe I owe that courtesy to J. T.

Go Navy—beat Army!

151

FAVORITE JUNIOR AND SENIOR HIGH SCHOOL TEACHERS

Rodney A. Sell

Rodney Sell was a University of Pennsylvania graduate who likely came from old-school money. He taught sophomore English. Mr. Sell was exceptionally well dressed, wearing expensive suits and handsome ties. He was well coiffed and shaved at least twice daily, as a familiar site midday was "Rodney" briskly walking down the hallway carrying his shaving kit.

Mr. Sell was bright, articulate, very prim and proper, handsome, and extremely passionate and knowledgeable about British and American literature. He was also private, and my sense is that he was not well integrated with fellow faculty, most likely because of his background. I never recall him working open houses or athletic events to earn extra money, as he probably did not have the need or the interest.

Mr. Sell was a solid instructor in grammar and construction. However, he excelled when discussing literature and assigned novels. I recall his love of Thomas Hardy's description of characters as displayed in *The Mayor of Casterbridge.* He was not impressed with my insistence that Mr. Hardy "get to the point." Mr. Sell's significant impact on me was in the way he analyzed plot and characters, and how he detailed written construction and technique. I view him now as more suited to teaching literature as a university instructor rather than at the high school level, since so much of his subject knowledge was lost on us.

Mr. Sell called all of his students by their last name: Mr. Bingham, Mr. Bower, Miss Spencer, etc., throughout the school year. I liked him, and he liked me. I frequently stayed after class when he had time to follow up on class discussion. Marjorie Spencer was another class favorite of his. Not that "Rodney" was an easy teacher, but I aced all four marking periods, primarily because he motivated me to do well in his class.

I do know this: he was my favorite teacher in six years of junior and senior high school. He definitely made an impact, especially on my formal reading practices as an adult.

Horace Laubach

Horace Laubach was my ninth-grade English teacher. He was middle-aged and very distinguished looking, always wearing a suit. He graduated from Middlebury College in Vermont.

The first day of his class was legendary. Mr. Laubach would randomly select a student and ask his or her name. His follow-up was, "How do you know?" After a standard response, such as "My parents told me so" or "It's on my birth certificate," he would follow up further with "How do you know? Do you believe everything people say to you or that you read?" And the race was on. The selected student felt some mild pressure, but Mr. Laubach used this creative icebreaker as a nontraditional way to launch the school year.

There were rumors that Mr. Laubach suffered shell shock in World War II and that he was particularly jumpy and on edge. I never saw evidence of this, despite some quasi-delinquent classmates deliberately creating challenges in class for him during the early weeks of school.

I remember Horace Laubach as approachable, dignified, and polite: a true gentleman and excellent role model. He was attentive toward students and always treated us with dignity and respect. It is telling to me that I recall little about his teaching prowess and style. What I remember best were his personality characteristics and how he treated students.

Mr. Laubach was not married. He lived with his mother on West Greenwood or Essex Avenue in Lansdowne. I know this because Billy Skinner and I often shoveled his sidewalk in the winter, and he always tipped us a dollar over our price. Funny how you remember simple acts of kindness.

Regina Stretch

One of my wisest decisions as a high school student was taking American History in summer school between my sophomore and junior years. The class met daily from about 8:00 a.m. to noon at LAHS for six to seven weeks. The class size was small, about fifteen students. I had no close friends in the class, although I naturally knew everyone because of LAHS's small size and limited enrollment. Regina Stretch was our instructor.

Summer school was a grind, and Ms. Stretch knew it. Not only did we attend class for three-plus hours daily, but we had daily reading assignments, and tests and quizzes were frequent. We were also assigned a major paper or oral presentation on a topic of our choice as approved by Ms. Stretch. I chose the infamous Confederate prisoner-of-war camp, Andersonville.

Teaching an intense, all-morning-long high school class during summer recess was a challenge. Ms. Stretch well understood the situation, and she made the class enjoyable and entertaining. She was also gracious about allowing a fifteen-minute break. Fellow classmates Jack Nalbandian and Alex Deveney and I took full advantage by running to and from the Jew Store four blocks away for a midmorning infusion of soda, candy, and/or Tastykakes.

I especially recall Ms. Stretch's support of my Andersonville paper/presentation. On several occasions, I spent afternoons at the Philadelphia Library reading, researching, and using a new coin-operated device (I used up a lot of dimes) known as a copying machine to duplicate photos and text. J. T. took an interest in the project as well. While I was naturally assigned major class papers to write in college and grad school, "Andersonville" was my first legitimate exposure to researching a topic in depth at the high school level. I did not stop at the Philadelphia Library, but based upon leads gathered there, I sent letters to historical societies and organizations to gather even more information. My enthusiasm for the project was significantly fueled by Ms. Stretch, with whom I frequently consulted as I gathered new materials.

We all need teachers who believe in us. Part of my drive and enthusiasm was linked to Ms. Stretch's interest and encouragement, although she probably thought me a bit possessed as well. I aced the paper and the course.

Raymond E. Spafford

Long before Ray Spafford served as my high school varsity football coach, I knew him as my seventh- and eighth-grade homeroom teacher (room 73) and eighth-grade American history teacher. Mr. Spafford was a fun teacher. Class was never boring or dull. He had a warm and comfortable style in dealing with students, although he also knew when to be hard and firm.

The only time I ever saw him tense was prior to a Lansdowne-Aldan–Radnor football game that had been postponed from the previous weekend to Monday afternoon because of inclement weather. He was a mess that morning.

One of our eighth-grade assignments was to memorize the "Gettysburg Address," which was a major challenge to me, but I survived. Much of eighth-grade American history was devoted to geography and maps and rivers and state capitols, so I was well within my comfort zone. Getting an A was easy for me, since I held such a strong interest in the subject material. My hand was always shooting up in class, probably to the point where I was an irritant.

I recall one test where we had to write out all fifty states and their state capitals. I received a 99 percent on the test because I spelled Connecticut incorrectly. (I used two t's at the end.) Mr. Spafford asked me to stay after class to discuss my test grade. As opposed to complimenting me, the native New Englander put his arm around my shoulder and, with a grin, pointed to my misspelled version of Connecticut and whispered softly, "What is wrong with you?"

152

THE 1964 PHILADELPHIA PHILLIES

Baseball was the major professional sport that I best followed as a youth. The Phillies, bar none, were my favorite team, with the Chicago Cubs a distant second. (I had already fallen in love with Wrigley Field via black-and-white television broadcasts of "The Friendly Confines.") The Phillies record from the mid-1950s to the early '60s was extremely poor, but in 1962 and 1963, the Phillies gained some overdue legitimacy and respectability within the baseball world. John Quinn served as general manager, and in that capacity, he hired Gene Mauch, a feisty, hardnosed, and aggressive field manager.

The 1964 team raised eyebrows with an 8–2 start, and they were in first place from opening day to the final games in September. The Phillies had solid starting pitching in Chris Short, Art Mahaffey, Dennis Bennett, and Ray Culp. The bullpen was talented and deep as well, with Jack Baldschun serving as an effective reliever. The team received a huge boost prior to the 1964 campaign when starting pitcher Jim Bunning, a five-time American League all-star, was traded to Philadelphia from the Detroit Tigers.

Offensively and defensively, the Phillies were stacked with accomplished veterans who could both field and hit. Major contributors in the field included Tony Taylor, Ruben Amaro, Dick Allen, Roy

Sievers, Wes Covington, Tony Gonzalez, Johnny Callison, and Clay Dalrymple.

Richie Allen won the Rookie of the Year award that year. Johnny Callison, my favorite Phillies player, had a career year that included a team-leading thirty-one home runs. Jim Bunning pitched a perfect game on Father's Day against the Mets at Shea Stadium, a game I actually watched in the final innings with J. T. and Esther. Three Phillies made the National League all-star team, including Chris Short, Bunning, and Callison, who won the game with a three-run homer in the ninth inning against Red Sox ace reliever Dick Radatz. I recall my intense pride and sheer ecstasy when Callison dropped that homer into the right-field stands to win the game.

All the pieces seemed to fit. Everything had fallen into place. During the '64 season, the Phillies led the National League by as many as nine or ten games. I attended more games that summer than ever. When the Phillies were on TV, I was watching. If the game wasn't broadcast on TV, I typically listened to games on the radio, including those late-night broadcasts from Los Angeles and San Francisco, courtesy of hometown broadcasters Byrum Saam, Bill Campbell, and Richie Ashburn. Though they were not baseball aficionados, J. T. and Esther actually showed interest as well, with J. T. becoming a Jim Bunning fan when he learned that Bunning was a fellow Kentuckian.

However, it all came crashing down in late September in one of the greatest—if not *the* greatest—collapses in major league baseball history. The Phillies had gone 12–9 until September 21, and they held a comfortable six-and-a-half-game lead over the Reds, their closest challenger. Philadelphia's win over the Dodgers on September 20 was their last win of the '64 campaign. The great "Phold" had begun.

The agony of that ten-game losing streak remains hurtful even today. As a sixteen-year-old, I intently followed every game in late September, even when I should have been more focused on my schoolwork or high school football. I recall Jimmy Bower and Billy Skinner being especially impacted by the skid as well. We all felt so horrible, so helpless. Panic set in, including Gene Mauch's over-reliance on all-star pitchers Chris Short and Jim Bunning. Or could it have been "The Curse of Chico Ruiz?" The Phillies' bats grew cold. How could this be happening? The tickets had already been printed. I cried more than once during that late September, but it all came down to a crucial weekend series against the Cardinals in St. Louis's old Busch Stadium.

The Cardinals cruelly brushed our red-and-white pinstripers aside, swept the series, and assumed first place for good. For weeks, months, and years, I despised the Cardinals and some of their key players: Tim McCarver, Bob Gibson, Curt Flood, Bill White, Ken Boyer, and even former Phillies pitcher Curt Simmons. The saddest reality of all was not that the Cardinals had won the National League championship in 1964. It was the way the Phillies—or "the Phiz Kids," as they were soon to be called—had lost it.

A. Bartlett Giamatti, the former commissioner of baseball, was credited with the following quote: "Baseball breaks your heart. It is designed to break your heart."

Mission accomplished in 1964 in Philadelphia. It's still breaking.

153

MOCK HEADLINE: "ELOISE SHINES AT STEWART FIELD IN LORDS' DEFEAT"

Lansdowne-Aldan was unusual in that it played its home football games on Saturday mornings at 10:00. During one of these games (Methacton in 1964), the actual game was upstaged by an overweight beagle.

In those days, our beagle Eloise roamed freely about the neighborhood. She was extremely friendly, fondly regarded by our neighbors, and well known in our section of Lansdowne. Eloise was a fun and spontaneous spirit. Many of my peers recognized her on sight. I especially recall a close friend in junior high, Ronnie Townsend, who was very high on Eloise. Whenever Ronnie visited our home, he would greet Eloise with an enthusiastic "Weezy, Weezy, Weezy," to her overwhelmed delight. Classmates Jim Bower and Billy Skinner were also major fans.

Anyway, back to the game. I started at offensive end my junior year, and at this point in the game, we were in offensive huddle. Some laughter was evolving from the home stands, at which time I saw Eloise loose on the field. (In retrospect, I suspect that Eloise entered the field either through some break in the cyclone fencing or by casually walking in through the Essex Avenue gate with some spectators.)

The referee called a time out in an attempt to shoo Eloise off the field. Eloise was having none of this. She disrespected the referee's efforts and continued to scamper about the field. At this point, an offensive teammate said, "Hey, Bingham, isn't that your dog?"

Eloise had now turned her focus toward the huddle, and serendipitously (I've always wanted to use that word), she stumbled across her boy master. With the crowd loving it, Eloise's attention now shifted to me. Here she was, vigorously wagging her tail, looking up at me with those adoring brown eyes, fully anticipating a warm greeting from her master. What was I to do? I had to do something, since the referee's efforts were worthless, and the game had to go on.

I promptly made an executive decision to grab Eloise and carry her to the home sidelines, where I believe an LAHS cheerleader assumed custody. It was one long walk to the sideline, but in doing so, I received the greatest ovation of my storied high school athletic career. I later learned that J. T., in response to events, left the game to hurry home and fetch a leash. A leashed Eloise took in the rest of the game with my parents in the home stands.

I would love to let the story stop here—but it doesn't. The teasing I received post-game and well into the next week was brutal. It came from all directions: from students, players, coaches, etc. Everyone had fun with it, including head coach Ray Spafford, whose needling was relentless.

Months passed, and the event was soon forgotten. Or was it? In the spring, as a member of the yearbook staff, I was terrified to learn that the student editors wanted to include a photograph of Eloise's escort off Stewart Field in the 1965 edition of the *Lahian*. My fragile teenage vanity got in the way, and I immediately accosted the editors. My begging and pleading was surprisingly effective, and they reached a decision to ditch any plans for including it.

And here's the irony. Fifty years later, I would now be so pleased to see that photo permanently posted in the 1965 *Lahian* in all its nostalgic glory. What a fun memory—not then, but certainly now!

By the way, we lost the game, 7–0. So much for home-dog advantage.

154

ROBERT VINCENT III

Robert Vincent—or Bob Vincent, as we called him—was a high school classmate. I met Bob in seventh grade when Green/Highland Avenue and Ardmore Avenue schools mixed their populations in junior high.

Bob was a tall, athletic, handsome youth with curly red hair and light freckles. He was a three-sport athlete in junior high, but in high school, he dropped football. He was active in the Boy Scouts and advanced fairly high in rank. He could be funny and eccentric at times, and I recall how enthusiastically he would do an Indian dance when called out. While not a frequent visitor to my house, he was known and liked by my mother, and his behavior toward her was always polite and respectful. Bob also attended Lansdowne United Methodist Church for a number of years, thus forging an even tighter bond with several classmates.

It was in Bob's sophomore or junior year that he learned he could no longer participate in interscholastic athletics because of a heart problem. This was no doubt difficult for him to accept, since athletics were a major component of his teen years. But Bob did not melt away because of this setback. He was still jovial and fun to be around. He was cleared to participate in physical education, but at his own risk.

The public address announcement in school on November 22, 1963, regarding President Kennedy's assassination rocked us all and was a moment we would never forget. LAHS classmates and I received a similarly shocking announcement on September 15, 1965, when we learned that Bob had collapsed while running the track in gym class and had died shortly thereafter. His fragile heart had given out, and now one of us from the class of '66 was swiftly gone.

All who knew Bob were disbelieving and saddened. A lot of tears fell that day and at Bob's funeral service a few days later at Lansdowne United Methodist. The school attended in force, both students and faculty. It was a somber event, made even more personal because many of us addressed our own vulnerability for the first time.

You might think that Bob's parents would attack the school and somehow claim negligence in his death, but they didn't. My sense is that they knew that Bob's years were limited, and from what I can recall, they received news of his passing with dignity and grace.

Bob was recognized in the senior section of the yearbook with his photo and the following inscription:

Robert Vincent III

April 21, 1948–September 15, 1965

"God's finger touched him, and he slept."

155

MINUTI'S

I recall Minuti's as the first Lansdowne-based pizza shop in town while I was growing up. So many of the pizza shops were on the periphery of the town in sections of Upper Darby or East Lansdowne.

This "first" came into being around 1962, with the shop hidden away in a drab, forgettable building in downtown Lansdowne near the bowling alley. Minuti's received absolutely no foot traffic, as it had no storefront on either Lansdowne Avenue or Baltimore Pike. I cannot even recall the shop having a discernible sign. You had to take a driveway off of Lansdowne Avenue or Baltimore Pike and wind your way back toward the bowling alley to access the store.

Minuti's was owned and operated by a sweet, first-generation Italian-American family. The mother and father, along with their children and perhaps other family members, worked very hard to produce a good and reasonably priced pizza. Their store had no seating and was strictly takeout. I cannot recall them offering anything other than pizza—certainly no hoagies or cheese steaks.

Minuti's was popular and was especially busy on weekends because of its novelty and its quality. I would give their pizza an A grade. J. T. was a big fan as well, and he could easily be convinced to fund the purchase of a large Italian sausage pizza on many a weekend. I lost track of the store when I went off to college, as other pizza shops opened in and around Lansdowne.

Minuti's seemed to have a short business life of ten years or less, but it ranks up there with the better pizza shops visited during my Lansdowne adolescence.

156

OPEN HOUSES

Open houses were frequent, casual dances held in the old gym at LAHS. They were popular social events designed for junior/senior high school students and were typically held on Friday evenings from early evening until 10:00 p.m. My recollection is very fuzzy here, but I believe open houses were separately scheduled as junior high events for grades seven to nine and senior high events for grades ten to twelve.

In the fall, the senior high open houses were often held the night prior to Saturday football games, and as varsity football players, my teammates and I had to leave early in order to make curfew. Admission was twenty-five cents, and the events were chaperoned by high school faculty. Light refreshments were available for purchase: Cokes and homemade treats such as cupcakes and cookies.

The open house venue was always the small, "old" gymnasium constructed as part of the original high school building in 1927. The old gym was just that: old, dingy, tired, musty, and less than attractive, with its ancient basketball standards and weathered climbing ropes secured in the gym's rafters. In the early and mid-1960s, it was still used for junior high physical education, junior high team basketball and wrestling, pep rallies, and all formal dances except the senior prom. However, the old gym with its limited bleachers and small, antiquated locker rooms—which also served as restrooms for open houses—was already well past its prime.

Attire was relaxed from the school dress code, but there were still no jeans. Guys typically showed up wearing letter sweaters and khakis. Girls, not surprisingly, emphasized makeup, hair, and dress. When not standing or dancing, students sat in gymnasium stands. Small, creaky, rollout wooden bleachers extended from the east and west walls. The north and south ends behind the main basketball nets were deeper and included permanent bench seating, but this area also doubled as a storage area for heavy wrestling mats. Despite its deficits, the old gym was a familiar, trusted setting, and we disregarded its numerous shortcomings out of appreciation for the event.

Student deejays spun forty-fives in a mix of up-tempo and slow songs, current and oldies, from a tiny confined booth located at the north end of the gym floor. Occasionally a special dance, such as a "ladies choice" would be announced. I especially recall Jimmy Nelson, class of 1966, efficiently occupying the role of deejay during my final years in high school, and I offer a special, belated thanks to Jimmy for his devoted work in cramped and less-than-ideal quarters. I occasionally brought a favorite forty-five of mine for Jimmy to spin, and he generally accommodated.

While I cannot recall examples, a student band might have performed, such as the Offbeats from the class of '65. Chubby Checker supposedly lip-synched "At the Class," a pre-"Twist" tune, at an early 1960s open house, which I did not attend.

The open-house protocol that existed at the time was for teen boys and girls to generally remain segregated. Genders stayed together, unless a pair was a serious couple. Students also pretty much remained within their niches: jocks, scholars, nerds, and hoods (as Esther called them). It was very common for girls to dance with each other to up-tempo tunes, as many boys considered fast dancing "not cool" and a girls' thing. This rigidity waned during my high school years, as trendy dances such as "the twist" and "the pony" became popular. As seniors, male classmates Harry Gicking, Jack Schultz, Jimmy Isgro, and Allen Reeps were admired for their up-tempo moves on the wooden dance floor. While I was an adequate "slow dancer," I had zero talent and no nerve or desire to dance to up-tempo songs.

Open houses were rich with gossip and drama. News spread like wildfire. Romantic relationships were born and publicly displayed at open houses. They also died there, as breakups spontaneously unfolded and hearts broke, seemingly before the entire world. On an occasion or two, I recall the scene of a teenage girl frantically running to the girls' locker room in tears because of a relationship just ending. On the other hand, it was not unusual for a girl to be seen enthusiastically displaying a recently received ring from a new boyfriend as evidence that she was now "going steady."

Eyes were always focused on the dance floor. Moves were made, and signals were sent. Who was dancing with whom, and what did that mean? If you were in a steady relationship, you balanced time between your partner and your close friends. If you were not in a steady relationship, you dared to experiment with the available field.

Guys occasionally got rowdy and animated on the floor. I cannot recall a single fight developing, although some must have taken place. Male faculty regularly visited the boys' locker room to deter smoking. Teacher/coach Ed Kolodgie was a major locker-room cop, as was teacher/coach Charlie Phillips. Sometimes couples daringly left the dance to "make out" with each other in the adjacent football stands and then return to the event. No doubt some students consumed alcohol outside the school as well, although I believe those instances were isolated.

I am confident that if you were to canvas LAHS classmates of my era, you would receive warm and positive responses to recollections of open houses. Many of my best high school memories, next to high school football, are linked to these wonderful happenings.

On a summer trip back to Lansdowne, I actually toured LAHS (now Penn Wood High School) while major construction was underway in the building. I wandered the halls, sat in the auditorium, walked on the stage, and eventually made my way to the old gym, the site of those glorious open houses. When I first walked into the old gym, I realized that it was no longer the old gym. It had been converted to a school library. I was stunned, almost sick to my stomach.

I had always hoped that one of my high school class reunions would be held in the old gym, but that wish is now permanently dashed. I don't want the Concordville Inn or a Sheraton or a Holiday Inn. I want that small, beat-up, brown-brick gymnasium, complete with dirty wrestling mats, hard bleachers, and scratchy climbing ropes dangling in the rafters.

The Penn Wood administration got it all wrong when the old gym was converted to a library. It should have been converted to a museum, worth the price of admission from thousands of former LAHS students.

157

MEMORABLE "OPEN HOUSE" SLOW SONGS

- "Til" by the Angels
- "Just to Be with You" by the Passions
- "Where or When" by Dion and the Belmonts
- "You Belong to Me" by the Duprees
- "A Thousand Stars" by Kathy Young
- "Once in a While" by The Chimes
- "Have You Heard" by The Duprees
- "Since I Don't Have You" by the Skyliners
- "There's a Moon Out Tonight" by the Capris
- "Hold Me, Thrill Me, Kiss Me" by Mel Carter
- "Chances Are" by Johnny Mathis
- "One Summer Night" by The Danleers
- "I Only Have Eyes for You" by The Flamingos
- "It's All in the Game" by Jerry Butler
- "I Can't Stop Loving You" by Ray Charles
- "Those Oldies but Goodies" by Little Caesar and the Romans
- "I Can't Help Falling in Love" by Elvis Presley
- "Angel Baby" by Rosie and the Originals
- "Only You" by The Platters
- "In the Still of the Night" by the Five Satins

158

RANDOM REMEMBRANCES VIII

This will sound extremely odd and perhaps even untruthful, but alcohol and drugs were largely a nonissue for me in high school. For one, the 1963 expulsion of four seniors—one being a neighborhood friend—from the varsity football squad for underage drinking was a galvanic event that assuredly got my attention and that of my teammates. The risk of underage drinking for me was simply too great and not worth it. Any thought of being released from the football team or track squad for being caught drinking was unfathomable to me. I would never take the chance, nor did I. I believe many of my close friends and fellow athletes felt likewise.

Was some underage drinking going on at LAHS? Very likely. But not in the jock crowd I associated with. Within my social circle, I never witnessed any hint of drinking until high school graduation. Marijuana and other street drugs were a nonfactor at LAHS during my years of attendance.

Yes, the Beatles hit America during my high school years. I recall watching their initial television performance on *The Ed Sullivan Show* in our living room on a Sunday evening in 1963. My girlfriend, Jeri-Anne Winner, was in enthusiastic attendance.

My grades through LAHS were good, but they could have been much better. I generally earned all As through grade school, and then some Bs appeared in junior high, primarily in math and French. I had all As and Bs in high school, with a few Cs popping up in math, and even a D in geometry during one disastrous marking period of my sophomore year. I also struggled with physics in my senior year, and classmate Mark Gilbert provided invaluable tutoring services.

Compared to Bill's valedictorian status, I was a major letdown to J. T. and Esther. I graduated twenty-sixth out of a class of 151, hardly a noteworthy status. I clearly underachieved. Nonetheless, J. T. and Esther did not tightly supervise homework, taking a very *laissez-faire* attitude about my study habits and grades. However, they were not supportive of my attending midweek sporting events during the winter season.

During the winter of my senior year, an ugly event occurred at an away basketball game with Chichester High School. I had considered going to the game but had declined because of homework and the lengthy commute to and from Chichester High School. It was good for me that I had not attended the contest.

After the game, football center and senior classmate Ray Heller and some other LAHS students were attacked in the school parking lot by some irate Chichester fans. Chains were involved, and Ray received several chain whips to the head and body. I do not recall the names of the other students, but they were not seriously hurt. Ray was medically treated and was bedridden for a few days after the attack. Several football teammates and I visited Ray at his East Lansdowne home during his recovery, and I still recall with horror seeing the chain bruises and indentation marks on his face.

To their credit, Chichester High School administration and students took the attack very seriously, and a few days later, Chichester High School representatives formally apologized for the shameful behavior at an LAHS assembly.

Esther liked to take our beagle, Eloise, along in the car as she ran errands. Weezie would have her head outside the passenger-side window the whole way, with ears wildly flapping in the wind as Esther covered her routes. Weezie was well-mannered and waited patiently in the car.

A walk-up Dairy Queen across from Upper Darby High School was a favorite stop for Esther during warmer months. There she would buy Weezie a small vanilla cone and feed it to her in the front seat. Eloise loved Dairy Queen, but she could only lick the cone for so long before her tongue got cold, forcing her to stop temporarily. Once the majority of ice cream was gone, Weezie would eagerly devour the cone. Sometimes students from Bonner, Prendergast, and Upper Darby were present, and this routine never failed to catch their attention. With students assembled around the car, Eloise put on her show.

J. T. liked waffles, and occasionally we would have them on the weekends with link sausage, bacon, or Scrapple, which J. T. preferred crispy. I have no memorable stories of pancake Saturdays, but a donut run to Montbard Bakery was always an option on weekends, especially after I had earned my driver's license.

Horn and Hardart was Lansdowne's primary restaurant of the two that were located downtown. It was a chain restaurant that had its roots in the Automat trade in the company's New York City and Philadelphia restaurants. To my recall, the Lansdowne restaurant did not have Automat service. It was a full sit-down restaurant that was open for breakfast, lunch, and dinner. Service was hardly enthusiastic. You can well imagine how eager H & H waitresses were to serve teenagers, since we weren't exactly major tippers.

For many years H & H was the only restaurant to frequent after attending a basketball game or viewing a movie at the Lansdowne Theater. The decor was Spartan and uninspired, but H & H was bright, very bright. We had absolutely no problems reading the menu. A major selling point for LAHS students was that H & H was cheap. Two toasted sticky buns and two Cokes cost less than a dollar. In the several times I ate at H & H, the only meal I ever consumed there was a toasted sticky bun and a Coke.

Despite its Quaker heritage, Lansdowne operated a bowling alley during my youth. It was located west of South Lansdowne Avenue adjacent to the Media local train tracks. It was a dumpy, grungy, smoky establishment that sported two distinct features: (1) at a time when automatic pin spotters were in use in most bowling alleys, Lansdowne's alley still used pinboys for setup in the early '60s, and (2) the alley did not include the customary eighteen lanes.

If our bowling party consisted of all boys, we took great delight in trying to nail a pinspotter with a hurried roll before he jumped to his perch out of harm's way. A more civil approach was taken when girls were in attendance.

There was no concession stand. Any refreshments were purchased from vending machines. An added plus to the Lansdowne lanes was the availability of Bireley's orange soda. Bireley's was a luscious, non-carbonated soda that was not common to the area.

J. T. was zealous about summer produce, especially sweet corn, melons, and peaches. Whenever I might be traveling to the Jersey Shore for the day, I was required to load up on these items on the return trip. He was never shy about handing over some bucks to cover the cost.

We had several cats while I was growing up. I do not remember Sylvia and Heathcliff, as I was an infant at the time. Joining our family over the years were Cassandra (tortoise shell), Ophelia (gray longhair), and Carolina (tan-and-white shorthair). Esther was especially fond of Cassandra, who was not a fan of me. The odd names were attributed to Bill, who liked to name pets after literary figures. Carolina was the exception.

My ordeal with math in high school was ongoing. I somehow survived tenth-grade geometry, but I met a major wall in eleventh-grade math class with Howie Freeman, who served as my instructor. Mr.

Freeman was a long-standing faculty member at LAHS, who always wore a chalk-powdered gray suit. He taught Bill as well, who surely aced the class with little effort.

I was another story. I struggled. I asked frequent questions in class. I feared attempting to solve a problem at the blackboard. I frequently stayed after school for tutoring. I believe Mr. Freeman grew as frustrated with me as I was with the subject material.

I somehow earned a C in the class, but Mr. Freeman's assessment of my limited ability in math was summed up by an unnecessary comment that he offered during an after-school session: "You sure aren't like your brother."

Sometimes I believe that J. T. and Esther were completely without hobbies. J. T. usually took work home from the office on Monday through Thursday evenings. His weekends were spent running errands and doing assorted jobs around the house. J. T. and Esther watched a lot of television at night. Neither took any interest in exercise or sports such as swimming, running, hiking, ice-skating, skiing, tennis, or golf. J. T.'s only occasional physical activity was some flower gardening.

J. T. and Esther were both mild readers, but they took disciplined interest in reading the morning newspaper, *The Philadelphia Inquirer*, which was delivered daily to the house. They did like to entertain and have couples over for dinner: the Quinns, the Pruitts, the Bermans, the Fullers, etc.

This may sound like a lame activity, but because of my interest in commercial aviation, I enjoyed taking periodic trips to the Philadelphia Airport as a teenager. In those days there were next to no security restrictions, and anyone could go to the designated gate to meet or send off passengers. Parking was about fifty cents, and for a few hours I could observe the different types of piston, prop-jet, and jet aircraft that were in commercial service.

Several airlines that serviced Philadelphia back then are distant memories and are no longer in service, such as TWA, National, Northeast, Eastern, Mohawk, and Allegheny.

To this day, the funniest experience of my life occurred when I was eighteen. The event was held close to high school graduation, so all pressure was off, including final exams. About a half dozen of us crammed into someone's car and drove to 45th and Market Streets in West Philadelphia to attend our first professional wrestling at the old Philadelphia Arena. The main match pitted fan favorite Bruno Sammartino against the evil Baron Mikel Scicluna. Other action included matches involving Bulldog Brower, Johnny Valentine, midget wrestlers Little Beaver and Ski-Lo-Lo, and lesser names. The event was a laugh fest from the opening match. At times, I did not believe that classmate Harry Gicking would survive from laughing so long and hard.

The night included Bulldog Brower eating a turnbuckle. "What d'ya mean? Open hand, open hand!" There were foreign objects hidden in wrestlers' trunks, and matches that spilled out into the audience, including the upper deck seating. We saw a female match, possibly involving the Fabulous Moolah, and the championship match between bad guy Baron Mikel Scicluna and beloved Bruno Sammartino. As was no surprise to anyone, Bruno won the championship bout, but only after Scicluna punished Bruno severely on his way to breaking every professional wrestling rule known to man.

The next day, my ribs actually hurt: the price one paid for such a riotous evening. And yes, Harry did survive.

When we lived on Essex Avenue, our principle neighbors were the McGraws and the Dormons.

The McGraws lived next door, to the east. I still recall Marge McGraw welcoming us to the neighborhood with a homemade chocolate cake. Jim McGraw, Marge's husband, was a local businessman. He was friendly and a bit of a prankster. He was very active in the Lansdowne Republican Party, and I recollect that he paid me to distribute anti-Kennedy materials prior to the 1960 presidential election. I don't understand why J. T. and Esther never socialized with the McGraws, since there was genial interaction across the cyclone fence between the two couples.

The McGraws had three children, and the two older girls were musically inclined like their mother. Jimmy, the youngest child, was two years my senior.

The Dormons lived in a very large, stone house on the corner of Essex and Wayne Avenues to our west. Bill Dormon was an energetic and active man who worked for Atlantic Refining in Philadelphia. He typically ran to the Lansdowne Train Station in the morning to catch the commuter train to work. He was fearless in completing home repairs using tall ladders to access the roof or clean gutters. He was also a skier who undertook challenging runs at ski resorts in New England.

Alice Dormon was a stay-at-home mom with very long, salt-and-pepper hair. She was extremely kind and deeply religious, almost Quaker-like.

Grandmother Dormon lived for several years next door as well. My remembrance of her is associated with a beautiful flower garden that she kept across the fence behind our garage. The garden contained numerous varieties of domestic and wild flowers, which were in glorious bloom throughout the summer months.

Bill and Alice had three children, all older than me: Billy, Jane, and Betsy. All three children attended a private religious school and had little interaction with neighborhood children.

The Twentieth Century Club of Lansdowne was organized in 1897 by a small group of women whose objective was "to create an organized center of thought and action among women, for the protection of their interests and for the promotion of science, literature, and art."

During my upbringing, the Twentieth Century Club was a vibrant and active organization of which Esther was a member. Most of the club's efforts appeared to be directed toward charitable or benevolent causes.

The Twentieth Century Club's attractive, Tudor-style clubhouse was located on Lansdowne Avenue just south of the train station. This facility hosted special events such as wedding receptions and even our annual high school football banquet.

Many of my LAHS classmates will recall etiquette and dancing instruction at the clubhouse that many of us attended in seventh grade. Much of this sad activity has been repressed, and my recall here is very spotty. Sessions were held once or twice a month during the school year, but I cannot remember the specific evening of the week.

Boys wore ties and coats. Girls wore dresses. The two genders sat on opposite sides of the dance floor. Our instructor, Mr. Keenan, guided us in proper dance etiquette, including how to ask a girl to dance. He also taught dance steps to traditional dance tunes played on a phonograph. "Step, step, glide" comes to mind.

Most boys hated these sessions, myself included. On one occasion, many of us threw exploding torpedo fireworks on the dance floor or casually dropped the torpedoes on the floor, knowing that they would explode when stepped on by an unsuspecting dancer. To say that

Mr. Keenan disapproved is an understatement.

Parents were periodically scheduled to chaperone these classes, and they paid a registration fee to the club for Mr. Keenan's efforts.

A favorite TV personality of mine as a child and teenager was Soupy Sales. Born Milton Supman in 1926, Soupy was an American comedian and television personality best known for his local and network children's television show, *Lunch with Soupy Sales.*

Lunch with Soupy Sales involved slapstick and improvisational skits. The pace was fast, and sketches frequently included characters such as White Fang, "the Biggest and Meanest Dog in the USA," who only appeared in a corner of the TV screen as a white dog paw. White Fang spoke in unintelligible grunts and growls, which Soupy then translated back to the audience for comic effect. Two of the funniest skits ever were White Fang training for the Olympics and White Fang as the mad chemist. White Fang was often the launcher of pies in the face when Soupy's bad jokes offended Fang.

Black Tooth, the "Biggest and Sweetest Dog in the USA," was seen only as a black dog paw with similarly unintelligible dialogue. Black Tooth's trademark was to lure Soupy off camera for loud and noisy kisses.

A hand puppet, Pookie the Lion, performed from behind a window while Soupy sat in front. A frequent greeting from Pookie was "Hey, boobie." Pookie often pantomimed to popular records during his sketches.

Another regular feature of the show was "the guy at the door." In these sketches, only a man's hand was seen, and the theme was usually an attempted sale or plea for help, to which Soupy usually obliged.

Soupy reached his greatest popularity in the early '60s when he had a network show on Friday evening from Los Angeles. One of Soupy's biggest fans was Frank Sinatra, who eventually received a pie in the face during a well-publicized episode.

159

JOHNNY CALLISON

Johnny Callison (five foot ten, 170 pounds) was a former professional baseball player who spent his best and most productive years with the Phillies from 1960 to 1969. His major league career spanned fifteen years and included stops with the White Sox, Phillies, Cubs, and Yankees. He batted left and threw right. He played right field and was an excellent defensive outfielder with good speed and a powerful and accurate throwing arm. For four consecutive years he led the National League in outfield assists. On several occasions I personally witnessed number 6 almost nonchalantly throwing runners out at third base or home plate.

As a teenager following the Phillies, Johnny Callison was my favorite ballplayer. I was not alone. He was a fan favorite, and why not? His career batting average was .264 and totaled 226 home runs and 840 RBIs. He led the National League twice in triples and once in doubles. He was the star of the 1964 all-star game for hitting a three-run walk-off home run against Boston reliever Dick Radatz at Shea Stadium. He was also runner-up for MVP in 1964 and surely would have won the award if the Phillies had not tragically collapsed late in the season. During 1964, his best year ever, Callison amassed 31 home runs, 104 RBIs, and a .274 batting average.

In 1997 Callison was named to the Philadelphia Baseball Wall of Fame, and in 2012 he was inducted posthumously into the Philadelphia Sports Hall of Fame.

When I attended games at Connie Mack Stadium, I would typically sit in the upper deck ($2.25 a ticket) in one of two places: (1) right behind home plate or (2) deep down the right-field line so I could observe Callison in the field. Without question, Johnny Callison was my very favorite sports figure while I was a teenager growing up in Philadelphia. He is still a hero for me today.

Upon leaving baseball in 1973, Callison did not secure a lucrative post-baseball career. He did not return to his native Oklahoma but bounced around the Philadelphia area with no clear vocational direction. In their book, *The Great Book of Philadelphia Sports Lists*, radio personalities Glen Macnow and Big Daddy Graham give the following account:

> He was one of the best players in baseball in the '60s and still had to work in the off-season bartending, selling cars, selling insurance. Soon after his playing days, the economics changed. You might think he'd be all sour and bitter, right? Wrong. I used to perform at a comedy club where Johnny poured cold ones, a nicer guy you never met. He was gracious and patient with every fan that approached him. Here's a man who had every right to wish that his mother had given birth just 10 years later, which would have made him a multimillionaire who wouldn't have to work the rest of his life. Yet Johnny kept his chin up and was grateful for everything the game gave to him. There's a lesson to be learned here.

Johnny Callison died at age sixty-seven in 2006, perhaps a better teacher by example than a professional baseball player. His 1968 Topps baseball card and the above Macnow/Graham quote are framed and adorn my basement wall as an ongoing, steadying example of how to live one's life.

160

WEATHER

The Philadelphia area, also known as the Delaware Valley, had four distinct seasons. Unlike some parts of the country where spring and fall seem only a few weeks long or even nonexistent, I recollect not being cheated on any of the seasons.

Lansdowne winters were relatively mild compared to Midwest climates in which I have lived as an adult. During my upbringing, I can never recall a temperature below zero. Rarely, but occasionally, temperatures dropped to single digits, but winter temperatures were typically in the thirties and forties during the daytime, and even briefly in the low fifties on infrequent occasions.

We received three to four snowfalls a year that might require shoveling (snowblowers did not yet exist). Accumulated snowfalls typically did not linger and soon melted. Esther was forever critical of local snow preparedness and snow removal, constantly comparing it to her years in Traverse City, which was naturally an unfair comparison. I do not recall any ice storms impacting the area, unlike events in the South.

I have the least recollection of spring, but I was always glad for its arrival. Track and baseball practices in early spring always demanded a warm sweatshirt, but by mid to late April, the air had warmed considerably. It seemed windier early in the season as well. The area naturally got its fair share of rain, so cancellations of track meets, baseball games, and tennis matches were not rare. Especially on weekends, neighbors started sprucing up their yards as they raked up winter debris, trimmed bushes, pulled early-sprouting weeds, planted flowers, and performed the initial lawn cut of the season. It was at this time that my grass-cutting business started in earnest, so weekends were especially busy for me in spring and summer.

I well remember summer as being hot and humid. Air-conditioning was usually only a guarantee in stores. Cars were not air-conditioned. If homes were air-conditioned, relief was typically delivered by window units. On Essex Avenue, we had a monster unit in the living room and one in the master bedroom. Esther liked the house cold, so these loud units were always cranked to capacity. For years I slept with a window fan cooling my bedroom, until a small window air-conditioner was added during my college years.

In recollection, it always seemed that daytime temperatures and humidity were jointly parked in the nineties or at least high eighties. Baths and showers helped, but such relief was only temporary. It wasn't so much the temperature; it was the humidity that drained and choked. Evening thunderstorms provided welcomed yet temporary relief. At no point did I feel the burden of temperature and humidity more than in full pads during late summer, preseason football practices. Football teammates and I always welcomed fall, since it meant more bearable temperatures and lower humidity at afternoon practices.

Fall was exhilarating and always my favorite season: cooler temperatures, smoke from burning leaves in the air, football practice extending into the dark as daylight saving time kicked in late in the season, the initial frost, etc. While Lansdowne did not sport the diversity of fall coloring common to New England or the Southern Appalachians, many parts of the town were heavily treed with mature hardwoods casting diverse blends of brown, red, and yellow leaves.

161

ROTARY INTERNATIONAL "SERVICE ABOVE SELF" AWARD

During my high school years, I repeatedly ran for class president. I always lost the elections, but barely. At the end of my junior year, I ran for student council president. I again lost, this time by two votes in a run-off.

At an assembly near the end of my junior year, I learned that the high school faculty had voted for me to receive the Rotary International "Service Above Self" award. The recognition was significant to me in light of my past election defeats, most importantly because it came from high school teachers and school administration. Without actually verbalizing their confidence in me, I perceived the recognition as my high school faculty's formal expression of trust and belief in me as a person. This honor, even so distant from the present, remains special to me.

A benefit that came with the honor was enrollment in Rotary Leadership Camp, a weeklong residential event held at a camp venue north of Philadelphia. Rotary sponsored the "Service Above Self" award at many Philadelphia area high schools, so in the summer of 1965, about one hundred fellow award recipients and I spent a week together at a residential camp located about an hour's drive from Lansdowne.

Upon arriving that Sunday afternoon, I quickly recognized a fellow camper: Carman Infante. Carman attended Chichester High School, which was a Section III high school like LAHS. I recognized him from sports, and we immediately hit it off. Carman was a three-letter sport athlete who quarterbacked the Chichester football team. He wasn't big, but he was quick, fast, and agile.

Carman and I had both arrived early, and while we were not originally assigned as roommates, we rigged the registration list so that we could bunk together. The two of us instantly bonded. We had a phenomenal time that week, and we constantly jabbed each other back and forth as to Chichester or LAHS dominance in sports. I had scored a touchdown in LAHS's 13–0 victory over Chichester in 1964, so I repeatedly reminded him of that feat. Carman assured me that the 1965 score later that fall would be different.

Another camper I met was Ned Coslett from nearby Swarthmore, another Section III school. For some reason, Ned had earned the nickname "Ned Nougat." Ned was a likeable and funny kid with whom I instantly connected. Ned played guard on the Swarthmore football team, and as rivalry tradition determined, I would play against him on Thanksgiving Day on the Swarthmore College field. I believe both Carmen and Ned were team captains.

The regimen at the camp was an emphasis on leadership development. Accomplished Rotarians would speak to small classes of campers and then lead discussions and assignments. There was a definite curriculum that the Rotary instructors followed. These sessions dominated the day, and while their format might sound boring, the sessions were informative, revealing, and even fun. We spent late afternoon and evening playing touch football and softball, swimming, and socializing. Carman and I teamed up several times as a football quarterback-receiver team in some highly competitive touch football games against talented competition.

The week at Leadership Camp was a memorable and meaningful experience. This week was perhaps the first time I actually envisioned myself as a leader. The course work, which included some light reading, was helpful and eye-opening. The comradery established with fellow campers was special, and I valued getting to know Carman and Ned as I did.

As an adult, I should have joined the Rotary Club. I felt I owed them that much for their belief in me in 1965. That membership never happened, and I fault myself for not following through. However, I provided numerous probation presentations to assorted Rotary Clubs over the years, and in doing so, I always recognized the club members and thanked them for Rotary's support and belief in me many years prior.

As for Carman Infante, he attended the University of Delaware where he played football. He later went on to become a highly successful high school football coach in New Jersey. Ironically, I briefly worked with his younger sister when she and I were both employed by the Delaware County Juvenile Court in the mid-1970s.

Ned Coslett attended Washington and Lee University in Lexington, Virginia, a school where I had been accepted and could have attended. Ned was disappointed that I did not attend W & L. He had hoped that we could play small-college football together. Upon graduating from W & L, Ned returned home to join the family real estate firm.

A now glaring aspect of my Rotary Leadership Camp experience was its all-male status. Fortunately, that has all changed. Rotary has accepted female members since 1989. The Rotary Leadership Camp commitment continues as well, and now with a coed population.

As for my leadership plaque, it continues to hang on the wall in my basement office.

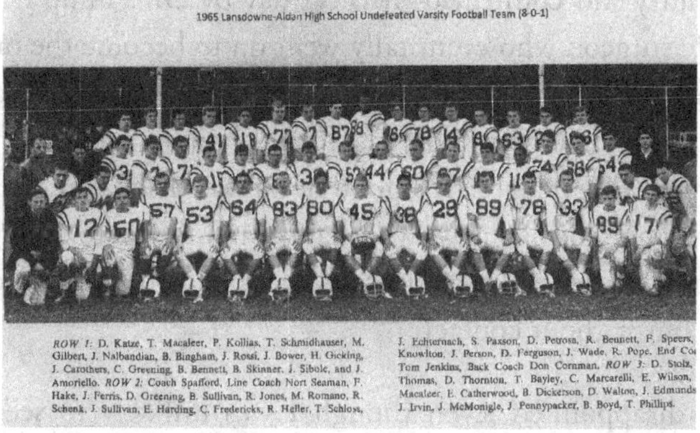
1965 Lansdowne-Aldan High School Undefeated Varsity Football Team (8-0-1)
ROW 1: D. Katze, T. Macaleer, P. Kollias, T. Schmidhauser, M. Gilbert, J. Nalbandian, B. Bingham, J. Rossi, J. Bower, H. Gicking, J. Carothers, C. Greening, B. Bennett, B. Skinner, J. Sibole, and J. Amoriello. ROW 2: Coach Spafford, Line Coach Nort Seaman, F. Hake, J. Ferris, D. Greening, B. Sullivan, R. Jones, M. Romano, R. Schenk, J. Sullivan, E. Harding, C. Fredericks, R. Heller, T. Schloss,
J. Echternach, S. Paxson, D. Petrosa, R. Bennett, F. Speers, Knowlton, J. Person, D. Ferguson, J. Wade, R. Pope, End Co Tom Jenkins, Back Coach Don Cornman. ROW 3: D. Stolz, Thomas, D. Thornton, T. Bayley, C. Marcarelli, E. Wilson, Macaleer, E. Catherwood, B. Dickerson, D. Walton, J. Edmunds J. Irvin, J. McMonigle, J. Pennypacker, B. Boyd, T. Phillips.

Lansdowne-Aldan High School Undefeated Football Team, 1965

162

LANSDOWNE-ALDAN HIGH SCHOOL VARSITY FOOTBALL (1963–1965)

Football was a huge part of my high school experience. I played all four years in high school. I started as both offensive and defensive end my freshman year on a team that earned a 4–2 record, guided by head coach Ed Kolodgie.

I started at offensive end and defensive end my sophomore year on the JV squad. However, early in the ten-game season, I broke a carpal bone in my right hand and both of my index and middle fingers while tackling Tommy Eztweiler in practice. (Tommy actually fell on my hand as a result of the tackle.) I knew by the force of the impact that something was very wrong, and the pain sent an undeniable signal as well.

The injury was confirmed the next day by Dr. Phillip Marone, an orthopedic surgeon who eventually went on to become the orthopedic surgeon for the Philadelphia Eagles. My fingers were taped, and I was fitted with a molded, removable cast for the hand break, which was well secured by ACE bandages. The good news was that I could remove the cast for bathing. The bad news was that the injury was to my right hand, and I would be sidelined for at least six weeks. I could still practice with the team, but without contact.

I was disappointed, even though I was unlikely to see much, if any, varsity time. I subsequently attended daily practices, performed limited calisthenics, helped with the scout team, and ran sprints at the conclusion of practice. Later in the season with my hand now healed, I did play in the Yeadon varsity game because of injuries to upperclassmen. I recall being so nervous when I entered the game that I had no clue as to whether we were on offense or defense. Senior linebacker Dave Renard helped settle me down, and I actually made a pretty good tackle on one play for a loss on an end sweep. At the Monday JV game against Yeadon, I caught two touchdown passes, both bombs. Our 1963 varsity squad endured a losing season (3–6–1) marred by the mid-season dismissal of four seniors for underage drinking.

My junior year saw me start offensively on the varsity. Our offense ran a seven-man line with both ends tight. Our offensive backfield consisted of a quarterback, two halfbacks, and a fullback. I was fortunate to play next to Greg Ellis, a powerful 235-pound offensive tackle, who was All-Delco and subsequently earned a full football scholarship to the University of Pittsburgh.

Our offense was primarily a ground attack with little passing emphasis. Between myself and the other starting offensive end, senior Paul Hample, we caught fewer than thirty passes between us. I scored touchdowns against Media and Chichester on identical twelve-yard curl routes. The 1964 squad had a much-improved record (7–2), which included important shut-out victories against Interboro (6–0), Chichester (13–0), and Thanksgiving Day rival Swarthmore (32–0).

A very memorable action took place at the Tuesday practice following the Interboro victory. Our only touchdown had involved a long run by halfback Earle "Butch" Mosley. As the run progressed, I was downfield, out in front of Butch, while two Interboro defenders were closing in. I had to carefully time my entry, or I could have been called for a clip. My hope was to cut off at least one of the Interboro defenders. For an offensive player not especially known for his blocking prowess, I timed this one perfectly, knocking one Interboro defender into the other and allowing Butch to scamper unimpeded for the touchdown.

The memorable event at the Tuesday practice was Coach Spafford sending Butch and me in early—before wind sprints as a reward for our efforts on our only touchdown. Butch and I were dumbfounded, as this was a totally novel action by Coach Spafford and one that I never saw repeated.

Our senior year in football held great potential. LAHS was considered a front-runner for the Section III crown, with Nether Providence, Interboro, and Chichester viewed as other formidable teams in the hunt. Jimmy Bower and Chris Greening, our cocaptains, were both two-year lettermen and very talented players.

I started again at offensive end, and I was allowed to line up as a split end on several plays to help split the defense. I did not play defense (good move by the coaching staff), but Coach Spafford unofficially anointed me cocaptain of special teams, so I was on the field a lot. Coach Spafford said he wanted me on the field for my speed to stop any touchdown runbacks on kickoffs or punts. Mission accomplished.

No Delaware County high school in 1965 was blessed with better running backs than ours. Jimmy Bower, Harry Gicking, and Billy Skinner were a punishing, talented trio that formed the basis of our offense. Our offensive line was inexperienced at tackle and small in size.

A real question was whether or not the offensive line could open holes for our skilled runners.

Our passing attack was very limited because of our dependence on the ground game, plus our starting quarterback, Danny Greening, was a sophomore. My primary role would be downfield blocking and running a lot of decoy routes. Defensively, we were undersized, but we were quick, athletic, and tough.

This is our varsity record for 1965.

	We	They
Garnet Valley	40	0
Media	13	6
Interboro	13	7
Nether Providence	7	7
Darby-Colwyn	7	6
Chichester	26	25
Yeadon	52	0
Sharon Hill	46	14
Swarthmore	20	7

I was the main receiving option, catching twenty passes and scoring one touchdown. My best games were against Media, Interboro, and Chichester.

Our 1965 squad went undefeated, earning Section III championship honors.

Bill Skinner and Chris Greening were All-County, with several teammates earning second-team status or honorable mention.

Lansdowne-Aldan vs. Interboro, 1965

163

LANSDOWNE-ALDAN HIGH SCHOOL VARSITY FOOTBALL: CHICHESTER FOOTBALL GAME, 1965

Going into the 1965 season, LAHS was considered by many to be a legitimate contender for the Section III championship. In those days there were no state playoffs, so a league championship was as high as a team could go. Our chief opponents in Section III would be Interboro, Nether Providence, and Chichester, all larger schools. In a stroke of irony, all three of these games were scheduled at home on Stewart Field in 1965.

We entered the Chichester game undefeated at 4–0–1, with our only blemish being a tough, disappointing 7–7 tie against Nether Providence the fourth week of the season. Our last game against Darby-Colwyn had been an embarrassing 7–6 victory against the worst team in the league, an undermanned squad with limited talent that we should have demolished. In retrospect, we were, at that point, a team that played to its level of competition. We had eked out a 13–7 win against Interboro in mid-September. Then we'd tied Nether Providence. And then we'd been humiliated, nearly losing at Darby-Colwyn.

We had short prep time for Chichester, since we'd played the Darby-Colwyn game the previous Monday because of rainy conditions on game day, Saturday. Our coaches surely were concerned about how we would match up against the bigger and talented Chichester team led by my Rotary Camp quarterback friend, Carman Infante, and running back Bill Clark, a fast and durable offensive threat.

The prep week for Chichester was more intense and more focused. The Darby-Colwyn game needed to be quickly forgotten, but with a lesson learned. The game with Chichester could well be for the Section III championship, so we had everything to lose. The entire school seemed especially excited about the upcoming contest as well, and we would certainly have a major crowd at the game, as Chichester fans would surely be there in high numbers.

Our home games were played on Saturday mornings at 10:00 a.m., and teammates Jimmy Bower, Jerry Carothers, Bill Skinner, Don Petrosa, and I established a tradition of having a broiled steak/baked potato breakfast at my house at 6:00 a.m. on all Saturday home dates. Esther supplied the baked potato and broiled the steak with her typical ease, and by 7:00 a.m., we were in the locker room, getting taped, checking equipment, mentally reviewing plays in our head, etc.

When we ran onto Stewart Field for warm-ups, the stands were nearly filled on both sides of the field. The Chichester Band, which was of state-championship caliber, pumped us all up with their rousing play, and personally, I never felt more excited prior to a varsity game. By game time, the stands were packed, and the track was completely rimmed by standing fans a few rows deep. I had never seen Stewart Field better attended for a varsity football game. There were several thousand in attendance, many of them Chichester fans who traveled well.

The suburban *Daily Times* newspaper covered the contest.

Lansdowne-Aldan Clips Chi, 26–25 in Classic
by Ed Gebhard, *Daily Times* Sports Editor

LANSDOWNE – You must have heard it a million times: The team that won't be beat, can't be beat. Lansdowne-Aldan High proved Saturday that the ancient adage is as true today as when it was first uttered many years ago.

Coach Ray Spafford's Lords twice were within a first down of defeat in the last period and both times L-A rose to the occasion, driving 67 and 61 yards against a fine Chichester team and the clock to earn a sensational 26–25 victory.

Because Lansdowne-Aldan wouldn't be beat, the Lords are in line for the Section III championship. It isn't official yet, but the Lords are being measured for the crown and can put it on by winning their last league game against Swarthmore (2–4–0).

Lord Heroes

The Lords' heroes were many Saturday but two in particular, fullback Bill (Mule) Skinner and halfback Jimmy Bower, were foremost.

Skinner scored three touchdowns, including the one which ended a wild four-touchdown fourth period and won the game. In addition, he played his usual great game as linebacker on defense.

Bower passed for two touchdowns—including the big one to Skinner—and, just as important, booted two extra points.

His second placement came with 0:45 on the clock and won the game.

For Chichester, Bill Clark lived up to his billing as the finest running back in Delaware County.

A tremendous clutch player, Clark rushed for 95 yards in the fourth period alone, ran for two TDs and an extra point and picked up 172 yards on 23 carries.

Great Period

In one of the finest fourth periods ever played, both Chi and L-A took turns driving for what appeared at the time to be the decisive TD.

First Chi went 96 yards to go ahead, then L-A rolled 67 yards to tie. Chi came back with a 34-yard march to go ahead again before Lansdowne, with only 4:20 to play, drove 61 yards to tie it again.

That's the kind of game it was until Bower's extra point ended it.

"No one gave up, they really hung in there," Coach Spafford said when it was over.

"We saw an opening in Chi's pass defense and exploited it," Spafford said. "When we

started to pass, Chi opened its defense and our backs were about to run."

Look for More

"From now on, you can look for more of the same from us—open them up with passes, then run 'em to death."

The classic schoolboy battle started slowly enough. Neither team scored in the first period, but early in the second, Skinner picked up a fumbled pitchout on the Chi 30 and dashed into the end zone untouched.

Bower's placement made it 7–0.

The TD apparently woke up Chi, for the Eagles took the ensuing kickoff and roared 65 yards in 9 plays. Two passes from Carman Infante accounted for 28 yards before the QB took it over from the 2 on a sneak.

A hard slice by Clark tied it at 7–7.

Late in the period, L-A took to the air, and with Jerry Carothers at the controls, drove from its 43 to the Chi 17.

Greening Enters

On the 4th-and-10 at that point, alternate quarterback Dan Greening entered the game, called for a draw and Skinner ripped 17 yards into the end zone without a hand on him. It was 13–7 at halftime as Earl Johnson blocked Bower's placement.

Midway through the third period, Chi tied after Tom Fry recovered a fumble on the L-A 26. Clark carried six times, including the final yard for the TD, but was stopped cold by Skinner for the extra point try.

Late in the third quarter, Chi began an 8-play, 86 yard drive highlighted by Clark's great running. Teammate Walt Boulden had 27 yards on two tries, but Clark got the TD on a fine run off left tackle of 42 yards. Clark was piled up on the PAT attempts but the Eagles had a 19–13 edge.

Then L-A came alive.

Bower's 22-yard burst ignited a 7-play, 67-yard march, which ended when, on 4th-and-8, Bower took a pitchout and passed 29 yards to end Bob Bingham. Bower's placement was wide and it remained 19–19.

Chi took the ball with 6:00 to play and went right in again, this time marching only 34 yards after a 30-yard kickoff return by Don Linn and a subsequent 15-yard penalty.

In four carries, Clark carried to the 3, where on a great third down call, Infante faked to Clark and pitched out to Boulden who circled right end standing up. A penalty nullified Infante's extra point run and a subsequent pass went incomplete: Chi 25–19.

That should have done it with 4:48 to play, but Lansdowne-Aldan was not to be denied at this point.

Taking the ensuing kickoff on its 39, L-A went right to work.

> Greening's pass to Bingham netted 30 yards and a first down on the Chi 25. Gicking ran three times and L-A had another first on the 14.
>
> A penalty made it 2nd-and-goal on the 4 and that's when Bower took a pitchout, ran right, then fired short to Skinner who caught the ball on the 2 and slammed into the end zone to tie it once again.
>
> That's when Bower stepped back and booted the extra point cleanly through the uprights to end as fine a high school game as you'll ever see.

The Chichester game was the best game of my high school career. I caught four passes for seventy-one yards, netting three important first downs, my longest catch, and my only touchdown of the season. I received a lot of double coverage, and it was obvious that the defense took me very seriously as a receiver.

On Billy Skinner's touchdown draw-play run in the second period, I was to run a corner pattern to help clear out the secondary. I took both the defensive back and linebacker with me, and subsequently, Billy had an easy, untouched seventeen-yard run for the score. A wonderful memory on that play was my looking over my right shoulder after I had run the pattern deep into the end zone—to see the Chichester head coach's clipboard flung high into the air with papers flying because of his surprise over the play call.

The newspaper account of the final point after touchdown is inaccurate. Jimmy Bower's kick nearly hit the right upright and just snuck in for the score. Chichester protested the referee's call, but I saw the kick perfectly from my position on the field. It was the correct call.

We were naturally thrilled to win, but Chichester was a very tough and talented team, and had the game been played on their home field, the outcome likely could have been different. Now, and even then, I felt that the two teams were equals. Bill Clark was the best offensive player we saw all year, being nearly unstoppable.

Subsequently, we scored easy victories against Yeadon (52–0) and Sharon Hill (46–14). The contest against Swarthmore was a disappointing 20-7 win in nasty weather on Thanksgiving morning against a team we should have crushed. Regardless, the LAHS 1965 varsity football team ended the season undefeated and Section III champs.

164

PRO

Starting during my high school years, a summer ritual developed at Stewart Field on Saturday and Sunday afternoons. A middle-aged man wearing a rubber sauna top, shorts, white socks, and sneakers would appear to run impromptu baseball practices for anyone who wanted to participate. He would bring all the gear: bats, a bag of balls, gloves, catching equipment, etc. We simply called the man Pro, because he had supposedly played baseball on the minor-league level. He was an Army veteran who had also played in and managed baseball teams on military bases during his years in the service.

Pro was short and compact and seemingly always tanned. He wore a close-cropped flattop. He looked the part of a veteran soldier, but more than anything, he loved and ate and drank baseball. Pro was the father to Glenn Rankin, a LAHS baseball player a year younger than me. While the Stewart Field practices were open to anyone (usually five or six kids participated, sometimes more), they were really intended for Glenn, who demonstrated tremendous promise as a baseball player.

I never played organizational baseball because of my family's track-and-field heritage, but I loved the sport. Talent-wise, I was very raw. I had speed and could play decent defense, primarily in the outfield, but I was a terrible hitter. In order to improve my skills, I joined these practices on many occasions. Pro took a liking to me, as he knew of my football and track contributions at LAHS.

After loosening up with calisthenics, Pro directed both infield and outfield drills, hollering out situations and desired responses. I usually played left or center field, because he told me early on, "You've got an outfielder's arm. Don't let anyone tell you any differently." I recall his instruction to me on how to field a potential sacrifice fly ball in the outfield, and even how to throw "low rockets" from the outfield. The man knew his sport, inside and out. He also told me on one occasion that my commitment to track was a waste, that I should have better spent my talents on baseball.

Batting practice was next, courtesy of Pro. He was most certainly a junk-ball relief pitcher, because he could throw a variety of off-speed pitches, including curves, sliders, screwballs, forkballs, and a decent knuckleball that I was never able to hit even once. When Pro pitched batting practice to Glenn, he upped his game, frequently directing Glenn as to which field to hit the ball. While Pro laughed and clowned with participants like me, he was all business with Glenn.

Pro had phenomenal enthusiasm, energy, and endurance. He must have dropped five pounds on those blistering summer Saturdays and Sundays. He seemed to thrive on high temperatures and humidity. Never wearing a hat, he would bake in his sauna suit in Philly's heat and high humidity for hours while directing weekend practices. When it was all done, he would distribute Popsicles from his cooler to the surviving players while recalling baseball stories from his past. He was never boastful in his accounts but was funny and candid.

The weekend practices eventually stopped when Glenn graduated from LAHS. While details are sketchy, I do know that Glenn did play major college baseball but only for a short time. Glenn Rankin was the best line-drive hitter I ever saw. Much of that talent he gained from his father on Stewart Field.

165

THE DELCO MEET

The Delco meet was the traditional, annual Delaware County track meet held near the conclusion of the season at Stewart Field. It was sponsored and administered by the Union Athletic Association, with over twenty high schools, large and small, competing. I have no knowledge as to why it was held at Lansdowne-Aldan. It made no sense to me, since I considered it an inferior venue, with its loose-cindered, one-fifth-of-a-mile track.

Competition was divided into A and B brackets. Lansdowne-Aldan was in the B bracket reserved for smaller high schools. My senior track team, which I captained, went undefeated during the regular season. I was undefeated in the 100-yard dash, but my competition was weak. Usually I took first or second place in the long jump, despite having terrible form. The 220-yard dash was my weakest event, as I generally ran out of gas at the 180-yard mark. I usually got at least a third place in the 220-yard dash, even though I was a poor finisher.

I was to participate in the 100- and 220-yard dashes, two relays, and the long jump. I easily won a preliminary heat of the hundred in the morning, which meant that I qualified for the hundred final event in the afternoon. We did well in our two relays, medaling in both. I took a third in the long jump, which pleased me, since I'd been winded from running the lead position in the 880 relay just minutes before the long-jump competition commenced.

Long before the meet, I had fantasized about winning the hundred, which was clearly my best race. I was not concerned with the competition from my morning heat, but the other preliminary heat involved a sprinter from Sharon Hill High School, who allegedly had been clocked in the hundred earlier in the year at 9.7 seconds on a prefab surface. While I cannot recall his name, I had seen the boy run before. He was taller than I and had a long stride, but I honestly thought I could beat him. In the short sprints, the start is everything. Without a solid start, my chances of victory were minimal.

I had an hour between events until the final, and I purposely disappeared into the old gym of the high school. In those days, long before sports psychologists and gimmicky motivational efforts, I did my very best on my own, in private, to think positively and pump myself up—but also to relax, focus on the start, rule out the Sharon Hill runner and his 9.7 time, and visualize victory. I also intended to avoid eye contact with any of the competing runners. I successfully ignored them and shut them out, which I do believe had a positive impact on my performance.

I drew lane four out of six lanes, which was perfect, because it gave me excellent sight lines to my left and right. The Sharon Hill runner drew lane two, which I liked as well. An added advantage was that Don Corbin, an exemplary music instructor at LAHS, was also a veteran and well-respected track official. He would start the race, which again was to my advantage. I was very familiar with his style and cadence from previous races over the years.

All cylinders clicked into place. I timed Don Corbin's start perfectly and had one of the best starts in the hundred of my high school career. I was the clear leader at twenty yards. I was never a come-from-behind sprinter. My style was to grab the lead through a swift start, fight off challengers, and maintain the lead. That was what happened at the Delco Meet in 1966, as I won the event by a yard with a time of 10.3. The Sharon Hill runner came in second. By comparison, the Class A hundred winner, Bob Jackson from Upper Darby, ran a 10.0.

My high school coach, Joe Pitt, was ecstatic, as was my head football coach, Ray Spafford, who was cheering me on in the stands. I accepted the first-place medal on the top tier of the awards stand in full view of J. T. and Esther and a crowded stadium.

Everything is relative. The state district track meet was held two weeks later, the Saturday after my Friday evening senior prom. I was scheduled to compete in Norristown against the best from southeast Pennsylvania. I got next to no sleep that Friday evening because of the prom, and I was nursing a tightly wrapped and temperamental right hamstring. In the preliminary heat, I finished seventh out of eight runners, as everything that could go wrong did. There's nothing like getting smoked on your final race as a high school sprinter.

166

USPS MAILBOX AT ESSEX AND HIGHLAND AVENUES

When we return to our hometowns, there are some locales and entities that we purposely visit and inspect upon arrival. These constants exist in our memories as unique reminders. We want them to be the same as we left them. Some of these images may be commonly shared with others: the high school, the train station, a favorite pizza shop, the bumpy railroad crossing in need of repair, a neighborhood park, the community swimming pool, etc. Some others, however, are more personal, more special, even private.

When these anchors to our childhood remain the same, we are reassured. When they change, we are forced to accept the fact that change is inevitable, that nothing as we know it or remember it remains constant. When community fixtures dissolve, we experience a sense of loss.

During my adolescent years and college summers on east Essex Avenue, I frequented the USPS mailbox at the intersection of Essex and Highland Avenues on dozens of occasions. It was a block and a half walk from the Bingham family's front door, which could be completed, round-trip, in a little more than five minutes. Decades earlier, Lansdowne had had a couple dozen mailboxes conveniently scattered throughout the town. Most of them were of the older variety: about the size of a small window air-conditioner, painted blue, supported on a concrete post. Boxes were fitted with a small slot and raised capital lettering that read "LETTERS" across the front.

In an effort to increase efficiency and cut costs, the US Postal Service drastically decreased the network of neighborhood mailboxes in Lansdowne and other towns and cities across the country. The style of mailbox described above has been nearly eliminated in favor of a much larger receptacle. It's still painted solid blue, but it can now also receive small packages. We no longer mail letters down the street. Instead we travel to the supermarket or the mall or the actual post office to complete the task.

During a visit back home several years ago, I suddenly realized that the familiar USPS mailbox at Essex and Highland had been removed. The site to me now appears barren. My response is not as strange as one might think, because for me, so many steps and stages in my maturation as a teenager and young man took flight from that mailbox. The site signified important decision-making for me on any number of personal and professional levels. Whether it was a college application, a job inquiry, a paid parking ticket, Christmas cards, or some occasional love letters, they were usually mailed at this neighborhood site just a few doors down from my home at 29 East Essex Avenue.

On my infrequent visits to Lansdowne, I want that simple remnant of my childhood to return. I still look for it, knowing that it vanished unceremoniously many years ago. And I will always continue to look for it.

167

LAHIAN NARRATIVE: LANSDOWNE-ALDAN HIGH SCHOOL, CLASS OF '66

ROBERT LAWRENCE BINGHAM
29 E. Essex Avenue
Lansdowne

"Bing" … Student Council,
Football, Sprinter for the
Thinclads … Folk music,
Roger the Dodger … Mad
Chef in the kitchen … Shuns
sloppy dressers …"Goldenwheels" …
Journalism or communications in college.

168

THE PAOLI LOCAL

The Paoli Local is a major SEPTA commuter line from center city Philadelphia to the western suburb of Paoli in Montgomery County. This route services the Main Line, the affluent string of suburbs that includes such towns as Bryn Mawr, Rosemont, Villanova, Devon, Berwyn, and Paoli, which is the end of the line.

Upon graduating from high school in June 1966, I worked a summer job at Fuller Typesetting's Radnor plant prior to heading off to Wake Forest. Having no car, I commuted from home by Red Arrow bus and the Norristown high-speed line to my destination stop in Radnor. On the way home, I reversed the process.

The high-speed station and Radnor plant were separated by a half-mile walk that included crossing over four tracks of the Pennsylvania Railroad's principle route to Harrisburg, Pittsburgh, and farther west. The outside tracks carried commuter traffic, and the Pennsylvania Railroad's passenger trains generally ran on the inside tracks. While not ideal, the only practical method of walking between the high-speed stop and the Radnor plant included crossing over the busy main outside tracks, which also occasionally carried freight traffic.

It was late summer, and I had just completed another week of grunt work at the Radnor plant. As I approached the railroad's roadbed, I began my scan of the tracks and immediately saw on my right an outbound Paoli local approaching on the outside track as it raced west, right to left. I continued walking another fifteen feet until I met and stood below gravel roadbed on the near track, which carried Paoli local trains to Philadelphia. I remained focused on the outward-bound train to Paoli, and as it was passing, I began to mount the near roadbed. At this same time, a Philadelphia-bound commuter train going the opposite direction from my left blasted down the tracks, throwing me off the roadbed.

While the returning, eastbound commuter train did not strike me, I was half a step away from being hit and likely killed. I recall landing on my feet and holding my knees after having been blown several feet outward from the exterior track as the train whizzed by.

With my eyes clenched tight, an instant, rapid slide show of my life and its key actors danced before me. Adrenaline instantly kicked in, my breathing raced, and sweat soon covered my face. I steadied myself, resting both hands on my knees for a minute or so, and struggled with understanding and accepting what had just occurred. I was in shock over what very nearly could have been. In my dazed condition, I eventually pieced together what had happened. While I was focused on the westbound train to Paoli, I had committed the major error of ignoring any potential eastbound traffic, associating any train horn blasts with the Paoli-bound train.

It took me a good twenty to thirty minutes to settle down. I contemplated taking the much longer walking route to the Norristown high-speed line station, which avoided any rail track crossing. However, I eventually gathered the courage to look in both directions a half dozen times before sprinting across the four tracks.

I was very quiet on the high-speed and bus rides home. Whatever plans I had made for that Friday evening I canceled. I spent a quiet evening, pretty much alone, further reflecting on the incident and my own mortality. I never revealed the incident to J. T. or Esther or anyone else, primarily out of embarrassment.

Elizabeth Jane Dunkle

169

ELIZABETH JANE DUNKLE

Beth Dunkle was an LAHS classmate whom I first met in seventh grade when Lansdowne's grade school population merged in junior high school with students also joining us from Aldan and East Lansdowne.

I was quickly attracted to Beth, and she was the first girl I ever dated, the first girl I ever kissed. There were only a handful of dates between us in seventh grade, but they included chaperoned bowling, some movies at the Lansdowne Movie Theater, and perhaps some junior high open houses. The story goes that I dumped her in favor of another girl at an Aldan summer party between our seventh- and eighth-grade years. Conveniently, I have limited recall on that happening.

In later junior high and high school years, Beth and I were friends, even though our social circles were slightly different. We had several classes together, including homeroom during our junior and senior years, twelfth-grade English, and publications. I admired her then and now as one of the better players on the field hockey team.

I recall a funny story about Beth's hockey exploits. She played halfback, a defensive position, but she actually scored a goal in one varsity game. While pleased with her play, the field hockey coach, Edna Hoffman, was not happy, since she was so badly out of position when she scored. I say, "Lighten up, Mrs. Hoffman. A goal's a goal."

Beth and her twin sister, Ruth, both played varsity tennis in the spring.

Beth's longtime high school boyfriend, Bruce Bennett, and I were teammates on the football team, and for our varsity years, our lockers were next to each other. Bruce was a good guy, quiet and reserved.

An unfortunate event I do recall with some clarity was when Beth's father died during our sophomore year at LAHS. I felt so sorry for her, and I intentionally yet awkwardly shared my condolences at an opportune time at school a few days after the funeral. What a horrible event to endure as a high school sophomore, and right in the middle of final exams.

On the brighter side, I always regarded Beth as neither cute nor pretty but as beautiful, and I still do. She was vivacious and a little crazy back then, as well as being likable, funny, and popular—traits that have lived on well into adulthood.

Beth's high school bio reads: "'Bethy' … Hockey, Intramurals, F.B.L.A., Choir, *Lahian* … M.Y.F., Young Life … Smedley picnics …

B.B. … Abhors Reese's Cups … Chocolate mint ice cream … college ahead."

Upon graduation, Beth and I lost touch, but we connected with each other accidentally one late evening during my senior year in college at a convenience store where Beth was searching for a cake ingredient. I followed her home and kept her company until 2:00 a.m. while she completed the batter and baked the cake. That unlikely meeting caused us to begin dating once again.

Approximately seven years later, Beth and I were married at the Bryn Mawr College cloisters on September 18, 1976. It was the best decision I ever made.

170

ARLINGTON CEMETERY

J. T. and Esther are buried side by side at Arlington Cemetery in the Drexel Hill section of Upper Darby. Arlington is a private, nondenominational cemetery located across from Upper Darby High School. It was a cemetery that I was well familiar with, having passed it hundreds of times. Arlington is large in size and handsomely landscaped with trees, shrubs, and flowers. It is a serene setting that beckons walkers and runners to pass through its peaceful grounds.

J. T. died first in Philadelphia's VA hospital on December 2, 1977. I was unable to be present at his bedside when he died. I arrived at the hospital about one hour later, and to my surprise, Esther had already left. The attending physician was brief and to the point, and in his defense, there wasn't much to say, since we knew J. T.'s passing was both near and inevitable. He suggested that should I want to visit my father one last time, he was still in his assigned room. In hindsight, doing so was a mistake, as I then viewed J. T. after he had suffered a major seizure immediately before his death. His face and upper body were grossly distorted, a grotesque sight I have fought hard to repress over the years. This was not how I wished to remember my father.

A military funeral followed a few days later at a plain and simple gravesite at Arlington Cemetery. Those attending were immediate family and a few close friends. Rev. William Budd, a retired navy chaplain and family friend of the Dunkles, performed the service, and he did the best job he could, considering that he had never met J. T.

A limited military gun salute followed, including the presentation of an American flag from the flag-draped casket to Esther with the customary words: "On behalf of the president of the United States, the United States Navy, and a grateful nation, please accept this flag as a symbol of your loved one's honorable and faithful service." While teary-eyed, Esther showed class, dignity, and solemn appreciation when receiving the flag. On so many occasions, I have thought about how incredibly gut-wrenching that acceptance must have been for Esther.

A short luncheon was held at our Essex Avenue home, and by midafternoon, all had left, including Bill and his family, who were scheduled for an early-evening flight back to Wisconsin.

Completely drained by events, Esther softly mentioned that everyone had left or was leaving. She looked lost and terribly alone. I asked her if she would like me to spend the night, and she would have nothing of it, but that evening was easily the worst of her life. Her beloved husband for forty years, the light of her life, was now gone.

Esther survived J. T. by fourteen and a half years and died in Traverse City, Michigan, the place of her birth, in 1992. Bill and I were both present for her death, which occurred in the afternoon.

We were by her bedside, holding her hand as she passed. Esther had been unconscious for approximately thirty-six hours prior to her passing. A funeral service was held on June 1 at the Ruggles Funeral Home in Traverse City. It was lightly attended by family and friends. I spoke, as did family members and some high school friends. The Reverend Ray Brown officiated the service.

Esther's remains were flown back to Philadelphia, and because of flight delays, inclement weather, and a lengthier-than-normal process at the rental-car counter, Beth and I almost missed the interment. I recall that it was a rainy, ugly day, with everyone holding umbrellas during a very short graveside service. Beth and I were the only family representatives in attendance. We unwound that evening with an unhurried dinner at a restaurant familiar to both J. T. and Esther—an appropriate closure to a trying day.

J. T.'s and Esther's grave markers are two undistinguished bronze plates that rest flat on the ground. The markers list my parents' names and birth/death dates. J. T.'s plaque recognizes his naval service. While the markers are simple and unremarkable, what I gain from the site is my parents' ongoing union as a couple and their deep love and unwavering commitment to one another. When I visit the gravesite during occasional returns to Philadelphia, I always leave Arlington with a continued sense of that love and dedication to each other, a wonderful legacy to have imparted to their two children.

171

EPILOGUE

I have often asked my children which town they consider home, since we moved frequently during their upbringing. Their responses have understandably been different. I don't have that dilemma, because Lansdowne was always my hometown, and it always will be.

Though it was certainly not perfect in the '50s and '60s when I knew it as a youth, Lansdowne's simplicity and conservative nature were comforting and reassuring. I always felt safe and secure on Lansdowne streets. Somehow I also felt the Quaker heritage of the community, possibly, in part, due to my mother's Quaker connection.

I loved the town's large Victorian style homes and the heavily tree-lined streets. I appreciated downtown Lansdowne for its retail offerings and the fact that the town had a legitimate downtown where we could shop for groceries, buy school supplies at an old-time five-and-dime store, sit at a soda fountain, buy a current forty-five record, go bowling, or attend a movie at one of the area's classiest movie theaters.

Lansdowne also held some memorable events, such as the Fourth of July festivities and the unique Burning of the Greens. LAHS open houses were simply the best, kindling warm and rich memories of innocent and better times.

The school system was adequate to good. I thought my elementary education superior to junior high school and high school. High school football clearly remains my fondest memory, including the school's 1965 undefeated season earned by undersized yet focused, hardworking teammates.

My biggest complaint about the town during my upbringing remains the lack of open space, parks, and neighborhood playgrounds—and issue that Lansdowne has finally addressed.

Lansdowne was squeaky clean, and while schools were integrated, residential neighborhoods were clearly segregated. That too has changed in recent years, with the town now being far more residentially integrated than it was during my growing-up years.

When I walk familiar streets upon my return, some loneliness revisits. I recall having parents who were older than most of my peers' parents; an indifferent older brother who largely reneged on his role with me; Andy Thompson's untimely move to Newtown Square; and the empty apartment years in between homes on Marshall Road and Essex Avenue.

More importantly, what I do hove is a strong base, some roots, and respectful appreciation, and I credit Lansdowne with molding me as much as my parents did. Lansdowne was good to me, and I trust that my recordings about the town have been fair and level.

Should you need to reach me when I next return to Lansdowne, I'll most likely be walking Albermarle or Wayne Avenue or visiting Stewart Field. That's where you'll always be able to find me.

About the Author

Mr. Bingham is a retired career probation administrator who teaches criminal justice courses part-time on the college level. He has authored dozens of professional articles during his career. *Growing Up Lansdowne* is his first nonfiction book to be published.

About the Book

Growing Up Lansdowne is a photo-illustrated account of the author's childhood and adolescence in the mid to late 1950s and eventful 1960s in Lansdowne, Pennsylvania, a conservative Philadelphia suburb.

The book is composed of 171 diverse essays depicting growing-up years in Lansdowne. Eight sections titled "Random Remembrances" record dozens of additional recollections. Assorted photographs are included to accent the narrative.

The book is part memoir, part social landscape, part local/national history, and part love story. The recollections reflect candor and vulnerability, and at times they are surprisingly personal. Essays present balanced portraits of family and community life and the general era without resorting to enhancement or exaggeration.

By its very design, *Growing Up Lansdowne* compels readers to make personal comparisons with their own hometowns and upbringing. The text touches upon memorable historical events and sensitive social issues of the times, and their impact on adolescent transition to adulthood.

Printed in the United States
By Bookmasters